DESIGN

DESIGN

PHILIP RAWSON

PRENTICE-HALL, INC.
Englewood Cliffs, New Jersey

North and South American edition
first published 1988 by
Prentice-Hall, Inc., Englewood Cliffs,
NJ 07632

ISBN 0-13-199886-2

This book was designed and produced by
John Calmann and King Ltd, London

Designer Richard Foenander
Typeset by Rowland Phototypesetting Ltd,
England
Printed in Hong Kong by Mandarin Offset

Front cover
CHARLES BIEDERMANN
Structuralist Relief, 1954–65 (detail).
Aluminum alloy painted in oil, 41¼ x 36 x
5⅞ins (104.8 x 91.4 x 14.6cm). The Tate
Gallery, London.

Back cover
LEONARDO DA VINCI
*Vitruvian Proportions derived from the
Human Body*, c.1490. Ink drawing.
Galleria dell'Accademia, Venice.

Half-title page
KAZUMASU YAMASHITA
Face House, Kyoto, Japan, 1974.

Title page
INIGO JONES
The Tulip Staircase in the Queen's House,
Greenwich, begun 1616.

CONTENTS

PREFACE   9

CHAPTER ONE
INTRODUCTION   10

DESIGN DEFINED 10   Materials 10   Processes 12   Form 13   Purpose and Function 14   Symbolic meaning 16   Ornament 19

THE HUMAN BODY AS SOURCE OF DESIGN 20   The head 21 Eyes 21   Ears 22   Hands 22   The brain 23

DESIGN AND HISTORY 24   Repossession of tradition 26

CHAPTER TWO
PROCESSES AND MATERIALS   28

WASTING 28   Wood 30   Stone 30   Precious and semi-precious stones 31   Silhouetted shapes 33   Other inorganic materials 33

FORMING 33   Clay 34   Painting 35   Ductile metals 36   Hot working metals 36   Glass 37   Flexible materials 40

MOLDING 41   Shaping the mold 41   Mold materials 42   Press molding 44   Poured molding 44   Ceramic casting 45   Electrolysis 45 Die-stamping 45   Vacuum molding 45

CONSTRUCTING 46   Heaping 47   Courses and bonding 49   Mass and inertia 52   Skeleton structure 52   Shells 62   Textile structures 63

CHAPTER THREE
FORM   72

FORMAL CONCEPTS 72   Form and meta-form 72   Design forms 74 Content 75

BASIC FORMS 76   Rectangle 77   Circle 79   Triangle 80   Other geometrical figures 83   Figure and form 83

LINEAR FORMS 83   Curves 84   Linear expression 85   3D functions of line 86

PROPORTION 87   Rectangle 88   Circle 90   Triangle 90

PATTERN 91   Grids 91   Counterchange 93

CONTRASTS AND COMBINATIONS 93   Contrasting qualities 93   Combinations of contrasting forms 97   Unifying arrangement 100   Surface, bulk, mass, and volume 102

BALANCE 103   Scale 103

SPACE 104   Limited space 105   Space as arena 107

CHAPTER FOUR
COLOR   108

COLOR AND PHYSIOLOGY 108   Color and substance 110

THE LIGHT SPECTRUM AND OPTICAL COLOR CIRCLE 112   Additive and subtractive mixing 114   Color opposites 116   Color enhancement 118   Warm/cold colors 119   Primary, secondary, and tertiary colors 119   Rood's color circle 120   Goethe's color circle 123

COLOR AND FEELING 124   Convention 125   Color values 125   Color significance 126   Color and expression 129   Color as splendor 130

CHAPTER FIVE
SYMBOL   134

DEFINITIONS 134   Structural analogy 134   Symbol versus sign 136   Context 137   Metaphor 139

LEVELS OF SYMBOL 139   Actual object 139   Represented object 140   Joint symbols 141   Imaginary symbols 142   Personification 142   Archetype, form, and symbol 143   Convention 146   Iconography and cultural echo 148

PHYSIOLOGY AND SYMBOL 149   The face 149   The body 150

CHAPTER SIX
DRAWING   154

DRAWING PROCESSES 154   Dry media 154   Wet media 154   Use of media 156   Drawing surfaces 158   Frottage 159   Collage 159

EXPRESSION 159   Line 159   Enclosure 160   Tone and texture 160

Volume 161   Space 161   Crosswise relation 161

RECOGNITION 163   Context 163   Expectation 163

CONTENT AND TECHNIQUE 164   Space as arena 166   Human drama 166   Landscape and cityscape 167   Framing the action 167   Story-telling 167   Cubism and Futurism 168   Photography and movement 171   Free forms 172   Virtual movement 174

LETTERING 177   Calligraphy 177   Free calligraphy 178   Standard forms 179

DRAWING AND DESIGN 179   Plans 179   3D projection 180   Artistic uses of projections 182   Optical perspective 183

CHAPTER SEVEN
PRINT

186

PRINTING BASICS 186   Tracing and pressure tracing 188   Monotype 189

RELIEF 189   The printing block 190   Methods of inking 190   Methods of printing 190   Coloring by hand 192   Drawing for relief print 192

INTAGLIO 193   Engraving 194   Etching 194   Drawing on the plate 196

NON-TRADITIONAL TECHNIQUES 196   Mezzotint 196   Aquatint 196   Sugar lift 197   Relief etching 198   Lithography 199   Stencil and silk screen 199

PHOTOGRAPHY 200   The camera 200   Black-and-white design 201   Monochrome versus color 202   Photography and actuality 202   Photography and painting 204   Movement and movies 205   Photography and design 206

GRAPHIC DESIGN 208   Sources 210   Simplification 210   Typography 212   Layout 215   Computers in graphic design 215

CHAPTER EIGHT
FINE ART

216

ART AND MEANING 216   Elements 216   Focal and subsidiary meaning 218   The notional image 219   The choice of medium 220

ART IN ITS SPACE 221   The two modes of space 223   Art and place 223

PAINTING 225   Ground color 226   Applying paint 226   Color handling 226   Color sequences 229   Color families 230   Modulation of color 231   Color dominance 232   Hyper color 233   Color and shape 233   Modelling with color 233   Chiaroscuro 234   Luminosity 234   Shadow and light 236   Atmosphere 236

SCULPTURE 236   Place **238**   Materials **238**   Processes **241**   Imaginative technique **243**   Surfaces **244**   Articulation **247**   Object and image **248** Freestanding sculpture **250**   Relief **252**

CHAPTER NINE
INTERIOR DESIGN   256

BASIC CONSIDERATIONS 256   Climate **256**   Custom **256** Wealth **259**   Display **259**

FOCUS 263   Wall focuses **263**   Fabrics **264**

STYLE 265   Form **266**   Color **270**   Motif **273**   Contemporary solutions **274**

ELEMENTS OF INTERIOR SPACE 276   Roofs **276**   Floors **279** Walls **281**   Lighting **284**   Acoustics **286**

FURNITURE 286   Furniture types **287**   Furniture structure **288** Furniture decoration **291**   Utensils **292**

CHAPTER TEN
ENVIRONMENTAL DESIGN   294

THE SHAPED ENVIRONMENT 294   Form and expression **294**

ARCHITECTURE 298   Dwellings **298**   Hall and monument **299** Articulation of inner and outer **306**   Façade and ornament **308** Post-Modernist ornament **313**   High Tech reaction **314**

ARCHITECTURAL PLANNING 316   Conceptual methods **317**   Modular construction **319**   Ground plan **320**   Walls **321**   Roofs **322**   Unifying factors **323**

EXTERIOR SPACES 324   Courtyards and terraces **324**   Gardens **326**

THE URBAN ENVIRONMENT 328   Rectangular plans **329**   Water **331** The cosmological diagram **333**   Economic factors **333**   Zoning **334**   Toward humane planning **337**

GLOSSARY 338

CREDITS 345

INDEX 346

PREFACE

This book is meant for everybody concerned with design standards, whether as student, practitioner, or consumer. It explains design as a basic human faculty which shapes all human artifacts, of all ages and styles, evolved to modify and organize the physical world for our benefit. As well as adapting the environment to give shelter, livelihood, and social cohesion, it can also give delight, satisfying our feeling for coherence and communicating meaning.

To understand and practice design properly we need to perceive its scope and depth, and not to think of it only in terms of contemporary fashion and styling. So this book takes account of the whole history of design, and considers modern design as one manifestation of that broad human faculty.

The designer works with four main elements: **materials**, which are modified by **processes**, according to **formal concepts**, to fulfill specific **purposes**. The first two, broadly speaking, are manifested in craft and industrial skills. The second two involve mental modelling which envisages problems and thinks through solutions. It is the designer's essential skill, whether it is put into immediate practice or communicated to others by drawings.

Purposes, of course, are of critical importance. They range all the way along a spectrum, from one pole of technical efficiency in pure industrial design to the other pole of emotional, intellectual, and aesthetic satisfaction in the arts. This book emphasizes the latter, though it expressly affirms the genuine continuity of method linking the poles. It also tries to clear up confusion inherent in theories of artistic "functionalism." It points out that the moment a formal design concept is realized in a material artifact, occupying a place in the real world, it acquires a constellation of human meanings, which the designer has to take into account; while even the most individualist gestural painting, exploring its own inherent expressive possibilities, is evolving ordering systems of its own which focus its aesthetic propositions. Great monuments of design, like cathedrals and palaces, can symbolize not only the principle of order, but also its value.

I should like to thank some of the people who have made this book possible, particularly my editor, Peter Zombory-Moldovan, who gave clarity and balance to the text. Susan Wagstaff and Eleanor van Zandt helped in valuable ways. Picture researcher Susan Bolsom-Morris produced inspired solutions to many visual problems; and the book owes its elegance to the designer, Richard Foenander.

CHAPTER ONE

INTRODUCTION

DESIGN DEFINED

Design is the means by which we order our surroundings, re-shaping natural materials to suit our needs and purposes. It arises at the interface between human-kind and raw environment and expresses human intentions, desires, and hopes.

The evolution of the human race depended on our developing successful ways of relating to our environment. Our brain evolved a special intelligence that enables us to plan and apply techniques for dealing with specific challenges posed by the natural world. In early times we learned to make tools and other equipment to hunt, to cook, to protect ourselves, and to make possible increasingly sophisticated ways of living. All of our artifacts, from flint implements to temples, bridges, and cities, and, in our own time, to computers and spacecraft, reflect that special kind of constructive intelligence we call design.

Design involves altering the forms of existing materials to make them suitable for what we want them to do. People being swept away by a flood may respond immediately by grabbing hold of a floating tree to save themselves. Design begins when we foresee that we will need a raft or, better still, a boat, and work out how to make one.

All design has four aspects: **materials**, real objects which we choose, change, and combine by **processes**, giving them new **forms** that we conceive to fulfill our **purposes**. The first part of this book deals with materials and processes; the second with the conceptual and psychological principles involved in changes of form; the third with human purposes and meaning as they are realized through different design media.

Materials

These are the natural objects and substances whose shapes and properties we modify in the design process. As designers we need to know what those properties are, so that we can conceive designs that will suit them and perhaps discover new ways of using them. Its hardness, softness, toughness, tensile or compression strength, ductility or rigidity, and color will all determine what forms a material will accept and what functions it will be good for. It is, however, quite common for one material to be adapted to functions traditionally performed by another.

1.1 Chartres Cathedral, the flying buttresses of the choir, 1194–1220.

Design involves the exploration of the properties of materials in order to discover their potential for form. The audacious traceries of Gothic stonework are an example of what such exploration can achieve.

1.2   ISAMBARD KINGDOM BRUNEL
Temple Meads Railway Station, Bristol, 1840–41. Detail of cast iron hammer beams.

These integral iron shapes are based on those of medieval structures in stone and massive wood, and were meant to recall them.

This can stimulate new design ideas and give new physical characteristics to familiar objects. Many technical innovations have resulted from adapting processes developed for working one material to working another.

Processes

These are the physical actions by which material is worked into designed forms. During most of human history, processes have usually been specific to materials, and the domain of the craftsperson. With small-scale enterprises such as making pots or simple furniture, the craftsperson has usually also been the designer, realizing formal ideas contained in his or her own head. Sometimes these ideas have been original; more often they have been traditional ideas routinely repeated generation after generation; occasionally new ones learned, for example, from pattern books.

For major enterprises, however, such as the building of a cathedral, the skills of craftspeople such as stonemasons and carpenters were always subordinated to an overall design; and these people worked to specifications provided by the designer. During the early industrial period, the manufacturing of products was broken down into even simpler separate processes, each one of which could be carried out by individuals who did not always need to be craftspeople in the old sense. Nowadays, the industrial designer and process technician, working with sophisticated machines to technical briefs supplied by customers who may not care how the result is achieved, have further eroded the scope and value of handicrafts in industry. Today, as a result, true crafts have become the exclusive province of people who process their own materials, design their own products, and see themselves as free artists.

Form

We can think of design as a kind of mental modelling, a variety of abstract thought derived from basic human activity in manipulating and reshaping the physical world. Some kinds of formal thinking, such as mathematics, are highly abstract. But the designer has to conceive forms that can be turned into realities with the available resources. Creative designers may set out to devise new forms with which to challenge established processes and materials; this is one of the ways in which design develops. Craftspeople at work may also discover forms not previously used.

1.3 Aboriginal branch shelter, northern Australia, mid 20th century.

Constructed from shaped branches, twigs, grasses, and bark, this shelter has been given a shape that is ideal to protect people accustomed to sitting on the ground. There is a surprising likeness to the roofs of the Sydney Opera House.

1.4 JØRN UTZON
The Sydney Opera House, 1957–73.

Built of concrete, the roofs are reminiscent of sails and were exceptionally difficult and expensive to construct according to the architect's original idea, which stretched the use of the material to the limits of feasibility.

The modern product designer sitting at a drafting table, planning a new reclining chair, and the aboriginal tribesman erecting a branch shelter against the rain are in the same business. Both are conceiving forms to serve their purposes. The aboriginal is planning to take account of the ground and water run-off, wind directions, and cooking facilities; he knows the materials available and how to fit them together. The professional designer is considering such factors as the strength of steel, the shape of the human body, and the force of gravity. Even though he or she has no part in the actual construction of the chair, he or she must model the design with a clear appreciation of how it can be realized. The drawings and specifications such a designer produces have to communicate to other minds the shapes, the components, and the materials needed to fulfill the intention. And although brick-building, for example, may condition what an architect is able to require, the architect's design is a product of the formal imagination. Because its formal order gives rise to physical shapes that other humans respond to, it becomes an act of communication.

Purpose and function

The form of an object is dictated, to a great extent, by its purpose – in many cases, by a number of purposes, both practical and psychological. At one extreme, for example, are the cheap radios cased in ordinary food cans, thought up in the 1960s for sale in the Third World. Besides serving their main purpose, they implicitly served several others by means of their small size, low cost, and relative toughness. Fulfilling these purposes precluded fulfilling others, such as sensory gratification. At another extreme lie great cultural monuments such as the Gothic cathedrals of France which were meant to serve not only practical purposes of shelter and enclosure but also a host of other purposes, including the aesthetic, the spiritual, and the political. Between these extremes lie an enormous variety of design tasks: styling automobiles, packaging cereals, laying out advertisements and PR handouts, setting up microchip formats, and so on. All of these designs are conceived to meet some human purpose.

We tend to think of function and appearance – the pragmatic and the aesthetic – as mutually exclusive, and sometimes find it difficult to see how the term "design" can apply to both aspects. In fact, the two belong to the ends of a continuous spectrum of purposes. Most people would agree that fitness for its purpose – or purposes – is the criterion of good design. The problem arises when we cease to be clear about the purposes our designs are meant to fulfill, and we allow one person's purpose – let us say, making money with a building or solving an urgent housing problem – to override the purposes of other people who want to live in a satisfying environment.

Purposes range from the simple to the highly complex; so do solutions. A good design solution can be complex, although the best design usually appears simple, belying the complexities of its formulation. Purposes, though, are rarely as simple as they can be made to seem by someone in pursuit of an easy solution.

Purpose and function are different things. At one end of the design spectrum there is the artifact that has a single physical purpose, which we *can* call a function: for example, the hammer, intended only for hitting things. At the other is the purely aesthetic artifact: for example, the abstract painting. It has no function –

it does not even depict the physical world, as a representational painting does – but it does have *purpose*: the expression and eliciting of feelings.

Machines fulfill clear-cut functions, using replaceable parts within tightly prescribed physical conditions. Thus we evaluate the parts of a machine in terms of narrowly defined function within a system, but the system itself in terms of human and social purposes.

The distinction between purpose and function was emphatically articulated by Alberto Giacometti, the great twentieth-century French sculptor. Giacometti

1.5 CHARLES EAMES and EERO SAARINEN
Competition Drawings, 1940. Colored pencil, wood veneer, and paper cut-outs on white poster board, 30 × 30ins (76.2 × 76.2cm). The Museum of Modern Art, New York.

This design won a first prize in a competition organized by the Museum of Modern Art and entitled *Organic Design in Home Furnishing*. It is carefully thought out, both as a lightweight plywood and steel structure, and as a comfortable support for the human body.

1.6   Jaguar SS100, England, 1936.

The lines of the joined wings, door edge, and scuttle are styled to produce a highly effective visual composition that expresses the idea of performance, rather than mere mechanical operation. This is a machine clothed in sculpture.

1.7   ALBERTO GIACOMETTI *Walking Man*, 1947–48. Bronze, 26½ins (67.3cm) high, edition of 6. Thomas Gibson Fine Art Ltd, London.

This spindly figure has no purpose save to communicate thoughts and sensations to the viewer, and to stimulate reflection about the human condition. Its animated clay handling has been cast into bronze.

explained why he had refused to accept money from a car manufacturer to declare an automobile to be a sculpture. The former, he said, was an object; the latter, expression. What he meant by "expression" was the communication of subtle, intangible qualities, such as a subject's character, or complex interactions between walking figures, as in his own sculptures. By contrast, an object, such as a car, exists only to be used – and when it is not in use it is simply waiting to be used again, not looked at for what it expresses. This is a distinction in terms of purpose. For "expression," unless purely self-indulgent or therapeutic, needs another person to receive what it is expressing. It demands to be contemplated for the sake of its content, form, and symbolic meaning.

Symbolic meaning

Anything designed and made by humans inevitably reflects in its physical attributes the attitudes and intentions of its makers. These attitudes may be unconscious, but they cannot be hidden. Observers or users can always read them through their own patterns of subjective response and can feel their presence in the object.

Consider these examples: one building may be constructed of well-trimmed stone and massive oak beams cut locally, so that it will stand for centuries; another may be made of thin deal timber frame clad in board and shingle and intended to be only temporary. These facts will be part of the *meaning* of the building. Some people may feel very positive about age and solidity; others may feel that it cramps their style and prefer something less emphatic that can easily be pulled down and reconstructed. But it is not unknown for buildings of the second type to be "styled" superficially so as to give the impression that they belong to the first. And it is very common for homes that are constructed in fundamentally similar ways, out of similar materials, to be styled with symbolic attributes, so as to look different and appeal to clients with different tastes. This practice can give rise to quite delicate problems of morality in design.

Every designed object falls somewhere along the spectrum of purposes between pure function and pure symbolic expression. A bridge, for example, has a clear primary function, and its design entails problems that must be solved by

1.8 Alfriston Clergy House, Polegate, East Sussex, 14th Century.

This half-timbered and thatched medieval hall was built to last. It displays the basic wall-frame of wooden beams which were filled with light brick and plaster panelling. Each wall was probably assembled flat on the ground, then lifted into position and joined to the other wall-frames, with floors and fill-in panels being added last.

1.9 Black tin chapel, Ganllwyd, Wales, c. 1945–50.

Standard commercial corrugated iron sheet has been nailed onto a wooden frame. The need for very cheap construction methods has produced a building with a short life-expectancy.

1.10 Demolition of Pruitt-Igoe public housing complex, St Louis, Missouri, in 1972 (built 1951).

The prize-winning complex stood empty for much of its short life, as the people it was meant for refused to live in it. Some see its demolition as heralding the death of Functionalism in housing design.

1.11

1.12

engineers. But great bridges are also expressive works of architecture, symbolizing human senses of place and activity. A hotel, whose primary function may present relatively familiar engineering problems, may be designed expressly to appeal to aesthetic and social desires.

The great Swiss-born architect Le Corbusier once declared that a house was "a machine for living in." Some people took him to mean that "living" is a single mechanical function carried out by human components whose activities the designer defines in advance, and whom he or she then slots into calculated positions. In fact Le Corbusier meant his phrase as an appeal to get rid of an old, cluttered lifestyle and adopt a new one. Misunderstanding of this potent phrase led to the development of the Functionalist theory of architecture, which left out vital aspects of humane design.

The human consequences of Functionalism have come under heavy criticism. Its failure was conceded in 1972 when the vast, low-cost Pruitt Igoe housing development in St. Louis, Missouri, was demolished by the city government. Designed in 1951 by Minoru Yamasaki, this development had won an award from the American Institute of Architects. Architectural theorists of the day loved its "purity of style." But the people it was meant for refused to live in it and vandalized it. Its calculated simplicities seemed brutal, and the buildings made their potential inhabitants feel like battery hens, unable to live individual lives and deprived of sensory nourishment. Pruitt Igoe failed to acknowledge the fact that design for human purposes always operates at a symbolic as well as a pragmatic level.

1.11   THEOPHIL VON HANSEN
Heinrichhof, Opernring, Ringstrasse, Vienna, 1861–2 (destroyed 1945).

An example of the excessive and pretentious ornament to which the Modernists objected. The frontage of an apartment house is made to recall a Baroque palace.

1.12   ADOLF LOOS
Goldmann and Salatsch Store, Michaelerplatz, Vienna, 1910.

Loos was among the first to reject ornament as it had been understood in the late nineteenth century. His designs embodied subtle proportions, and allowed the visible qualities of fine materials to be the only ornament.

Ornament

One of the ways in which artifacts appeal to our aesthetic faculties is by ornament. Even "functional" design pays more attention to ornamental qualities than we often realize. An object can look terrible and still work well, an example being equipment mock-ups in a science laboratory, which no client would accept as finished products. A large part of the cost of any product actually goes on making it look good for the customer, according to criteria having nothing to do with function.

Until recently, avant-garde designers, trained under the influence of the Bauhaus school of design in Germany, believed that decoration was wicked, and that people who wanted "something extra" on what was intended as a beautifully functioning artifact were merely suffering from undeveloped taste. They did not recognize how much of what they themselves did was, in fact, ornamental. Modernism emphasized its "engineered" look and bare cladding for symbolic value. The naked geometry of straight edges and flat surfaces was taken to mean "cleanliness" and "freedom from stale convention." Many painters and sculptors in the early decades of the twentieth century, including the Russian Constructivists and some Futurist painters, were fervently optimistic about the miraculous benefits that science and mechanization would bring to society and filled their works with non-functional references to the shapes of technological wonders.

What purpose does ornament serve? It obviously satisfies some profound human need. All over the world, in every age, people have ornamented their own bodies with tattoos, jewellery, badges, non-essential bits of clothing, haute couture; their dwellings and shrines with pediments, plaster-work, mosaics. Such embellishments do more than make the person or building look good: they are intended to communicate inner qualities of the person or object to others – or on a deeper level, actually to induce those qualities by a kind of symbolic magic. If the ornament is to "work," as communication or magic, it must, to some extent, follow convention: one would not decorate a ballroom with religious symbols, for example; nor would an executive wear flowers in her hair to a board meeting.

In fact, ornament – interpreted in its broadest sense – is the language the designer must use in order to communicate with the public. Barely functional objects can even achieve the status of great art almost entirely through decoration. The landscape of Italy, for example, is dotted with superb decorated porticoes through which no carriage ever drives; Michelangelo's great Porta Pia in Rome is the supreme example.

1.13 UMBERTO BOCCIONI
Unique Forms of Continuity in Space, 1913. Bronze (cast 1931), 43⅞ × 34⅞ × 15¾ins (111.2 × 88.5 × 40cm). The Museum of Modern Art, New York, acquired through the Lillie P. Bliss Bequest.

The forms of this work invoke speed and multiple-exposure photography, and convey limitless optimism for the mechanized future.

1.14 MICHELANGELO
BUONARROTI
Porta Pia, Rome, south side, 1561–
1564.

This extravagant gateway is a cultural
symbol rather than a practical entrance.
It shows the artist's deliberately
unconventional detailing, allied with
careful design in terms of proportions
and the use of diagonals.

Most of what we recognize as fine art is rooted in ornament. The nineteenth-century theorist John Ruskin argued that the fine arts of painting and sculpture had their origins in the decorative arts and suffered if they lost contact with their original purpose. Ruskin held that good ornament is an additional layer of formal imagery developed out of the basic pattern of the object, rather as good musical extemporization develops the basic material of a tune.

THE HUMAN BODY AS SOURCE OF DESIGN

The structure and functions of the human body influence our designs in countless ways. Everything we make is, of course, a product of our physical and mental capabilities; but its form is – or should be – also designed to appeal to those same capabilities. As designers, we need to understand how the human body moves and responds and how its characteristics impinge upon our work.

The head

Besides holding the brain, in which all the functions of the person are co-ordinated (and whose structure and role in design will be examined later), the head is also the determining factor in the body's posture. We always feel the apex or peak of something to be special, and we find images suggesting a headless body particularly disturbing. The front of the head, the face, carries the four main organs of sense: eyes, ears, nose and mouth. Their symmetrical arrangement gives a special emphasis to the center-vertical in all human perception and creation.

Eyes

The two eyes focus upon objects in the world and help us to maintain our upright posture and our spatial relationships with those objects. The eyes also enable us

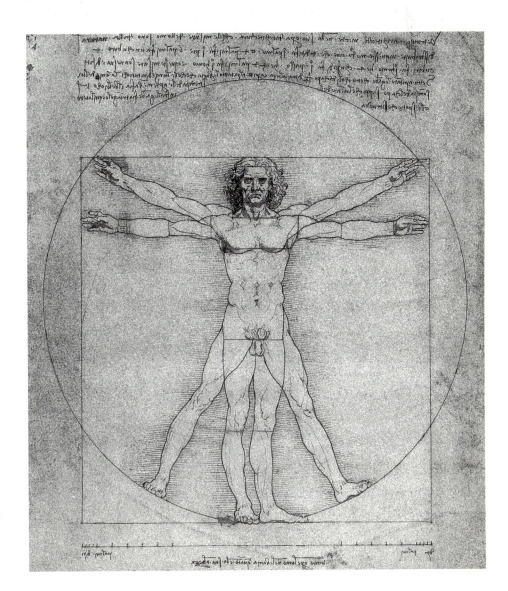

1.15 LEONARDO DA VINCI
Vitruvian Proportions derived from the Human Body, c.1490. Galleria dell'Accademia, Venice.

A drawing from Leonardo's notebooks represents one of the guiding principles of design in the Renaissance: that pure and ideal proportion were the basis of the human form, and could be derived from it.

to see objects up to about thirteen feet (four meters) away in three dimensions, partly because each eye sees part of one side of any object, as well as the front. The eyes' constant adjusting of focus and continuous scanning of the world by pulls of their muscles play an important part in our reading of 3D space.

Ears

Although the ears do not have the same degree of precise focus as the eyes, our hearing is to some extent directional. In an enclosed space we are able to gauge distances and heights from the timing and resonance of echoes – a faculty important in appreciating architecture. The balancing organs in the ear keep us upright, and thus indirectly influence our perception of balance and stability in design.

Hands

Evidence suggests that the versatility of the human hand played a major part in the evolution of the human brain. Not only can we raise our hands up and forward to any level, we can also do two things with them at the same time. One hand, with its fingers together, can shove, club, or poke; it can form itself into a blade to shovel loose earth or sand. The hands can grab things, break or pluck them; they can squeeze, throw, or roll things. Two hands together can carry water or loose material such as sand or grain. They can twist things or pull them apart. The hands carry out most of the designs the brain conceives – either directly, by manipulating the materials, or indirectly, by drawing, writing, or tapping a computer keyboard. Also, the acute sense of touch of the hands is essential to our appreciation and understanding of design.

The limitations our hands possess we compensate for in the numerous tools we have invented. These act as extensions of our hands, and so, although artifacts themselves, they occupy a middle ground between our own physical dexterity and the artifacts we produce with their help. Potters may use the shaped pads of their fingers and thumb, and their nails; but they also use a whole range of beaters, scrapers, and blades made of wood, stone, shell, and metal.

One area of sensory perception – that of touch – is often overlooked by designers in favor of the purely visual. We live in a world containing many objects that make scarcely any appeal to our sense of touch and rarely satisfy it. They thus have a remote or even repellent quality.

The tactile quality of an object is not limited to its surface texture. It also involves a whole complex of shaped surfaces, measured distances, volumes, and extended structures, which we understand through the various ways our bodies relate to them – by different hand-grips and finger-pressures, or by the amount of resistance we encounter if we rest our weight upon an object.

To give an artifact a highly tactile quality can also give its visual appearance an added power. Great architecture of the past implicitly acknowledged this fact. Even if we cannot physically reach most of its components, we are able to read their tactile implications. The craftspeople who carved these moldings and capitals used their hands as organs of their shaping intelligence – as we also should.

By contrast, mass-produced designs, even interior furnishings, often seem

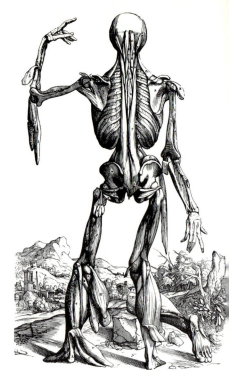

1.16 ANDREAS VESALIUS
The Thirteenth Plate of the Muscles from The Second Book of *De Humani Corporis Fabrica*, 1543.

From the Renaissance to the end of the nineteenth century, most European artists sought to build correct anatomical detail into their human figures; and designers have discovered prototypes for basis structures in the human anatomy.

1.17

blank, ungrateful, and uninteresting to the hand and body: raw-cut, featureless edges hurt hands; rolled-over plastic rims have unappealing curves; railings of featureless iron pipe that easily rusts cannot be gripped in wet weather. This repelling of human touch effectively wipes out a whole area of communication. Once we recognize the problem, however, we can take steps to deal with it.

The brain

The human brain is a mass of different cell structures performing an immense complex of interacting functions, some of which medical science has located in special areas. From the original brainstem (which controls the main automatic functions of the body) the higher parts of the brain developed to fill the skull with a multitude of complex folds. The outer envelope, with its deep convolutions of grey matter, is the cerebral cortex, in which many specialized functions take place. It contains two white-matter hemispheres where specific functions are performed. In right-handed people, motor functions, speech, and the ordering of space and time seem to be governed by the left hemisphere, whereas other more passive and emotive functions, including the appreciation of color and the perception of wholes, are carried out in the right. In left-handed people the situation is reversed. The nerve cells and pathways in the grey-matter cortex appear to consist of millions of sets of input and output columns, cross-linking with, and bridging, related cell groups in the two hemispheres. These give the potential for a colossal variety of interactions, which consist physically of patterns of electro-chemical discharges.

These multiple patterns of "firing" establish among themselves sets of customary reactions, building up what we know as our stock responses and our recognition and memory patterns. These learn to "fire" in many parts of the brain together, in association with particular patterns of immediate sensory response.

The principal regions of the cortex control movement, sight, hearing, and – oldest of all the senses – taste. The region concerned with smell is, as we know from experience, connected with quite complex emotions. There is also a large region that processes and stores associations and memories of touch and movements of the body, in particular of lips and eyes. It may therefore be the main resource area for such hypercomplex movements as those involved in speech and craftwork.

All of this demonstrates that what we subjectively experience as a world of colors, moving things, shapes, and vistas, extended into space and time, is an electronic construct within our brain. The images we perceive are, in effect, "translations" of the objects themselves. And since science has revealed many realities that we are unable to perceive at all, it seems likely that our mental image of the world is incomplete. Nevertheless, it is what we have to work with; we guide our actions by it; and the structures we are able to discover in that imaged world are reflected in our designs.

We shall probably never find any simple pattern of correspondences between perception, creative act and artifact; for each single apprehension or act involves an immense pattern-linkage through not one but several regions of the brain. Creative reflection, therefore, probably consists of directed searching among our stores of firing-pattern for matches and affinities of form. In designing, our brains

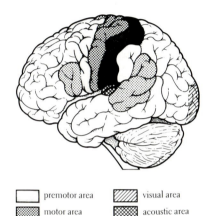

premotor area		visual area	
motor area		acoustic area	
sensory area		speech area	

1.18 Diagram of functional areas of the human brain.

1.17 Gudea, a Sumerian ruler, from Lagash, Iraq, c. 2100 BC. Hard mottled stone, probably quartz diorite, 29ins (73.6cm) high. The British Museum, London.

This dedicatory portrait sculpture was meant to eternalize Gudea's devotion to the deity of a temple. The forms are highly polished, but appeal very strongly to the hand. (The head has been incorrectly repositioned in restoration.)

use both inherited and learned techniques for converting the resulting pattern complexes into reality.

Designers thus think in terms of mental models: abstract combinations of form which they develop by mentally combining and adapting them in various ways to suit the requirements of the projected artifact. The designer needs to develop this visual modelling faculty of the imagination. Paper sketches can then serve as notations of models which take shape in the mind. Even a 3D designer may record ideas in 2D on paper; but 2D images should not determine his or her thinking. The modelling imagination needs to keep clear sight of the artifact as a real object.

1.19   RENÉ MAGRITTE
Mental Calculus, 1931. Oil on canvas, 26 × 45¾ins (66 × 116.2cm). Private collection, New York.

The artist portrays a landscape into which austere and basic geometrical volumes intrude, their smooth unreality dominating the simple tile-roof homes.

DESIGN AND HISTORY

No designer ever starts from scratch; he or she has inherited a basic language of design which humanity has been developing for thousands of years. What matters is what each individual designer is able to say in that language. In a truly creative piece of design the fundamental elements of the language are varied, combined, and/or adapted to produce an original statement.

Each personal or traditional style can use only some of the possibilities. Many may, in fact, be incompatible with each other. But novelty in design results from actively using the existing language of design, not by trying to invent a completely new one. Very rarely a genuinely new pattern may be found – as when

Keith Critchlow discovered a new interlock space-filling shape. But designers, like the users of any other language, need to work with basic forms and relationships that everyone can recognize, simply in order to make artifacts that will both work and be understood.

If we study in depth great designs from the past, we find them to be works of live design intelligence akin to our own, capable of revealing to us ideas that may have been forgotten. We may enjoy a wonderful feeling of being part of a great community of humans who speak to each other in form across time and space. But we belong inevitably to our own era, since we are heirs to discoveries after which design could never be the same again. Among these are the invention of the wheel, writing, the printing press, power transmission, steel frame building, photography, and the computer. We also now have access to many great designs from the past that people did not have even in the 1950s. We have seen a great upsurge in publishing, which has enabled us to experience, if only at second hand, all kinds of exotic design; and museums, travel, and tourism have offered us the chance to experience directly artifacts from many other cultures. This has had both positive and negative effects on our sense of design.

First the positive. We are now able to see ourselves as growing shoots on a living tree of design and to learn from and incorporate into our consciousness a great variety of good design images from the past. We have also learned a certain humility in the face of old aesthetic achievements from which our pursuit of sheer technological efficiency may have alienated us. The fine art end of design has long been trying to restore lost aesthetic modes to us.

On the negative side, however, this cultural repossession has resulted in

1.20   FRANK LLOYD WRIGHT
Ennis House, Los Angeles, 1924.

A monumental concrete structure whose 3D exterior is subdivided according to a single dominant grid of squares, and ornamented with rows of pre-cast features.

1.21

1.22

some dilution and generalization, because we have developed the feeling that so long as we can respond to a design idea at the formal level, we have understood it. We often therefore incorporate echoes of fashionable exotic designs – Aztec, Moorish, African, Gothic – into our own artifacts, without questioning at all whether we are genuinely grasping the cultural meaning of the original forms. We have been led to think that all appreciation is bound to work at that superficial level, and carry out our designs accordingly.

Repossession of tradition

Nearly every serious designer now feels that we need urgently to find our way back to authentic design statements of our own, which will take account both of our technological achievements and of what we have learned from the aesthetic expression of other cultures. This involves a new and special kind of investigation of the roots of design as a whole.

   To read intelligently not just the forms but also the meaning of what was done in the past has always been one of the best ways of stimulating new ideas. Some of the most superb examples of design have been inspired directly by works – or even by theories – from quite remote eras which suddenly revealed new potential in the imaginations of later designers. In the eleventh and twelfth centuries, for example, Romanesque art and architecture were believed to be maintaining the true spirit of ancient and civilized Rome after a period of barbarism; later, the works of Palladio and other sixteenth-century Renaissance architects revived the same spirit in quite different forms; Robert Adam, in the eighteenth century, incorporated concepts from the newly discovered ruins of Roman Herculaneum in his buildings; and in the following century the designers of Washington's public buildings chose classical forms to reflect Roman civic virtues in the capital of their new republic.

   Besides understanding structural and decorative forms for their intrinsic value, the modern designer needs to use them to communicate with his or her

1.21 The Baptistery, Florence, mainly 11th and 12th centuries.

1.22 PALLADIO
Villa Rotonda, near Vicenza, c.1566–70.

1.23 ROBERT ADAM
South front of Stowe House, Buckinghamshire, 1771.

1.24 THORNTON, HALLET, HADFIELD, LATROBE, and BULLFINCH
The Capitol, Washington, initial building 1792–1827; dome 1855–56 by Thomas Ustick Walter.

As successive ages reinterpret a design tradition, they cast that tradition into forms that are meaningful in the cultural terms of their time; and each reinterpretation of the tradition itself becomes a part of that tradition.

1.23

1.24

clients, who will have their own sets of attitudes and responses to design-forms. Unless the designer has some feeling for what clients expect, where their ideas come from, and what lies behind their attitudes towards their environment, he or she will not satisfy them.

In particular, the designer needs to understand the feelings people have in relation to the new and the old. In some periods, reverence for the past has inspired designers to make fresh versions of long-established types. But nowadays many people feel that "old" means "worn and shoddy" – an attitude that advertising generally tries to encourage. This attitude permeated the thinking of designers – both commercial and fine artists – in the 1950s. Designing came to be seen as continual undirected experiment with materials and processes, aimed at creating something totally new. Each piece was expected to demonstrate that it was in no sense a repetition of an earlier design. The cult of the random and of total individualism as the aesthetic way out of social conformity itself became an easy new conformity. Now we are again feeling the need for fresh and valid design ideas rooted in genuine creative method.

CHAPTER TWO

PROCESSES & MATERIALS

Processes are the fundamental factor in the production of designed objects, in that they emerge directly from the capacities of the human body to act upon the world. We change the forms of materials by applying energy or force to them using one or more of four categories of technique: wasting, forming, molding, and constructing. **Wasting** means removing parts of the original material, as in carpentry or stonecarving. **Forming** means altering the shape of the material by pressure, bending, or stretching. **Molding** means applying the material to another object which is already shaped, so that the material assumes the shape of that object. **Constructing** means connecting already-shaped sections (not necessarily of the same material) by means of joints, welding, or adhesives. Some of these processes entail changing the properties of materials, if only temporarily, as, for example, when we melt metal to a fluid, make fibers out of glass, mill wood into wood pulp, or make cement out of lime, slag, and clay.

The first three modes of processing – wasting, forming, and molding – produce from a single material one-piece 3D objects that stand on their own. Everything depends on the art that goes into the shaping; and certain materials are suitable for each mode. The fourth mode – construction – produces complex objects made of previously prepared pieces and often incorporating several different materials.

WASTING

All wasting processes involve striking or cutting parts of the original material away either by direct hammering; or by grinding with abrasive tools such as stones or sandpapers; or by cutting with edged blades such as axes, saws, adzes (transverse axes), point tools, or chisels, which may be either pushed by hand, driven by blows, bored, or milled with rotating drills and bits. Machine power may be used to perform any of these functions. The commonest example of this is the lathe, in which a solid mass of material is fixed on an axis and rotated swiftly against a

2.1 Michael Casson, a modern English potter, at work throwing a large clay vessel. Craftspeople like him are their own designers, often working with traditional forms, but also exploring the resources of their material.

held or fixed blade which cuts it into a sequence of circular sections following a given profile. Usually designed in advance, the profile may be cut to follow a template, which is offered repeatedly to the material or, nowadays, programmed into an electronic control system to cut a specified pattern. Different materials call for different types of implement to apply the wasting force.

In contrast to the live irregularity and worked surfaces of handcraft, the geometrical shapes of most modern design are conditioned by the general use of jigs. These are devices that automatically produce straight lines, right angles, arcs and mathematical curves. Such linear shapes are easily measured and translated from the drawing board to artifacts by mechanical processes; and components so conceived readily fit together. All drawing implements are jigs. So, too, are the engineer's matching equipment, ranging from calipers, gauges, guides, and templates, to all kinds of machine-tools.

Wood

The various kinds of wood are cut with sharp blades, usually of metal. Ancient peoples used a sharp-edged flint blade, whereas tribal people today often use glass. In some cultures, the woods of particular trees are also believed to have magical properties. Some smell beautiful, such as sandalwood. Woods vary in their resistance to rotting and to insect pests; generally the harder woods resist better than the softer ones. The hardest and most resistant woods, which can be cut only with difficulty, are *lignum vitae*, such as old oak, ironwood, and teak. The softest woods are baobob and balsa. Wood craftspeople include carpenters and joiners, who make structures; cabinet-makers, who make fine pieces; and sculptors, who carve objects directly from (usually) a single piece of wood.

Wood is normally sawn first into logs directly from the tree. These may then be further sawn into lengths of rectangular section – blocks, beams, or planks – by hand or machine. Logs and blocks are the shapes from which sculptors usually work; beams and planks supply structural components. The faces of all these can be planed smooth and/or carved in relief. Structural members may also be lathe-turned. Long members may be given profiled surfaces or edges with a profile-plane whose blade is shaped or adjusted to cut a specific section.

All woods have a natural grain which must be respected in hand carving with chisel or gouge and mallet: downward-slanting crosswise cuts are used; otherwise the wood might split off in strips. Whittled and shaved to shape, then ground smooth and polished, some woods reveal fascinating grain patterns. Sculptors use this quality to enhance their work; and furniture-makers often glue veneer of fine-grained and beautifully colored wood onto poorer woods. Veneers are cut by special rotary machines which slice thin sheets of wood across the grain of the log as it rotates eccentrically.

Stone

This may be coarsely split to shape by sheer percussion, by wedges driven into lines of drilled holes, or by explosives. It can be more finely cut to rectangular shapes by special hand or mechanical saws. Many stones, including some hard ones, can be trimmed to finer shapes by hand-chiselling; but very hard stones,

2.2 Egyptian figure of servant girl, 18th dynasty, 1570–1293 BC. Boxwood, 5⅛ins (13 cm) high. Durham University Oriental Museum.

This tiny figurine, found in a tomb, is cut and polished almost entirely from a single piece of wood. Her hair curl (recently replaced correctly on the other side of the head) and the jar lid are separate.

2.3 GEORGES VANTONGERLOO *Construction of Volume Relations,* 1921. Mahogany, 16⅛ins (41cm) high, 4¾ × 4⅛ins (12.1 × 10.3 cm) at base. The Museum of Modern Art, New York. Gift of Silvia Pizitz.

This carved wood-sculpture is an exercise in pure right-angled proportions in three dimensions.

2.4   Figures from the Temple of Konarak, India, early 13th century.

This stone carving of heavenly lovers, carried out with simple flat and pointed chisels, renders the figures as purely convex volumes with sensuously smooth surfaces.

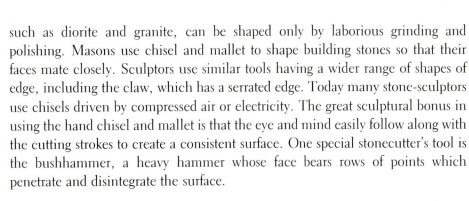

such as diorite and granite, can be shaped only by laborious grinding and polishing. Masons use chisel and mallet to shape building stones so that their faces mate closely. Sculptors use similar tools having a wider range of shapes of edge, including the claw, which has a serrated edge. Today many stone-sculptors use chisels driven by compressed air or electricity. The great sculptural bonus in using the hand chisel and mallet is that the eye and mind easily follow along with the cutting strokes to create a consistent surface. One special stonecutter's tool is the bushhammer, a heavy hammer whose face bears rows of points which penetrate and disintegrate the surface.

Precious and semi-precious stones

The shaping of gemstones is achieved by two techniques: splitting along a natural crystal plane with a hard, sharp edge; and grinding with an abrasive tool, drill, or wheel fed by a powder of the hardest stones – diamonds and some silicates. In the Middle Ages many precious stones were left uncut and merely polished to bring out the color. Since then it has become normal for all gems to have flaws cut away and the remaining bulk ground and polished with one pattern of facets on the upper face, and a different pattern on the lower, so that the mutual reflections of light among the facets produce effects of brilliance or "fire" in the stone. The basic patterns used on the upper face are: *cabochon*, a single curved or elliptical dome; rose-cut, a dome ground to a top rectilinear "crown" facet surrounded by concentric bands of triangular facets called the *pavilion*, usually six on the upper, twelve on the lower, steeper band; step or trap-cut, a rectangular crown with parallel facets sloping away around it; table-cut, used especially for diamonds, made by grinding the stone into an octahedron and grinding off one corner into a crown-facet half the width of the whole stone. Each stone requires specific facet-angles. Plain or colored glass can be cut into facets, grooves, and volumes with much greater freedom than can precious stones.

2.5 The Regent Diamond, Apollon Gallery, Louvre, Paris.

This spectacular diamond of 140 carats is one of the purest and brightest in the world. Found in the 18th century in central India, it was cut in a European workshop.

2.6 KURT SCHWITTERS
Red on Red, 1924. Collage of paper elements, 7⅞ × 6⅛ins (20 × 15.5cm). Marlborough Fine Art (London) Ltd.

The design deliberately avoids pure right-angle layout, and plays perceptual tricks by setting off overlapping edges against contrasted tones and colors which seem to advance or recede.

2.7 MICHELANGELO
BUONARROTI
Slave, c.1519. Red wax, 10½ins
(26.7cm) high. Victoria and Albert
Museum, London.

This little preparatory study for a
colossal stone-carving was modelled in
the hand out of wax, probably softened
with a drying oil, and filled with resin to
give it body when dry.

Silhouetted shapes

One simple type of wasting used for flat sheets of materials such as leather, cloth, paper, and cardboard is to cut silhouette shapes with a knife or scissors. Thin metal sheet and strip can be cut with shears, and so can wood veneer. The resulting silhouettes can then be applied to other materials. For example, cut or torn colored paper shapes can be stuck onto other sheets of paper – a technique called collage or *papier collé*.

Other inorganic materials

Lumps of set **plaster** or **concrete** can be carved like stone with stone tools; **plastics**, with sharp knives and chisels; **metal**, with chisels of a harder metal, a process called "chasing." The face of a hard material can be incised with a channel-like design. Special versions of this technique are used in printmaking (see pp.190–194). Panels of softish metal can be cut with pierced designs, a process called filigree.

FORMING

Forming involves applying forces to materials to change their shape without removing any of their substance. The materials have to be either ductile or flexible. Ductile materials include those that can be squeezed or pressed into shape by hand – like wet clay or warmed wax; malleable materials, such as gold, silver, copper, and their alloys, which can be pressured or hammered while cold; and harder materials, such as iron, which become malleable when hot and can be hammered or molded into shape. Flexible materials can be bent by hand or with tools into shapes which they can then be induced to retain.

Heat is an essential element in many forming processes. It may be used for softening a substance to make it malleable, as in melting the silica and fluxes used for glass-making; or for fixing the final shape of a naturally soft material – an example being the firing of clay, whose crystals fuse at high temperatures. Wooden components of furniture can be bent in steam. **Wax**, which never becomes very hard, usually needs to be softened by warming and perhaps by mixing with other ingredients such as lanolin and powdered resin; **plaster**, **cement** and **clay** are mixed with water to retain workable wetness for a time (see also molding, p.41). All these can be used for **modelling**, which involves not only squeezing and pressing with the hand or with shaped, spatula-like tools, but also cutting and applying smears or pellets of the material to build up surfaces. Modelling plastics work like wax, but most are thixotropic – they must be softened by kneading; you harden them by heating at normal oven temperatures.

Many modelling materials need armatures – skeletons of rigid materials enclosed within them for support. These can be metal bars, wire, or wood, held together with net or burlap, according to the strength needed. Large, heavy models and extended parts, such as arms of figures, are most likely to need support. If the modelling material becomes self-supporting once it hardens, an external, removable prop may do the job of a temporary armature. With internal ones you need to allow for shrinkage and cracking as the material dries and sets.

Warm wax sticks to itself; so does wet clay. But plaster and cement have modelling limitations. They come in dry powder form and have a setting time, during which they remain plastic before combining chemically with their mixing water into a stone. Set plaster is softer, cement harder, and is also mixed with silica sand. When correctly wetted, plaster is easier to work in some bulk; cement tends to flop and works best in thinner layers. Both can attack human skin, so hands need protecting; and both materials are best applied with metal tools. Since they adhere to each other only mechanically, fresh layers can be applied over a water-based adhesive, such as PVC emulsion. Both can also be used in molding processes.

Clay

Clays are found in natural beds and consist of alumino-silicate crystals combined with other silica and inorganic substances which both color and act as fluxes, reducing the temperature at which the clay melts. Once modelled, clay becomes hard, though not very strong, as its water content evaporates. Unless it is of equal thinness it also tends to crack as it dries. When it is fired in a kiln it becomes much harder.

The various kinds of clay, with their different chemical structures and properties, combined with appropriate firing techniques, produce a wide range of types of pottery. These include earthenware and terra cotta (low-fired particles remaining separate), stoneware (medium-fired particles partly fused) and porcelains (high-fired particles fully fused). The colors of clays are the result of different combinations of ingredients and temperatures. Mixed with a great deal of water, or less water and a chemical agent, clay can become a soup-like slurry, called slip. This can be used for jointing pieces when they are partly dried, for coating the surface, and for casting (see p.45). It can also be colored by the addition of special materials. Stronger colors are achieved with glazes, silicates, and fluxes combined with metallic compounds, which are applied to ceramics in powder or fluid form and then fired to the body at specific temperatures.

Because of its wet softness and other properties, clay needs to be built into masses carefully. When it is "leather-hard" or "green-hard" (with some moisture left in and workable only with tools), it can be shaved, cut with wire, scraped hollow into shells of more or less equal thickness, or joined to another piece with slip.

The potter's art is based on forming hollow shells of wet clay. This can be done entirely by hand: large, perfectly symmetrical pots are hand-modelled by some potters, who may then complete the work by beating the walls between a smooth rounded anvil held inside and a beater held outside. Or the shape can be "thrown" on a potter's wheel. The wheel spins the wet clay on a vertical axis, running it between the potter's wet hands, so that he or she can squeeze it into a circular shell of even thickness. Clay worked in this way will take and hold all sorts of elaborate shapes, including flanges and lips. It is then cut and lifted off the wheel carefully. The circular section can be modified by pressing the shape

2.8 CLAUDE MICHEL, called CLODION
Cupid and Psyche, c.1775. Terracotta, 23⅛ins (58.8cm) high. Victoria and Albert Museum, London.

This sensuous table-sculpture shows the heights of subtlety that clay modelling as a final medium can reach. It displays a very wide range of types of touch, cut and volume. Its sweetness matches its subject: the human soul carried away by love.

2.9

while it is still wet. Still another method of working clay is to press sheets of wet clay into open molds (see p. 44).

When a pot is green hard, the potter can put it on the wheel again and shave off some of its clay by scraping with a tool, or invert it and hollow out its foot. In this state the clay can also be carved freely with a blade – to form an undulating edge, for example. Extra elements, such as handles, modelled plaques, or crests, can be stuck on with slip. Several individually thrown sections can also be stuck together with slip to compose a single piece.

From the design point of view, the "drawing" of the lines that shape the pot surface is all-important. The surfaces can then suggest contained sequences of intelligible and subtle volume within the pot. The curves and rhythms, the depth and weight of bulges and narrowings, can be imbued with bodily expression – as implied by the names traditionally applied to parts of pots: body, neck, lip, belly, and foot. The placement and shape of handles and other protrusions relate to and amplify the expression of the main volumes.

Painting

In a sense painting is a type of modelling. A ductile material is applied to a surface which it adheres to. Paints are made by mixing pigments with binding media – in effect, adhesives. Water-soluble adhesives give transparent watercolors and gouache – watercolors made opaque with white. They are usually re-soluble, but dry quite quickly. Oils, such as those pressed from linseed or poppy seed, give oil colors, which set far more slowly. Egg yolk, white, or both become very hard by thorough drying; casein, made by mixing dried and crumbly skimmed milk with unslaked lime, when it turns fluid, is one of the best and toughest known glues. Nowadays we have the various polymer emulsions, notably PVA (acrylic) and PVC emulsions, which mix and thin with water, dry quickly, and remain effectively re-soluble.

The natural pigments traditionally used in paints are still the best, because they are relatively immune to fading, but are now very expensive. They include ground-up crystalline metallic salts, some of which have been heated to specific temperatures to take on different colors. A few, such as lapis-blue, are actually a single mineral found only in one area of the world. Others are produced naturally in volcanic regions – reds of Siena and Pozzuolana, for example. Some, such as the cadmium oxides, are manufactured by modern processes. A few traditional colors without metallic counterparts are organic – notably purple, from the murex shellfish or lac insect, and brilliant Indian yellow from the urine of cows fed on

2.9   Wine ewer standing in a basin, Sung dynasty, 12th century. Both porcelain with pale blue *ying-ch'ing* glaze, 9⅞ins (25cm) high. The British Museum, London.

Porcelain is capable of extremely delicate refinement of form, and Oriental porcelain is full of formal allusions to the shapes of flowers and fruits. Its glaze recalls "the color of distant mountains."

mango leaves. Sepia comes from the cloud-sac of the octopus, and black inks from oak-galls steeped in water.

Artificial dye pigments are now universal. They are chemical substances derived from tars which lack body, so have to be precipitated either onto fabrics or onto inert fillers such as chalk to make pigments. Used over white grounds their colors have a wider range and more brilliance than the traditional substances. Their main drawback is their tendency to fade over time.

Different kinds of pigment are applied in different ways. Dyes bonded with acrylics can be run as fluids onto raw canvas, paper, or other white absorbent grounds; but bulks of precipitated dyes can be used almost as if they were thick oil paint.

Ductile metals

Gold, silver, copper, and other softish metals can be made harder by being alloyed with another metal. Copper also work-hardens under sustained hammering, eventually becoming brittle and losing its ductility. This property can be used to give a working edge to copper tools; or it can be relieved by heating the piece to an appropriate temperature (annealing), when it will regain its ductility. Ductile metals can be beaten into almost any kind of continuous shape with special hammers and punches. They can be drawn out through a series of progressively smaller holes in a plate to make wire. They can be shaped simply by pressing and rubbing them with a tool called a burnisher. In liquid form they flow without losing consistency. Pieces of such metals – especially gold – can be pressure-welded together. Gems can be set into small craters of metal and held in place by burnishing. A sheet of metal can be hammered from the back into broad forms, then finished on the front with small punches and chasing – a technique called *repoussé*.

One special gold surface treatment is granulation. Small granules of the metal are stuck to the surface with a fluxing agent (see p.55) and then heated so that the granules melt onto the surface where they touch.

The principal way of shaping any ductile metal into hollow ware is to hammer out a cake of it over a specially shaped anvil called a stake. The smith gradually beats out a curved metal shell, relieving any work-hardening by annealing it at intervals. Pieces made in this way can be welded or soldered together – the body and foot of a bowl, for example. Metals can also be formed by spinning a cake on a lathe pressed against a shaping tool, when the metal will spread and curve under pressure. Metals can also be spun into concave molds (see p.44). These processes have an affinity with clay forming and can produce broadly similar shapes – although metal can be naturally thinner and sharper than clay.

Hot working metals

Certain metals become ductile and malleable only when they are red or white hot. Among these, iron is the most commonly used. To forge iron one needs a furnace to heat it (usually a shallow basin or bed of charcoal blown with bellows to a very high temperature), a block-like anvil on which to beat it out, heavy

2.10

2.10 Cast Tumbaga pendant from the vicinity of Popoyan, Colombia. Gold, 11½ins (29.2cm) high. The British Museum, London.

One of the reasons why gold has been highly prized by all cultures is its extraordinary ductility, which means it can be worked with relative ease into almost any shape. The other is its unique resistance to tarnish.

hammers, several kinds of pincers to grip the hot metal, and punches to shape it. The iron is beaten out from billets and bars. Hot iron will not flow as readily as cold-ductile metals, so the forms it will take are more limited, and the working process is heavier and slower. Pieces will weld together under the hammer. Iron heated repeatedly in the furnace-bed of charcoal absorbs carbon, so that its outer surfaces case-harden into steel – a basic factor in steel technology. Commercially available steel sheet, rod, and girder are now used with little modification by many artists, simply cut to varied lengths and welded together.

Glass

Worked as a glutinous fluid at extremely high temperature, glass hardens and becomes transparent as it cools, and once formed must be annealed slowly to release stresses in its shape. It is made of sand or quartz mixed with wood-ash, lead, or soda as fluxes. Fluid glass can be drawn out into sinuous shapes or molded (see p.44). A hollow piece of glass can be formed by dipping a clay core into the hot fluid one or more times, then chipping out the core once the glass has cooled. More often, hollow ware, or vessels, are made by blowing.

A glassblower picks up a blob of molten glass on the end of a long iron tube. He or she blows out a bubble, then shapes it as it slowly cools and sets by swinging the tube to lengthen it, by twirling the tube or rolling it along the flat arms of a special chair to open it, and by rolling it out on a slab of slate to flatten its walls into a cylinder. With pincers one can narrow a stem while rolling the bubble, or shape flanges onto it. Other blobs of glass can be applied and drawn out into delicate shapes.

2.11 LOUIS COMFORT TIFFANY
Iridescent glass vase, c.1900. 7½ins (20cm) high. Private Collection, London.

A *tour de force* of the glassblower's craft, this piece required the addition of tiny blobs of colored glass to the incandescent mass before blowing.

2.11

Glass can be colored with metallic salts; one color of glass can be "cased" over a bubble of another color; rods of colored glass can be worked into the surface of a bubble and then twisted and rolled into the substance. While it is still soft the shape can be trimmed with metal shears. The finished piece is placed in an oven to cool very slowly.

Another way of making glass is to blow glass bubbles into hollow molds (see p.44). Commercial bottles are made in this way by machine.

Flat glass for windows used to be made either by dropping a blob of glass to spread on a hot slab (bottle glass) or by cutting a blown cylinder vertically and opening it out while still pliable. Nowadays flat glass is made by running it out hot by machine onto the surface of a tank of molten tin. Three-dimensional glass pieces can be made by heating sheet glass over mold shapes until it softens and slumps onto or into them.

2.12 A glassblower from Dartington Glass in England draws out and shapes a bubble of hot, ductile glass on the end of his hollow rod. Elements such as stems and handles can be added at a later stage.

2.13   Crystal stele, 7½ins (19.1cm) high.

Designed by Cho Chung-yung of Taiwan and made by Steuben Glass, this facet-cut piece of crystal glass is a fine example of a work made by craftspeople to the design of an independent artist. It is engraved with a saying of Confucius.

Glass can be cut in two ways: as sheet, by incising a line on its surface with a diamond or tungsten point, then tapping it, causing it to break along the line; or as bulk, by pressing it against a spinning wheel whose sharp edge is fed with an abrasive powder suspended in oil. Wheel cutting is used to form the patterns of cut glass. Patterns can also be etched with acid, on either the front or the reverse side. Another technique is to cut through one layer of cased color to reveal the color beneath. Extraordinarily complex glass sculptures can be achieved by repeated blowing, adding, casing, and cutting.

Stained glass is made by cutting out pieces of flat sheet glass of different colors, then assembling them, sometimes on top of a drawn design, or cartoon, and joining them by setting the edges into H-section lead strip, which is then bent tightly around them. Joins in the strip are soldered, and large pieces may be strengthened with iron bars. Some glass colors need to be cased between plain glass to protect them from atmospheric corrosion.

Enamels are another form of colored glass. Many porcelain glazes are in fact enamels. But enamel is also applied to metal, usually gold or copper alloys, using glass-powders mixed with fluxes to bring their melting temperature to the level that gives the desired color. In two of the most widely practiced methods, *champlevé* and *cloisonné*, carefully judged quantities of powders are placed into shaped hollows, either chiselled into the face of the metal or made of wire soldered onto it, respectively. The piece is put into a kiln, heated to the right temperature to make the glass melt, flow, and fuse. When the work has cooled, the surface is ground and polished.

Mosaic is made with little tiles of different colored glass, cut from rods. The tiles are fixed to a base, either with lime plaster (if it is a wall) or with glue (if it is a board).

Flexible materials

In the case of flexible materials, forming is achieved by means of pressure. Some materials may need to be subjected first to a wasting process – for example, cane or wood veneer – or to hot working – as with metal tube. To bend woods and other organic materials such as tortoiseshell one may need to soak them in water or heat them in steam to prevent them from breaking. Metals are bent according to their ductility: gold and copper cold, iron hot. Once bent, they may need to be fixed into their new positions – either by being incorporated into stressed structures in which their natural spring plays a part, such as basketwork or bentwood furniture (see p.288), or by being heated to relieve their inner stresses so that they keep their new shapes, as is often done with metals.

2.14   Stone mold for terracotta images, Iraq, 2nd millennium BC. Approximately 7ins (18cm) wide. Durham University Oriental Museum.

Known as a single-valve mold, this piece was meant for making relief impressions on a thick sheet of clay.

MOLDING

The basic principle of molding is the same for all materials. You prepare a 3D surface shaped as the reverse image of what you want to produce, usually hollow. This is the negative mold. The material for the positive shape is applied, in a ductile state, to the mold surface-shape and allowed to harden; then the two are separated. If the negative is shaped carefully of strong material, without undercuts, a number of positive impressions can be taken from it. There are thus four main factors involved: first, how the mold is shaped; second, the constitution of the mold; third, the material and constitution of the positive; fourth, the method of bringing the two together.

Shaping the mold

You can waste the mold by hollowing out its face. The most familiar of such molds are semi-precious gems intaglio-cut with drills, often mounted on rings, and used to stamp relief images in sealing wax. Early Greek artists made the most beautiful intaglio seals; they also used to cut hollow negative molds for coins. The intaglio technique is still important in casting jewellery. When hollowing out an intaglio mold you need to think of the image in reverse – which can produce

2.15   ANDREA BRIOSCO, called IL RICCIO
A Satyr and Satyress, c.1507–1516. Bronze, 9⅛ins (23.2cm) high. Victoria and Albert Museum, London.

This small image was modelled with extraordinary vivacity of surface, probably originally in wax. The couple may symbolize unredeemed but guiltless natural love.

surprising results. Nowadays, intaglio molds of tough metal for runs of commercial products are made by computer-controlled cutting machines, which reverse the design automatically.

The second, commonest way of shaping molds is first to model or carve the original object either in something soft and disposable, such as wax, or in something hard and permanent, such as plaster. A modern way of making very large positives is to cut parts of the rough shape out of sections of thick polystyrene foam with a hot wire tool, then stick the sections together and do the final modelling with plaster. The negative mold is then made by applying some soft, hard-setting material to the positive (first coated with soap, light oil, watery clay, or powder to prevent the surfaces from sticking). If the core material is hard, you must make sure the mold will draw off without damage. If it has undercuts, or is fully 3D, the mold must be made in two or more pieces, which will individually draw off, and can then be fitted together like a 3D jigsaw. The inside faces of such piece-molds can be worked in intaglio to produce detail or surface ornament on the final artifact.

Mold materials

If the final piece is to be of plaster or concrete, the mold can be made from a mix of setting plaster or of clay which is then fired. If the object is to be of a setting plastic, and large, the mold can be made of plaster or of fiberglass; if small, both natural and synthetic rubbers and other plastics are good, since their elasticity allows the removal even of pieces with undercuts. These materials are particularly good for making a number of copies of the original. But if the final piece is to be one-off, it can go into a waste-mold – one which is chipped away afterwards.

A mold must always be strong enough to hold the positive material without deforming. If the final piece is to be of metal, which has to be poured molten and very hot into the mold, the latter must be made either of heat-resistant clay or casting-sand in a steel box, which can be heated to receive the hot metal without shattering. In **cire-perdue casting** a model is made of wax (French *cire*) and a clay mold built around it. The wax melts out and is lost (*perdue*) by burning away when the mold is fired. Extra vents or risers must be provided in the mold to allow gases to escape when the molten metal is poured in through the main hole, so that it can fill all the spaces of the mold. These are formed by little wax rods added to the original that lead out through the mold and melt away.

Molds for other materials are often made of wood. One of the ways of making precious metal jewellery is by cutting an intaglio image into the face of a board of hard wood, then with hammers and punches, or even a burnisher, pressing into it a sheet of precious metal. The back of this can then be filled with some setting material so that it keeps its shape. Wood can also be used for large-scale molding: an important type of wooden mold is the elaborate constructed shuttering used to shape the reinforced concrete of modern buildings.

The material of the final positive has to be pliable when brought into contact with the negative mold; and thereafter it must harden. Mold and positive must be prevented from sticking together. Most positive materials that are mixed with water shrink a little as they dry and/or harden, as does hot metal when cooling. This helps the separation.

2.16   Ritual wine vessel or *hu*, c.1300–1100 BC. Chinese, from Anyang, Honan Province. Bronze, 9⅞ins (25cm) high. The Metropolitan Museum of Art, New York.

The bronze would have been cast in a negative piece-mold of the main bulk, into the interior of which the complex raised patterns were incised. The casting was then chased.

2.17   JOSÉ LUIS SERT Fondation Maeght, Saint Paul de Vence, France, completed 1964.

The complex concrete shapes, including the *jali*, or sun grille, were poured into carefully constructed wooden shuttering. The surfaces are enriched by the texture of the planking from which these were made.

Press molding

Some materials can be pressed by hand either into or onto a mold. This is often done with ceramic clay to produce single-face terracottas and open bowls. Very large bowls may be first shaped upside down over a convex hump of, say, polystyrene foam, then removed and worked on by modelling or throwing. Hollow or hump molds made of clay can be thrown on the wheel and perhaps incised ornamentally, then fired. Wet clay can then be thrown onto or into them, using a separator. The natural shrinkage of drying clay allows you to pull the result away from the mold.

Poured molding

By far the commonest positive materials used in the arts are those which are poured into the mold in a fluid state, either cold or molten hot. In order to make sure the mold is strong enough, it may be necessary to bind it with cord or wire. The principal casting metals include **bronze**, an alloy of copper and tin; **brass**, copper with zinc; **pewter**, tin plus antimony, lead, and copper; and very soft **lead**. They melt at different temperatures. When the metal has cooled and the mold has been either chipped off or separated, the piece will almost certainly need polishing; it may also need to be patched by hammering in lead and finished by chasing parts that were cast thick for safety, and perhaps washing with acids to color it.

Other principal artistic casting materials are **plaster** and **cement**. Both are powders consisting of calcined stones based on calcium: plaster of Paris from alabaster, cement from ground limestone and slag. Both are mixed with water; they then return to the condition of stone over a period of time. Lime mixed with water glass (sodium silicate) will set similarly. Cement needs to be mixed with sand, usually in the proportions of one of cement to three of sand by bulk. Additives can also be mixed in, which both accelerate the setting process and waterproof the result. The principal use of cement today is for casting architectural members, even entire structural units, within molds built of wooden shuttering. But it is also good for sculptures. It needs reinforcement bars, supplemented sometimes by expanded metal net, iron, aluminum or zinc. Both plaster and

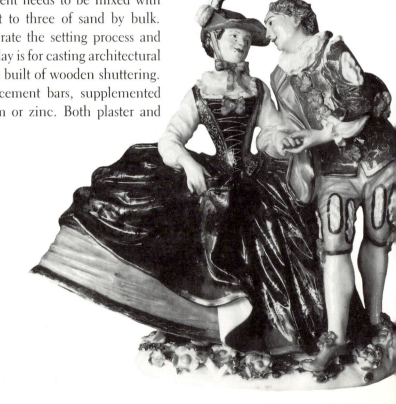

2.18 *Harlequin and Columbine*, painted porcelain, Meissen, c.1741. 7⅜ins (19.37cm) high. Victoria and Albert Museum, London.

The complex piece-mold from which this table-decoration was slip-cast would have been taken from a wax original and reassembled for re-use many times over.

2.19   George II five-guinea piece, 1753. Obverse, actual size. The British Museum, London.

Die for five-guinea piece. Obverse, actual size. Royal Mint, Wales.

This is the only surviving example of this coin, shown here with the concave die from which it was struck.

cement are poured in the form of a heavy, porridge-like slurry, which needs to be thoroughly and evenly mixed with water.

There are several proprietary **plastics** that are cast in molds; some require a catalyst to make them set, whereas others set when heated. They produce positives that are far lighter than those made of more traditional materials and can be mixed with metallic powders to give the effect of metal.

Ceramic casting

A special type of ceramic casting is to take piece-molds in plaster from the surfaces of originals either thrown in clay or lathe-turned in plaster: purely circular forms readily divide into half-shell molds that have no undercuts. You bind the shells together, dry them, then pour in liquid clay slip, which you swill around the interior. The dry plaster absorbs water from the slip, and a layer of drier clay builds up on the inside. When the layer is thick enough you pour out the excess and let the slip layer dry out. This is particularly good for porcelain wares whose body material is too slimy and lacking in bulk to throw properly.

Electrolysis

Often used for duplicating jewellery and industrial components, electrolysis involves first making a negative mold of some conducting material, backed up by non-conducting material, attaching it to the negative pole of an electric circuit. This is then immersed in a bath of metal solution along with a positive pole. Metal will then gradually deposit from the solution onto the negatively charged form as thickly as required. Metal objects can be silver-plated in a similar way.

Die-stamping

Another important way of mold-shaping metals is by **stamping** them. Coins, especially, are made like this. An intaglio image, called a die, is made in a block of metal. In the case of coins a second die is made for the reverse side. You then sandwich a small piece of ductile metal between them, hit the upper die hard with a mallet, and part them. This process is now carried out by machines for duplicating many kinds of shaped object – not by percussive force but by pressure. The die is often combined with a closed shearing edge that detaches each piece from its metal sheet or strip. The force can be applied either by direct die or by roller. The original intaglios need to be very carefully made so that the products do not stick in the die.

Vacuum molding

In this important modern technique, a sheet of plastic is placed over an open mold; its edges are sealed; it is heated; and a vacuum pump evacuates the air from the mold side. The plastic is thus sucked into very intimate contact with the mold. It is important that the shapes lack undercuts or overhangs, so that the positive will withdraw without damage.

2.20

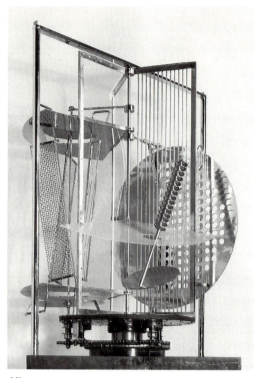

2.21

CONSTRUCTING

Unlike the processes of wasting, forming, and molding, which involve working with a material as a coherent mass, structural processes involve joining separate pieces of material or, sometimes, pieces of different materials. They are thus 3D diagrams of the forces they resist.

In most cases, of course, the materials used in a construction must first be treated in some way. Very seldom are we able to use materials structurally "as found." There are, however, some exceptions: tree branches may have shapes that turn out to be just what is needed, say, for an angled barn beam or a cart shaft. In the East the naturally tapered and flexible poles of the bamboo are tied or split to fulfill an extraordinary variety of functions. Other materials used more or less as found are the various fibers and thatches – banana leaves, tree bark, bracken, heather, reed, and wheatstraw. Most important of all are probably the naturally layered and fracturing sedimentary limestones, sandstones, and slates, whose fragments stack naturally.

The detailed execution of any structure depends upon the characteristics of the materials from which it is made, the loads and forces it will have to sustain, and whether or not the facts of the structural method need to be apparent to the spectator. In some modern architecture and structure-art these facts may be a vital part of the image. But in most high-grade furniture and automobile design they are meant to be concealed.

One striking aspect of structural design is the way its designers – even more than those in other areas – project images of the working fabric of their body into their technology. There are, of course, many features of design that we generalize from principles abstracted from the natural world. But since design takes place at

2.20 ISAMBARD KINGDOM BRUNEL
Clifton Suspension Bridge, Bristol, 1837–64.

The weight of the bridge and its traffic is carried on catenary-curved iron bars, linked and guyed through structural towers of masonry.

2.21 LÁSZLÓ MOHOLY-NAGY
Light Space Modulator, 1923–30. Mixed-media kinetic sculpture with electric motor, 59½ins (151.1cm) high, 27½ × 27½ins (69.9 × 69.9cm) at base. Fogg Art Museum, Harvard University, Cambridge MA, gift of Sibyl Moholy-Nagy.

Steel, plastic and wood are among the materials incorporated into this sculpture, which is made to move by an electric motor. Despite the elaborate structure, the sole purpose of the piece is aesthetic.

the interface between human being and environment, it is not surprising that the principle of extending the faculties of the hand into tools is carried through to quite sophisticated levels, and that mechanical patterns in the structure of the body are projected into the structure and function of artifacts. To take one example: we imitate the leverage and bracing systems of bones and muscles in the rigid jibs and hydraulic pump-systems of earth-movers and diggers. The great French writer Paul Valéry said, "the painter takes his body with him." So too does the structural designer.

Heaping

The simplest kind of structure is the heap. Any pile of material – sand, stones, earth – settles into a slope natural to it, its sides following its particular "angle of repose," according to the weight of its particles, their shape and size, and the friction and cohesion between them. Dry, round stones or sea sand lie in flatter heaps, because they roll off more easily than coarse gravel or sharp sand that locks together.

A heap structure may stand more or less vertically and follow a specific plan on the ground if made of a substance such as wet clay or other earths. Because they are naturally tacky or contain adhesive substances, they keep their wet shape when they dry; and you can make walls, even overhanging arches and domes out

2.22   Chapel, restored 17th century, Núpsstadur, Iceland.

This traditional and ancient structure of turf, supported by wooden members, provides warmth and shelter in a bitterly cold climate.

2.23   HIERONYMUS BOSCH
Adoration of the Kings, c.1500. Oil on canvas, 39½ × 29½ins (100.33 × 74.93cm). Petworth House, West Sussex.

The structure of the house is revealed where it is broken, notably the wattle-and-daub infill panels between the main frames. This technique of building was used in northern Europe for at least 1,000 years.

2.22   2.23

2.24   House at Skara Brae, Orkney Islands, 3200–2200 BC.

Even the furniture of this dry stone house – cupboards, beds, and tables – was made of stone slabs, since stone was a far more abundant material than timber on these barren islands in the North Atlantic.

of such materials. The process is closely akin to modelling (see p. 33). Eskimos still use **hand-modelling** to make huts of snow to shelter in when they are away from home. In some parts of the world quite elaborate architectural projects are hand-modelled in mud. The grainstores and great mosques of northern Nigeria are beautiful examples. So too are the *adobe* structures – churches, monasteries, settlements – of the Spanish-American south-west.

Such works may appear as unitary aggregates without conceptual seam or join. They often have a comfortable concavity of interior surface that fits the shapes and attitudes of the human body far better than rigidly rectangular planes do. The disadvantage of this kind of work is that rain washes off its outer layer, and it has to be continually resurfaced. But there are even parts of rainy Britain where entire villages used to be made of lime-rich earth pounded into walls between planking, the walls being then protected with a skim of plaster.

This kind of material holds together better if it contains fibers to bond it. Turf is an earth naturally full of fibers, and an excellent building material. Turf houses, very similar to those made by bronze-age Britons, were made on the American Great Plains in the nineteenth century. Roofs could be made of turf laid over timbers. Any turf stack naturally rots in time. But while it stands and is kept warm inside, it sheds water, is quite windproof, and makes an adequate home.

One version of the wet-earth modelling technique is so-called **wattle and daub**, used all over the world. Fiber or twig basketwork is daubed, on one or both sides, with clay or lime-rich earth, and sets as it dries into a satisfactory wall panel to keep off wind and sun. Modern plastering on battens or canework derives directly from this technique.

Locked heaping depends on an interaction of friction and gravity. Using variously shaped and proportioned angular stones, one can build a **dry stone** wall by matching stones so that they lock together without cement. A development of this sort of work involves grinding or cutting flat the irregular meeting-faces of the stones so that they mate almost exactly and lock without interstices. The outer face may also be flattened. This is called **Cyclopean masonry**. It was used, for example, in Ancient Greece, in Peru, and in the plinths of Japanese castles of the sixteenth to eighteenth centuries, being particularly suitable for lands shaken by earthquakes, because, if shaken, it tends to lock together even more tightly.

One way of using natural flat stones is to set very large ones up on edge, leaning and wedged together, to create box-like containers, which can be roofed with similar flat stones. In almost treeless regions of the world – for example, the Scottish islands of Orkney and Shetland – people assembled cupboards, beds, cradles, and entire houses from slabs of natural split stone, either dry stone walled, or set on edge.

Courses and bonding

One of the most familiar building materials is the rectangular **brick**. The flat faces of rectangular shapes stack easily. In the ancient Middle East, vast temple and palace structures were first made by the Sumerians, Assyrians, and Egyptians out of millions of flat bricks, manufactured cheaply from dried river mud. At first these were simple hand-formed cakes. Then they were made in wooden molds, usually by slave labor. As each mud brick dried in its mold, it shrank, and so came out easily. In the Bible we encounter the fact that bricks need straw (i.e., fiber) in them to hold them together. This method implies two fundamental

2.25   Polygonal masonry from Delphi, early 6th century BC.

The crude techniques of earlier Cyclopean masonry were refined until each stone was cut to match its neighbors exactly and interlock with them, forming an impregnable and durable structure that even earthquakes could not shift.

2.26   Dry stone walling, near Richmond, Yorkshire.

On the open moors of England, where stone is plentiful, walls have long been made by matching and rough-hammering natural pieces, with special long stones tying the structure together. Such walls resist animals and weather for centuries.

design concepts: first, the mass production of objects of uniform size and shape; and second, the use of a rectangular layout for elevation, ground plan, and structural components.

The next development in brickmaking is associated with pottery: **fired brick**. Dried mud brick dissolves back to mud when it is wetted by flood or rain; fired clay bricks resist this process. In the third millennium BC in the Middle East it first became common to use fired bricks for facing large masses of mud brick; later, for building entire structures. Fired bricks, of course, are more expensive than unfired; and in the past, in areas of the world where there was little forest, wood to burn for brick-firing was scarce.

To make bricks stick to each other you use a layer of mud, cement mortar, or plaster in every joint. The bricks are best laid on level "courses" or rows; and the bricklayer's skill lies in making joints and courses so correct that the finished wall stands vertical and even. **Bonds** are used to give stability. In the simplest – the stretcher bond – each end joint is placed at the centre of the brick below. But since few walls are only one brick thick, each thickness of brick needs to be bonded onto the adjacent thickness. Some of the bonds used for this – such as the English and Flemish bonds – require a brick twice as long as it is wide. It is possible to design more complex bonds.

Over the centuries stonemasons have developed enduring and sophisticated methods of building in courses. Layered stone that splits along a natural plane of cleavage can be broken into flat pieces which can be laid immediately in rough courses and joined by varied *ad hoc* patterns of bond. This means that the characteristics of each piece have to be individually considered. Dry stone walling can be done this way. Often good coursing need only be used for the faces of the wall, while the inside can be filled out with rubble that develops a natural interlock as it settles. Extra bonding elements, such as sets of larger stones at intervals, or tie logs, can be built in to strengthen the faces and to tie them together. Wooden logs, of course, rot long before the life of the wall has ended. So, too, do the iron ties often used in eighteenth- and nineteenth-century buildings; since rust expands, slotted-in ties can actually split apart the stone structures they were originally meant to hold together. Lead links, though softer, last far longer.

Nowadays structural stone is usually sawn at the quarry by powerful machine-saws, to standard sizes that approximate the individual neutrality of bricks, either as blocks or as facing slabs. These can be laid in the same way as bricks. But heaped walls can still be made from natural pieces of stone. A good mason will cut each one of them accurately to the best proportioned rectangular shape, which will enable it to be mated with others into a fitting fabric of stone. The mason uses a right-angled straightedge and, to measure each piece exactly for the place it is to fit, a pair of calipers. These implements have become the emblems of mason-craft. The variety of size and shape among the stones, and the mason's careful fitting, can work as a bond. Mortar may be used, but really true flat-cut masonry does not need it. A mason is able to use the relative weights and lengths of different pieces of stone to engineer the balance and locks of the structure. Cornerstones are usually large, and are laid with their long axes projecting alternately into the fabric of first one and then the other wall. The mason keeps the natural strata horizontal, to prevent water from running down between and into the layers and frost from splitting them.

2.27   Flemish bond in bricklaying.

2.28   The West door, Qalbloré, Northern Syria, c. 500 AD.

The main structure is assembled from painstakingly shaped and decorated lintel and arch members, which combine the two simplest formal elements: rectangle and circle.

Mass and inertia

All the techniques mentioned so far for erecting heaped structures depend partially or wholly upon the accumulated weight, as well as the fit, of the components to hold them steady. A stable mass stands balanced on its base. A vertical line dropped from its center of gravity must fall within the area of its base. The moment it ceases to do so, the mass develops a sideways topple, or thrust.

A wall that is in danger of falling to one side can be kept up by a **buttress**; this consists of a mass of material, which is itself unstable and which leans in the opposite direction, thus exercising a thrust that counterbalances the push of the wall. This counterpoise constitutes one of the basic principles of all structures. It also plays a part in our appreciation of structural sculpture; for example, when some part of the work leans so far over that it has to be bolted to the floor, it conveys the aesthetic impression of some unanalyzable force at work.

Architectural engineering has to solve the problem of opening spaces in a solid wall without the structure above collapsing into them. One solution is simple: to insert above the opening a **lintel** of wood or stone strong enough to carry the whole weight of the wall built above it, and pass it to the two **jambs** or posts on either side. Some examples of vernacular and classical architecture, such as Renaissance palaces, play very sophisticated games in leading weight down through a stepped series of posts and lintels to the ground. And, of course, versions of the post and lintel are the basis of modern steel architecture.

A more sophisticated solution is the **arch**. The evolution of the arch was of central importance in the history of Roman, Romanesque, Gothic, Byzantine, and Muslim architecture. The arch diverts the thrust of weight above it along its curves down into the jamb-posts. The jambs sometimes had to be fortified by being fitted with weight-carrying pillars of especially tough stone. Elaborate combinations of arches could carry almost the entire weight of a structure, allowing the walls to be lightened and opened with broad windows.

There are several standard types of arch. First is the **triangular** arch, made of a pair of lintels leaning together; second, the **corbelled** arch, built by projecting the blocks of each course a little farther across the opening, until they meet. Third is the **round-headed** arch, which has to be independently built as a line of stones laid in a curve independent of the main courses. It needs a wooden support (centering) until the weight on its center block locks it into position. Fourth is the most efficient, the **pointed** arch, found in Arab and Gothic architecture.

In architecture the **roof** is the commonest source of problems. The weight of sloping rafters and tiles on a gable roof exercises an outward thrust at the top of a wall. The usual remedy is to tie these together by carpentry into a solid structure which thus becomes a uniform vertically acting weight which the walls transmit to the ground. End-gable walls can help to carry the thrust and exert a contrary folding-in force on rafters that hang from the main beam. Beautifully conceived roof structures are among the great glories of cathedrals in the West and temples and palaces in the Far East.

Skeleton structure

The transition from the stacking principle to the notion of the load-carrying

2.29   A lintel stone incorporated into rough masonry.

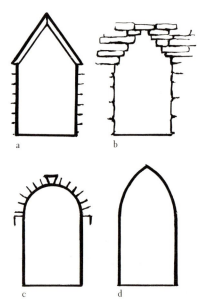

2.30   Different types of arch: (a) triangular (b) corbelled (c) round headed (d) pointed.

2.31   Typical roof structure.

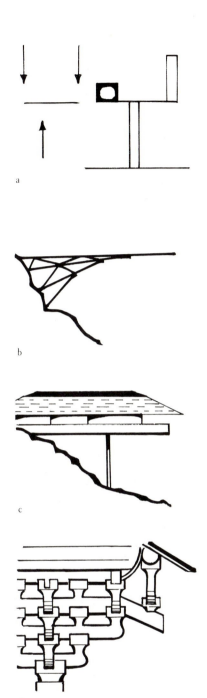

2.32 The cantilever: (a) representation of forces in a basic example (b) early architectural realization (c) functional architectural realization (d) ornamented architectural realization.

skeleton or armature is marked in the history of architecture by the evolution of the Gothic arch system. Medieval builders learned to conceive lines of thrust through which they could lead the weight of their buildings through the ribs of vaults and around the frames of openings into piers and columns. Most of the decoration carved on such buildings punctuates and enhances the elements of their structural design.

The **ground** itself is always an integral part of any skeleton structure, not only receiving weight but holding the footings of the building in constant spatial relationships to each other. The ground plan functions as a main constituent of a structure. And whereas in traditional architecture the ground plan is more or less the widest part to cope with the "center of gravity" problem, with a skeleton or armature it is perfectly possible to make structures that stand on bases far narrower than the main structure, so long as the bases are firmly rooted and balance the whole.

The basic elements of any coherent skeleton structure, with their anatomical analogues, are: rigid extenders (bones), joints and bracers (tendons and muscles), and casing (membrane or skin). All can be made of various materials, amplified in various ways, and elaborated or decorated. They can even, to some extent, exchange functions.

Extenders are the principal elements that give any skeleton structure its overall form and dimensions. In architecture we may classify as extenders the main lines of the ground plan, the inner and outer vertical corners, the main thrust lines, and the roof beams. Extenders are most obvious in post-and-beam architecture, in which vertical posts carry horizontal cross-beams. But many structures use a variety of arrangements. Extenders may be straight or curved. They must sustain the main weights and stresses including their own weight; so you choose different materials according to the job to be done and the needs for maintenance and replacement. Stone posts, for example, may carry wooden rafters and joists; reinforced concrete pillars may carry steel or aluminum girders.

The properties of the materials used for extenders must match their loading. To carry weight, verticals may need to have great compressive strength (resistance to compression), but little tensile strength (resistance to sideways snapping pressure). Horizontal extenders may need opposite properties. Steel has both, although one or the other may be greater according to how it is forged or rolled, giving it a particular crystalline structure. The flexibility of steel also makes it good for long vertical members. In a high wind it will yield slightly to sideways pressures and return – several feet in the case of a tall skyscraper. A disadvantage is that a steel structure can pick up vibrations from traffic or from air-conditioning plants and resonate enough to cause discomfort to its occupants.

Extenders can be compounded out of different materials, so as to combine their physical qualities. Reinforced concrete, for example, is made by pouring concrete into molds around clusters of thin steel bars or high-tensile wires. When the concrete sets hard it gives high compressive strength to vertical posts and rigidity to horizontal beams, complementing the tensile strength of the steel.

The shape of extenders contributes to their structural properties. Wood simply needs to be thick and dense to be strong. Metal tube, I-beam, H-beam, or L-angle section steel girders have a built-in resistance to the bending or crosswise flexing which a simple flat section would permit. The function of extender can be performed by areas of cladding, if it is broad and rigid enough, as in furniture made of board, or the cardboard used in architectural model-making. Lightweight girders of great strength can be constructed by using complex open-work bracing with relatively thin components.

One important dynamic aspect in the use of tensile strength in extenders is the principle of the **cantilever**. This involves supporting a horizontal or quasi-horizontal extender at a point part-way along its length, weighting down one of its ends and requiring the other, unattached end to support a lesser weight. Another version of the cantilever is really part of the process of **bracing** (see p. 56), since it uses a right-angled component, one of whose arms is attached to a vertical extender, while the other arm juts out to carry the weight. One ancient use of the cantilever in building is for supporting on extended beams an upper story projecting beyond the lower.

The two principal kinds of skeleton structure are the **cage** and **armature**. The cage is an external frame supporting weight inside itself; the armature an inner tower that carries its weights hanging cantilevered around itself. The two types, which may or may not be rectangular, are occasionally combined. Nearly all wooden-framed buildings are post-and-beam cage frames. The extenders that hold up a cage are footed at the outer corners of each cell; and weights are carried on internal flooring. This is the pattern followed by commonplace modern building, using reinforced concrete posts or pillars and prestressed concrete transverse beams. The cage is a very stable pattern, capable of extension in all directions over the ground, and of supporting its loads inside itself.

The armature structure demands a very strong and relatively narrow column that serves as a trunk resting on feet, its horizontal branches being cantilevered out. It can be of any coherent shape, a cage or even a single post. It requires only lightweight external cladding; but it does need to be virtually symmetrical, so that its center of gravity is always balanced over the area of its narrow footing. High inner loads such as machinery need to be carried close to the central tower and counterbalanced. An armature is capable of interesting aesthetic elaboration, as in Frank Lloyd Wright's Johnsons Wax Building.

Extenders have to be **jointed** together, either end to end or at an angle. Good jointing is vital to stability. Some jointing techniques are material-specific, others can be applied to a variety of materials.

One type of joint is the simple **lug and slot**. On a joint closed by weight, one or other of the parties to the joint is given a male projecting lug, and the other a matching female slot. The second is the **peg** or **nail**. A peg is usually of softer material than a nail, and it needs to have a hole drilled or cut for it if inserted into a harder substance. Members of the timbers of a boat can be pegged together. A large part of the strength of all joints comes from the closeness with which the joined faces meet each other and bond by pressure and friction. Herein lies the virtue of the **screw**. Its thread cuts its way into the holed material – usually wood or metal – and it can be pulled out only by dragging its thread off or tearing out part of the material.

The master joint is the **bolt**. It can be made to any size, suitable for anything from watch movements to sixty-ton girders. It can be given a thread and screwed into a hole cut with a matching negative version of its own thread in the lower of the two members to be joined; or it can be run into a nut, which may be locked

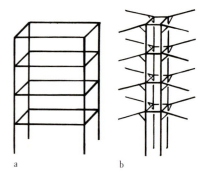

2.33 Skeleton structures: (a) cage (b) armature.

2.34 FRANK LLOYD WRIGHT Administration building and laboratory tower for S. C. Johnson & Sons (Johnson Wax), Racine, Wisconsin, 1937–9 and 1946–9.

The night-time lighting shows how the armature structure can carry cantilevered internal floors independent of the external cladding.

on by a second lock-nut pulled tight behind the first. Automobiles, machines of all kinds, bridges, and skyscrapers are full of metal nuts and bolts. The strength of any such construction depends to a great extent on the quality of the bolts and the skill of the bolt-hole layout designer. Some famous accidents, such as that to the mezzanine in John Portman's San Francisco Hilton, have been attributed to defective bolts.

Riveting is used especially for sheet metal, but also for beams. The basic principle is that both ends of a metal peg slotted through matching holes in two members are spread by hammering, so that neither will pull back through its hole. There are two forms of riveting. In one, a cylindrical plug of metal with a mushroom head is pushed through holes in the members to be joined – if made of steel, the rivet is red hot and so malleable. The other end is then hammered – if steel, usually with a compressed-air-driven riveting hammer – into a matching mushroom head. Once fixed, the joint is solid. The other form of riveting uses a more malleable metal collar or cap which, when hammered onto the rivet end, expands it and flattens the collar behind the expansion.

Welding is perhaps the commonest method of jointing metals. The parts to be welded are cleaned and coated with flux before being melted together. The skill of the welder, helped nowadays by computers and X-ray checks, is to ensure that the joined surfaces have flowed completely into unified metal, with no incomplete fusing or hair cracks. Welding is used on a minute scale, for example, in jewellery, as well as for joining the enormous steel structural members of bridges, ships, and oil rigs.

One vital joint which depends on the principle of the loop is the **hinge**. The basic hinge usually consists of a pair of interlocked loops, or a single peg attached to one member which slots into a loop attached to the other member, loosely enough to turn within its clasp. This type of simple hinge can be unhooked. Many collapsible temporary structures make use of hinges; and they are good friends to the inventive set designer.

The **ball and socket joint** is directly derived from the human anatomy. It enables the ends of two extenders to revolve against each other. In one version of this joint the ball forms the end of one extender and the socket the end of the other. In another version the ball is held loose between two sockets. Ball and socket may be fixed in a given relationship by a tightening screw, as in a camera tripod, for example.

The **sleeve joint** consists of a tube that fits over the ends of both extenders, as on some tent poles. It is one of the best ways of joining extenders lengthwise to keep them rigid. The sleeve is also an important mechanical principle, used as a bearing to hold rotating parts in position, as in the motor distributor, or in the piston-cylinder combination.

Wood joints can be the most fascinating of all the jointing methods. Nowadays few variants are cut. But in the days of wooden ships and huge wooden roof structures for churches and barns, very complex locking joints were devised. Wood sculptors have recently become interested in the expressive possibilities of joints.

The commonest wood joint is the **dovetail**, used in carpentry. Once knocked into place it can only be disassembled by being knocked apart in exactly the opposite direction; it will resist other forces. The **locking joint** is one in which

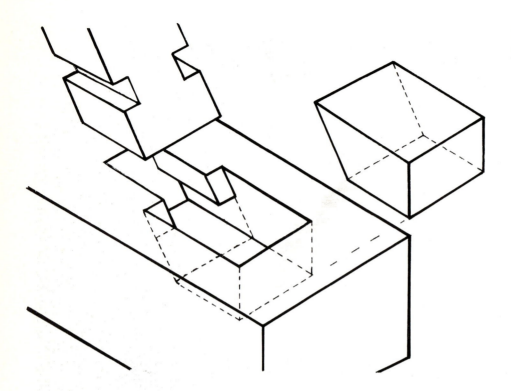

2.35 Locking joint for wood members.

the shaped pieces are slotted together, and then held in position by a single peg or wedge, which bears no strain. Unless that is removed, they can never be separated. The shapes of the pieces may be devised to take strains in specific directions: the joint that hangs a heavy beam from a truss will be different from one that connects two stressed beams end to end, or one that locks a truss to a sloping rafter.

Bracers reinforce the tensile strength of extenders, and operate between extenders or between extenders and their base. They work by receiving either thrust or pull. The prop receives thrust; its commonest variant is the **bracket**. Props have to be rigid – secondary extenders, in fact. Pull-bracers may be rigid, or flexible like rigging ropes and wires.

In an open right-angled post-and-beam structure, any sideways force exerts a powerful breaking strain on the angle joints (which is why the backs of so many welded-tube chairs break away). A simple diagonal bracket or **thrust bracer** straddling the angle will redirect the side thrust downward. The point where a bracket meets a horizontal beam extender serves as a firm fulcrum point across which the beam works as a **cantilever**. If its inner end is held firm, it can carry a considerable weight on its outer end, which is redirected through the bracket down onto the post extender. It is important, incidentally, to follow the bracket principle so far as possible in the placing of nails, screws, bolts, and rivets.

The principle of diagonalizing thrust appears in the triangular arch (see p.80). In effect, two extenders leaned together redirect a part of the weight they carry sideways into downward thrust. This is the principle on which many bridges are built, the earth itself taking the sideways thrust. But an integral structure can convert thrusts into patterns of cantilevered tension. This system is incorporated in the light compound girder. Each horizontal extender, which would individually bend or break under the weight it carries, is braced to the other in such a way as

2.36 JULIAN SCHWARZ
Eight Inch Circle, 1978. Yew wood, 13½ × 11¼ × 11¼ins (34.3 × 28.6 × 28.6cm).

This wooden sculpture makes a feature of carefully cut lock-joints to hold its carved components together.

2.37 THOMAS FARNOLDS PRITCHARD
The Bridge at Ironbridge over the river Severn, Shropshire, 1779.

This earliest surviving iron bridge of the industrial era is constructed of individually hand-forged components assembled upon a perfect semi-circle, buttressed with masonry towers.

2.38 The Great Central Pagoda at Mount Koya, Japan, Haian style, AD 794–1185 (later reconstruction).

The building is entirely of wood, though roofed with tiles. The "wings" of the roof-structure are carried outward on very complex multi-cantilever wooden brackets.

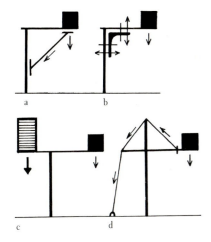

2.39 Load bearing structural techniques: (a) prop (b) bracket (c) cantilever (d) tensioner/guy bracing.

2.40 North façade of the Palace of Chosroes, Ctesiphon, near Baghdad, Iraq, mid-6th century.

The huge catenary arch is built of brick, and is one of the earliest of the great brick buildings of Persia still standing. This is a 19th-century photograph; much less survives today.

to convert horizontal load into a pattern of diagonal thrusts and pulls, which operate through fulcrum points.

The principle of the bracket can be developed in a variety of directions. Perhaps the most aesthetically sophisticated is in the roof-system of the Chinese or Japanese shrine. Here whole sets of curved cantilever brackets extend the weight-carrying reach of the structure far out beyond the footings of the posts. Each lesser cantilever bracket is weighted by the inner structure to bear up the thrust of the outer eaves.

By contrast, the curves of the understructure of fine western bridges embody progressive angular bracketing forming a curve, so converting the bridge into a lightweight unified structure, and consolidating its stresses.

External **pull-bracing** is best exemplified in the old-fashioned guy-rope tent, in ship mast-rigging, and in the suspension bridge. The wires with which early multi-plane aircraft were strung were designed to accept forces beyond the tensile strength of the main extenders, which had to be slender and light. A number of modern architects have adapted the tent and suspension principle using steel wire or rod to carrying very large lightweight roofs over sports arenas or conference centers. The weight carried is transmitted to the upper end of a strong extender. From there it may be either transmitted directly downward from both bracers, if the weight on either side of the vertical is equally balanced, or passed on at one side as pull through the second bracer to a fixed mass.

A characteristic shape for long **suspension bracers** is the catenary curve: the shape that any flexible length hung from both ends adopts as a consequence of

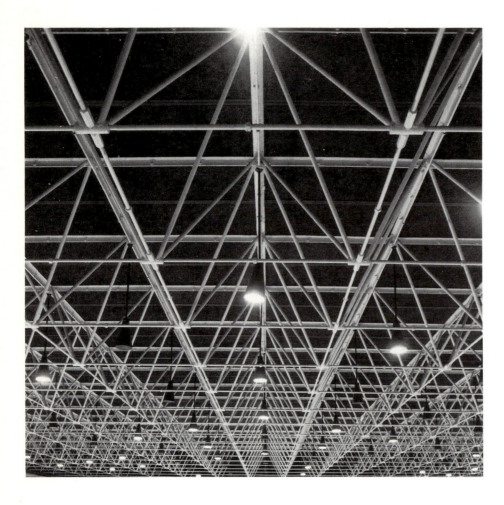

2.41   PHILIP MIDDLETON and PARTNERS
Internal roof of Durham University Oriental Museum, 1958–60.

The space-deck roof is a single girder of tensioned steel rods which spans a broad open space.

the distributed pattern of its own weight in relation to its fixing points – a "droop," in fact. This shape, inverted, is an exceptionally good curve for a supporting arch that takes thrust rather than pull. Its earliest known use was in the great palace of Darius at Ctesiphon, near Baghdad in Iraq. Nowadays many road bridges across gorges use a flattened version of the inverted catenary curve.

Frame and armature structures may need **casing**. According to its attitude and position, casing has to do different jobs. Floors have to carry inert weight; so, if they are of wood, they may consist of sets of thick joists of wood or metal running parallel from one side of the walls or weight-bearing cage-extenders to another, carrying planks. If they are of concrete, they may be in the form of pre-formed reinforced beams. Nowadays expanded sheet metal may be used, ridged for rigidity.

Roofs have to be strong enough to carry the weight of their own structure and its weather-resistant cladding. If the cage structure is a simple one, a flat roof need not be very different from one of the floors; just coated with weather-resistant materials. But if it is to span a large area, either open or subdivided into rooms, a roof needs to be an elaborate independent structure of jointed extenders and bracers. To shed heavy rain or snow its outer surface needs to slope, and that slope may need to carry quite a weight of, say, tile. The main frame may therefore consist of rafters, trusses, and tie-beams; the slope, of rafters and battens; the outer skin, of overlapping tiles pegged to the battens.

The space deck, used especially to cover large, open areas, is a three-

dimensional girder composed entirely of alternating upward and downward pointing rectangular pyramidal cells. These can be realized in terms either of rods or
of planes of sheet occupying the triangular spaces. Its strength comes from the
way it spreads load throughout its interwoven sets of bracers, diminishing individual stresses and converting them into thrusts and pulls that each bracer can
sustain. One interesting adaptation of this principle is the modern development
of solidified foams. These range from expanded polystyrene to the newest metal
foams used for space structures. They have a similar kind of strength to that of
natural aggregates of shells, such as coral.

Exterior **vertical casing** has the nature of a barrier, separating inner from
outer. It may be of plank or vertical beams, of wattle and daub, of brick, of bronze
and/or glass set into frames, or of any of the many commercial concrete and
plaster boards. To resist heat or cold it may need to be multiple, or insulated. It
need not carry weight, so it needs no great strength. Internal partitions may be
even lighter.

Geodesic construction, which is based upon the girder principle of multiple
extenders that brace each other, has recently become very important. It is the link
between linear member and shell structure. Sets of short extenders are arranged
to form a continuous series of closed identical polygons that shape an integral
and continuous outer skin that has great integral strength. It was used in the 1940s
for the bodies of military aircraft; more recently it has been used to construct
enormous dome structures, sometimes combined with the space deck principle.
The most notable recent designer to use it is Richard Buckminster Fuller.

**2.42   RICHARD BUCKMINSTER
FULLER**
United States Pavilion, Expo 67,
Montreal. 200ft (60m) high, 254ft
(76.2m) diameter.

A complete geodesic dome structure by
the master of this form, who also
designed such huge examples as the
Houston Astrodome.

2.43 Fiesta assembly line, Ford Motor Company, Dagenham.

The modern mass-produced automobile has no chassis: the monocoque method of construction means that the body-panels of the car form a pre-stressed shell.

Shells

The prototypes of shell construction in the natural world are the shells and carapaces with which many creatures surround themselves. Insects have external skeletons of chitin; crabs and molluscs form protective coverings within which to live. As spatial structures shells can have great tensile and torsional strength. They consist of continuous, more or less equally thick curving skins of material that contain definite volumes of space and follow three dimensions so as to embody multiple bracing functions in their shapes. They are thus far more rigid than a flat sheet of similar material would be. All molded cast forms amount to shells, even including automobile engine-blocks. Clay and plastic vessels are shells. But the most familiar are the bodies of modern automobiles, made on what is called the "monocoque" principle.

Older automobiles were built on a chassis. This was a braced skeleton frame of lengthwise extenders, maintaining the constant geometry of engine, drive and axle, and resisting engine torque. It had crosswise extenders added to support vertical extenders which carried the cladding of body panels. The strength of the structure was contained in its skeleton, which tended to be heavy. The monocoque method dispenses with the skeleton and uses shaped body panels, each of which is a shell, welded together along the edges into a semi-rigid structure stiffened by the pairs of welded edges. Panels are usually cold-pressed from steel, a process which stresses the crystalline structure of the metal, thus adding to the strength of the whole. Recently, cars have been built with lightweight fiber glass bodies, which have little intrinsic strength, so requiring chassis frames once more.

A vast number of our molded plastic and pressed-metal appliances are now shell structures. Some entire habitation units have been designed in the form of plastic shells. Their strength depends upon careful bracing and reconciling of structural stress planned into their supporting ridges, flutes, flanges, and tension-rings.

Textile structures

Nature offers a wide variety of fibers from which textiles can be made. The hair of sheep, camels, llamas, cattle, and other animals – even that of humans – has been used for this purpose. Various grasses can be used entire; so can many kinds of whole or split cane. Fibers can be extracted from the stem of flax and treated to make linen; cotton fiber comes from the heads of the cotton plant; there are fibers in barks and woods of all kinds, such as reed, bamboo, and pine.

Once any fibers have been separated – often by some form of shredding or beating – they can be used either in their natural condition or bleached, softened and/or dyed with one or more colors. Interesting textures can be achieved with plaiting and weaving patterns; but it is when different colors are combined that the most interesting designs appear.

The simplest way of combining fibers, **felting** is a technique used primarily with animal hairs. It involves stirring fibers together, usually in water, that sometimes contains some sort of glue, until they tangle intimately together. The resulting mass is spread out evenly on a flat surface, and then beaten or pressed flat while it is drying out. This produces a stiff cloth that can be cut into shapes. If made well, it will stay intact as clothing or decoration. In the first millennium BC central Asian peoples were making marvellous designs in cut felt.

A development of the felting process led to the invention of **paper** by the Chinese around AD 100. The technique was passed on to Europe via the Islamic world in the Middle Ages. Paper is felted from vegetable fibers, which you can see if you tear a piece of paper apart and look at the edges with a magnifying glass. Formerly these were relatively strong and long plant fibers, such as flax, cotton, and bamboo. Rags were a common source of such fibers for centuries. The Chinese used to fortify their paper with fibers of silk as well. But nowadays wood pulp usually provides our paper fibers. The fibers are mixed with water and glue into a tangled slurry, often with the help of chemicals and other materials. A person making paper by hand then lifts out an accurately judged quantity of the

2.44   Detail of a felt saddle cover. Scythian, 5th century BC.

The design is carried out in cut and appliqué felt, and represents an eagle-griffin attacking an ibex – a typical Scythian theme. It was discovered, its fibers and colors miraculously preserved by the permafrost, in a tomb in Siberia.

slurry in a rectangular sieve. The main skill is to run slurry over the sieve so that the sheet has an even thickness all over. The water drains out, and the layer of felted slurry dries into a sheet. Recently, quite a few artists and craftspeople have taken to making their own paper.

All these processes have now been mechanized. Wood is processed through pulping mills; the slurry is combined with various chemicals and bleaches and emerges as a continuous sheet running over huge drying cylinders. These sheets can be given a variety of thicknesses; they can also be given different surface qualities and textures by being passed over toothed rollers. They may be hot-pressed, which gives a glazed, compressed, less absorbent surface, or left looser and more absorbent or naturally "rough." They are then cut into the standard rectangular formats we are all familiar with.

The structural processes of **basketry** are based upon twisting together moderately rigid, but still flexible, fibrous canes. The resulting structure will stand independently. The principle of the simplest baskets is to set up stakes which act as supports – radiating in a floor, becoming upright in a wall. Binding canes are then threaded in and out of the stakes, passing behind (A) and before (B) alternately, in either a simple ABABA pattern, or in a more complex sequence. The structure retains its integrity through the complementary effects of the flexed tension in the components and the friction induced between them.

More complex baskets may be made out of suppler fibers such as grass, which may be twisted together either singly or in bunches to make substantial main members. These are then integrated by looping together binding members, or simply interlaced into a continuous texture. The softer baskets depend for their structural integrity upon being woven into continuous shell forms, whose internal tensions maintain the shapes. Tensions are thus intimately related to shape, to a much greater degree than with most other processes and materials. The softer baskets tend also to use far more strands; and it is therefore possible, by using strands of different colors, to produce striking patterns incorporating rhythmic blocks and sequences.

All kinds of fiber can be spun into continuous **threads**. Before they can be spun, the threads have to be combed out parallel to each other using special combs. With wool this is called carding. Spinning consists of teasing out the fibers and twisting them together so that they form an even, unbroken, continuous thread, or ply. Once they are twisted, it is the friction between them that holds the fibers together. The tighter they are twisted, the stronger the friction, and the more resistant they will be to being pulled apart.

Spinning can be done with the fingers alone. But more often a little circular weight with a shank – called a spindle – is fastened to the end of the twist, and kept spinning with the fingers. The spun thread can then be wound onto the spindle. Spinning machines, either domestic and worked with a foot-treadle, or industrial and powered, do a similar job, but much faster.

The twist in a single thread has a tendency to untwist itself and lose its friction-strength. So more complex yarns may be made by twisting two or more plies together in a direction opposite to the original twists, thus keeping the friction high. Cords and ropes combine many complexes of tight countertwists; it is this that gives them their strength. The length of the fibers is another important factor. One of the reasons why parachutes used to be made of silk was that because its

2.45 Basketmaker David Drew, at Higher Hare Farm, Somerset. The springiness of the long upright willow poles (called "withies") is tensioned together in the twisting and setting of the woven components.

fibers are very long indeed, it relies very little for its strength on pure friction. Today synthetic fibers, such as nylon, can be made in continuous lengths which have a very high breaking point and great elasticity.

A variety of different **knots** have been invented for different purposes. Many were developed in the days of sailing ships with their elaborate rigging, when a sailor's ability to tie a quick, sound knot could be literally a matter of life or death. Some fantastically elaborate knots were developed for symbolic and decorative purposes. Renaissance artists such as Leonardo da Vinci and Dürer were fascinated by intricate knots and designed very extravagant ones. Nowadays some textile artists construct whole fabrics with patterns of knots – a technique called macramé. Knotting extra threads into a woven base is the basis of most carpet-making (see p.71). One practical application of repeated knotting is in making nets, which may be knotted by hand with the help of a smooth sliver of wood; but nowadays most nets are machine-made.

Starting with an uneven numbered set of threads, you fasten them at one end for single **plaiting**, at both ends for double. In single plaiting you will have a set of free ends. But in double plaiting, with both ends fastened along a frame to begin with, you will naturally build up a corresponding reverse plait from the other end as you do your twisting. A finished piece of single plaiting will need to be carefully knotted up at the end to prevent it from unravelling. Double plaiting must be secured in the middle, by running extra thread along through the final picking to stop it unravelling. An extra transverse thread added at every picking will produce a very dense and substantial fabric. Plaiting is perhaps the oldest technique for making belts. Baskets can be made by plaiting stiffer fibers or canes. If you plait with different colored threads, patterns which embody the interplay of numbers can emerge. These patterns have often been imitated in designs not produced by plaiting – painted on pottery, for example.

Knitted fabrics are particularly elastic, and they can be made double thickness. They follow two principal types: weft knits, which are looped horizontally; and warp knits, which are linked vertically.

Most **weft knits** can be produced by hand, using needles. They consist, basically, of two kinds of loop, or stitch, that link the thread horizontally: the knit stitch (sometimes called "plain"), in which the yarn is drawn through another loop to the front; and the purl stitch, in which it is drawn through to the back. The wrong side of a single row of each of these is identical to the right side of the other. These two stitches can be combined and adapted in various ways to form literally hundreds of textured patterns. By using threads of different colors it is possible to produce multicolored fabrics.

Warp knits, which link the threads vertically, can be done only by machine. They include tricot, lace-like raschel, and crossed diagonal milanese. These fabrics are especially useful in garment design, for they drape well.

In **wild knitting**, done usually by hand, elaborately varied textured patterns can be produced by casting on and off varied thicknesses of threads in bunches and knots, to produce inspired one-off designs.

Most textiles are produced by **weaving**. At its simplest, it consists of first fastening the ends of one row of threads onto a continuous taut thread or bar. These are the warp threads. You then pick up every other warp thread, and pass the end of a continuous additional thread – the weft – across and through the

2.46 ALBRECHT DÜRER
Woodcut from the *Six Knots* series, c.1505–7.

Dürer made a series of copies of engravings from the Academy of Leonardo da Vinci intended as patterns for embroidery. Knots, especially those with no beginning or end, fascinated many Renaissance artists, for whom they represented arcane symbols of eternity.

space to the other side. Usually this new thread is unwound from a smoothly streamlined piece of wood called a shuttle, which slides easily through the spaces between the warp threads. You then drop the first lot of warp threads, pick up the others, pass the shuttle back between the new space, and so on. The tension of all threads must be exactly right, and the weft threads must be packed tightly against each other after each throw of the shuttle. Different patterns of weave can be made by picking up different groupings of warp threads each time.

Usually the warp threads are thinner spun and stronger than the weft. If the weft is looser and fluffier, it will effectively hide the warp, which makes it possible to weave textiles with colored patterns using different colored threads only for the weft. You can also pass two weft threads through each lift of the warp. To weave patterned tapestry you can keep several different shuttles, each wound with a different colored weft, and pass each one through only the appropriate group of warp threads before you pick up the next one to carry on the weft line with the next color.

All weaving patterns depend on counting threads: the numbers of warps to pick up each time and the number of wefts to pass through those warps to give

2.47   JUDITH DUFFEY
Masquerade: Sheep in Wolf's Clothing, 1986. Wool, machine knitted.

This contemporary work is a virtuoso display of knitting technique to create a witty visual, material, and verbal pun.

the right-sized area of color. This gives the weaving process a natural rhythm. Since it is easier to count threads in batches, color areas tend to be rectangular in hand-woven textiles. Even very sophisticated Turkish and Persian carpets tend to favor rectangular forms, and curves have to be made by graduated counting of small rectangular blocks of threads.

Weaving has long used mechanical devices. Since early times looms have been set up with sets of heddles – bars carrying loops that pick up in groups the warps that have to be lifted at once. These could be actuated in turn to give rise to patterning. In the early nineteenth century a Frenchman named Joseph-Marie Jacquard invented a loom whose program of pickups by multiple heddles could be governed by a pattern of punched holes on a card, planned in advance by the designer on graph paper. The Jacquard loom was able to execute long and complex patterns with a multitude of fine threads, far beyond the memory skills of the ordinary weaver. It was the prototype of the modern computer controlled looms.

Sewing was originally used by primitive peoples for joining animal skins, but is now used to join and decorate cloth in many different ways. In essence it consists of piercing a hole in the fabric with a sharp implement, then passing a thread through the hole. The earliest implements were augurs, usually pieces of sharpened bone, which would make the holes in the leather, the thread being passed through by hand afterward. Later the augur was given an eye to become

2.48   Embroidered roundel from a Chinese court robe, 18th century. Satin, 10¾ins (27.2cm) diameter. Victoria and Albert Museum, London.

The dragon is represented as a symbol of cosmic power. Mostly carried out in running stitch, using many colored silk and metallic threads, such roundels were worn as emblems of the power that went with high official status.

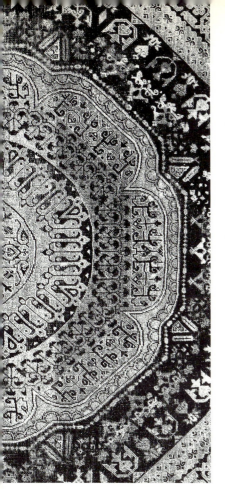

the needle we all know in its many forms, including that incorporated into the sewing machine.

Many different stitches are used in sewing; most of them can be used both functionally, to join pieces of fabric, and decoratively, for embroidery. The simplest of all – running stitch – consists of taking the needle regularly in and out of the fabric at regular intervals. In backstitch, each new stitch overlaps half of the previous stitch. Both of these can be used to join fabric, although this task is now normally done by machine using two threads, one in the needle and one underneath in the bobbin, which interlock as the needle pierces the fabric. Another often-used hand stitch – overcasting – is worked spiral-fashion over an edge to prevent it from fraying. A decorative alternative to overcasting is blanket stitch, which involves forming loops on the edge; when the stitches are worked close together this is often called buttonhole stitch.

Embroidery may be considered "pure" sewing, since here the stitching is an end in itself, rather than a means of joining fabric. Countless stitches can be used to form all manner of designs. One of the most popular, chain stitch, consists of lines of joined loops. Used extensively in both oriental and western embroidery, this can be worked quickly and lends itself to cursive design, following the immediate inspiration of the embroiderer. Satin stitch covers small areas of fabric with straight, parallel stitches; a variant, called long-and-short stitch, can be used

2.49   Detail from the *Simonetti Carpet*, probably from Cairo, Mamluk period, 1450–1500. Wool, whole carpet 29ft 7ins (11.65m) long. The Metropolitan Museum of Art, New York.

One of the medallions from this great woollen knotted carpet reveals the complex interweaving of geometrical patterns into an overall temple/garden image.

2.50   Detail from a silk quilt, English, 1839–42. The Castle Museum, York.

Skill and care were lavished on pieces such as this, created to grace the home of the maker.

2.51   Pieced calamanco, American, late 18th or early 19th century. 112 × 99ins (285 × 250cm). The American Museum in Bath.

Calamanco is a woven woollen fabric with a checked design showing on one side. A sophisticated and striking pattern has been achieved in this patchwork. This side panels are feather-stitched.

to fill larger areas, producing a modelled effect. In couching, long threads are attached to the surface of the fabric with tiny stitches. Other often-used embroidery stitches include herringbone, feather, and various knotted stitches.

One popular version of embroidery is **quilting**. The best known form of quilting involves stitching together two layers of fabric with a layer of padding sandwiched between them. The stitching forms decorative patterns with a relief effect caused by the padding. In Italian and trapunto quilting the design is first stitched through the two fabrics only, then yarn or bits of filling, respectively, are inserted into parts of the design.

Embroidery on canvas (popularly but misleadingly also called needlepoint or tapestry) entails completely covering an open-mesh fabric with stitches, often using wool thread. The smallest and most popular stitch, tent stitch, is worked over one intersection of canvas threads; it is often called *petit point* when worked on fine canvas, *gros point* when worked on relatively coarse canvas. Tent stitch can be used to form extremely intricate, many-colored designs. Other, more textured stitches are often used in modern canvas embroidery.

Appliqué is another use of sewing, often combined with embroidery. Shapes are cut from fabric or leather and stitched down onto the fabric base. Partly because of its freedom and variety of texture, appliqué has wonderful potential as a fine art medium today. A combination of appliqué and embroidery, called stump work, involves creating images in deep relief with padded appliqué, bits of applied canvas work, and highly textured embroidery stitches. Stump work was highly developed during the sixteenth and seventeenth centuries in Europe and is much used by textile artists today.

Patchwork, like appliqué, involves sewing small pieces of fabric; but in this case the pieces are normally joined to each other, rather than to a background fabric. In the American block method of construction, small units – most often squares, diamonds and/or triangles – are joined into progressively larger units, forming complex geometrical designs. English patchwork uses mainly repeated single shapes, the pattern emerging from the contrast of fabrics.

Sewing pieces of fabric together is also the essential skill in **dressmaking** and **tailoring**. However, because the end product is 3D and must fit the human body, many other skills are involved, especially in tailoring, which has a highly sculptural quality and requires a mastery of many seaming and shaping techniques. The design of clothing demands not only an aesthetic sense but also a thorough understanding of the ways different fabrics behave; how a given fabric will drape if pieces are cut on the straight grain, or on the bias (diagonally to the grain); how different contours can be joined; and how fullness can be controlled through such methods as gathering and pleating.

There is a wide variety of techniques for creating patterns by altering the structure of the fabric. Among them are drawn-thread work, in which some threads are withdrawn from the weave and stitches worked over the remaining ones; and eyelet lace, or *broderie anglaise*, which is made by piercing holes in the fabric and overcasting the edges to create an openwork design.

Perhaps the most important textile technique artistically has been **carpet-making**. This was invented in central Asia, perhaps with the intention of imitating animal fleeces. The basis is a strong but relatively open-weave fabric of wool, cotton, or burlap. Into each space of this weave loops of dyed wool or silk are knotted and cut off on the upper side. The best carpets have as many as 1,000 knots to the square inch ($2.5\,cm^2$), more ordinary ones about 250. The resulting surface has a shaggy pile consisting of the loose ends of the knots. This is carefully trimmed with shears to an equal overall length. The carpet may then be washed several times to make it pliable. Nowadays carpets of synthetic fabric may be machine-woven and the pile heat-welded to the base cloth.

Today textile artists make free use of any group of these techniques. You can machine-embroider woven areas, knot-in pile elsewhere, stitch appliqué elsewhere and fill out parts of the design in the manner of stump work. You can use a wide variety of different threads in many thicknesses, either with minute care or with broad freedom. Indeed, you can combine many different techniques into 2D, 3D, or free-hanging compositions. There is no limit to the possibilities once you know the techniques.

CHAPTER THREE

FORM

FORMAL CONCEPTS

Forms are ways of arranging and articulating material in space, just as syntax and grammar arrange words into language. They exist first of all in the mind, classifying experiences of the world. The moment you manufacture a thing according to a formal idea, what you make is no longer a true form but an embodiment or expression of it. For instance, the pure mathematical idea of a cube is abstract. But physical objects we call "cubes" are made of cardboard, concrete, metal, and so on and are never pure cubes, but have "cubeness" as one of their qualities.

Forms are the concepts of design, material shapes its expressions. The formal thinking behind design is mental modelling; and it implies other minds to understand its arrangements. The moment you apply formal ideas to shaping and arranging objects, even lines in diagrams, they cease to be mental and acquire physical content – and hence meaning.

Form and meta-form

Forms are constant recognition factors or qualities by which we distinguish parts of our everyday experience and make sense of it. The basic set of 2D forms – circle, rectangle, and triangle – are the most general differences of shape we recognize. We also employ sets of formal concepts closely related to those we use to analyze and classify nature. Wing-shapes we learn first from birds; propeller-shapes from wind-borne seeds such as sycamore; patterns of mechanical structure from animal bodies.

We also have access to a subtle realm of meta-form which links the forms of phenomena that are not immediately connected in nature. We recognize meta-forms in extended or inverted shapes or affinities of process. They may link, for example, a feathered wing under stress with a slide of soft eroded soil below a cliff, patterns on lichened tree bark with markings in crystalline stones, straw hats with volcanic cones. But individual forms do not have to correspond with complete objects or organisms, such as people, walls, or chairs. Forms can appear in parts of things, collections of things, and even relations between things.

3.1 Church of San Miniato al Monte, Florence, begun 1018. Detail of the façade (upper part 12th century).

The use of a restrained but inventively varied repertoire of pure geometrical forms is the hallmark of Classically-inspired design. Proportion, scale and module are rigorously controlled and logically derived.

3.2   LEONARDO DA VINCI
Studies of water passing obstacles and falling into a pool, with notes (RL 12660 V), c.1510. Pen and ink over traces of black chalk, 11¾ × 8⅛ins (29.8 × 20.7cm). Royal Library, Windsor Castle.

These studies of the forms of curls and coils in flowing water connect with other studies of the forms of women's hair. Leonardo was fascinated by repetitions of certain forms in different phenomena.

Design forms

Design *starts* with forms and then modifies materials into shapes that embody them. A truly creative designer combines forms to arrive at new realizable images. The less creative use simple, single forms or follow routine combinations, as often happens with projects where many people have to take decisions, or where the product has to compete in a mass market. It is, however, well known in physics, that only extremely rarely is any fundamental unit discovered that is intrinsically new; newness usually lies in arrangements or combinations. So it is in poetry, which uses the same old worlds but juxtaposes them in original ways. Likewise in design it is our new arrangement of old fundamentals that generates new meanings.

Content

It is often said that form and content cannot be separated. This does not mean, however, that "contents" of forms do not exist. The idea of content helps to explain many artistic phenomena, including the difference between styles. Early Italian Renaissance architecture, for example, used as its primary forms ordinary rectangles, circles arranged in rectilinear rows and sharing common centers, and sets of simple proportions. Mayan monumental art and much Modernist architecture used quite similar arrangements. But their content, subsidiary forms, and detail differ. For the moment any set of forms is actualized and combined with others it gains its own meanings from the physical nature of its materials, and from its new contexts of other forms.

A simple example shows what this involves. A specific rectangle can serve either as the plan of a huge plaza, or as the format of a page. Plaza and page can both be subdivided in ways that would look very similar on a diagram. But the realized plaza may be paved with stones, surrounded by buildings, and planted with tall trees, which give it one kind of meaning. The page may have blocks of text and pictures laid out in its subdivisions which give quite another meaning.

3.3 FILIPPO BRUNELLESCHI
Interior of the Pazzi Chapel, Church of Santa Croce, Florence, begun c. 1430.

The proportions of its design, based on rectangles and circles, are governed by the diameters and radii of the circles. Brunelleschi was the first Renaissance architect, and one of the greatest.

3.4

3.5

BASIC FORMS

Human beings adapt themselves to the direct downward pull of gravity by standing at 90° to the apparently flat surface of the earth. That is the *vertical*. Their horizon gives the *horizontal* base line in relation to the body's vertical; so we abstract the right angle. Anything set up in balance – a pillar or post – stands at 90°. A standing person rotates to survey terrain within the horizon: from this we abstract the circle around a center. When the vertical person moves and runs the body leans. So most people experience a slanting line, a diagonal, as somehow "dynamic." Without support anything that leans tends to fall. The most general abstract design-forms derived from basic human experience of vertical and horizontal, center, and slant, are the rectangle, circle, and triangle.

The **rectangle** seems intrinsically static, though it can be given dynamic qualities by changing its attitude to the base line. The **circle** has the value of an area uniform in all attitudes, and its quality of rotation gives its outline implications of movement in either direction around the center. The **triangle** need not even stand on a base line, and the slants of its sides give it varied dynamic qualities, also implying movement up or down their slopes. Each of these geometrical concepts classifies a host of direct human experiences.

Traditionally these geometric forms are discussed in the order: circle, rectangle, triangle – the circle standing for the unified whole, the rectangle for the

3.4 PIET MONDRIAN
Composition with Red, Yellow and Blue, 1939–42. Oil on canvas, 28⅝ × 27¼ins (72.7 × 69.2cm). The Tate Gallery, London.

The black rectangular grid deliberately avoids asserting any of the simpler, more easily recognizable numerical proportions; the different colored areas play an important part in in the asymmetrical balance.

3.6

3.5 Front view of Yoshimura House, Habikino, Osaka Prefecture, Japan, 17th century.

A traditional Japanese farmhouse, which uses structural wood framing laid out according to an irregular plan not unlike Mondrian's. It is likely that Mondrian knew this kind of Japanese imagery from photographs.

3.6 LUDWIG MIES VAN DER ROHE and PHILIP JOHNSON The Seagram Building, New York, 1954–8.

This remains one of the best known and most influential examples of purely proportioned Modernist architecture based on steel frame and glass cladding.

static pairing and symmetrical balance of elements, and the triangle for dynamic movement based on developing asymmetry. But because it dominates our design culture we shall discuss the rectangle first.

Rectangle

The rectangle is the pattern for design structures with implications of permanence. It is mathematically simple, with four identical angles, each a quarter of the total rotation of 360°. Its sides can easily be measured, lengthened, or shortened, their proportions altered to give stable shapes anywhere between the square and the long shaft. One rectangle can be added to or made to overlap another with minimal adjustment. Rectangles integrate readily into grids.

All our space-measuring procedures, theoretical and applied, are based upon two or three coordinates or axes at right angles to each other, conceived as an enclosing frame or inner skeleton. These make it possible to locate any point in

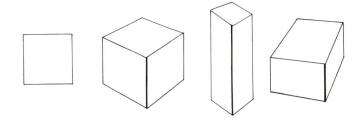

3.7 3D developments of basic rectangles.

3.8 One of the wheels of the
Temple of the Sun, Konarak,
India, c.1230.

These great decorative wheels convert
the whole temple into an image of the
heavenly chariot of the sun god. The
decorative carving was done after the
masonry was assembled.

space by measuring its position from fixed points on the coordinates. Draftspeople plan their designs on rectangular paper, often printed with a grid, knowing that it will be possible to transfer any given set of points in their drawings to corresponding sets of points in reality, using a standard scale of enlargement. Nowadays entire designs can be stored as computer data in the form of points measured along given coordinates. Specified lines connect each set of points, and the linear image can be displayed from any aspect.

The rectangle offers us ready control over all kinds of objects – not only single formal units but whole environments. Vast stretches of wild prairie in the Middle West have been subdivided by the government's rectangular grid systems, which you can still see from the air.

The 3D projections of the rectangle are the **cuboid** or, if square, the **cube**. They offer the same kind of conceptual convenience as the basic rectangle: they can be added to each other or subdivided using the same measuring procedures. Cubic shapes stack on level ground in conformity with gravity; hence bricks and masonry have adopted these shapes. Open cubic frameworks have been humanity's chief structural resource, although they may need diagonal bracing to resist sideways-acting forces. Finally, the cube or cuboid is the simplest of that group of fascinating uniform shapes that lock together into 3D space-filling grids.

Circle

The circle is derived mathematically from its center point, around which another point rotates at a fixed radius. It is thus a function of revolution and represents both the area it embraces and the rotary movement by which it is produced. It stands for completeness. Most early peoples imagined the world as a circle, bounded beyond its continuous horizon by a remote river or ocean. Wheels rotate

3.9   Stonehenge, Salisbury Plain, England, c. 2100–2000 BC.

This circular complex of huge standing stones may have been a combination of temple and calendar reckoner, a center of cult and power.

around their axis without hindrance; and the cycle of the seasons has often been interpreted as a wheel-like circling. The center has a special symbolic value. Used in a ground-plan or as the base of a dome, the circle has been given a cosmic significance. Circular openings in a plane surface have the value of passages, perhaps suggesting the act of widening or narrowing. This active implication can be increased in a series of concentric circles, perhaps progressively more widely spaced, or by a spiral. The chief ways in which circles can be articulated are by intersection; by concentric or eccentric arrangement; or by being subdivided regularly or irregularly by radii.

The **semicircle**, often realized in the arch, also has "passage" significance, although it has also purely structural value, and will articulate with rectilinear shapes.

The 3D projection of the circle is the **sphere**. Often thought of as the shape of perfection, the totality of the divine cosmos, it is a flawless, 3D enclosure, without beginning or end, top or bottom, right or left. Cut anywhere by a plane, it always gives a circular section. Seen from outside, its curvature refers to its interior. Seen from inside, it confines attention completely within itself.

Hemispheres, or half-spheres, may have, according to their attitude, the value of bowls, domes, or shells.

The only modifications of both circle and sphere are towards the **oval** and **ovoid** by the regular extension of one diameter as principal axis. Such an axis gains special dynamic value. An irregular oval or "drop" shape can be thought of as amalgamating two circles of different radius.

Triangle

The triangle is capable of infinite variation in shape and dynamic quality, according to the relative lengths of its sides. It is also an intrinsically stable structure since it cannot be distorted. This makes it especially appropriate, for example, to the construction of girder systems. A structure on three feet, one at each point of a triangle, will stand on any surface, however irregular. Triangles whose sides are all equal in length are called **equilateral**; triangles with two equal sides, **isosceles**. Both are symmetrical, the first around three axes, the second around one. You can assemble both into continuous grids; and they have often been so used in surface design.

The **right-angled triangle** has special mathematical properties. Its sides have the Pythagorean relationship, i.e. that a square on the diagonal (hypotenuse) equals in area the sum of the squares on the other two sides. A right-angled triangle the lengths of whose sides stand in the proportion to each other of 3:4:5 has been used down the ages as a major controlling factor in design, especially to generate overall proportional schemes for complex buildings.

3.10   LEONARDO DA VINCI
Plan and drawing of centrally planned church, c.1490–1519. Institut de France, Paris, MS 2037 3v [Codex Ashb. II].

Leonardo covered many sheets with such drawings, illustrating how an architectural complex can be constructed according to basic 3D forms, rising from a ground plan which establishes the overall proportional scheme.

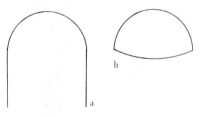

3.11   Uses of circles: (a) semicircle used as an arch (b) hemisphere used as a dome.

3.12   Uses of triangles: (a) equilateral (b) scalene (c) isosceles (d) right angled (e) trapezium (f) parallelogram.

3.13   JUAN DE COLONIA
The fretwork spires of Burgos Cathedral, Spain, 1442–56.

Pierced masonry spires of triangular shape are subdivided geometrically and decorated with moldings, recesses, and crockets.

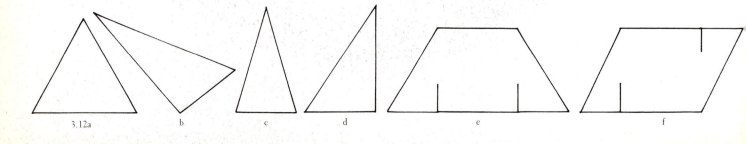

3.12a   b   c   d   e   f

3.14

The basic 3D projection of a triangle is a **tetrahedron**. Like the triangle it can take an infinite variety of shapes. Tetrahedrons are particularly important for shaping volumes in sculpture. Volumes projected from equilateral triangles will interlock alternately to fill space.

Other geometrical figures

Trapezoids are developed from rectangles and squares by adding right-angled triangles to them; **rhombuses** are made by joining two similar triangles along a common base line; the "diamond" shape is one of its commonest uses. Islamic art often used **hexagons**, **octagons**, and eight or twelve-pointed stars, arranged to create complex grid-patterns.

3.15 Geometric figures: (a) hexagon (b) octagon (c) complex star.

 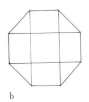

a   b   c

Figure and form

Combined projections of the plane forms give basic 3D forms. Four triangles on a square plan or three on a triangle give a **pyramid**. A rectangular elevation on a triangular plan gives a **prism**. On a circular plan any rectangular elevation gives a **cylinder**. On a rectangular plan, various combinations of triangles, rectangles, and truncated triangles may give volumes such as the shapes of pitched roofs. Even more complex volumes can be projected from multi-sided plans, including **stars**. Late Gothic wooden spires realized such complexes. But perhaps the most intriguing of the 3D forms is the **cone**, a triangular elevation raised on a circular plan. Plane sections cut through the cone at various angles give an extraordinary variety of mathematically fascinating curved shapes.

3.16 Geometric forms as projections from figures: (a) square pyramid (b) triangular pyramid (c) cylinder (d) cone.

a   b   c   d

LINEAR FORMS

So far we have taken for granted the lines that enclose shapes as the straight lines or arcs of geometry. But a line can also be considered as a record of a track, called in mathematics the *locus* of a moving point. The number of possible tracks a point can follow to generate lines is infinite. The same continuous line can follow

3.14 Dome above the *mihrab*, Great Mosque, Cordoba, Spain, c.961–976.

The octagonal layout of the arches is formally elaborated, and the surfaces are covered with ornament in a variety of techniques, all based upon complex geometrical schemes.

any number of directions, not only in 2D, but also in 3D, as a kind of drawing in space.

There are two basic types of line: the straight and the curved. Straight lines differ only in length and direction; but curves can differ absolutely in their inflection.

Curves

There is a group of progressive curves standard in geometry. Two of these that are important for us are the catenary curve and the exponential spiral.

The **catenary** is the curve a drooping rope or chain takes when suspended by its ends (the Latin word *catena* means "chain"). It has been followed structurally in the design of suspension bridges, and more recently in some roof-structures that are hung from wires, like huge tents. The catenary curve has special structural values when it is inverted to shape an arch or vault.

The **spiral** represents the locus of a point rotating around a center, increasing

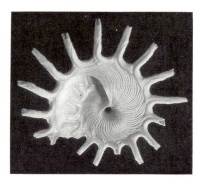

3.17   Sunburst Carrier Shell (*Stellaria solaris*).

The 3D spiral, or augmenting helix, is one of nature's most fundamental and universal forms. Versions of it appear in the seed-heads of flowers and in the structures of the human inner ear.

3.18

3.18 INIGO JONES
The Tulip Staircase in the Queen's House, Greenwich, begun 1616.

It is formed as a pure cylindrical helix. Jones believed that the beauty of a building lay in the clarity and harmony of its forms.

its radial distance from that center as it goes. One 3D version is the **helix**, or screw-like spiral in space, which may either increase or decrease in diameter as it rises along the axis of its center. Bud and leaf-base points in plants may occur at regular intervals on a helix. All spiral staircases follow the helix form. So does the rising ramp-like floor of Frank Lloyd Wright's Guggenheim Museum in New York. Some of the great sixteenth-century castles of the Loire region in France contain beautiful helix stairways in masonry.

Since a curved line is capable of infinite inflection, it can make any shape to which it is applied unique. You can give to basic shapes normally composed of straight lines or surfaces either convex or concave sides, or both. You can also give to oval curves varying, rather than regular, inflections.

Linear expression

This brings us to the realm of dynamic expression, as contrasted with static structure. For when you combine curved forms you are creating unique, not

3.19 FRANK LLOYD WRIGHT
Interior view of the Solomon R. Guggenheim Museum, New York City, designed 1942–3, built 1957–60.

The helix here defines the form of a whole building: the museum is essentially a shallow helical ramp with exhibits hung around the outer wall.

3.19

standard, shapes. The leading and inflecting of curves is one of the most potent ways of giving shapes referential and symbolic content.

Individual lines can have specific kinetic meanings. Thick-and-thin variations of pressure applied by a drawing hand, and the way a line rises or falls, floats or retreats, in relation to any surrounding format, convert it into a symbol crystallizing acts of perception that our eye and mind have performed. Of relevance here is the fact that technical design and architectural drawing are done with jigs and an unresponsive point which suppress kinetic expression. Linear expression is more fully developed in freehand drawing.

3D functions of line

Continuing from the moving point to the line that is its locus, we can go on to thinking of loci of lines. This is the basis of analytical 3D thought.

Think of one face of a cube. It can be described mathematically as the locus of an unchanging straight line that moves in a straight line at right angles in the

3.20   NAUM GABO
Linear Construction No. 2, 1970–71. Plastics, 45¼ × 32⅞ × 32⅞ins (114.9 × 83.5 × 83.5cm). The Tate Gallery, London.

The shapes are produced as the loci of the straight lines "moving" and "twisting" through space, the movement being symbolized by the series of visible filaments representing successive positions of the line.

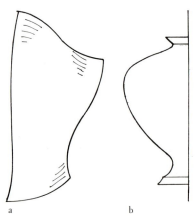

3.21   3D functions of line: (a) surface moving freely in space as a function of a changing line (b) pot-shape as a "function of revolution" of a particular line.

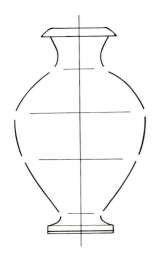

3.22 In a ceramic piece the volumes may change their character along the vertical axis at each level.

3.23 Neck amphora, Athens, proto-attic, orientalizing period, 675–650 BC. *Combat between Herakles and the Centaur Nessos.* 42¾ins (108.5cm) high, 22ins (55.9cm) diameter. The Metropolitan Museum of Art, New York, Rogers Fund, 1911.

The shape of any wheel-thrown vessel is a "function of revolution" of one of its profiles rotated around its vertical center axis.

same attitude across its own length. The whole cube is contained by six such surfaces. Now consider the profile outline of a thrown pottery vase, which is a complex curve. The surface of the vessel results from this line revolving in a circle around the axis at the center – the axis of the throwing wheel in actuality – as the locus of the line. The line may be quite complex, but its movement is simple rotation. So we call the abstract shape of the pot surface "a function of revolution" of the line. But a moment's thought will enable us to realize what a vast number of different forms potters have been able to produce using this relatively straightforward procedure.

Now think of a line that moves freely in space, not just revolving around an axis: first a straight line. Quite a number of twentieth-century Constructivist sculptors – Naum Gabo and Antoine Pevsner, for example – have constructed their works from surfaces embodying spatial loci of straight lines moving relatively freely.

Now think of the surface that a more complex line may create by moving through space freely. Then take the further step of conceiving a surface in space that is the locus of a line that *changes* as it moves, as in the hull of a racing yacht. These are the kinds of infinitely variable surface with which the most advanced sculptors have always worked, developing linear expression in all directions over the surface.

All surfaces that we can define as the loci of moving lines we shall call, for the purposes of this book, **shells**. They may be closed, open, or undulant and follow a whole variety of possible convolutions. The important point about them is that each surface maintains its consistency and unity as a locus, while it is also capable of being individually complex in shape. In this way shells meet the greatest challenge of design – variety in unity.

A logical step beyond the shell is **volume** – quite a difficult concept to grasp, partly because we can never actually see one. We have to infer the presence and shape of any volume from surfaces which we do see. Some volumes, such as cylinders and ovoids, are simple and easily intelligible. But some kinds of design offer us not only single volumes within shells that are complex, but also linked sequences of differently shaped volumes. Fine ceramics, certain types of metal-work, and some kinds of sculpture work like this. Volume has nothing intrinsically to do with mass; defined volumes may or may not convey mass (see p. 102).

In designing logically linked complexes of shape – line, shell, and 3D volume – it is important to take into account the challenge of contrast and active variation of shape. This is where real creative thinking takes place.

PROPORTION

Proportion is one of the most important unifying elements in the designer's formal equipment. It can make or mar any design. There are no hard rules for good proportion, only guidelines. In the last resort the designer's intuition discovers which of the possible solutions works best.

Proportion is a matter of relationship between lengths, not actual measurement. You can apply any proportion on any scale. So a practical designer may have to take the required dimensions of the artifact and discover ways to combine and subdivide them according to proportional relationships that will make the object look as good as possible. A brief giving strict overall and internal dimensions – say for a refrigerator – may be very difficult to organize visually. By contrast, a domestic architect may have a much freer hand. Only experience teaches you how to think intuitively in terms of extending and varying proportional relationships.

An extraordinary quantity of the world's art and design is based upon the use of **unit-modules**: absolute measured lengths which the viewer's mind can identify and keep hold of. They bring schemes of proportion into the real world of measured scale. For example, if "m" (the module) = 6 feet, then $\frac{1}{3}$m = 2 feet, and 4m = 24 feet. If m = 6 feet = 1, then $\sqrt{2}$m = $\sqrt{12}$ feet = about 3.47 feet. Such sets of relations are the raw material for *generating* designs (not just controlling them), basic elements of the language of form in terms of which we "utter" our design propositions. Most important, they help to build up those interesting rhythms among features and parts that vitalize all good design. For rhythm does not consist of unvarying repetition of a single measure, but of shaped meters (in the poetic sense of the word), which the eye can readily pick up as giving variety to spacings, areas, and volumes within an overall unity.

Rectangle

The mind recognizes proportional relationship between two or more measures as a fundamental unifying element. The pairs of sides of a rectangle can have many different possible relationships of length. The simplest is when they are equal, in a square. When they are unequal we can call the length of the shorter side "m". The longer sides may then be 2m, 3m, or 4m, all of which give a horizontal row or vertical stack of squares, each m × m. Squares stacked together into a grid, as in a chessboard, have often been used to lay out the overall designs of environmental spaces such as gardens. But rectangles may be given more complex and interesting proportions, such as m × 1½m, or m × 2⅓m. (We can describe these as 1:1½ and 1:2⅓; or as a 1½ rectangle and a 2⅓ rectangle.)

Perhaps the most interesting are the so-called **irrational proportions**. Designers have used them extensively down the ages. They are 1:$\sqrt{2}$, 1:$\sqrt{3}$, 1:$\sqrt{5}$, and the Golden Section. You can use both the rectangles and proportional measurements derived from them as constructive elements in any artifact. At present they are used, for example, in European paper formats. Standard A4, for example, is a $\sqrt{2}$ rectangle, whereas foolscap is traditional and has the proportional relation 4:7. A $\sqrt{4}$ rectangle, of course, is a double square. You can construct all of them without using arithmetic.

You construct the $\sqrt{2}$ rectangle from a square by taking its diagonal and, using ruler and compass, extending one pair of sides to the length of the diagonal, and then completing the rectangle with a straight line joining the two points to which the sides were extended. A $\sqrt{3}$ rectangle is generated by using the diagonal of a $\sqrt{2}$ rectangle to extend the longer sides in a similar way; a $\sqrt{4}$ rectangle by using the diagonal of a $\sqrt{3}$ rectangle; a $\sqrt{5}$ that of a $\sqrt{4}$.

There is a reverse constructional technique in which you proceed by subdividing internally a large square, by drawing a diagonal inside it. Then, using as a center point one of its corners, you draw an arc of a circle to intersect the diagonal,

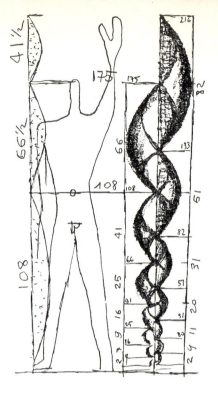

3.24   LE CORBUSIER
Modulor, as in Le Corbusier, *The Modulor: A harmonious measure to the human scale, universally applicable to architecture and mechanics*, London 1954.

Le Corbusier's proportional system for architecture is derived from the main proportions of the human body. It invites comparison with Leonardo's scheme (1.15).

3.25   FRANCESCO DI GIORGIO
Drawing, 16th century. Cod. Magliab. II I 141 c.42v, Biblioteca Nazionale, Florence.

The Italian Renaissance architect illustrates how the proportions of the ideal church ground-plan can be derived from human bodily proportions. We still speak of the "head," "body," and "feet" of a church.

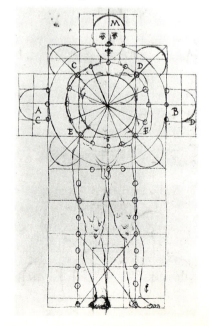

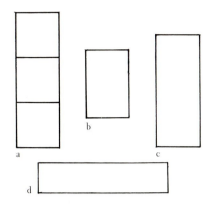

3.26 Rectangles based upon different modular proportions: (a) 1:3 (b) 1:1½ (c) 1:2½ (d) 1:4½

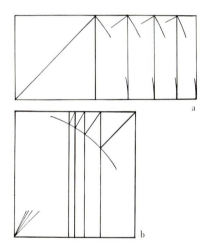

3.27 Techniques for generating square root rectangles: (a) extending them from a given square (b) developing them inside a given square.

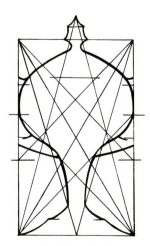

3.28 The Golden Section used in the design of a goblet.

taking the length of one of the sides as the radius. Through the point of intersection you then draw a straight line parallel to one pair of sides. The larger of the subdivisions will be a √2 rectangle. You obtain a √3 rectangle by drawing in the diagonal of the √2 rectangle and then drawing a further straight line parallel to the two sides through the point at which that diagonal cuts the arc inscribed in the original square. You obtain a √5 rectangle by repeating the procedure, using the point at which the diagonal of the √3 rectangle cuts the original arc. The square on the longer side of a √2 rectangle is exactly double the area of that on the shorter; on a √3, three times; on a √4, four times; on a √5, five times. In this way, although the lines are incommensurable in terms of linear measure, their areas are commensurable.

There is one other irrational rectangle of proportion that has been especially important in all design: the **Golden Section**. You construct the rectangle by first drawing a square, then adding both its diagonals. Through the crossing point of the diagonals you draw a straight line parallel to one pair of sides of the square, that is, through its center point. This divides the square into two smaller rectangles. You then draw one diagonal in one of the smaller rectangles, and extend both its shorter sides to the length of that diagonal, perhaps using a compass with its point placed where your central dividing vertical cuts the sides of the square. This gives the Golden Section; in that the side of the square is proportional to its total extended length as its new extension is to the original side of the square. Basing your proportion on this construction you are able to use the measures of the originating square to link Golden Section developments to other proportions based on the same square or its subdivisions.

All of these proportional concepts have to be capable of being realized in terms of actual measurements. You use proportional rectangles in two main ways. First, you can inscribe your designed object within its borders and determine the placing of the main features of the design either in terms of the simple numerical relationships of measure, ½, ⅓, ⅕ etc., or in terms of subdivisions based upon the same proportion applied to one half of an original rectangle, for example. You achieve this very easily by again using diagonals. You draw a diagonal of your original rectangle, divide it down the center, then draw other diagonals parallel to the original diagonal. The points at which the new diagonal straight lines cut the verticals and horizontals will give you the corners of fresh rectangles having the same irrational proportions as the original.

Diagonals can be very important. They can be used to determine page layout, the placing of windows in a façade, or the extent of projection of eaves. In all these various developments you can retain conceptual unity by using a consistent numerical scheme. Because this kind of thinking emerges most naturally at the

3.29 Constructing a rectangle of Golden Section proportions: (a) divide a square into two equal rectangles (b) draw a diagonal in one rectangle (c) extend the short side of the rectangle to equal its diagonal and complete the figure. AB:BC:AC:AD

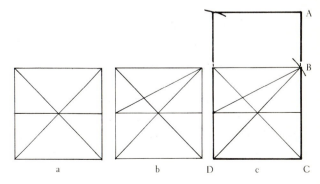

drawing board, some designers believe that direct 3D design cannot exist; whereas, in fact, the intuitive creative thinking of an experienced craftsperson can come up with subtle forms that give up their proportional secrets only on later analysis, and which have tactile and symbolic values of their own.

Circle

With the circle we can use a module in only two ways, as radius or diameter, radius being either m or ½m; the perimeter will be $2\pi r$; the area πr^2. A 3D projection of the circle, however, such as a **cylinder**, can have a height given by some other numerical proportion of m as radius or diameter – for example, 3 diameters. The number 3 may then be used as a subdividing factor for subordinate features. Circular objects, such as arcades or round towers, can be derived from, and related to, rectangular features by using derivatives of m or ½m. One useful method of deriving proportion by means of the circle is by inscribing squares within a circle. The side of the square, the diameter of the circle, and the radius of the circle all have proportionally related lengths.

Triangle

The diameter of the circle that encloses the square, as just described, is the same as the diagonal side of the right-angled triangle formed by dividing the square in half diagonally. If that diagonal is extended to the corners of a square inscribed

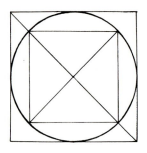

3.30   Squaring the circle as a basis for design proportions.

3.31   Tile decoration in the Alhambra, Granada, Spain, 1354–91.

Forbidden by the Koran to represent the human form, Islamic artists developed the world's most sophisticated language of geometrical design as a way of representing the mystical harmony of God's Creation.

outside the circle (and tangential to it, so that its sides are the length of the diameter of the circle), that generates a further measure which is proportionally related to the radius m. It was much used in the Gothic period as a basis for design, when the mystique of mathematical and Pythagorean formulae, and their relationships with the harmonic frequencies of musical sound, fascinated theoreticians. There is, however, a much more ancient way of achieving a three-valued proportional scheme for use in both 2D and 3D design.

This is the cord with thirteen knots and twelve spaces value m in it. This was probably widely used for design in ancient cultures that did not have either writing or mathematical notation. Its special value is that it gives sides and diagonals that can be expressed, and grasped by the eye, as single whole numbers. Place the end knots of the cord together. Pull it out into a triangle at the third and seventh knots, and the result is a right-angled triangle whose sides have the values 3m, 4m, 5m, the diagonal being 5m. If that right-angled triangle is backed onto a similar triangle, so that they share the same 4m side, then the resulting equilateral triangle will have a height of exactly two-thirds of its base line; and if the 5m side is treated as the diagonal of a completed triangle, that will have sides of 3m and 4m. This matrix, applied through combinations of rectangles, circles, and triangles, has generated many of the world's greatest designs, whose proportions the eye and mind easily and intuitively accept. Such a matrix can still be effective on a broad scale even when the execution is not mechanically precise.

PATTERN

We use the term "pattern" to describe repetitions of form which are usually symmetrical around at least one axis. We talk of patterns in snow crystals and in "standing waves." Because Nature is so full of certain basic patterns – the arrangement of six equally spaced radii around a center in a snow crystal being found in the petal arrangement of many flowers, for instance – it is likely that the ability to recognize and respond to patterns is one of our most deeply rooted perceptual faculties.

Grids

Grids play an important role in design. A grid is made by ruling two or more sets of straight lines parallel to each other at equal intervals. Most grids are symmetrical in both directions. Two sets running at right angles to each other and identically spaced give a square grid; dissimilarly spaced, they give a rectangular grid. Running diagonally they give a diamond grid. Three sets of lines give a triangular grid. Additional sets give grids of higher order plane figures: hexagons, octagons, and so on.

You can use grids to construct many kinds of design, because they define a large area in terms of equal intervals (the grid itself can be removed later). You can lay out a sprig or diaper pattern on fabric using a grid, or plan a geometrical garden using proportional numbers of squares on a grid. You can use 3D grids to organize spatial volumes.

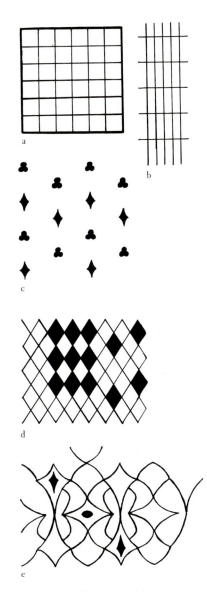

3.32 Overall patterns: (a) square grid (b) tall rectangular grid (c) diamond grid with counterchange patterns (d) diaper on grid (e) pattern developed using different elements in a grid.

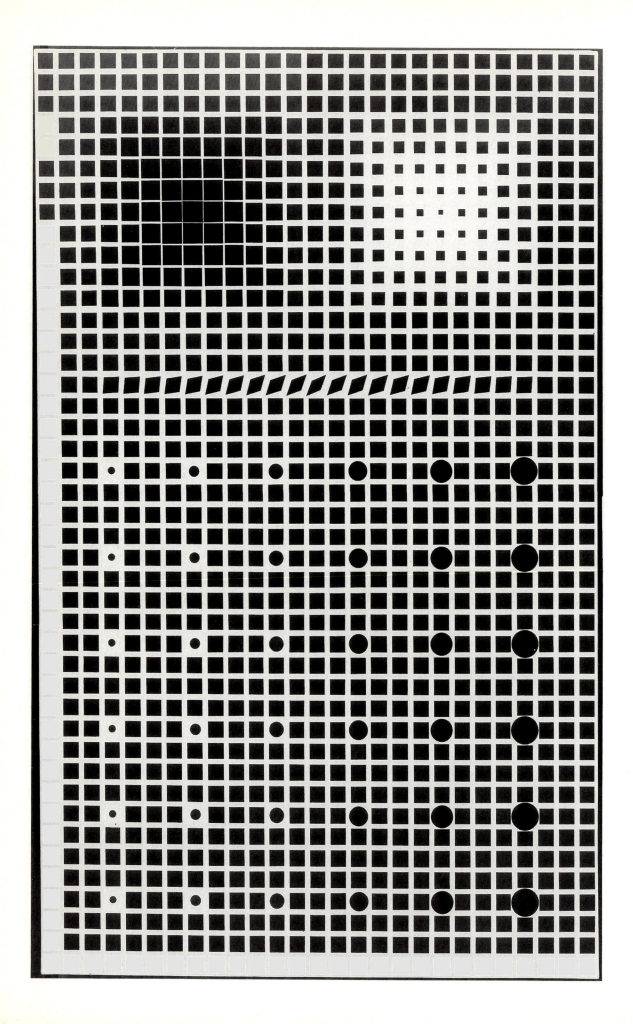

3.33 VICTOR VASARELY
Supernovae, 1959–61. Oil on canvas,
94¼ × 60ins (241.9 × 152.4cm). The
Tate Gallery, London.

This painting is based on a grid, the
cells of which are magnified
progressively along each horizontal and
vertical file.

Counterchange

One of the most important processes in developing patterns consists of alternating the units of a grid, together with their alignment. A chessboard is a simple counterchange system of black and white in alternation on a square grid, in which like squares align themselves diagonally, rather than horizontally or vertically. Counterchange elements can also be units of color or shape-content, such as little birds or subdivided "flag" patterns. If flag patterns are used, regular changes in the direction, of say, stripes can introduce new elements into the counterchange system.

If the units composing a pattern differ, you will get more elaborate counter-changes such as, for example, one large and two small units; two reds, then three blacks; three squares and five circles; wide dark bands, several smaller bands, and so on. If such lines are offset, they will generate diagonal lines of the same units. Into this area of pattern-making you can introduce all kinds of interesting numerical variations, counterpointing, say, odd against even numbers. For example, in two or more parallel rows you can place one row of three varied units beside a row of two others. At every sixth place, horizontally, a matching pair of units will occur; with three and five only at every fifteenth place; and so on. If you then introduce variations, of say, intensity or referential content among your formal components, you can add further elements of frequency-coincidence, which a reader may "feel" but find difficult to decipher.

These kinds of numerical systems, which you simply set going and allow to interweave as they may, are called **parameters**. You can in fact include as a component among your parameters some progressive widening and/or narrowing of the units along either one or both axes of a grid, which can generate very interesting overall shapes. If they are executed at a certain level of scale, and in colors very close to each other in tonality, you can generate **moiré** or optical dazzle effects. Certain designers have devoted themselves to exploring the possibilities of these methods; the Hungarian artist Victor Vasarely is perhaps the most prominent.

CONTRASTS AND COMBINATIONS

All effective combinations of form are based upon qualitative contrasts which the design harmonizes. Without the challenge of contrast, a designer's powers of formal invention will not be stretched.

Contrasting qualities

You first need to develop a lively sense of how the qualities of shapes can contrast with each other. Since some of these have to do with *handling*, you need to analyze the range of contrasts possible within the limitations of a specific material and technique: graphics, wood, concrete, and so on. You can then devise ways of combining them into single images. It may be helpful to try out the contrasts listed here in any specific medium using figurative or non-figurative imagery.

Possible contrasts are: straight/curved, area/line, geometric/organic, angular/rounded, large/small, broad/narrow, thick/thin, solid/transparent, heavy/light, and single/plural (all related to *shape*); static/mobile, smooth/rough, light/dark, and high/low (all related to *surface*); standing/lying and rectangular/slanting (all related to *positioning*).

Perhaps the most general contrast is that between **straight** and **curved. Area** and **line** reflect two different kinds of perception. To make and read a line we follow it along its length, whereas we perceive an area as centered, although we may scan it actively. We may also state or understand an area by following its outline. It may be 2D on a flat surface, or a sector of curved surface. Or it may be bulk, mass, or volume.

Areas or bulks may be **geometric** or **organic.** That is, they may either have clear shapes which we know in advance, and apprehend as soon as we see them; or they may have hazy or wandering contours which we may need to study carefully before we can grasp the whole as an entity. This contrast is closely related to that between **hard** and **soft**.

Shapes may contrast or combine **angular** or **rounded** inflections. Angular lines add up to zigzags. Angular 2D areas or 3D volumes are sharply faceted – or sometimes star-shaped, with indentations as pointed as the projections. Curved lines change their directions gradually, either in one direction continuously, as in an arc, or alternating to form undulations; either may enclose rounded areas or volumes.

Both lines and areas may be **large** and **small** in relation to each other. Large size can give weight and expression, even coarseness to one element; small size, fineness or insignificance. This contrast may be apparent only when we can compare elements in terms of scale. Although forms can look large or small only in relation to each other, they may *seem* large or small in relation to the format or context in which they are placed.

All kinds of form may show contrasts of **broad** and **narrow** in relation to their length. Lines, of course, are virtually defined as narrow. But between areas broad/narrow can also be a contrast. Similarly 3D bulks may be **thick** or **thin**.

Forms may be **solidly executed** or **hazy** and **transparent.** A pale wash can contrast with a bar or block of dense pigment; a block of stone with a sheet of gauze netting. This contrast may also appear as **heavy** or **light** application – for example, of beads onto fabric.

Single forms may stand out in contrast to **plural** ones, either of the same kind or of other kinds: say, one major bulk against flocks of dots, or an area against lines.

Forms or groups of forms may appear **static** or **mobile.** Generally the static is defined as the regular, geometric, and solid; whereas the mobile involves clusters of marks with implicit directions, which give them a kinetic sense – agitated, looping, and so on. This is closely connected with a regular/irregular contrast, as between synthetic and natural forms, for example.

The **smooth/rough** contrast relates to the apparent quality and depth of surfaces. A smooth surface prevents the perception from penetrating to any depth and appears continuous and cold. A rough surface is defined as one having

3.34 JOHANNES ITTEN
Representation of contrasts, from *Design and Form*, Thames & Hudson, London, 1963, pages 10–11. German original edition *Gestaltungs und Formenlehre*, 1955, by Otto Maier Verlag, Ravensburg, Germany.

A set of designs illustrating different kinds of formal contrast combined into single images, used by the artist for teaching.

3.35   FRANZ KLINE
Vawdavitch, 1955. Oil on canvas, 62 × 80ins (157 × 203cm). Private collection, New York.

The broad, black strokes stand in stark contrast to the white ground, and are reminiscent of high girders reaching across the sky.

perceptible crests and troughs. Because it does not take heat so easily from the skin, it seems warmer than a smooth surface. It does not seem continuous. It may be natural, like fractured stone; or it may be manufactured as regularly chipped or scratched "rustication." Mock roughness can be made on a paper surface by **frottage** (see p.159).

   Light and **dark** is another contrast. Depending on the tone of the background against which you are working, either may seem more emphatic in relation to the other by reason of clear shape. It is also possible simply to outline shapes in dark on light, or light on dark.

   With reference to the positioning of a figure, three possible contrasts are those between **high** and **low** in relation to your eye level; **full** or **empty** in terms of the amount of ground it occupies; and whether it lies **inside** or **outside** an enclosure.

One final pair of contrasts depends upon our reading the forms in relation to a fixed rectangular context. The first is between **standing** and **lying** – that is, vertical or horizontal. The second is between either of these two **rectangular** attitudes and a **slanting** attitude.

Contrasts between colors are discussed in Chapter 4. Here, too, the basis of invention lies in setting up a sense of opposition which is then reconciled.

Combinations of contrasting forms

It is possible to combine contrasting pure shapes, but not so easy as it might seem. A more useful approach is to begin with real objects having different physical characteristics; place them together, then derive shapes with corresponding qualities from these originals. You might, for example, lay a mossy branching twig

3.36 ADOLPH GOTTLIEB *Thrust*, 1959. Oil on canvas, 108 × 30ins (274.3 × 76.2cm). The Metropolitan Museum of Art, New York, George A. Hearn Fund, 1959.

This painting sets off against each other two shapes of violently contrasted form.

over the edge of a sheet of bright colored tin, or scatter coins or playing cards across a blouse.

From these physical contrasts you derive your images, not by copying, but by finding media equivalents for them. The twig suggests energetic dark strokes, both large and small, hard and soft, regular and irregular; the tin, forms that may be smooth, hard, light, or angular. The coins and cloth imply a contrast of many versus one, hard versus soft, geometric shape against softly organic. Subjects such as still lifes, draped bodies in rectangular settings, and rocks with trees, became traditional partly because they offered exactly such kinds of contrast.

Contrasting forms can be combined in several ways. First and simplest is by **addition** – laying forms with different qualities next to each other, so that none modifies the others. The American Abstract Expressionist painter Adolph Gottlieb does this, standing two distinct types of shape one above the other, one deep red and the other black, both contrasting with the ground in terms of light and dark. Here the proportions of the placing are all-important.

Second is simple **repetition**, often controlled by grids. The commonest kind is the repeat pattern, laid out either in bands or as an all-over pattern. The motif may be almost any kind of design theme, from clusters of dots to elaborate figurative shapes. The lines of a grid may be featured, or simply used as a system

3.37   KISHO KUROKAWA
Agricultural City Project, 1960. Model exhibited in *Visionary Architecture*, Museum of Modern Art, New York, 1961.

The layout of this ground plan is based upon squares of standard size added to each other, intercut or stepped back by half a side.

for arranging the repeats of the motif. You can also make grids that progressively enlarge and/or decrease in size along one or both of their axes. These may give a strong sense of movement and change.

You can use any grid to lay out the 2D plan of a project, by joining up clusters of components out of the grid upon which to base your image, obliterating the rest of the grid. In your chosen clusters you may also incorporate proportionally related step-ons or step-backs of one area into another. This is especially common in architecture. For example, the ground plan of a large institutional building may be based upon squares added one to another. The squares may be irregularly clustered and incorporate bands of step-backs or step-ons – say, by one-third of a square or Golden Section. Such irregularities add interest, while still keeping in touch with the proportional scheme of the building, especially if the same proportions are used elsewhere in the structure to locate other features, such as internal subdivisions and window placements.

Rectangular 3D grids naturally articulate level floors and ceilings, vertical walls and other components. Subsidiary proportioned grid patterns may be developed for smaller details. Other varieties of grid may be projected into the third dimension by simple vertical extension. But others may be developed, like egg-boxes, for example, into interlocked decahedral shells.

Each of the basic 2D forms (rectangles, circles, and triangles) can be combined into patterns, in either regular or irregular ways. Squares and other rectangles can be added to each other. **Subdivision**, another method, is done either by lines parallel to the sides, or by diagonals, which may or may not intersect in various ways and follow specific proportions. A central cross-band is one common version. Circles may be arranged concentrically, or subdivided by radii either regular in number (e.g. 4, 6), or irregular (e.g. 3, 5), to produce diameters. It is also possible to subdivide basic shapes with curved lines.

Shapes may be *inset* into each other to produce internal spaces: a circle into a square or rectangle, a square or rectangle into a circle, two circles or an oval into a rectangle, a cross-shaped set of squares into a circle, and so on. Linear designs based on any curve may also be fitted into any of the basic shapes. If you add shapes together in irregular ways, using proportional schemes and modules, you can generate interesting spatial images – especially if you incorporate triangles.

Perhaps the most interesting and important way of combining basic shapes is by **overlapping** and **intercutting** them. The resulting shapes may not be simple, but may have sound formal identities. One of the simplest intercut forms is the ellipse, generated by the overlapping of two circles of the same or different radii. Perhaps the most interesting overlap/intercut combinations arise when you intercut circular with irregular straight-sided forms.

Normally you cannot simply add the circle to either of the straight-sided sets of forms. Unless it is merely to touch a straight side, you need to add extra segments to make the two forms combine, or one of the pair will have to cut into the other. Typical real-life architectural solutions to this problem are the traditional ways of adapting a cubical volume to the cylindrical base of a circular dome using squinches and pendentives. When you cut 3D volumes into one another you generate new contours and shapes along the joint.

Perhaps the most sophisticated 3D inventions are **3D combinations** of more than two complex shapes: for example, a conical helix with a pyramid of

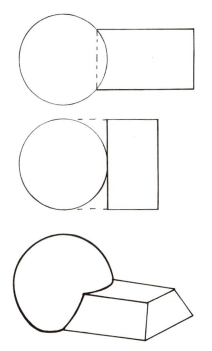

3.38 Ways of interrelating circular and rectangular shapes.

diamond-shaped flanges. The Baroque architects of Rome, in particular, intercut circular, elliptical, and rectangular plans and volumes to create complex interior spaces. It is also possible to develop 3D volumes having surfaces that are rectangular at one end, and, say, elliptical at the other; or to raise on a rectangular ground-plan an elevation based on catenary curves – common in modern utilitarian architecture.

Some of the most aesthetically interesting and profound 3D volumes combine **crystal** and **fruit** aspects into a single form with rectilinear and organic inflections. Crystal means that volumes can be read in terms of plane facets; fruit means continuously curved and inflected shells. Major sculpture articulates sequences of such volume. So does ceramics, and, more rarely, architecture.

3.39 Crystal and fruit: how a facetted crystal-shape can strengthen the layout of a rounded fruit-shape.

Unifying arrangement

Subsidiary forms can be connected externally by means of certain specific arrangements. The commonest and easiest is making lines or surfaces **parallel** to each other. We saw how all rectangular grids and frames do this naturally. But sloping or slanting forms can lie parallel. You can also make them lie at different angles to each other, unifying them either by repeating the same angular difference, or by developing them into series of increasing or diminishing angles. You can interlock two or more of these series; or repeat the same series using contrasting physical qualities.

A second way is by using **geometry** to control subdivisions within a frame and a degree of **projection** beyond the frame by means of lines parallel to given diagonals. This is very common in architecture; Le Corbusier made it the keystone of his method. The geometry and projections do not have to be based only upon rectangular proportion; they may also be based upon repeated angles, radiating series, or even curved vectors. The simplest and most obvious case is the vertical central line, parallel to the sides of the rectangle. On the façade of a building, for example, it may position the center of the door, or a portico hood, or a window; at roof level, it may locate the central supporting member.

Interesting designs use **projected** and **parallel lines** based on diagonals. In a rectangular format you can start with a diagonal springing from the center of the base to an upper corner. To this you may add a parallel line springing from the

3.40 Classical use of diagonals, parallels, and right angles for establishing the layout of a façade.

3.41 The nave of St Mark's Cathedral, Venice, begun 1063.

The vast interior consists of cells of contained space articulated into a single continuous, intelligible, and limited volume.

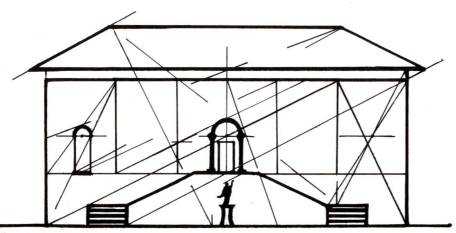

3.40

base line according to an appropriate proportional scheme – say from one-third of the distance from center to edge. Where this line cuts either upper or side edges it establishes, respectively, a horizontal or vertical point that you can use to determine the placing of some feature. A projection of such a diagonal beyond a side edge on the façade of a building may establish the projection point of the eaves. If circular and oval forms are involved, and such reckoning by projection and parallels is extended into the third dimension, very powerful effects may result.

Surface, bulk, mass, and volume

When forms, their variations and combinations are realized, they take on qualities that need to be conceived as part of the original design. Something that may feel right when realized eight inches tall in cardboard may look either brutal or ineffectual a hundred feet tall in concrete. Scale in relation to human feeling is of the essence.

You can infer the shape of a volume only from its **surface**, and this requires the surface to read as continuous – not necessarily smooth, just consistent. Surfaces also need to be interesting; strictly schematic geometrical ones may not be. The flat, smooth faces of cubes, however useful from the engineering point of view, are virtually identical, so our minds skate over them easily and only note the general geometric category. Well-invented mobile lines and modulated surfaces invite the eye to scan and follow them, vitalizing any design of which they form a part.

Three key space factors in any realized design are bulk, mass, and volume. **Bulk** is the general feeling of physical presence a designed object conveys. **Mass** is the sense of contained weight and/or expansive pressure it suggests. **Volume** is the spatial shape produced through the interpretation of bulk and mass.

We all have some sense of the weight natural to particular materials, such as concrete or sheet metal. But one of the important factors in our reading of bulk and mass is how much we are able to see into the solid depth and around the corners of the main surfaces. We may, for example, feel a powerful sense of bulk in a rough-hewn stone, such as one of the megaliths at Stonehenge, because we can actually see into the irregular thicknesses and depths of the surfaces and around the sides. On the other hand, we can design a heavy object such as a freezer or even a house so that it looks far less massive than it is by enclosing it in smooth, flat surfaces, which meet at tight angular corners.

Volumes, which can be either solid or void, can be inferred only from surfaces (see p.87). Our imagination has to move beyond the surfaces to grasp any volume as an interesting 3D entity. West African wood sculptures, for example, display each of their highly individual component volumes as completely as possible, so that they can be readily understood. But Western art is accustomed to using geometrical volumes so familiar that they need only be hinted at, such as ovals.

One important aspect of volume in all 3D design is void space between linking solids. All sculpture works its voids most carefully. Not only the proportions but the actual *shapes* of the void volumes between closed masses can be essential to the visual logic. In major works of architecture – for example, Angkor Wat or

3.42 Altar figure, Yoruba, Nigeria. Late 19th or early 20th century. Wood, c.18ins (46cm) high. Private collection, London.

The volumes of this work are individually distinct, complete, and formally characterized. Their shapes can be understood from many points of view. Their layout is based on proportionally set out and clearly shaped empty spaces.

Giacomo da Vignola's Roman churches – the shaped voids complement the solids to generate the overall image. They count not simply as spaces *in* which solid volumes are set, but as void volumes *with* which the design is composed.

All three factors of bulk, mass, and volume, varied and combined, create the distinctive qualities of any spatial construction, whether it be, for example, open shelter, enveloping nest, display hall, or maze.

BALANCE

One criterion often applied in design is "balance." We know from our own bodies what balance means – a sense of security in not falling over. We refer most works of design to our human anatomy, which is what gives them their feeling of life. So our inner fabric of sensation and experience interprets the placing of relative weights, bulks, masses, and volumes in relation to our sense of human symmetry, equalizing them on both sides of a center line.

In 3D design we feel two blocks of equal weight flanking a larger or smaller central block to be in obvious balance. We also feel that a substantial mass can "carry" a smaller extra mass at one side without difficulty, and that a squat bulk can balance a taller, slender one. A large bulk to one side of a central point can balance a smaller one lying farther out – implying the principle of the lever. All of these estimates depend upon our feelings for actual or notional mass and weight in the components.

In 2D design we can read in a similar way relations between imaginary bulks and masses. Blocks of dense text on an advertising page can balance a photographic image far larger and off-center but much less dense. A small area full of detail can balance a larger, less emphatic one. An area of empty space can be defined by being balanced by a smaller, emphatic element placed off-center. In a painting a few energetic and mobile strokes may balance large, relatively inert areas of plain color. Artists may work by first deliberately setting up a series of imbalances between thrust and inertia, weights and densities, advancing and retreating colors or textures, which they then resolve. Such solutions may not be amenable to planning by proportional and numerical schemes, but accessible only through our experience of bodily sensation and activity.

Scale

The articulation of complexes of form depends upon one or more scales. A scale is a set of degrees or levels by which you define basic relationships between formal units throughout a composition. Rather as a musical scale does, it gives both breadth and coherence to your design statement. In any substantial work that reaches the status of art you need more than one scale; but you also need a clear idea of what your scales are, or you end up with a formal blur.

Here are the principal qualities for which you need to set up scales: relative size, length, and width of parts; prominence or projection, relative to the viewer (either actually in 3D or fictionally in 2D); linear direction; slant of surface, in relation to the viewer; color, as a graded set; tone, as a set of intensities or densities;

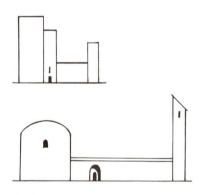

3.43 Symmetrical balance in structures.

3.44 Asymmetrical balance in building blocks.

3.45 Asymmetrical balance on a graphic sheet.

finally, shape, the most problematic, as a set of transitional stages between one definite shape and another.

Some scales have natural terminal degrees: direction has the vertical, horizontal, and depth axes; slant of surface, the pure flat face and the invisible direct recession at a right angle; tone has the extremes of black and white. In the case of prominence or color, however, you establish your own terminal degrees (you can also choose your own, narrower, limits for direction and slant). Size usually depends on proportion; your maximum is obviously given by the whole artifact, although you need to be very clear in deciding on a minimum degree for its component parts. Shape you need to establish for yourself, though the basic forms can serve as a guide.

Within terminal degrees, you must decide how many other degrees you need along each scale you are going to use, and on the relative distances between them. You can, though, incorporate passages of extra degrees as, for example, of size in decoration on architecture.

Scales work by connecting different elements of a composition, as well as by providing an intelligible overall spread for each set of elements. Separate lines or surfaces may lie parallel to each other. The degrees of color that combine in one area to produce a particular effect may combine to produce quite a different effect in another part.

SPACE

The moment forms are realized as shapes they produce a sense of actual space: that which they occupy individually and that in which they are contained. For the designer and artist there is no such thing as neutral, featureless space like that

3.46   Rhythms: (a) by stress
(b) by counting unit *m*.

employed conceptually by science. All their spaces are concrete, forms *of* space not *in* "space". The designer can only create a sense of space to share with the viewer by laying out and handling solid things. "Space" and "thing" are functions of each other. So the particular space each designed object creates arises from the rhythmic placing and punctuations of its material surfaces, volumes, bulks, and substances.

Space appears in two principal modes: that which defines limits, marking off and enclosing static areas; and that which is an open arena, without limits, revealed by things extending into it. The two modes may coexist, though they lose some of their clarity in combination. A design that works with closed forms may imply the space around it also in terms of enclosed area; whereas design that generates a sense of open environment usually implies both infinity and mobility of time as well as space.

Limited space

The Egyptian and Mayan pyramid, the fortified castle, and the prison detention block all refer primarily to the space they define. So, too, do those rectangular volumes we use for building offices, housing, apartments, and virtually all interiors. It is all too easy to think of design primarily in terms of containing rectangles and their 3D projections, only slightly varied by circles and triangles. We draw on drafting tables and within paper formats that are rectangular; so we do much of our thinking in terms of 2D subdivisions and placement within those rectangular formats. The most wildly expressionist paintings are usually confined

3.47 Teotihuacán pyramid, Mexico, before 600 AD.

A focal point of the Mayan empire, and an example of a shape that defines the space around it.

3.48

3.49

3.48 After KUO HSI
Winter Landscape, 13th–14th century.
Scroll painting 21¹¹/₁₆ × 189¼ins
(55.1 × 480.7cm). The Toledo
Museum of Art, Ohio, Gift of Edward
Drummond Libbey.

This composition was probably done
originally around 1050. The mountain
forms "open and close," their solid
shapes revealing and shaping the empty
spaces between them.

within rectangular frames which fit them into the rectangular spaces of galleries
and rooms. The few painters who "break" the rectangle accept it implicitly as a
limitation to be broken.

Space as arena

The natural environment is never rectangular, and planning that starts with the
irregular landscape as its "given" has its own special qualities. Many people find
that to experience an art that pays no regard to the limiting rectangle can be not
only a relief but life-enhancing. The ceiling of the great hall covered with paintings
at the paleolithic cave site of Lascaux in France is one example; its beasts "stand"
at all angles. It is probable that the charm of the work of the Spanish architect
Antoni Gaudí, and of "naive" art such as the Watts Towers in California, results
partly from the feeling of release from the rectangle which they give.

Design that reveals space as open, endless arena is rarer than limited space,
and more difficult to achieve. It arises when the designer works outward from a
number of separate foci. An architect may design a house opening onto vast
terrain, say, for people who own a good deal of land. It was the natural mode for
pre-modern Chinese and Japanese art. Traditional Chinese ink-painting revealed
it by drawing fluid shapes expressly to show what is *not* there. Their implied space
extends beyond the edges of any format. Traditional Japanese painting features
cloudy-spaces (*kasumi*) for a similar purpose, as positive images of voids. Some
of the Japanese prints that influenced nineteenth-century European painting,
notably the long-format "pillar prints," cut off their figures in scenes in an
apparently careless way, implying that action continues outside the limits of the
picture.

On a larger scale, space as arena is generated in Chinese and Japanese
gardens, architecture and furniture. Far Eastern architecture and furniture were
thought of as open frameworks, supporting roofs or flat tops and permeated by
space. Internal subdividing was achieved by means of lightweight screens or panels
rather than solid masonry. In eighteenth-century England, Capability Brown,
influenced by Chinese garden designs, designed private landscapes with fluid
spaces, irregularly shaped tree plantations, and stretches of water running off into
a distance whose boundaries were invisible.

Outer and inner space in this mode do not have to be direct formal imitations
of each other. A whole family of twentieth-century architecture fathered by Frank
Lloyd Wright, many of whose ideas came from Japan, developed the concept of
mutually interpenetrating interior and exterior, breaking down distinctions between closed room-space and open garden-space. Much Californian beach and
junk-architecture is meant to amalgamate outside and inside.

Some people like the interiors of their houses or apartments to be "open
plan." Even architects who have had to work within fundamentally cuboid
block-volumes have been able to develop interesting free-flowing interior spaces,
like the vast open foyers of the American hotel architect John Portman. The
architects of high-rise cuboid office blocks have used vast areas of glass as a way
of opening up the interiors to light and panoramic vistas to help overcome the
imprisoning effect of the rectangle, while from the outside, the acres of glass
reflect the sky and moving clouds, so helping to vitalize their strict shapes.

3.49 FRANK LLOYD WRIGHT
Kaufmann House, Falling Water, Bear
Run, Pennsylvania, 1936–7.

The architect articulates the rectangular
inner volumes with the exterior
environment, the levels reaching out to
"take possession" of the natural
landscape.

CHAPTER FOUR
COLOR

COLOR AND PHYSIOLOGY

In most books on art and design color is discussed primarily in terms of the spectrum of visible light scientifically analyzed as wavelengths; but we now know that we need to incorporate a new physiological understanding of color into our conception of its role in design. It used to be believed that our sense of color was purely the result of our eyes registering the differing wavelengths in light. Recent neuro-physiological research, however, has shown that a much more complex and interesting phenomenon is involved – one that, in a sense, validates the old Greek definition of color as "that which always accompanies form." This phenomenon is called **color constancy**.

At the back of the human eye, on the retina, three types of cell-cluster that convey visual information to the brain, via the optic nerve. One type, called rods, records form and depth in terms of monochrome definition. Another registers movement across the field. The third, called cones, responds to color.

There are three sets of **cones**: one sensitive to light in the red frequencies, a second to those in the green, and a third to those in the blue. Each set of cones registers a pattern of relative light intensity within its own frequency band, from bright to dark across the field presented to it. This pattern is transmitted to the brain. There the three intensity patterns in each of the color bands are combined and constructed into an image of the whole colored field. Each individual color is registered as a compound of brighter or darker parts in the overall pattern of all the three main frequency fields, not as a spectrum wavelength of its own. In right-handed people this is constructed in the right hemisphere of the brain; in left-handed people, in the left hemisphere. The brain then combines this joint pattern of three light-dark color systems with the overall monochrome light-dark space-structure pattern which is registered through the rods in the opposite hemisphere.

One reason why color is not read as pure spectrum-wavelength is that in the course of evolution humans needed to identify separate things in the environment, as predators or prey, by their color as well as by their shape; and each color had to appear constant under all kinds of external conditions of light and shadow, which alter actual wavelengths. If the brain had not developed the faculty of discounting rapid changes of wavelength, the world would have seemed to consist

4.1 JOAN MIRÒ
Foundation's Tapestry, 1979. 24ft 7ins × 16ft 5ins (7.5 × 5m), made by J. Royo in the Maeght workshop of Tarragona. Fundaciò Joan Mirò, Barcelona.

Powerful primary colors, black, and subtle earth-grays are combined in this vibrant work. The figure of a woman has been abstracted into an almost, but not quite, two-dimensional pattern of chromatic arrangements.

of constantly shifting colors, and we would be unable to concentrate on specific objects at all clearly. What the brain seems to do is continually to reconstruct the colors of perceived objects by balancing out the three different patterns of relative light intensity in the red, green, and blue wavelengths, along with the patterns received by the rods of monochrome light and dark. This means that perceived color is constructed in the brain and is not a quality "belonging to" the object. Furthermore, no color area can be read alone. It must always be identified as one element in the whole field of colors we continually scan. So even if overall brightness diminishes, and an object moves from, say, bluish daylight to greenish shadow, the pattern of *relative* brightnesses among the areas of colors remains the same to the scanning eye. Painters have long known that the quality of each color in a composition is affected by the neighboring colors. The theory of color constancy disposes of an old assumption that sheer brilliance of individual lights or pigments can make a composition interesting.

Color perception is only one element in the brain's response to visual stimuli. It also sees movement, as the wavelength patterns move across the retina, as well as form, which is registered by the rods. By varying the application of colors, an artist can suggest movement in an object. Great artists are also able to lead the eye along specific paths in the image, thus helping to intensify its sense of color-modulation.

The form and depth faculty is also involved in color composition, for outlines greatly assist the eyes' grasp of relative brightness. A strong 2D outline-structure in black and white can actually enhance the color image produced in the brain.

Color and substance

Since there can be no shape that is not colored, one of the most important

4.2 MASACCIO
The Rendering of the Tribute Money,
c. 1425–1428. Fresco, Brancacci Chapel, Church of Santa Maria del Carmine, Florence.

This shows an important basic function of color: distinguishing different objects from one another – faces from garments, the folds of one robe from those of its neighbor.

4.3 *St Luke*, from the Gospel Book of Otto III, c.1000. Bayerische Staatsbibliothek, Munich, MS Cod.lat.4453 fol.139 v.

The richness and strength of the color system in this miniature from the monastery of Reichenau is meant to carry across to the viewer the splendor and importance of the images depicted.

functions of color in design is to unify and distinguish objects and substances – green grass, blue sky, red fire engines, pale violet lilacs, yellow lemons. Much of the world's greatest art has used plain hues to define and distinguish objects in this apparently naive manner. For example, the frescoes of Masaccio and Michelangelo employ restrained, plain colors to unify separate areas of outlined surface which correspond to flesh, clothing, hair, buildings, and earth.

Early eighteenth-century Indian miniature paintings made at the court of the Rajput rulers of the state of Basohli use the principle of color identification in an interesting way. The picture is divided into areas of quite unrealistic colors, often of a hectic brilliance, which are meant both individually and collectively to evoke passionate responses in the viewer. Colors not only identify objects but invite heightened responses to them. The Ottonian illuminators of Reichenau

और the Rhine Valley in the ninth to twelfth centuries produced comparable color inventions of rarely matched splendor.

A related color technique was employed by Fernand Léger, who worked for several years in the United States. He limited his palette to flat areas of the bright and simple colors he loved – also used in the popular arts of the fairground and animated cartoon: red, blue, green, yellow, orange, and some purple. He added these to an emphatic black-and-white design, often leaving large areas white, which also took on the value of color. In his later works Léger often applied his color in bold, clearly shaped independent patches and bands cutting across the black outlines of objects.

4.4 One of a set of illustrations to Bhanudatta's Rasamanjari, painted in the Basohli state palace, Punjab, India, c.1660–70. Gouache on paper, 7 × 10⅞ins (18 × 27cm). Victoria and Albert Museum, London.

In this picture the colors are used to symbolize a range of intense feelings, to which the viewer is meant to respond immediately. The correspondences between particular colors and feelings are well known in Indian tradition.

THE LIGHT SPECTRUM AND OPTICAL COLOR CIRCLE

The sun's energy reaches us as a spectrum of electromagnetic radiation of different wavelengths. Within this spectrum the red, green, and blue bands of wavelengths appear to us as visible light. Mingled together they amount to clear, white luminosity. Even though our eye-brain complex responds only to the three color wavelengths and constructs intervening colors in terms of them, we can nevertheless think of the spectrum range, for practical purposes, as a visual continuum.

In the 1660s Newton and Leibniz both discovered techniques, including the use of glass prisms, for splitting white light into a range of colors. They realized that this is just what happens when one sees a rainbow: water droplets in the atmosphere "diffract," or break up, the light into its different wavelengths. So, too, do iridescences, as found on the feathers of some birds. Since these split-spectrum iridescent images are rare, we instinctively feel that they signify some special glory or transcendence. God's Old Testament promise to Israel was symbolized by the "bow set in the clouds." Iris, the ancient Greek goddess from whose name "iridescence" comes, was one of the messengers of the gods.

When a ray of white light is passed through a prism, it is diffracted into a graduated band of colors according to their wavelength-order. Traditionally we isolate and name parts of the band as follows: deep red, crimson, or carmine (long wavelength, 750 millimicrons); vermilion; orange; yellow; pale green; bluish green; blue; and violet (short wavelength, 350 millimicrons). It was Newton who

4.5   FERNAND LÉGER
Two Women Holding Flowers, 1954. Oil on canvas, 38¼ × 51⅛ins (97.2 × 129.9cm). The Tate Gallery, London.

The few and simple colors applied to a black image on white give color value to the entire image. The colors gain intensity from the black borders.

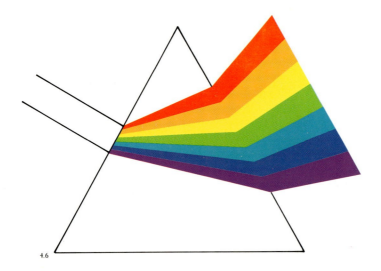

4.6

4.7

conceived the notion of arranging the spectrum band into a circle of equal sectors of color for theoretical purposes. In reality, the color sectors are of different widths; moreover, the circle artificially joins deep red and violet, the two wavelengths that are actually the farthest apart, to make a purple that does not exist in the spectrum. Although, strictly speaking, inaccurate, the color circle remains a useful artistic aid.

Additive and subtractive mixing

When red, green, and blue light are superimposed, they make white. Other cunningly spaced triads of single colors of light can also combine to form white light, the most effective being magenta, cyan blue, and chrome yellow, now the basic group of ink colors used in color printing. Mixing lights is called **additive mixing**, because the more colors you put in, the more light you get. This is why the colors of, say, sunsets or fire appear especially intense.

Pigments do not radiate light but display color by absorbing wavelengths selectively, reflecting back to the eye only the wavelengths they do not absorb. Mixing pigments is called **subtractive mixing**, because the more pigment colors you mix, the more light is absorbed. Eventually you get mud, then dull black. Many artists and designers these days use as few pigment mixtures as they can,

4.6 White light entering a glass prism is split up by refraction into the spectrum of its natural constituent colors.

4.7 The optical color circle, as devised by Isaac Newton. Combining any two colors lying opposite each other will, theoretically, produce the neutral gray in the center.

4.8 The additive mixing of colored light primaries produces lighter secondaries and, finally, pure white.

4.9 The subtractive mixing of primary color pigments produces darker secondaries. All three together make black, or the absence of reflected light.

4.8

4.9

4.10 SONIA DELAUNAY-TERK *Study in Light: Electric Prism*, 1913. Gouache and conté crayon on cardboard prepared with gum-based white paint, 12⅜ × 8⅜ins (31.4cm × 21.3cm). Victoria and Albert Museum, London.

This is a kind of hymn to the rainbow color-spectrum, meant to display it as the ultimate source of the painter's art.

Sonia Delaunay Terk 1913

N° 37

4.11   PETER PAUL RUBENS
Landscape with Rainbow, c.1635.
Panel, 37¼ × 48½ins (94.6 ×
123.2cm). Alte Pinakothek, Munich.

Rubens, like many seventeenth-century
Dutch painters, knew how to use small
touches of red – a sleeve, a bodice – to
intensify the effect of large areas of its
color opposite, green.

preferring to lay single pigments onto white grounds to allow them maximum
brilliance. Old masterpieces always look dark to us at first sight, because the artists
organized their tonal scales in a lower key to compensate for the effects of
subtractive mixing of their optically "impure" pigments.

Color opposites

The color circle enables the designer to pick out, virtually at a glance, the colors
diametrically opposite each other. Artists have intuitively used color opposites,
or complementaries, for centuries. The seventeenth-century Dutch landscape
painters, for example, understood how a patch of red – say, a person in red
clothing – could intensify the visual effect of masses of green foliage. Red and
green are one of the principal pairs of complementaries. But it was only when
the French chemist Michel-Eugène Chevreul published a book dealing with the
theory of color in 1839 (reissued in 1889) that the whole system was clarified and

made easily available to artists and designers. Chevreul focused our attention on color as an optical phenomenon, giving colors meaning primarily in relation to each other in the circular spectral system.

The system works like this: in the human eye the color receptors get fatigued by looking at a single bright combination of wavelengths and gradually register it more feebly. You can test this for yourself by doing the well-known experiment of staring at a patch of strong color – say, orange – and then abruptly transferring your gaze to a white sheet or wall. On it will appear a similarly shaped patch of blue, the color opposite of orange. What happens is that the patch of color receptors on the retina which have been bombarded with orange light have become temporarily "blind" to orange. The white light being reflected from the wall is therefore perceived as deficient in orange – which the brain interprets as a corresponding predominance of its opposite, blue.

4.12   By staring at the orange triangle for approximately 30 seconds and then transferring your gaze immediately to the black dot below, you will "see" a blue triangle of the same size. This well-known phenomenon is the result of "color fatigue" on the retina.

4.13   JAVIER BELLOSILLO *Figure*, 1986. Porcelain dinnerware, large plate diameter 12ins (30.5cm). Manufactured by Swid Powell Design, USA.

The effect of using small amounts of one color set against a large area of its opposite is well illustrated here: the jagged strip of blue seems fairly to crackle as it crosses the orange and ochre. There is a further vibrant contrast between the dark of the blue, and the white laid beside it.

If you juxtapose color opposites in a design, they make each other seem more intense. This effect is enhanced if you use them in substantial blocks and areas. If you add a small patch or stripe of one color to a relatively large area of its complementary, the main color will seem more intense, as in those seventeenth-century Dutch landscape paintings. If you mingle sets of color opposites in little dabs you can make optical greys, which seem especially luminous because they consist *not* of subtractive mixtures of pigments, but of additive combinations of multicolored flecks of light that blend optically. This technique was developed especially by Seurat and other "Pointilliste" ("little dot") or "Divisionist" painters. We shall discuss other aspects of their technique later on (see p. 120).

Color enhancement

Another aspect of color opposites is color enhancement. If you place a patch or ring of one bright color on a neutral ground, say, a grey, the grey surround takes on a kind of glow of the opposite color of the applied color. Chevreul pointed out that the color opposites that appear in response to any strong color do not consist only of the diametrically opposite wavelength group but also include colors adjacent to that color opposite. This is entirely consistent with the theory of color

4.14 VINCENT VAN GOGH
The Night Café, 1888. Oil on canvas, 28½ × 36¼ins (72.4 × 92.1cm). Yale University Art Gallery (Bequest of Stephen C. Clark, 1903).

A mood of anxiety verging on nausea is deliberately evoked in this work in disharmonies of red, green, and yellow, and by the juxtaposition, in van Gogh's own words, of "soft Louis XV greens and malachite, contrasting with yellow-green and harsh blue-greens, and all this in an atmosphere like the devil's furnace, of pale sulphur."

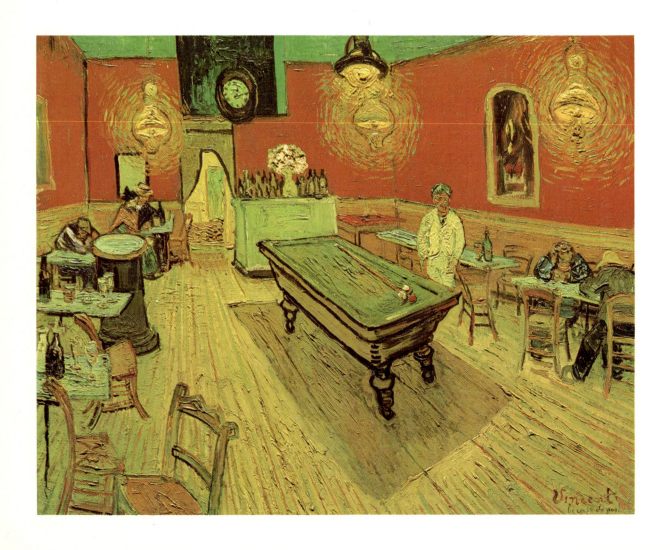

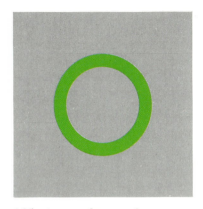

4.15   An area of strong color sets up a kind of glow of its opposite on a neutral ground. Other colors may appear to be present: in this example, you may get a sense not only of red, but of orange also.

constancy. Thus, when strong green paint is put onto a neutral ground, the glow the ground takes on is not just a simple red but also includes what we interpret as deep red and orange. It is of course possible to produce subtractively a wide variety of different looking greys by mixing color opposite pigments. Not all work equally well with different commercial materials; experiment will show you which work best with your own palette. Furthermore, if the ground the color is laid onto is light – for example, white – the color itself will seem lighter than exactly the same color laid onto a darker ground.

The painter who followed the full implications of the nineteenth-century discoveries regarding complementaries most thoroughly and creatively was Vincent van Gogh. In a letter to his brother Theo he wrote, "I have fallen into the full metaphysic of color." In many of his late pictures van Gogh used a wide variety of color opposites, combining light and dark versions of the hues not only in the same work, but also in works he meant to hang in groups of two or three.

Warm/cold colors

The warm-cold distinction describes a subjective but valid response to colors. It is determined by drawing a diameter across the color circle from yellow to violet, the colors on the red side being usually felt as warm, probably because of their proximity to the infra-red heat-radiation band of the frequency spectrum, while those on the green-blue side are perceived as cold. Designers of all kinds have used this distinction for their own purposes.

One modern artist-theoretician, Carlo Suarès, devised a color diagram called a hyperbola which combines the physical facts of the color circle with the psychological facts of the warm-cold division. He based it upon the two "axial" colors that artists have often used to produce luminous shadow – purple (horizontal) and green (vertical). The two curves approach both axes, but in opposite directions. You find color opposites by drawing a straight line from one color through the crossing of the axes. The relevant point about this diagram for artists is that it gives two different maximum "lights": for the cold, bluish sector, white; for the warm, reddish sector, gold.

Primary, secondary, and tertiary colors

By long-established convention red, yellow, and blue are thought of as the **primary** colors out of which all others can be subtractively generated. This was partly the consequence of the chemistry of naturally occurring pigments. Good strong reds, blues, and yellows were available; other colors were not. The term primary is still often used to refer to this group of colors. Some twentieth-century artists, including Piet Mondrian, based their color system on it. We know now that these are not the physiological primaries. In principle, any three colors at 120° intervals around the 360° color circle should be able to act as primaries. As lights, additively, they can; though the imperfections of the dyes used to color the transparencies through which we have to project our colored lights make some primary groups work better than others. We have already mentioned the best, the magenta-cyan-yellow group.

Secondary colors are made by mixing the primaries. The secondaries of this

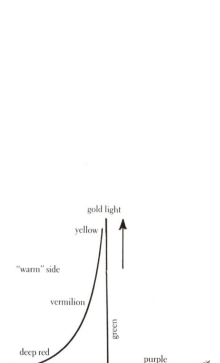

4.16   Carlo Suares's color hyperbola.

group are deep violet (cyan plus magenta); vermilion red (magenta plus yellow); and green (yellow plus cyan). The secondary colors that result from combining the traditional primaries are orange (red plus yellow); green (yellow plus blue); and violet (red plus blue). Each secondary color in this system is thus the color opposite of a primary: green of red; orange of blue; violet of yellow. This is the system that most practical designers still follow.

Used additively as light, the system works reasonably well. But used subtractively, by mixing pigments, it has the annoying defect that, by definition, subtractive secondaries have to be duller and darker than the primaries from which they are mixed. Manufacturers of artists' colors have therefore concentrated on trying to produce strong secondary color pigments, which eliminate the need for such mixing. The Pointillistes found another solution. They put spots or delicate strokes of red and yellow, or yellow and blue, or blue and red, side by side in overlapping clusters, to approach the effect of additive combination without losing brilliance. By adjusting the relative numbers of dots, modulated versions of the secondaries could be suggested. From this method was developed the basic technique of color printing, which uses screens to produce a set of plates covered with dots printing each color of the magenta-cyan-yellow group, plus black – which would not be needed if the three primary color inks were optically perfect.

Tertiary colors have the subtractive mixing problem to an even greater degree. They are made by mixing a secondary with one of the primaries next to it on the color circle. Modern technology has now produced some pigments giving colors styled "tertiary" that have good properties. Tertiaries only have other tertiaries as color opposites, of course, which can limit their use.

Rood's color circle

Excellent accounts of what more can be done artistically with color circles were given by two other theorists: the American physicist Ogden Nicholas Rood and the German poet Johann Wolfgang von Goethe.

Rood's discoveries concerning color, developed and applied by the English designer Barrett Carpenter, are not based on optics but relate to the effects actual coloring substances have upon our human responses. You can easily check them for yourself by experiment.

Rood pointed out that there is a kind of natural order of light and dark built into the color circle as it appears among the natural range of pigments and dyes. This order is therefore identified through the retinal rods as well as the cones. The darkest tone is deep violet-purple, the lightest is yellow. Around the color circle in both directions the colors can be graded into a tonal series upward from purple to yellow. From purple the red, warm side runs counter-clockwise through crimson-carmine, red, and orange to yellow; and the blue, cold side runs clockwise through violet-blues, cyan, green, and yellow-green to yellow. It is perfectly possible to carry out convincing shadow modelling – in a still life, for example – only using colors in a "natural" tonal order. Artists have done it for centuries. Rood called the effect of juxtaposing colors from either or both sides according to their natural tonal order **harmony.**

We know that we can lighten any color by mixing white with it. So we can make pale versions of the naturally darker colors – pale violet, pale blue, pale

4.17 A greatly enlarged detail of Figure 4.18, as printed, shows clearly the "rosettes" characteristic of four-color lithographic reproduction. There is an obvious similarity between this technique and that of the Pointillistes.

4.18 GEORGES SEURAT
Study for *Le Chahut*, 1889. Oil on panel, 8½ × 6½ins (21.6 × 16.5cm). The Courtauld Institute Galleries, London (Courtauld Collection).

The Pointillistes, or "little dot" painters, sought to overcome the inevitable dulling of colors in the subtractive mixing of pigments. Their solution was to apply separate dabs of bright primary color that the viewer's eye would combine optically.

red, pale green, and so on. We can also darken the lighter colors by mixing them with black, or with their color opposite. To lay colors next to each other out of their natural tonal order has an effect that Rood called discord. The discord is increased the farther apart on the color circle the juxtaposed colors lie. Thus, to lay a pale violet next to a dark orange is more discordant than to lay a paler orange beside a darker yellow. This effect (for which there are optical-cerebral reasons) has expressive potential for the artist and designer. It allows us to use color "harmony" and "discord" for expressive purposes. We can, however, use lightened or darkened versions of color-opposites together – for example, dark purplish red with dark bluish green – with little sense of discord, since both share a strong blue element.

You can juxtapose colors either in harmony or in contrast. Harmonic groupings consist of colors from the same sector of the color circle that follow the "natural" order of tone. Red, orange, and yellow, for example, create an agreeable harmonic group, as do blue-green and yellow-green. But to introduce a pale blue into the first group, or a pale rose into the second, introduces an element of discord, as well as of contrast. The relative proportions of one color or the other in the group affect the values of the group as a whole. You can combine two harmonic groups into a single scheme; and if you preserve the "natural" tonal order among all the elements of both groups the combination will be harmonic. It can contain several interesting discords if more than one of the colors appears out of its "natural" order of tone. Here again, relative quantities are very important.

The relative quantities of juxtaposed color opposites strongly influence the effect. Taking yellow-green and violet as an example, a very different effect is given by small patches or lines of violet scattered on a light yellow-green ground, from the opposite; similarly with blue and orange.

a

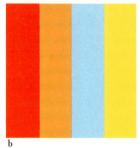

b

c
4.19

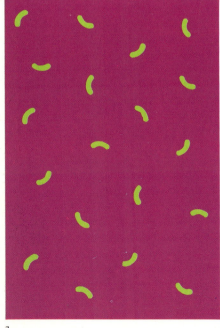

a
4.20

b

4.19 (a) Red, orange, and yellow lie in the same sector of the color circle and make a harmonic group.
(b) Introducing a pale blue produces an effect of discord as well as contrast.
(c) However, the relative proportions of one color to another will affect the values of the whole group.

4.20 The relative quantities of juxtaposed color opposites strongly influence the effect. (a) Flecks of yellow-green against a violet background produce a sensation of contrast quite different from that of (b) violet against yellow-green.

4.21   MAISA TIKKANEN
Broken Red and *Broken Blue*, wall
hangings, 1986. Appliquéd pieces of
felted wool, 59 × 79ins (150 ×
200cm).

Color discords, set up by the
juxtaposition of "warm" and "cool"
colors widely spaced on the color circle,
can be used to produce effects of vibrant
luminosity. The relative amounts of
these disharmonious colors need to be
very carefully judged if the result is not
simply to be jarring.

Goethe's color circle

The great German poet, dramatist, and novelist Goethe was also a considerable
artist and color theorist. He was particularly interested in what he called the
"moral" effects of colors, or what we would call their sensuous, psychological,
and emotive effects. Goethe believed that when a person perceives colors, he or
she does not simply take in raw sense-data, but builds in a whole complex of
psychological experiences. For this reason optical science has largely discounted
Goethe's ideas – although the recent realization that color is a mental construct,
not a distinct objective fact, implies that it has much in common with the
emotions, exactly as Goethe believed. We now know that the perception of any
phenomenon by a human being stimulates a whole range of connected memories
and expectations. Color is just such a phenomenon. The designer can therefore
combine colors to symbolize subtle feelings.

Goethe recognized how the deeply satisfying and pleasing feelings evoked by
colors affect the whole organism. He wrote about the energizing effects of reds,
oranges, and yellows, the pacifying effect of colors of which blue is a component,
and especially the mysterious and disturbing quality of purple, which is, as we

saw, not a pure spectrum color at all. Goethe saw it as the "root" of all color. But to identify schematically the "moral," sensuous, and emotive qualities of colors is far from easy. Psychological research, commissioned largely by the advertising industry, has tried to isolate the specific effects of individual colors, so that they can be used to persuade people to buy particular products; and there is now a vast literature on the subject, but little general agreement.

COLOR AND FEELING

Since we never normally experience a single raw prismatic color, designers of light-shows often use such colors to create unusual experiences. At rock concerts violent changes or mingling of wavelengths may be produced by lighting technicians. And lights may be projected by rotating heads or through fluid media so that they change in random fashion with any movement of the source. The effect seems to be to disorient the audience and temporarily impair their normal responses to color. Computer images on TV screens tend also to use simple color as light, not yet with much complexity either of mixture or of composition; though there are still many possibilities to explore. Many painters and printmakers, notably those working in the United States during the 1960s and 1970s – for example, Jasper Johns and Andy Warhol – used to apply raw dye-tints to otherwise fairly simple images in the hope of achieving something like the disorienting effect of light-shows.

It has now become very hard to avoid cliché, the new banalities of color-hype.

4.22 and **4.23** JASPER JOHNS
Figure 3 and *Figure* 7 from the *Color Numeral* series, 1968–69. Lithograph, edition of 40, 38 × 31 ins (96.5 × 78.7 cm).

Johns uses the raw energy of pure and saturated colors to transform his deliberately banal "subject-matter" into heightened and almost hallucinatory icons.

4.22

4.23

All commercial design, especially advertising, has bombarded us so intensively with violent color that we have become partly de-sensitized to any subtler effects. This kind of color usage has been based on the assumption that quantifiable physiological excitements are our primary responses to particular separate colors. We know this is not the case with art.

Visible color always refers us to an inner field of color experiences. When we see, for example, the rosy breast of a bird in the wild, the impact of the actual color may not be all that vivid. But our mental associations may enhance the perception to the level of quite a powerful experience. We may therefore have to make some inward effort to discover how genuine feelings are related to color phenomena if we are to use color more effectively in design.

Convention

It is impossible for all people of different backgrounds, places, and times, to agree precisely on the effects colors have upon them. Purely personal experiences may have conditioned the responses of individuals to particular colors. Different societies use different colors, for example, to mourn the dead: white, black, yellow, and blue are the commonest. The Lüscher Color Test asks people to express preferences from among a group of cards of complex dulled colors and assesses personality on the basis of that selection. As yet the test appears to have little reference to creative design, although in advertising it may help to pinpoint the most generally appealing tints.

Colors nevertheless seem to have broad symbolic reference to feelings. We may not be able to find accurate one-to-one matches between a specific color and a specific feeling; but this may be partly because our words for feelings and colors are inadequate. Our color responses are nevertheless the raw material that design employs. The job of the designer-as-artist in exploiting the palette is not just to enhance the appeal of artifacts but to differentiate and weave together feelings. So some insight is needed into the "palette" of feelings in relation to the palette of pigments.

Color values

From the emotive point of view, white and black work as colors. It is easy to lose sight of their color values, because we see them and use them every day in contexts where we have to treat them as neutral. Newsprint is black on white. We write and draw things with black ink on white paper – even things that we may know to be colored, or that we may intend to execute in full color.

White symbolizes the unsullied basis for other drawn marks and color areas. All other colors will be laid on it or reflected from it without suffering change. White can therefore be used to symbolize purity. Many peoples have felt it as somehow bodiless, the color of ghosts and spirits. Used as the color of an image in a darker-colored field, it gives that image a kind of negative presence almost like an inversion of reality.

Black is the absence of light. It is picked up only by the rods in the human eye, since matte black surfaces absorb all color wavelengths. Only a glossy black surface reflects any light. Normally we associate black with night – a time when we sleep and when unseen dangers can threaten us. Used in large areas – as, for example, in some paintings by the American artist Mark Rothko – it can convey fear and uncertainty. But if it is surrounded by other colored features it can "receive" luminous impressions which our minds transfer to it from them, as if they were "light shadows" of nearby shapes. Applied in small quantities – in lines and dots to white surfaces – black can simply interrupt the natural luminosity of the ground. Graded proportions of dots or grains blend optically in photographs, or in printing screens, to give a variety of greys. Black may naturally stand for shadow.

In fact, we use black far more as line than as anything else. Black outlines are the commonest kind of drawing. As line, black on white is emotively neutral. A black line on white paper, or a white line on dark, is the most basic way in which we can record for the eye either printed letters or the outlines of objects.

The warmth and coolness of colors are psychological effects. Warm colors – reds, oranges, and yellows, either singly or combined – seem to advance toward the viewer, whereas cold colors recede. And, as Goethe pointed out, many people find warm colors more stimulating. They are thus well-suited to brightening up chilly or depressing environments. The cool colors – greens and blues – are more suitable for surroundings in which people need to relax – a dentist's waiting room, for example. This also connects with Goethe's idea that a design that works only within the cool blue-green range will lack vividness and spiritual energy. Good results come, he said, when the designer learns to take the "royal road" from blue to yellow through the violet-red sector, bringing in some of the warm colors. Paul Cézanne learned to do exactly that in his later landscapes. Earlier, Eugène Delacroix had written, "Yellow, orange, and red represent the idea of joy and richness." Other artists, among them Paul Signac and Vassily Kandinsky, have quoted this phrase with approval.

Color significance

If we combine written evidence from several great artistic traditions, including the Indian, Chinese, and Muslim, we will find agreement about the general effects of particular color groups.

Yellows are, quite naturally, connected with sunlight and even – in the work of van Gogh, for instance – with the radiance of love. It has a strong association with gold. To most people sunshine is intrinsically joyful. But in very hot countries, such as India, intense yellows that verge toward orange can suggest a brilliance and heat that are almost intolerable. Emotively the range remains one of high spirits, pride, and exaltation. Yellows that tend toward green are what we see in spring foliage, forsythia, and daffodil, and so evoke lighter, less turbulent feeling.

Yellows that are "killed" – neutralized with an admixture of black or violet – have a distinctly negative effect. They seem to suggest disappointment and sometimes a clay-like affinity with the earth. In many countries ochre is the color of mourning. However, following the principles of color contrast, we can experience ochres set off by violets as close to the luminous reference of the purer yellows.

Reds are usually connected with extremes of passion. Some people revel in

4.24   WILLIAM NICHOLSON and JAMES PRYDE, called THE BEGGARSTAFF BROTHERS
Poster for *Harper's* magazine, 1895. Victoria and Albert Museum, London.

The stirring, emotional effect of red is cleverly exploited by this innovative team of designers to produce a poster that is eye-catching, exciting, and memorable – all the things a poster needs to be.

4.25   ERNST LUDWIG KIRCHNER
Self-Portrait with Model, 1909–10 (dated 1907). Oil on canvas, 59 × 39½ins (150 × 100cm). Hamburger Kunsthalle.

The German Expressionists explored the use of "unnatural" color to create works that are charged with sometimes unsettling tensions. Feeling is expressed directly through the choice and combination of color.

this quality. The Indian miniature painters usually framed their pictures in a border of strong red, so that as you step mentally into the picture you are at once in the realm of heightened feeling. By contrast, Chinese scholarly tradition tended to feel uncomfortable with reds. The Chinese word *se* means both "red" and "vulgar" – that is, "popular", and hence, as it does with us, "communist"! A large area of red by itself can be simply violent, suggestive of blood or fire. Orange-red, or vermilion, is at the very center of the hot sector of the color circle. But in combinations, and in modulated forms, reds can evoke less violent emotion and even spirituality. The setting sun, the brilliance of certain flowers, such as geraniums and poppies, all have their own notes of rich and varied feeling.

The killed reds, red-ochres, are also colors of earth and clay, but are not lifeless. To people who knew few other reds, such as desert nomads, the red ochres can have much of the value of our familiar reds. The reds that tend toward purple always share something of the darkness of purples and dark blues. But attempts to imitate their multiple color mixtures with dyes and pigments are rarely successful, resulting in hues that have few overtones of feeling.

Color and expression

One particular adaptation of the relationship of color and shape has been very important in twentieth-century art. It was used notably by some early German Expressionist painters and sculptors, and by Henri Matisse and other Fauvists. It raises psychological issues that can lead designers in interesting directions. The method involves employing colors to unify and define object areas in the design (see p.111), by using not the "right," conventionally accepted colors, but "wrong" expressive ones: blue hair, red landscape, and so on. You can use this kind of color expressly to disrupt convention. The colors you select will not be merely

4.26   FRANZ MARC
Blue Horses, 1911. Canvas, 44 × 33¼ins (112 × 84.5cm). Städtische Galerie im Lenbachhaus, Munich.

"Unnatural" color is used here to transform familiar subject-matter into something symbolic. These great glowing beasts have the power of dream-images.

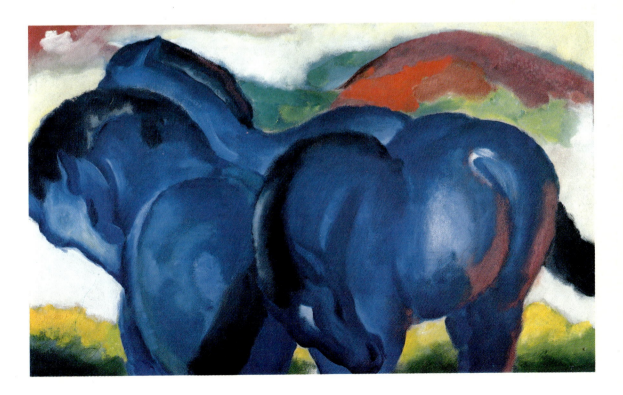

arbitrary. You can suggest, for example, special conditions of light and atmosphere: the sky may seem green or yellow at times; at sunset some flowers may seem almost black; a tungsten light may intensify the yellow in a tablecloth, or a strip light intensify a blue to violet or turn coffee a khaki color.

You can also use "unnatural" colors to give special emotional overtones to a particular part of your image – generally not alone but in expressive combinations. You can suggest baking heat with orange foliage in a red landscape. You can set off a magenta nude, say, against a black sofa with orange-yellow cushions. You can draw the features in a green face with red lines, and set it against purple trees. Part of the effect of such coloring will depend upon the spectator realizing that at least one color is deliberately "wrong" and therefore that color constancies cannot be directly matched with the norm.

The effect is greatest if it is part of a human being or familiar object that is unnatural in color. The green face may be part of an image of a cool interior, amplified by pale greys and blues, shaded by the dark foliage beyond the window. This may actually correspond to a "true" reading of visible brightness uncorrected by the brain. But if the other colors give special variant readings of their own, it may suggest sickness or it may merely be a result of fashion, like some kinds of make-up. The German Expressionist Franz Marc turned his violent red and blue horses into powerful symbols of joined earthly and unearthly vigor. Clothes and furnishings, walls and draperies, have no natural or unnatural colors. So you may choose their colors mainly for what they do along with the rest of the color group. Unnatural coloring can also be a powerful means of creating a sense of space, using the capacity of particular colors to "advance" or "retreat" in relation to each other. Individual pigments vary in this respect, and you need to experiment attentively with your own palette.

Colored line is one especially effective way of combining graphic design with color which has great potential for the future. It consists of executing linear images purely by means of lines that are themselves many-colored: a single continuous line can even change color as it moves. Chinese woodcut designers of the late Ming dynasty used it; so too did that great inventor of techniques, Pablo Picasso – especially with crayons. Cunningly employed, it can suggest between the lines areas of color that do not need to be overtly stated. The quality of its coloring can become part of the expression of the line itself, which we then feel as the trace of a changing colored energy.

Color as splendor

Certain colors – clear blue lapis-lazuli, delicate green jade, gold of various colors, the pinks and violets of Terra Pozzuolana and lac, an orange-yellow made in India from the urine of cattle fed on mango leaves – have been cherished by artists and designers over the centuries, because they do something unique for an artifact. They give it an intrinsic splendor, which turns it into a beautiful and valuable thing in its own right, quite apart from any graphic or craft skills the maker may deploy. They are metamorphosed by the context to stand for something else, which is then invested with the borrowed beauty of the substance. The designers of Byzantine mosaics used colored glass tessarae, gems, and lustrous shell to wonderful effect. Byzantine painters often used transparent paint over a

4.27 *Karaori* kimono, Middle Edo Period, c.1700, Japan. Brocaded silk, 60ins (153cm) long. Tokyo National Museum.

The garment was worn by a male actor playing the part of a woman in the traditional and formal *Nō* performance. The motif of autumn grasses on the three alternating rectangles (of which no two are quite alike) is metamorphosed by the intrinsic beauty of precious materials – silk, silver, and gold.

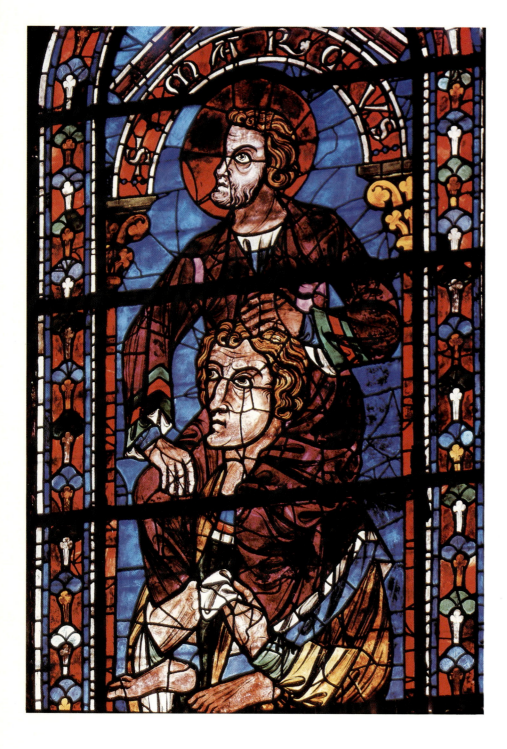

4.28 St Mark the Evangelist, stained glass window, 13th century. Chartres Cathedral.

Stained glass had a double symbolism for medieval artists: it glorified the hand of God by transforming everyday light into luminous color; yet, because each color was darker than the original light entering the window, it could also represent the dimming of divine light in our imperfect world.

gold ground to achieve luminosity. The stained-glass masters of northern Europe also achieved splendid colored lights. Renaissance painters, such as Botticelli, used to glaze one fine transparent color over another to give resonant depth to individual areas, or lay gold leaf into, for example, the lines of blonde hair to give it an otherworldly sheen.

It is rarely possible to buy such substances now. Materials and color manufacturers these days produce and deal only in substances and pigments that are either chemically pure and/or manufactured according to the dominant optical theory.

This prescribes that pigments must reflect light so as to conform as closely as possible to given degrees on the color circle – which we now know to be physiologically problematic (see p. 108). The resonances of older precious materials and pigments were due partly to the presence of a large number of what the modern commercial chemist would call impurities.

A few twentieth-century artists, such as René Seyssaud and Georges Rouault, have attempted to produce beautiful surfaces by brushing together complexes of colored paint to "stand in" for substances – rocks, trees, flesh – to which they want to attribute an intrinsic splendor. They are obliged to use modern pigments to attempt it. But far the commonest way today is to interpret splendor in terms of a luminous iridescence achieved by compounding several lines into a single area of color which corresponds to no single identifiable tint.

4.29   GEORGES ROUAULT
Grégoire, c. 1956. Oil on panel, 28¾ × 22¾ins (73 × 58cm). Formerly in the artist's collection.

The working, reworking, and combining of pigments here reaches for the luminous effects of stained glass, and produces compound colors which are far more than simple tints.

CHAPTER FIVE

SYMBOL

DEFINITIONS

A symbol can be defined as a thing that *means* more than it *is*. We use symbols most often to convey meanings too complex or subtle for verbal language. When we are designing with symbols, or reading someone else's symbols, we have to rely on our intuition and take time over feeling our way into their meanings. Symbols of this kind do not have right or wrong single meanings. In some of the sciences we may agree that "*this* sign stands for *that*." But this is not our kind of symbolism. In using the symbolic language of art you cannot stop at the convention that, for example, a white rose stands for purity. "Purity," in this sense, is only an abstraction. What a white rose may actually symbolize includes a multitude of experiences each person may have had of such roses; all those meanings that he or she remembers being applied to it in the past; and, finally, a halo of other things that resemble it.

Every mark, stroke, cut, surface, shape, or color we produce by design is a symbol. It means something different from, and more than, what it actually is. A pencil line may mean a trace of shadow, the edge of a table, a crease in a face; a curved surface, part of a face, a cabbage leaf, or the undulation of a cloud. The meaning of any of these may lie beyond words, being purely sensuous, optical, and intuitive. It is through the context of other symbols into which the mark or shape is integrated that the viewer can interpret it. This narrows down its possible meanings to those relevant to the total image. Learning to use and read these kinds of symbolic language is what art education is about.

Structural analogy

Works of art and design convey their meanings through shapes similar in form and color to other elements of our visual and tactile experiences. Words do not usually sound like the things they mean, but visual symbols may look like what they mean. Even a standardized road sign meaning "steep hill" may follow a form resembling a steep slope. ◢ This is structural analogy. It means that you can match parts of the symbol with parts of an actual thing, so that one thing can stand for another. The shape we use in mathematics to mean *equals* (=) derives from a pair of rods of the same length laid side by side. But to stop us thinking

5.1 Crown of Charlemagne, made for Otto I (936–73) and remodelled for Otto III (d. 1001). Height at front 6⅛ins (15.6cm). Kunsthistorisches Museum, Vienna.

The multiple symbols here include the Christian cross, the idea that the head it adorns is the container of radiant power, and the notion that, as its jewels are fragments of the coloured lights of the stars, the royal head reaches to heaven.

5.2 FRANCISCO DE GOYA Y LUCIENTES
Self-Portrait with Dr Arrieta (detail), 1820. Oil on canvas, 45½ × 31⅛ins (115.6 × 79.1cm). The Minneapolis Institute of Arts.

The painted touches on the canvas symbolize the faces of the suffering artist and his caring doctor, wearing expressions that both symbolize feelings and evoke sympathetic responses in the viewer.

of actual rods, the graphic symbol cuts out everything but the abstract aspect that matters: the equal length. But since a design symbol is not usually meant to indicate only one specific thing, you need to offer a match broad enough to awaken in the mind of your beholder the meanings you want, but not so broad as to be too general.

In art you may find symbols for forms that appear in very different things. For example, you may use a shape like this ⟨⟩ to refer to patterns found in a whirlpool, the skin on the balls of your feet, and growth marks on a tree's bark. The overall meaning of the form will not be confined to any one of those things, but all the instances will be part of the meaning. They create, so to speak, a "halo" of resonance through structural analogies with each other. Such **metaphor** gives works of art their special quality of aesthetic radiance.

Symbol versus sign

It is important not to confuse "symbol" and "sign". A sign refers to something you already know, and is a signal for action to which you have been conditioned. If an official points you to a space in the car park, you drive into it. If you see a picture of a pointing hand, you go in the direction it points, reading it as a similar sign. But when you see a pointing hand portrayed in a painting, you consult your inner reference systems to discover what it could mean as a wider symbol in the context of this picture.

The same thing can thus be both symbol and sign in different contexts to different people. Take, for example, a particular occurrence of a phrase in an opera. For a singer waiting in the wings, who has heard it hundreds of times, it

5.3 Early Chinese script, from L. Wieger, *Chinese Characters*, Hsien-hsien, Catholic Mission Press, 1927.

The graphic shapes symbolize objects which refer to acts: a hand with three fingers holding up a fragrant offering, a mountain range where the ancestors live, and a sky-dragon sending down flood waters.

may be just a sign to walk on and start singing. But for the audience it may be a symbol for subtle feelings.

This suggests that some signs may actually be symbols that have become degraded through familiarity. One of the aims of good design may be to reawaken people's awareness of the symbolic value of certain things. For example, we may normally think of a doorway as just an opening to go through. But at another level the door works as a symbol; a church door, for example, may be designed to evoke extra references by its shape and ornament.

Information theory suggests that the mind constantly filters out from everything that reaches it what is important from what is not, distinguishing "signal" from "noise". So in using ordinary things we normally notice only their functions, and take them as signs for action. But in designing a thing well we are inviting people not just to treat it as a sign but to contemplate it as a symbol and perceive anew how it fits into and focuses a wider world of relationships.

Context

The same symbol can have different meanings according to its context. A woman holding a baby in an advertisement means something quite different from a woman holding a baby in a picture of the Massacre of the Innocents by Herod. Many symbols may be so summary that you simply cannot know what they mean without first knowing their context or **region of discourse**. Symbols can, in time, die or revive, along with their regions of discourse and social relevance.

Designer and beholder need to entertain similar models in their minds as frames of reference for any particular symbol. Men and women, for example, may read quite different meanings into the same symbol. The designer, in formulating his or her preliminary mental model, has to feel for the meanings beholders are likely to read from the finished work. Matching the two mental models will be easier to the extent that the two parties share common experience of the world and of other design.

However, in museums or in art courses we often encounter what we know to be valid symbols, but which refer to things we can never have experienced in reality. We may easily recognize the symbolic values of an object consisting of colored pigments smeared on a board as a painting. When we realize it "represents" a seventeenth-century scene on a Venetian canal we are recognizing clusters of strokes as symbolizing people wearing clothes we have never seen worn, not even in the movies; and we suppose from the arrangement of coloured smears that they must be standing in front of houses like none we have seen, in what we assume to be sunlight. We build up our responding image out of memories of similar things we *have* encountered. We can never be sure whether anything like that image did exist, or even could have existed. That does not matter, provided the whole image works symbolically.

Our world-wide trade and communications have made us superficially familiar with symbolic art and design from many exotic cultures. Usually the objects alone give us very few clues as to what they actually meant to the people for whom they were made. We may have no access to the social customs and attitudes underlying their symbols. Because we cannot grasp their symbolic references, we may fall into the trap of believing they never had any that mattered.

Some twentieth-century artists and designers who admire the strong "abstract" forms of exotic artifacts have concluded that nothing but their formal arrangements matter. As a result they were inspired to make art of their own similarly empty of reference. Anthropologists and art historians, however, are able to tell us where to look in our own experience to discover the kinds of meaning exotic symbols may have had. They can often help to show what the symbolic imagery of, say, African masks, Japanese textiles, Chinese or Etruscan pots meant to their makers. Properly used, factual knowledge can help to enrich our sensuous and emotional responses.

5.4 GIOVANNI ANTONIO CANAL, called CANALETTO
Venice: A Regatta on the Grand Canal, c.1735–1741. Oil on canvas, 48¹/₁₆ × 72ins (122.1 × 182.8cm). National Gallery, London.

We have never witnessed this scene actually taking place; but we accept the picture as a true representation because it refers us to our memories of similar things we *have* seen.

Metaphor

Things may not look much like each other, yet awaken similar feelings. When a phenomenon evokes a feeling or emotion, it may also call up a response proper to different phenomena, connected only through some common felt quality of movement or attitude. Poetic metaphor often works this way. A poet sees the waning moon in the sky behind moving clouds. It evokes feelings similar to those evoked by a boat on moving water. So the poet may write, "The moon is floating on the blue sea of heaven," although the two do not really look at all alike. Such metaphoric reading may give us a sudden insight into the deeper, unconscious structures of our minds and the inner world they shape. Art can awaken us to similar mysterious and unexpected regions. A piece of jewellery worn as a pendant may resemble a bird with opening wings, and may also convey references to sun and planets by its gold and ruby substance, all worked in filigree. Once you get accustomed to feeling analogies between quite different things and processes, you can discover that the world around you is full of symbols for indefinable but real meanings. Even pragmatic, functional design will inevitably evoke some resonances and comparisons of feeling, because the inner process of matching and comparing experiences is involuntary and goes on all the time (see p.72).

LEVELS OF SYMBOL

There are different levels of symbol; art and design often use them combined in the same piece. We shall follow them through in order of relative abstraction: actual object, represented object, joint symbol, imaginary symbol, and archetype.

Actual object

Actual objects, such as a piece of fruit, a cord, a foot, or a stick, are defined first

5.5   Dogon dancers, Mali or Northern Nigeria (members of the Fire Society, masked at a funeral).

All human societies make use of symbols, particularly in situations that are charged with special significance. The actual choice and use of symbols goes a long way to defining cultural identity; thus the symbols of one culture may be incomprehensible to members of another.

of all by the context in which we normally meet them and what we habitually use them for. Many artists nowadays try to baffle our normal expectations about objects, either eliminating their old contexts, so that they become simply "instances" in a formal arrangement (Constructivism), or combining their contexts to produce novelty and surprise (Surrealism).

We have certain expectations about designed objects that are essential for us to carry on our lives; but these expectations can become very inhibiting, and certain artists have set out to liberate us from them, by demonstrating other possibilities of symbolic meaning in objects that already have well-established functions in our social systems. Marcel Duchamp removed a urinal and a bottle drainer from their familiar contexts and relocated them in the art gallery, calling them *Fountain* and *Bottle Rack*. The pleasure we get from looking at such work comes partly from experiencing the re-jigging or reversal of reference systems in our heads. The effect depends not only on the formal affinities of the object but also upon its original identity and purpose, which we recognize and then reassess radically. Many other artists have elaborated on this idea – among them, Claes Oldenburg, with his soft colossi, and Surrealists such as Meret Oppenheim, with her famous cup, saucer, and spoon of fur.

We also use objects symbolically by convention. Red roses are given as a token of love. In Britain during the First World War, a young man not in uniform might be given a white feather, meaning "You are a coward." If we hand over currency bills, people will give us goods in return. Behind each of these uses lies a history that explains why it works. Roses once suggested the blood of the heart; the white feather implied biological submission; a currency bill is the vestigial record of a contract between the bank and its customers.

We normally depend on our entire verbal and visual culture to keep alive our language of symbolic objects. The meanings of many symbolic things have obvious bases: sun and moon, for example, meaning day and night. Others have suggestive forms or functions: in Chinese symbology a bursting pomegranate evokes the ideas of wealth and fertility by means of its internal mass of ripe, red fruitlets.

Represented object

The next type of symbol, the representation of a person or object, can work in two ways, which may not involve personal feelings. First, the representation may be of something that was already symbolic before it was represented, like the printed image of the British Queen on a banknote. Second is the thing which only becomes a symbol by being depicted, perhaps in a specific way. Raphael's painting of Plato and Aristotle in *The School of Athens* fresco in the Vatican turned these two long-dead philosophers into potent visual images of cultural and theological meaning. A vast amount of art symbolism works like this. Photography as art depends almost entirely on presenting pictures of ordinary things as symbolic. And the very act of isolating some ordinary thing, perhaps stylizing it to emphasize one aspect, can give its image a powerful symbolic value. A child standing in a field of brilliantly colored flowers can be stylized so as to stress particular features and eliminate others: for example, curved rosebud mouth, nose freckles, distinct curls of hair, flat blue dress and blue sky, flat green field with blobs signifying

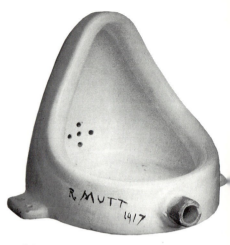

5.6 MARCEL DUCHAMP
Fountain, 1917. Selected object, 24ins (60.9cm) high.

Showing this urinal as a signed work of art was both a mockery of the art-gallery system, and a challenge to the viewer to overcome a stock response to a familiar and practically symbolic object.

red, magenta, and orange flowers. Designers are often asked to stylize an image of a company's product – steel tube, say, or clay tiles – into a logo to be printed on letterheads and packaging.

Joint symbols

We can also combine into joint symbols images of identifiable objects that do not – maybe never could – occur together in nature. A simple example would be a graphic image of an orange surrounded by rays of the sun. The combined image then becomes something imaginary which yet draws directly on the basic meanings of the actual objects referred to.

The way you execute such images can influence their meanings. If the sun-orange is done as a flat color-graphic on, say, boxes for a brand of oranges, the company is simply trying to make you respond positively, not to convince you that the orange is really the sun. But in dealing with the world's great myths, many artists have aimed to convince you of just that: Titian, for example, painted

5.7   CHARLES MOORE
Piazza d'Italia, New Orleans, 1975–80. View from above.

Built as a celebration of the contribution of Italian Americans, this public space incorporates a map of Italy into an elaborate symbolic statement that also includes a temple front in Classical style.

5.8

5.8 TITIAN
The Rape of Europa, 1559–62. Canvas, 73 × 81ins (185.4 × 205.7cm). Isabella Stewart Museum, Boston.

The great god Zeus, disguised as a bull, carries off Europa, mother of all Europeans. For a Renaissance artist, these figures from pagan mythology had a purely symbolic significance; yet Titian reanimates them by the conviction with which he represents them.

5.9 PAT BRODERICK and DOUG MOENCH
Frame from *Lords of the Ultra-Realm*, No. 6, 1986, © DC Comics Inc, New York.

Comic illustrations make full use of symbolism. The traditional symbol of Death, a skeletal figure armed with a scythe, is straight out of the Middle Ages, and can be traced back to Roman art. The fact that we instantly recognize its significance shows that this particular symbol has lost none of its power.

Europa, mother of all Europeans, being carried off by a huge white bull, the great god Zeus in disguise, swimming across the waves of the ocean to the shores of Europe; and he tried to give it the same kind of real presence and spatial conviction as the figures in his portrait of the Pope and his nephews.

Imaginary symbols

There is another kind of symbolic object that claims to be real but only exists in representations. A good example is the Chinese dragon. Originally it stood only for the fluid energy permeating nature, which is present in the forces of storm, wind, cloud, rain, and river. Later, it came also to refer to other kinds of power, including that of the state. All of these forces are real and have something in common, which the image of the dragon symbolizes. In the modern West we have similar, if less potent, symbols, such as the unicorn, the angel, and Father Time. Cartoonists use them a great deal. Most have some kind of tradition behind them. It is very difficult indeed to invent one from scratch, because hardly anybody would get the point.

Personification

One symbolic technique that has had a great influence on the whole western tradition is the custom of personification: starting with an idea, and then finding a human image for it. The image may be a real person or an imaginary one. Kings, queens, and presidents stand for the power of their respective states, as do

characters such as Uncle Sam and John Bull. The explanation of this custom is tied up with the history of ritual and theatrical performance. It implies that special persons – once perhaps animals, too – were the focus of great complexes of projected significance. In medieval times people used to take part in pageants and festivals dressed up, say, as the goddess Flora signifying Summer, as Virtues, Vices, Planets, Cities, Heroes, and so on. Personifying an otherwise abstract area of experience makes it somehow alive and active.

Archetype, form, and symbol

Some psychologists and scholars of religion, such as Carl Gustav Jung and Mircea

5.10 JAMES MONTGOMERY FLAGG
Recruiting poster, 1917.

Uncle Sam has become a conventional personification of the USA. Part of the impact of this famous and much imitated poster derives from the unsettling effect of being addressed personally by a familiar symbolic figure.

Eliade, have interpreted the major symbols of humanity as following certain patterns called archetypes. These appear universally in myth, dreams, and art and take on different specific shapes in different cultures. The hero archetype, for example, can appear as a knight or a cowboy; the spirit as a familiar bird, such as a dove or peacock; the trickster as Brer Rabbit or a clown. The "center" can be marked by a column, a shrine, a fountain, or a flowering vase, and is especially important in design. The archetypes are thus patterns lying behind actual imagery, rather than the images themselves.

Archetypes may be part of everyone's mental and psycho-physical make-up, like body organs and behavioral patterns, and emerge through unconscious processes or a society's rituals, to shape the individual's life experience. Because they are more deeply rooted than purely personal thoughts, their projections always have a special haunting power; and each individual experiences the archetypal contents of his or her own unconscious mind differently. Because we readily project archetypes onto people and events in the real world, we need to be able to recognize these projections as parts of ourselves and to re-assimilate them. One of the chief functions of symbolic ritual and art may be to help forward this process of reintegration by enacting it before our eyes.

There is a tradition, shared by many religions, known as the Perennial Philosophy, in which standard geometric forms are used along with numbers to refer to archetypal ideas which recur in the mythologies of those religions. Among these are the square, referring to the protective enclosure for the spiritual self; the cross, meaning the union of opposites; the circle, completeness. (These descriptions are, of course, gross simplifications.) Used in designed symbols, such forms always carry with them undertones of their philosophical meaning. One example is the circular shape with radii found in the Gothic "rose windows," which is so-called because the petals of a single rose also follow this shape; together they add up to a symbol of universal creation. The square may appear as a rational enclosure – for example, a city wall – opposing centrifugal or invasive forces; and the cube may symbolize the power of reason – what theology calls the "rational soul" – or organized space.

Some important kinds of symbolism work through the physical qualities of materials and objects. Color, texture, and shape contribute their qualities. But there are other basic components of the real world, used especially by modern sculptors, that connect with and symbolize experience.

One category of these physical qualities contains what are, broadly speaking, **things**: pillars and trunks which can carry weight; projections from or hollows into surfaces; holes through things – either small or big enough to serve as entrances; caverns and nests one can enter; blocks which are flat-faced, even cubic, and thus stable; sharp points up or down; smoothly flattened surfaces; circular shapes like globes and discs which imply rolling; things that hold or contain other substances; components that are tucked into or encircle others, gripping tightly or loosely; lips or edges from which water, objects, or people could fall; margins or transitions between one kind of area and another, like the seashore or a river bank.

Another category consists of **energetic qualities**. We can think of these in contrasted pairs: balanced upright or leaning; supported by something else or threatening to fall; standing on or hanging from; standing tall or lying flat;

5.11 The western rose window, 13th century. Chartres Cathedral.

An archetypal symbol, the circle, is combined with the opening flower that represents the crossing over between realms of existence.

structurally arranged or chaotically piled; gathered together or scattered; long and thin or squat; squared-off or rounded; flattened and spreading out or turned in on itself; arranged in long lines or radially; close or distant.

All of these symbolic forms can be treated independently, combined, or induced to add their force to any part of a figurative composition, especially in unconventional usages. Whereas artists have conventionally used bulging, trunk-like forms for the human torso, a roundish globe for the head and pointed ellipses for eyes, one could instead use a tall, concave form for a torso, and squarish projections for eyes on a flat, spreading crest-shaped head. Such deliberately unconventional applications of symbolic shapes are characteristic of much twentieth-century art, and reflect ideas which artists such as Picasso and the Expressionists learned from African sculpture.

Convention

When any symbol is used repeatedly it may become conventional and visually stereotyped. We then find it difficult to regain any sense of its original live meaning. This has happened with many of the symbols in our western vocabulary of decorative themes. We may use them on our textiles, for example, without feeling any flicker of response to their true significance: the Tree of Life, the tulip, the three feathers, and the knotted ribbon. We may not know what they are, let alone what they mean. But for the designer who explores their traditional meanings, they can come alive once more.

Convention can also work through **sign codes**, whose meanings are established by common consent. A good example is the Morse code of long and short sounds to represent the alphabet. The radio distress call SOS, ···---···, can have a strong emotive effect, though neither the shape of the image nor the sound has any structural relationship with the meaning. Another type of purely conventional symbol is the national flag to which all citizens of a state are meant to respond. The component parts and colors of certain flags may reflect some aspect of the nation's history – as with the Stars and Stripes and the Union Jack – but many flags have had to be made up simply out of shapes and colors not already used by another country. Only by usage in specific contexts do flag images gain real emotive force.

One final category of conventional symbols, **words** and **letters**, can be very important in design. Words mean what they do almost entirely by convention. There is nothing horse-like about *horse*, *cheval*, or *Pferd*. But we may develop strong emotional responses to them because of the contexts in which they are used. Words constantly used in, say, political slogans may become quite highly charged – "Freedom," "Love," and so on. A word may even come to stand for and evoke the experience it is connected with; and the designer can link that experience with the rest of the imagery he or she is using. Advertising uses emotive words all the time, trying to engage our feelings with its selling message (and eventually degrading the responses it trades on). Many painters in the 1960s and 1970s – for example, Jasper Johns and Larry Rivers – also used words as symbolic components in their images; and conceptual artists from Duchamp on have used not only words but phrases and whole sentences in a similar way.

Recent research has shown that both speech sounds and the forms of letters

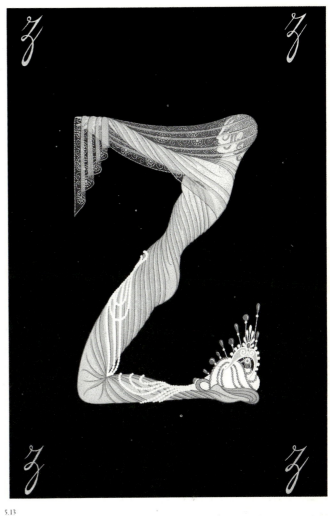

5.12

5.13

5.12 and **5.13** ERTÉ
Two letters from *The Alphabet*, 1977.

These figurative interpretations of the letters of the alphabet invite us to see their familiar forms afresh. Structural analogies with the human body are suggestively and ingeniously explored.

may have more than casual meanings. A designer can emphasize and shape the letters of words to capture some part of those meanings. There are three aspects to this kind of meaning. First, there is the pure history of the letter; second, its shape; third, its contexts, which come from the words in which it plays a leading role.

In all **scripts** letters seem to have started life as pictures of things and mimicry of actions; and many scripts evolved from a pictorial imagery which we also find on related pottery or bronzes. Such is the case with Mesopotamian, Mexican, and Chinese scripts. Our capital A was once ∀, the face of an ox. The Hebrew *bayt* ⊐ was an enclosure; our B was △△, a house, and so on. We may have long forgotten the pictorial aspect of our language scripts. But the Chinese culture has preserved a powerful sense of the visual imagery embodied in traditional letter forms and their meanings. ⫸ is the "water" radical, used to distinguish the fluid aspect in the meanings of Chinese sounds. ⟋ comes from ⌒, referring to "covering." Artists have often interpreted our Roman capital letters as human figures. Any designer is free to modify the shapes of letters, suggesting any kind of movement, or to make them structurally analogous to recognizable things.

Iconography and cultural echo

The term "iconography" refers to the whole complex of symbols used by an artist or designer. An icon was originally a representation of a saint into which some of the holiness of the subject was supposed to have passed. When the icon was of a single figure – say, the Virgin – it could serve someone kneeling before it as a direct access to the transcendent person. But the combination of several figures could invite quite complicated theological interpretations. Later iconographic paintings, such as those of Botticelli or Poussin, convey profound meanings by their figures and arrangements which scholars can tease out.

Nowadays "iconography" refers, more generally, to any grouping of symbolic images that conveys more than any one symbol would alone. This is not the same as the subject illustrated; for it includes many subordinate elements as well, such as inanimate objects, the clothing worn by the figures, and the style in which the various elements are depicted.

The last kind of symbolism has played a part in many art styles, especially recently, in the deliberate use of shapes and combinations that evoke echoes of the admired art of other cultures and periods. The symbolism can be either detailed or general, and is especially common in architecture. During the nineteenth century, for example, architects set out deliberately to work in imitation of Gothic and/or Italian Renaissance styles. Sir James Barry submitted designs in both styles when applying for the commission to design the British Houses of

5.14 SANDRO BOTTICELLI
The Birth of Venus, c. 1482. Tempera on canvas, 68⅞ × 109½ins (175 × 278cm). Galleria degli Uffizi, Florence.

Much debate has taken place on the iconographic complexities of this great painting. The central figure of Venus denotes Love; the Wind is the Creative Spirit; and the goddess Flora may be seen as the robing of human flesh in Divine Love.

Parliament. Modern architects have borrowed features and combinations from fifteenth-century Italian Renaissance architects, who had, in turn, borrowed them from ancient Roman styles. Many modern designers of furniture and ceramics have given their work strong echoes of seventeenth-century Japanese work.

Artists may use such established imagery because patrons appreciate it, or because they feel the need to "correct" their own invention, or because, transformed and integrated into a modern context, it makes an original statement. Through its echoes, the borrowed style then becomes a symbol that contributes to the expression of the new work.

PHYSIOLOGY AND SYMBOL

Our most intense interest focuses naturally on images of the human being. In design we use them to carry many different types of symbolism. Since we know the body and its expressive organs from the inside as well as the outside, symbolic human images can speak to us with a special directness.

The face

Facial expression is perhaps the most basic and powerful way of conveying feeling, and the range of possible expressions is very wide. Even before developing spoken language, human beings probably relied on facial codes to express and read

5.15 and **5.16** CHARLES LEBRUN *Fright* and *Despair*, from *Expressions des Passions de l'Âme (Expressions of the Passions of the Soul)*, c.1680.

This famous set of facial expressions symbolizing basic emotions, supposedly derived from Classical art, influenced artists and actors for over two centuries.

5.15

5.16

feelings – hostility, anger, submission, welcome, grief, enjoyment, and so on. To read the reactions correctly could have been a matter of life or death. Today, in any social situation, we still look first at each other's faces. So we have evolved sophisticated facial codes for expressing not only social response, but refined nuances of emotion. Sometimes we use them automatically – as instant reflections of our feelings – but they can also be used deliberately. Politicians and officials may take great pains to cultivate particular expressions, both to give them face-to-face dominance and to enhance their TV image. Magazines and book design give great prominence to faces; movies and TV to emotive close-ups. Masks and puppets isolate and emphasize particular expressions.

Facial expressions centre on the mouth and eyes. Different expressions produce creases: most important are those between and around the eyebrows, as in frowning, smiling, or expressing alarm. The shapes of each group of creases, combined with the complementary shapes around the other main features, give each expression its own specific character. Involuntary responses add to these expressions, such as the dilation of the pupil of the eye that indicates sexual interest.

Figurative artists have always made special use of facial expressions as symbols. In the sixteenth and seventeenth centuries Italian and French painters who based their imagery on the drama developed a repertoire of face types, based on ancient Roman sources, to a recognized set of "passions." The French seventeenth-century Classicizing painter Charles Lebrun designed a standard set which was copied in engravings that were widely distributed throughout Europe and much imitated by actors as well as painters. To us they may seem corny. But we have our own corny sets, including that hectic unreal smile often used by fashion models. Fashions in face types and facial expressions have succeeded each other with the generations and have been reflected in the conventions and stereotypes of commercial design. A major element in the graphic artist's repertoire of skills is being able to capture the current ones.

We also sometimes read faces – **simulacra** – in trees, buildings, wallpaper, and other objects because some arrangement suggests the standard pattern of eyes, nose, and mouth. Such images can even suggest particular expressions. Advertising deliberately uses hidden face images to influence people. So, too, may architecture, in its arrangement of windows and doors.

Faces and their imagery can thus be important symbols. In western cultures we are reluctant to exaggerate the proportions of the basic elements of the face too far from the ideal. But other cultures, and some twentieth-century western artists such as Picasso have cultivated methods of dividing up the face, exaggerating some parts and eliminating others, to produce "unrealistic" images which are nevertheless truthful in their own way.

The body

The body's expressive qualities include general characteristics we respond to. Conventional ideals of beauty and proportion are obviously important, but different eras see these differently. Current ideals are heavily conditioned by fashion and advertising images. In other times and places, for example, people have admired plumpness as symbolic of prosperity; and associated thinness with poverty. Such ideals are always reflected in art.

5.17

5.18

5.17   A "face" of rock on a north Cornish cliff, England.

The human mind readily picks up resemblances between natural phenomena, especially those involving the human face. Such formations are often regarded as possessing mysterious significance.

5.18   A street scene in Biella, northern Italy.

Two men are making hand signs to each other which have a conventional meaning in their society. We can guess at their general meaning, but it is the actual context in which they are used that gives them specific communicative significance.

The **spine** is the central shaping factor in the human body. Seen from in front and behind, the body is symmetrical around its center line; seen from the side, asymmetrical. These different presentations of the body have strikingly different meanings. Frontal address implies some kind of human contact; turning the back implies its refusal. Side presentation converts the viewer into a detached observer. The body needs to be in sideways balance to avoid falling; so sideways displacements need to compensate each other, as in the classic pose with one leg rigid with its hip out and the corresponding shoulder dropped and opposite knee relaxed forward. Carrying a weight to one side, or with a limb stretched out, the body must lean in the opposite direction. Seen from the side, the body's balance reflects the active will. Leaning forward implies "going," backward "falling."

We respond to **body images** with a kind of inward imitation. Stances, postures, and twists evoke in us matching sensations, feelings, even emotions, related to shadowy responses in groups of our own muscles, bracing, pulling, and clenching. These responses lie at the roots of the meaning much figurative art conveys.

Gestures belong primarily to the arms and hands, although they spring from movements of the head, trunk, and legs. Some gestures are almost universal: one or two hands offering and giving; arms open in self-surrender or despair; the forward stride of dominance; the finger pointing to the closed mouth in secrecy; the hand or hands raised in appeal; the arm lifted, palm out, fingers up, offering protection; the head flung back in superiority to look down on another; the drooping head, hands, and slack knees of fatigue and sorrow; the clenched fist. Baldly stated, these particular gestures may sound over-simplified, but they are capable of considerable refinement by variation. In Italy, for example, a wide repertoire of extravagant gesture has long been in existence. But in other western countries gestures tend to be far less expansive and often confined mainly to the interplay of the hands on their own.

Some figurative arts, such as Baroque sculpture, illustrate postures, twists, and gestures so extreme that no person could ever execute them. Here, the exaggeration is meant to intensify expression. Art that shows blatant bulges in particular sets of muscles may cause us to respond with the implied stress-pattern in appropriate parts of our own musculature; sometimes this kind of expression can seem excessive. Michelangelo, for example, showed virtually all the muscle clusters of his nude figures bunched up and fully contracted. This symbol for what everyone feels as his overwhelmingly violent expression can make spectators quite uncomfortable.

We readily see features and attitudes of the human body symbolically realized in artifacts, especially those made on a human scale: furniture or ceramic vases, for example. The designer always has to take this into account and to imply relevant human postures and gestures even in the design of such things as buildings and automobiles which people, in any case, feel to be extensions of their persons. Some artifacts, like refrigerators, seem almost to confront us as another body would.

It is part of the designer's business to make sure that artifacts "read" appropriately for the kind of job they have to do. You can make sure that the human attributes of the artifact are appealing rather than threatening, athletically poised rather than baggily slumped, balanced and alert rather than lifeless. Positive attitudes that can be recalled are a reaching and climbing C curve; twisted balance, arms extended; perhaps a flying leap or head-on dive. Fashion may dictate others. The aesthetic judgments we make about the placing of graphic design images on pages can also reflect bodily feelings in relation to placing and assessments of poise. Features that may not be obviously anthropomorphic, such as elements of landscape, can actually address us in the same way. Rocks may "heave"; tree branches may "reach" or "gesture." A line of hills may take on the secret undulations of a reclining body.

Bodily similarities can be reinforced by specific features in the shape of an object. One may stand in for its **head** – the stopper of a decanter, for example. The different ways in which that head is related to the bulk of the object, as well as its own qualities, also contribute to the specific expression. It may, for example, be rigidly vertical, drooping, pointed, or domed.

The human **neck** has its own symbolic importance, as witness the way we so often decorate it with a collar or necklace. Necks of one type or another play an important role in all kinds of design. We talk of the "neck" of a column or of a vase; mechanical components also have necks.

5.19 MICHELANGELO BUONARROTI
Day, 1525–34. Marble, c.7ft (215cm) long. Tomb of Giuliano de' Medici, Medici Chapel, Florence.

The power-filled expression of this great sculpture comes partly from the way we respond to its fully-contracted musculature with involuntary mental rehearsals of corresponding tensions in our own bodies.

5.20 BARTOLOMEO RIDOLFI
Fireplace in the Palazzo Thiene,
Vicenza, mid 17th century.

The gaping fireplace is here interpreted
as an image of a leafy nature-monster
(or Green Man) consuming its own
progeny – logs of wood. Such ingenious
conceits of symbolism were much
admired in this period.

Shoulders contribute to the posture or gesture of all kinds of designed objects, including pots, shovels, and some musical instruments. We tend to feel that broad, strong shoulders represent physical strength. We also use our shoulders as supports for various objects: bags, clothing, harnesses, weapons, and armour.

Together **trunk** and **pelvis** constitute what we normally think of as the main bulk of the person. When we refer to the "body" of something – say, a pot or a building – we are invoking by analogy this substantial and relatively inert but vital segment of the anatomy.

The **waist** is marked in the human consciousness far more by the way it is traditionally used in relation to clothing than by its anatomical importance. Nevertheless, "waisting" of one kind or another is a common feature in the design of all kinds of object, graphic image, and appliance. Pronounced waisting can add an especially feminine character to forms.

All kinds of artifacts have **bellies**, especially containers. One modest feature of the belly plays a quite disproportionate role in design consciousness: the **navel**, which has a profound symbolic importance as marking the "center" of the body. All figurative art treats the navel as a major feature of its system of proportions. Sacred sites are sometimes referred to as "the navel of the world."

The body's **sexual organs** also occupy a central position in design. We often use the terms "male" and "female" for paired components of which one enters or locks into the other. All sorts of physical characteristic can be designed into objects to give them a male phallic aspect – long, stiff, and pointed or round-ended – or a female aspect – parting, receptive, hollow, and containing. The female breasts are constantly referred to in designs of different kinds. Advertising art is full of metaphorical allusions to sexual shapes, deliberately intended to evoke positive responses from a particular target group. A large part of the world's mythology about the origins of things, which has inspired so much art, is rooted in metaphors and abstract versions of the physical facts of sexual intercourse and generation.

The **legs** support the body against the pull of gravity, and carry it about. Legs form basic components of all kinds of design, from furniture and machinery to buildings and bridges. The shapes and attitudes of their legs give expression to objects, as does the apparent relationship between the weight they carry and their thickness, length, and bracing-angle. Legs on objects such as furniture can be given either substantial or token feet to mark the load-bearing point of contact. Two legs do not give fore-and-aft stability to what they carry, unless they have projecting feet. Four legs give much greater stability on a genuinely flat surface (most of us can remember having to shove folded paper under one foot of a cafeteria table on an uneven floor). Three legs give total stability on any kind of surface whatever; although the height of the center of gravity in relation to the width of the base triangle can also be important. But most objects with three-point support convey a natural feeling of stability.

5.21 JACQUES LIPCHITZ
Figure, 1926–30. Bronze (cast 1937), 85¼ × 38⅝ins (216.6 × 98.1cm). The Museum of Modern Art, New York, Van Gogh Purchase Fund.

This work has a "face" that "looks" at us; but its looped shapes convey distinctive meanings of their own for which we have no words.

CHAPTER SIX
DRAWING

DRAWING PROCESSES

Drawing can express the most profound concepts with the simplest resources. You can draw with anything that will leave a mark on a surface – your finger or a stick in sand or dust, a hard point in soft clay or wax, a lump of earth or charcoal on a rock, a wall, or a piece of paper. Marks and lines take time to make, and so have a beginning and an end. Every line is bound to have value as a directed movement, even if it consists only of a twirl of the point. All need some support or ground, which they modify. Color and relief add other dimensions. Drawing is therefore, in the words of Paul Klee, an "active line on a walk."

Dry media

The media of drawing are either dry or wet. The dry media consist of pieces of softish material such as charcoal or earths. They are applied by being rubbed over a surface to release some of the material. They must then be sprayed with a fixative to make their dry, fragmented texture adhere to the surface. Some dry media are mixed with an oily, waxy, or greasy base; these do not need fixing.

Wet media

These are primarily inks, some made of iron compounds, and dyes. All of them, including nearly all the dye inks used in modern ball-point and fiber-tip pens, will fade in time to some extent. This may or may not matter to you. Of the relatively permanent inks, the best by far are made of finely divided pure carbon suspended in water. They may need fixing. Some can be used in fountain pens, but waterproof carbon inks mixed with a resin cannot, although they do have the advantage of not needing fixing. Chinese ink comes in blocks that you rub down with water; western inks come in bottles ready mixed. Wet media need not always be used with a pen or a brush. It is worth while experimenting with various other implements to find which suit your purposes best. Try your fingers, a shaped stick, grass, or a toothbrush. You can draw directly with wet blocks of Chinese ink. And you can, of course, draw with any painting medium.

6.1   ALBRECHT DÜRER
Head of Apostle Wearing a Hood (Heller Altarpiece), 1508, detail. Brush, heightened with white, on green grounded paper, 12½ × 8⅓ins (31.7 × 21.2cm). Graphische Sammlung Albertina, Vienna.

An intensive study of the three-dimensional shapes composing a ravaged face, using bracelet-shading in both dark and light media. Especially important is the way it grasps the central, nearest parts of the image.

6.2   PAUL KLEE
Drawing from *The Thinking Eye: The Notebooks of Paul Klee*, London, 1964.

Interlocking lines are meant to reveal the functional activities of an organism; this is not a drawing of a thing, but of movements recorded as linear tracks.

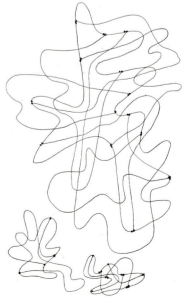

6.2

6.3 TAO CHI
Lone Boat on a Stream, 1793. Ink and colors on paper album leaf, 18½ × 12⅛ins (46.8 × 30.7cm). Museum of Fine Arts, Boston, William Francis Warden Fund.

Varied densities of fluid medium convey spatial depths. A few brush-lines define major edges; the rest is composed of collections of loose dots and spikes, allowing our imaginations to complete the implied image. The writing is part of the composition.

Use of media

Most drawing media produce lines that are clearly defined and relatively narrow, although you can lay a piece of chalk or charcoal on its side to make broad, squarish strokes. Wet media can be used either loosely or precisely. You can flood or splash ink or paint onto canvas or paper either as areas of toned wash, or as blot and trickle marks. When you use a good and flexible implement, such as a

Chinese brush, to lay a liquid medium you can draw especially interesting and expressive lines. If you use a pen with a hard nib, a fine fiber-tipped pen, or a drafting pen, you make fine lines of regular width. Felt-tipped pens also produce a line of regular, but broader width. It is often convenient to begin a design in a paler medium, and then go over it to complete it or bring out salient points with a darker one. Ideally, you ought not to obliterate any of the earliest marks that still show, because the process of making each image forms part of its character.

Drawing marks can be used *en masse* as texture. You can scribble loose

6.4   JEAN FOUQUET
Portrait of a Papal Legate, c.1464.
Silverpoint on paper, 7¾ × 5¼ins
(19.7 × 13.3cm). The Metropolitan
Museum of Art, New York, Rogers
Fund and Exchange, 1949.

This portrait study was probably done in
preparation for a painted portrait which
the artist could work on in the absence
of the sitter. It uses, principally,
modelling tone.

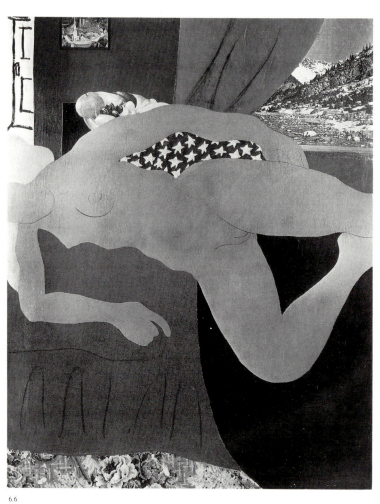

6.5

6.6

marks; you can group more definite strokes of various kinds, such as dots, parallel lines (hatching) in any direction, and wandering or stabbing strokes. You can lay strokes on your surface and later rub them into an area of tone. You can draw areas of tone that have definite overall shapes, either by outlining them or by working a texture outward.

Drawing surfaces

Different surfaces, or supports, respond in different ways to the marks you make on them. A very smooth surface gives marks with clear and definite edges. Liquid media used on a soft, absorbent surface, produces marks with irregular blot-like edges. On a rough surface, marks made by dry media acquire texture as they are interrupted with white flecks where hollows and crevices in the surface remain untouched. Paper with such texture is said to have "tooth." One special technique in which the response of the paper is part of the process is **silver point**. This was first used during the Middle Ages, before pencils or fine chalks existed; but today some artists have taken it up again for the sake of its fine, pale grey line. It involves coating the paper with a layer of opaque white and drawing on it with a point of pure silver. The two substances interact chemically to produce the mark.

6.5 MAX ERNST
From *Histoire Naturelle*, 1925, reproduced 1926 by photogravure, original engraving 19⅝ × 12¼ins (49.85 × 31.3cm).

A composition of frottages taken from different materials laid under paper and rubbed over with pigment, which was then further combed and scratched.

6.6 TOM WESSELMAN
Great American Nude #2, 1961. Gesso, charcoal, enamel, oil, and collage on plywood, 59⅝ × 47½ins (151.5 × 120.5cm). The Museum of Modern Art, New York, Larry Aldrich Foundation Fund.

A combination of techniques, including collaged illustrations, furnishing fabric, a flatly silhouetted nude, and casual line-drawing in the curtain and door.

Frottage

One process for producing graphic textures which you can build into drawings is *frottage* (French for "rubbing"). You take some object or collection of objects that offer interesting surfaces, and lay over it a piece of thin paper. You then rub the paper with a drawing medium. The medium will rub off especially strongly where humps and ridges stand up and will leave a clear image on the paper representing the raised 3D properties of the original. You can be on the lookout for likely surfaces, such as rough wood, chiselled stone, or natural rock, or make them from things such as seeds, bark, leaves, loops of cord, or burlap.

Collage

Sticking anything to a drawing is called *collage* (French for "gluing"). You can cut up frottaged paper and then stick it down. You can construct entire pictorial compositions by cutting the elements out of printed matter such as magazine illustrations. You can make surprising designs by cutting up technical plans or illustrations; perhaps photocopying multiple versions of each piece and laying them out in sets. You can arrange formally on a surface such things as shells, twigs, feathers, strips of colored or textured cloth, old paper money, tickets, sand, and so on. Some discrimination, however, is essential; the image formed should be interesting and the individual shapes expressive.

You can also draw in a light medium on a dark surface, as well as dark on light. And you do not have to draw only on flat surfaces. You can draw on irregular rock faces, or the curved surfaces of ceramic vessels. Such rough surfaces offer interesting challenges. You can draw by incising with pointed tools on metal or stone. You can draw with special media on the body, on costumes, curtains, furniture, or glass. You can draw by brazing wire to a metal surface, or by building up lines in solid relief.

EXPRESSION

The expressive power of drawing comes from six principal factors: line, enclosure, tone and texture, volume, conceptual and visual space, and crosswise relation. They work together in collaboration with the format, which is normally rectangular (but can be circular, fan-shaped, or even quite eccentric). Lines convey meaning by evoking in the spectator echoes from his or her own stock of memories of past experience, especially the kinetic – referring, that is, to shapes of movement and change in the world, as well as to the scanning of visual reality we all perform continuously.

Line

There is literally no limit to the different lines you can draw. All belong to one or more of four basic types: the straight; the equal curve, such as a segment of a circle; the angle; and the altering curve, which opens or closes as it progresses.

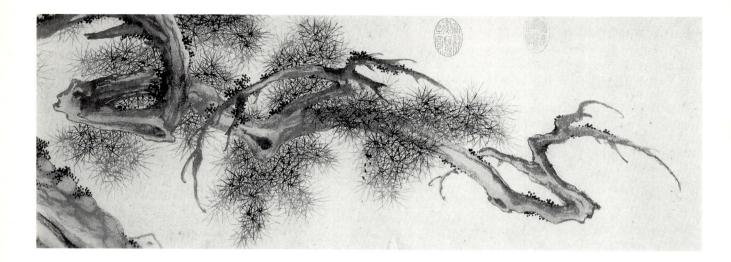

Longer lines get their variety and expressiveness from the combination of different lengths, variations, and inflections of these types; from the ways in which they change direction and undulate or spread. The rhythms you embody in them – savage, harsh, tender, or suave – are the most potent element in their appeal.

The first two types – straight and curved – are fixed in shape, though not in length or width; the second two – angle and altering curve – can vary widely. In free drawing even the first two can be given different expression by visible variations of speed and thickness, slight deviations from sheer accuracy, and the way the medium responds; and the other two types are capable of great variety. Such expressive qualities, however, are inappropriate in planned project drawing, which demands, above all, measurable accuracy and fine lines.

The meaning of lines also depends on the relationship of their movement to the format. You can usually give free lines a sense of direction so that they seem to rise or fall, float or sag, drop or crawl along one edge, for example. They can also do things in relation to each other: collide, crisscross, pick up each other's movements across an interval, twine together, splay apart, and so on. There is immense scope for experiment with linear expression.

Enclosure

One of the principal functions of lines is to enclose. Such enclosures can be fluid, organic shapes or can follow – not necessarily strictly – the basic geometric shapes discussed in Chapter 3. They can be closed or open. You can articulate them to make very complex sequences, and you can stand them any way up on the paper you choose. You can make complete figure compositions by assembling sets of quite simple enclosures.

In project drawing, however, you must normally confine yourself to geometrical enclosures strictly related to vertical and horizontal axes.

Tone and texture

You use these as essentially flat layers. Scaled tone is flooded or brushed on either freely or carefully to fill in an area, to rim it, or to stripe it. You can also define

6.7 WÊN CHÊNG-MING
Old Pine Tree, Ming Dynasty, first half of 16th century. Detail from a handscroll, ink on paper, 10¾ × 53½ins (27.3 × 135.9cm). The Cleveland Museum of Art, Andrew R. and Martha Holden Jennings Fund.

The vivid line, varied stroke pattern and ink color, multiplied needle-touches, and flocks of dots combine to give a deep sense of growth and endurance through time.

6.8 Varying characters of line.

6.9 Varied component lengths of a complex curved line.

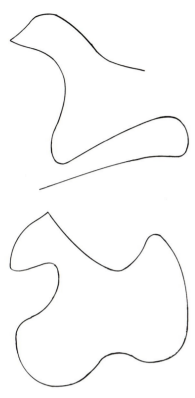

6.10 Vital lines follow different curvatures along their lengths, both when they are open ended and when they make enclosures.

6.11 Bracelet shading of oval volumes.

a shape by working it over with vivid linear activity, or vitalize it by treating it with repeated small graphic features. You can use tone in various densities and ways, including hatching, to define shadows. This means that you must first decide which parts of your enclosure system correspond to solid volumes; for only solids are modelled by shadow and cast shadows.

Volume

The moment you isolate part of a drawing surface as an enclosure it tends to be read as a solid, the rest becoming a void; that is, *figure* set against *ground* (to use terms common in the psychology of perception). The weight of the tone or the qualities of the texture can attribute distinctive character to the solid. But you can also make an enclosure or a set of enclosures read as even more solid, either by drawing the contours slightly bowed out, or by turning them into a diagram of a 3D stereometric body in one of the ways discussed below. A solid we can call a positive volume: empty space around it we call negative volume. The effect of a good drawn design can come as much from the negative as from the positive volumes.

As soon as you establish drawn symbols for solid bodies you not only define volumes inside the solids, you also imply a space in which they must exist. The drawing surface becomes a kind of space, either conceptual or visual.

Space

Conceptual space relates its bodies to each other in terms of their relationships on the drawing surface, such as above, below, to left or right, inside, outside, larger, or smaller. It does not attempt to suggest much depth or an actual visual field. **Visual space** is produced by implying a coordinated scale of depth. The three principal techniques are overlap, volume, and shading.

As we look at reality, what we see in front overlaps what lies behind. So if you make the edges of enclosures *overlap* each other you create a sense of implied solids that occupy not just a sideways extent of space, but also a depth. You can develop sequences of contour to suggest not only single volumes but also linked series of volumes running into one another, or clustering together in the depth of the picture space. If you cluster them, you will not be able to draw both contours for every volume; so you may need to complete some of them either with tonal shading, or with "bracelet" shading. Tonal shading defines areas of the drawing surface as "shadow," where light interrupted by solid volumes does not fall. Bracelet shading, invented by Albrecht Dürer, was taken up by engravers. It consists of running loops of line-like sets of bracelets around the main axis of rounded shapes. The loops can be exaggerated to increase the sense of bulk. They can also be clustered so as to work as shadow.

Crosswise relation

When you draw several lines, they relate to each other not only in terms of their lengths, but also in terms of their placing. These relationships result from the

6.12

6.12 CLAUDE GELLÉE, called CLAUDE LORRAINE
Landscape with Narcissus and Echo, from *Liber Veritas*, 1644. Pen, brown and gray wash, 7¾ × 10¼ins (19.6 × 26cm). The British Museum, London.

The deep space of the landscape is calculated in terms of optical perspective and recorded as a series of depth bands. These run from the lying figure, through the rocks and trees, to culminate in the luminous sky and clouds set off by contrast with the dark foreground.

6.13 MARCEL GROMAIRE
Nude Study, 1957. Drawing, 13³/₁₆ × 10ins (33.5 × 25.5cm).

The image has precipitated out of agitated pen-strokes, which measure off distances, angles, and spaces from the edges of the sheet.

6.13

6.14 Chinese tangrams are made up of pieces from a square sheet. The same pieces stand for different objects at different distances in space, according to the context in each design. From a 19th-century Chinese woodcut Tangram book.

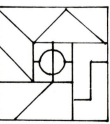

6.14

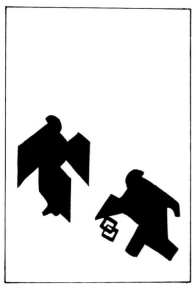

angles at which they lie to each other and the rhythms of the intervals between them. When you create a drawing you need to make your angular directions varied and interesting, and the rhythms of your sets of intervals effective. Such rhythms are analogous to the punctuating rhythms of music.

One particularly important use of crosswise relationships is to define where objects stand on a surface that seems to rise up into the distance. This is the clearest way of fixing the relative position of an object in deep pictorial space. You can position objects on a floor according to rhythmic "ladders" rising from the lower edge toward the horizon and readable as measures of distance. To register the floor as a bond between these two limits is part of the process of projection (see pp. 180–5).

RECOGNITION

The graphic artist must bear in mind that any drawing he or she produces will derive part of its meaning from the powers of interpretation brought to it by the viewer. These powers are a function of two elements: context and expectation.

Context

There are two kinds of context. One is the external context in which the image is placed. We may see it on an advertising page in a magazine, framed in an art gallery, among a pile of similar works, or stowed away with a lot of junk in an attic. Each context helps us to know how to read what we are looking at.

The second kind of context is that which the components of an image give to each other. Two dots and two lines, if positioned in a certain way, add up to a face. In the Chinese game of Tangrams you are supposed to make up a wide variety of images from a single set of stock shapes. Each shape "becomes" or "means" a different visual fact according to where you place it. This is because your mind is always busy making connections between what you are looking at and what you have already seen.

The properties of objects we recognize in a drawing (face, woman, automobile, gun) become strong clues to the expression of the work, and their scale in relation to each other can be especially important. A head can be made to seem a gigantic dream vision if it appears to hover over a miniaturized landscape. We need to be able to refer to combinations of movement, feeling, luminosity, distance, size, and impact, as well as to single objects. On the other hand, if we are "abstract" artists we may need expressly to prevent our viewers from identifying our shapes too exactly with individual common objects, if we want them to have multiple readings.

Expectation

There is another and less obvious factor at work in recognition. Since our minds tend to complete images of what they expect to see from surprisingly slender clues, forms already present in the mind can be awakened to interpret even random markings. The artist's task is to structure shapes in such a way as to enable viewers to read images combining elements from their own expectations. Each viewer thus participates in appreciation as a creative act. This partly explains the appeal of open and rough drawings, such as Chinese *I-pin* (uninhibited style) or late Rembrandt works which leave a great deal to the viewer's imagination. The good designer will have an interesting stock of forms, well tried and tested, that stimulate viewers to recognize and complete connections between things, conformations, spaces, and even actions, using material from their own unconscious memories. The formal aspect of design is what integrates these otherwise scattered references.

CONTENT AND TECHNIQUE

There are important techniques of drawing identifiable entities which are not solid objects. The first technique uses the principles of 3D structure (see p.86). You construct one or more entities in terms of straight lines that compose skeletons of jointed extenders occupying an imaginary 3D space. The skeletons can be laid out quite freely according to regular or irregular 3D linear polygons, or in any spread attitude you choose; and they can inhabit imaginary plane frames in space. Their extenders can radiate or hang freely, since they are not obliged to support themselves as actual structures are. The extenders can carry clusters of other extenders, or purely graphic features, such as ellipses or circles, clusters of lines, dots, or blobs; you can clothe them with drawn volumes to constitute figures of animals and people.

The second method is to treat each shape as a skin which appears stretched by external forces. You can make it seem to interact with other entities to emphasize inner or outer volumes. Normally we think of a body as pressing outward from within. But we can also think of external space as molding solid shapes.

Another technique presents shapes in space as presences by implication without defining them precisely by either structure or outline. You can cover the surface of your paper, say, with small, fairly indefinite strokes of different lengths which cluster together in some places and separate quite widely in others.

You can treat small lines as surface texture, and spread one particular kind of line across each area of a drawing. In a figurative drawing you can use each kind of line to illustrate nothing but the dominant feature of one area of the represented image. Van Gogh, for example, sometimes drew the surface of a field by means of little scattered flower signs; background rocks with clusters of short straight lines; or trees and sky by clusters of special curved strokes. You can treat dark line-clusters as standing for shadow, and so create an image of overall enveloping and varied luminosity. Rembrandt, in his etchings, would cover the surface with flocks of lines running in many directions that added up to mobile darks, their shifting intensity producing the impression that the light is actively "falling" onto the scene. Other artists may even use loose lines as if they revealed magnetic fields, clustering together to produce a shaped density where objects lie, and thinning out to signify looser interaction across intervening spaces.

6.15 VINCENT VAN GOGH
The Rock: Montmajour, 1888. Pencil, pen, reed, brush, and black ink. 19¼ × 23¾ins (49 × 60cm). Vincent van Gogh Foundation, National Museum Vincent van Gogh, Amsterdam.

The immensely varied pen-strokes give different qualities to each part of the landscape image, and their movements fill it with life.

6.16 PIERRE BONNARD
Still Life with Fruit, 1935. Black lead, 11⅝ × 12¾ins (29.5 × 32.5cm). Gustav Zumsteg, Zurich.

The loose flocks of delicate pencil scrawls give a sense of luminosity and texture, defining very few hard edges.

6.17   EDGAR DEGAS
Dancer Adjusting her Stocking, c.1885.
Charcoal on paper squared for transfer,
9⁹⁄₁₆ × 12⁵⁄₁₆ins (24.2 × 31.3cm).
Fitzwilliam Museum, Cambridge.

The chalk outlines combine shape and
tone. The dancer extends herself over
an undrawn, invisible floor and out into
the surrounding space, almost like a
sculpture.

Space as arena

If we consider our personal experience of actual spaces, we realize that space may
appear as a kind of field or arena which is defined by the movements we can
imagine taking place within it. Our everyday sense of the openness of the world
we live in is generated partly by our going from here to there, reaching out to
touch things, and following paths to more distant places.

Western art has long been accustomed to invoking this sense. It has often
asked the viewer to recognize figures doing things that take time and interacting
– walking, dancing, gesturing, falling, reaching toward each other, pulling and
lifting each other. Good artists poise their figures at exactly the right points in
their implied movements to tell us what has just happened and what is likely to
happen next. If the whole image tells a story that viewers know well – one, say,
from the Bible – the viewer can even complete a past and a future in their minds
on the visible evidence of a single static image. We may know that Christ is going
to lift that ill woman upright, or that this temporarily blinded man on a country
road will become a disciple. Painters now usually leave such kinds of dramatic
image to the movies; but its potential nevertheless remains immense. Drawing
can also imply movement in figures we know to be solid by allowing the rhythmic
and kinetic lines that compose them to cut across each other, so suggesting
complex 3D activity.

Human drama

The methods of dramatic composition that were traditional in the West were
mostly based upon images of complete human figures that confront each other

6.18   KORYUSAI
Girl Teasing her Dog with a Samisen,
c.1770. *Hashira-e* color print, 27½ ×
4¾ins (69.5 × 12.1cm). Victoria and
Albert Museum, London.

This pillar print represents a girl
musician and the moon as if through a
half-open door, implying that the scene
extends beyond the cut-offs.

striking postures, making gestures, and wearing facial expressions that tell the spectator clearly what each of them is feeling about what is going on. In elaborate compositions the protagonists are supported by other figures disposed theatrically around the principals, gesturing to each other and looking in directions that help to develop the drama. They may interact as groups and emphasize incidents by the ways they arrange themselves. Contemporary developments in theatrical production and stage design influence painters, whose conceptions in turn influence the theatre.

Landscape and cityscape

These pictorial elements were evolved in order to provide logical definitions of space and time in which human dramas could take place.

From the earliest times down to the eighteenth century in Europe, landscape was thought of primarily as a setting for dramatic action. The seventeenth-century artists Nicolas Poussin and Claude Lorraine did not paint pure landscapes as subjects in their own right, but drew the Roman countryside because to them it was the setting for the great historical and mythical events of Classical literature. Even without figures their wonderful bouquets of trees and heaped up rocky mountains are magical locations where wonderful events took place.

The development of landscape and cityscape purely as images in which the imagination could dwell began with the eighteenth-century Venetians, such as Canaletto and Guardi, French court painters, and the English watercolor topographers such as J. R. Cozens and Thomas Girtin. These artists were working mainly for travellers who wanted reminders of splendid places they had visited. The artist's aim was always to realize the charm of the locations as completely as possible. This tradition survives today. Artists still draw reminders of picturesque or historically important places; and amateur draftspeople (and photographers) eagerly capture likenesses of scenes with romantic associations.

Framing the action

A radically new way of presenting dramatic action was invented during the nineteenth century under the combined influence of Japanese art and photography, notably by the Impressionist painters, and then by Post-Impressionists such as Degas and Toulouse-Lautrec. Their interest in actual life in vivid progress led them to depict figures cut off at the edge of the canvas, caught in mid-movement, glimpses from above or below as through a door or window, and combinations of very near and very distant with no in-between. Such images convert the picture space into a fragment of momentary reality, interrupted and emphasized by the frame but continuous with the rest of the everyday environment. Nearly all of these techniques have been assimilated into the modern movie and comic.

Story-telling

One very common story-telling device used in both East and West adds an extra dimension of time to drama. It shows successive episodes enacted by the same actors in different parts of the same setting, which gives coherence to the story.

6.19

The most magnificent development of this idea appears in Japanese *Emakimono*, story scrolls painted from about AD 900. On a single scroll, up to 60 feet (18m) long, are depicted all the phases of an extended story. It is read as it is unrolled, a little at a time. Early *Emaki* were partitioned into self-contained episodes punctuated by passages of written text. But in the most splendid of all, made about 1200, the story appears as a complete visual continuity, filled with court scenes, expanding and contracting crowds of running and fighting figures, flaming buildings, stretches of vast river and distant mountains.

Nowadays the strip cartoon and the drawn storyboard used in planning movies are an important part of commercial design not yet developed in the fine arts. Sections of storyboard for movies that do not go into production are often printed as comics; and, conversely, movie ideas can originate as comic strips. Both use successive separate frames to illustrate successive stages of action. In good comic page layout the frames may vary in size and shape, sometimes elongated horizontally or vertically, wrapped around each other or locked together; while successive frames may contain parts of the same moment of action, some in close-up and others seen from a distance.

Cubism and Futurism

Between 1909 and 1912 Picasso and Braque developed the technique of implying a moving observer by combining into a single image profiles of the same set of objects which could only be seen from different points of view. To coordinate

6.19 *Tales of the Heiji Insurrection,* Kamakura period, early 13th century, detail. Bodycolor and gold on paper, c.16ins (41cm) high. Museum of Fine Arts, Boston.

Crowds of figures drawn with springing lines in positions suggesting vigorous movement lead our attention away to the left, far beyond the edge of this section.

6.20 FRANCIS SCHUITEN and C. RENARD
Detail of a page from "At the Middle of Cymbiola," *Heavy Metal* magazine, 1982.

The original pencil drawings take a series of different views of the progress of the story, in a movie-like manner: they could actually serve as part of a movie storyboard. The images combine on the page to produce a powerful atmosphere of mystery.

6.21

6.21   PABLO PICASSO
Nude, 1910. Charcoal, 19¹/₁₆ × 12⁵/₁₆ins (48.4 × 31.3cm). The Metropolitan Museum of Art, New York, The Alfred Stieglitz Collection, 1949.

An early Cubist drawing which articulates overlap-segments of the figure according to right-angle axes. The segments derive from parts of the figure's surface, isolated and brought up parallel to the picture plane.

6.22   GIACOMO BALLA
Study for *Passing Car: Abstract Speed*, 1913. Gouache on cardboard, 2³/₄ × 3¹⁵/₁₆ins (7 × 10cm). Stedelijk Museum, Amsterdam.

An image by a Futurist artist obsessed with speed, meant to give the impression of things flashing past the windows of a speeding automobile. The dynamic diagonals and swish-lines have been widely adopted by commercial illustration.

6.22

these they built them around grids of horizontals, verticals, and regular diagonals. They also opened up the interiors of objects to define them with plane-sections.

More extreme techniques for implying a moving spectator were evolved by some of the Italian Futurists. Gino Severini and Giacomo Balla drew and painted fragmented images of cityscapes that imply that the viewer is either reeling about or being borne along at high speed in a vehicle, so as to derange the continuity of vision. Many of the Futurists' methods were derived from developments in photography.

Photography and movement

During the late nineteenth century photographers provided artists with new ways of representing the movement of figures. Eadweard Muybridge and Thomas Eakins took the first accurate sequences of instantaneous photographs showing the actual postures of people and animals in movement. Artists were enabled to see how literally inaccurate some of the traditional conventions for expressing movement were. The most famous of these errors is the impossible posture that generations of artists had given to galloping horses, with front and back legs in the air simultaneously. Such photographs were thereafter used by artists everywhere who were seeking to give a feeling of genuine life to their figures. Degas drew repeatedly from Muybridge's horse sequences.

Marey first developed the multiple-exposure image on a single plate, so that moving parts of the body appeared as a series of superimposed blurs. Many artists, especially the Futurists, developed their own versions of such images; perhaps the most famous is Marcel Duchamp's *Nude Descending a Staircase*. Duchamp applied the conventions of Cubism to clarify and fix his multiple-exposure image first in drawings, then in paint. He laid out the principal start and stop edges as radiating diagonal straight lines, eliminating the bounding contours of individual limbs, defining the movement of each limb as the plane described by its series of positions across space. The procedure, however, is most effective when applied to a single figure and depends heavily on photography, which shows only the exteriors of objects. Moving versions of this technique are common today, especially in the fields of film and computer graphics.

Free forms

Today our attitude toward drawing techniques has been influenced by newly discovered physical phenomena recorded in photographs. These have enabled us to envision reality as a structure of interacting forces, which drawing is uniquely able to record as freely interpenetrating linear shapes.

We are now quite accustomed to the idea that the world around us is filled with invisible waves and currents of energy and that the energetic life of forms reaches out beyond the visible limits of their apparently solid bodies. We have seen photographs of the magnetic fields of objects, animals, and the earth itself and diagrams of the orbits of planets and comets. We know what instantaneous electrical discharges and lightning look like. We have seen time-lapse movies of plant growth and cloud formation; and we have seen visual images of sound

6.23   VASSILY KANDINSKY
Drawing from *Point to Line and Plane*, figure 19. First German edition 1926.

The complex of lines suggests how reality should be understood in terms of patterns of movements, rather than of a collection of static blocks.

6.24   BORIS ENDER
Untitled: 19 July 1924. Pencil on paper, 7⁹⁄₁₆ × 7¹⁵⁄₁₆ins (19.2 × 20.1cm). © 1981, George Costakis, Princeton, New Jersey.

This avant-garde design is meant to give an analytical, general view of compositional principles rather than an image of any specific reality.

6.25 MU-CH'I
One of *Eight Views of the Hsiao Hsiang*, 13th century. Ink on paper. Private collection, Japan.

The brushed ink tones are intended to reveal the transitory nature of visible reality, appearing and disappearing before our eyes.

6.26 JOSEPH WILLIAM MALLORD TURNER
A Swiss Valley, c.1840. Pencil and watercolor, c.9½ × 15ins (24.1 × 38.1cm). The Tate Gallery, London.

This vivid brush drawing of atmospheric processes in nature is imbued with the energy of light; it implies that the mountains themselves are a part of the process of universal change.

spectrograms and of heat and electrical current exchange between living organisms and their environment.

It was the Russian revolutionary painters, notably Kandinsky, who first began to cut lines free from their role in defining objects. Kandinsky's interest in theosophy led him to conceive reality as "spiritual," consisting of free flows and vectors of energy. By 1912 he was trying to symbolize these by turbulent swerves, sweeps, and knots of interacting brush lines, often in different colors. Eventually these lost any reference to identifiable objects, although he did strive to give them a 3D character. Once he had cut free from objective representation he developed a language of mobile abstract shape.

Kandinsky's Russian contemporaries explored the interaction of multiple enclosures particularly intensely. Such images can seem to execute an immense variety of reciprocal activities: enwrap each other; reach out to touch; press up against or penetrate; crush or support each other. Many of these actions go far beyond what objects could do in reality.

Kandinsky and his contemporaries were influenced by calligraphers and painters of the Far East, who had already cultivated the line as a track of energy in time as well as space. For centuries these artists had built up their images from interwoven lines and touches of ink. They were conscious of the possibilities of reading invisible continuities in nature and of symbolizing them with brush and ink as actual or implicit lines and complexes of line condensing into objects. The philosophical assumption was that the object-separations we see in nature are only transient patterns in a continuous web of change. Mountains, rocks, and trees, they felt, were – like clouds – brought before our eyes by currents in an invisible river of energy. An artist's job, therefore, was to follow these currents in movements first of the mind and then of the brush. The Chinese and Japanese painters sought a sense of depth in space and time so as to increase our sense of actuality.

It is possible to combine the idea of free linear movement with some of the western concepts of volume and space already considered. Spatial whirlpools and aggregations of bracelet shading, for example, can imply fascinating 3D images of mass and hollow. And aggregates of "lines of force" can do something comparable. The greatest artist to work in this vein was Turner. His vortices were based upon his experiences of British weather, with its turbulent interactions of water, cloud, rain and snow, land, and light.

Virtual movement

Whereas lines are traces of an actual movement of the hand, virtual movement arises only in the viewer who reads along sequences of forms that imply no particular order of making. Those dramatic figure groups we discussed (see pp. 166–7) produce a special type of virtual movement. But the twentieth-century interest in kinetic structures has also developed ways of working up the kinetic implications of sets of static abstract shapes. Most of these implied movements depend upon the viewer actively reading rhythms and relationships over long series of shapes. Five principal kinds of interaction are associated with the names of leading artists.

First is **rotary motion**, which Sonya and Robert Delaunay developed in Paris between about 1906 and 1926. They composed irregularly concentric bands, which were disrupted at intervals so as to suggest vigorous circular movements. Their sequences of luminous colors based on the color circle (see p. 114) increased the feeling of rotation.

Second is the extraordinary **open space imagery** developed by Russian Constructivists, and especially Kasimir Malevich. Using only flocks and flights of ruled rectangles, Malevich was able to imply many kinds of process and interaction in a deep space which anticipated and influenced science fiction imagery.

6.27

6.28

6.27   JOSEPH ALBERS
Planar Sections, 1928. Study on paper.
Bauhaus Archiv, Berlin.

A study of how optical deformation of
simple banding, as if by a circular lens,
can give rise to fascinating shapes.

6.28   KASIMIR MALEVICH
Splitting of Construction, 1917. Pencil,
12¾ × 9⅔ins (32.5 × 24.5cm).
Stedelijk Museum, Amsterdam.

This work, by one of the leaders of the
Russian Suprematist movement, is
meant to suggest swift movement
through reaches of cosmic space.

Third is the development, especially by Joseph Albers in his Bauhaus classes
in the 1920s, of a sense of **sideways** or **rotary movement** by carefully phased major
interruptions of regular banding or grid patterns.

The fourth mode was developed by Victor Vasarely in France. It depended
upon the progressive alteration or **deforming of grid motifs** according to mathematical parameters, horizontally, vertically, and diagonally, giving rise to optical
effects that seem to shift as they run across the grid.

The fifth mode has been developed by artists such as Carlos Cruz-Diez and
Bridget Riley and is based on the optical **dazzle effects** of moiré patterns (see p. 93)
resulting from the mutual interference in the eyes of light filtered through
superimposed screens, or of close banding punctuated by wavy patterns. Some
artists, including the Israeli Yaacov Agam, took up a related technique, also
promoted by Vasarely, of working on a surface that is corrugated vertically. The
left faces of the corrugations bear one design; the front faces another; the right
faces yet another. So as the viewer walks from one side to the other, the three
images appear in succession. Many designers have explored the possibilities of
virtual movement and optical dazzle, and there is a wealth of fascinating leads to
follow up.

Musical graphics is a special type of design involving virtual movement. It
came to prominence in the 1950s and 1960s, among its best exponents being the
Greek composer Logothetis and the American Moran. Musical graphics consist
of arrangements of 2D graphic shapes which are intended to be translated by

6.29

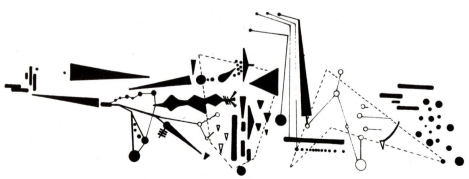

6.30

6.30 ROBERT MORAN
Four Visions, 1964. Detail.

This musical graphic design lays out, from left to right, the overall shape of a musical composition, to be realized by skilled musicians.

6.29   BRIDGET RILEY
Right-Angle Curve, 1966. Gouache and pencil on graph paper, 23½ × 22ins (58.5 × 55.9cm). Juda Rowan Gallery, London.

An intriguing study, by one of the leading practitioners of Op Art, of the progressive deformation of bands passing through right-angled curves according to a set system, and the optical effects they produce.

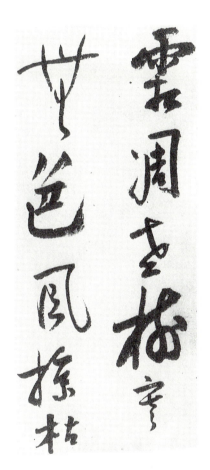

6.31   Chinese calligraphy, from T. C. Lai, *Chinese Calligraphy*, University of Washington Press 1975, page 135.

Each character is carried out as a specified pattern of strokes. The whole adds up to a sustained dance of the brush.

6.32   IBN AL-BAWWAB
Detail of a page from a Koran, Baghdad, 1001 AD. 7 × 5⅜ins (17.7 × 13.7cm). Chester Beatty Library, Dublin, MS 1431 f.9v.

The lines of script are read horizontally from right to left, and their shapes indicate rhythms and durations for chanted recitation.

instrumentalists into appropriate sounds, sometimes very freely. The shapes may even stipulate movements of the musicians around the hall. In a sense, even traditional musical notation is "musical graphics," for it consists of clear visual shapes that are intended to be realized as sequences of sounds. Some of the best of the innovative musical graphics have a powerful visual effect and offer an interesting avenue for designers to explore.

LETTERING

Letters of the alphabet, which are graphic images, represent speech sounds; an ordered series of letters stands for a spoken word. In the West we read and write from left to right down the page. Arabs read from right to left down the page, and Chinese and Japanese traditionally read each line from top to bottom, moving from right to left. Our method of reading words also conditions our reading of visual imagery – which has important implications for design and layout.

Calligraphy

Different scripts have their own beauties and expressive capacities. Western calligraphers have usually aimed at producing and repeating perfect individual letters. Scribes have sought both good horizontal combinations of letters and, more subtly, vertical groupings across the lines, which can involve slight deformations of component letters. In book-jacket and advertising design the shapes of individual letters can be quite radically deformed for effect.

In China and Japan calligraphy is considered the most important art. This is because the different pictographic letter forms of the basic Chinese script are very numerous – more than 8,000 are used in classical Chinese – and acquiring the skill to write them makes every writer a potential graphic artist. Different types of Chinese script evolved between 300 BC and AD 400. The earliest pictographs became squarish images, each occupying its own square. Finally the script became very free, and the calligrapher was able to invent new simplifications and arrangements of shape for each character in any sequence and to give them

overtones of resemblance to other phenomena – a "meaning beyond the text" revealing the depth and tranquillity of the writer's spirit. This could be highly complex, since the elements for the characters were themselves originally pictorial; the calligrapher could refer to such phenomena as the plunging of dolphins, the flight of swallows, or the gestures of aged pine trees.

Another eastern tradition of calligraphy as high art is Arabic. Its letter forms can convey expressive vocal cadences and lengths of melodic chant. The rhythm of the script is governed by numbers of notional dot-spaces, each signifying a basic unit of time. Letter lengths can vary from one to six dot-lengths. In Islam the clarity and rhythmic beauty of a script is taken as a visible demonstration of the devotion and stability of the writer's inner heart. It can lead the heart of a reader to a similar condition.

Free calligraphy

One especially interesting type of twentieth-century design is derived directly from eastern calligraphic prototypes. You use the brush or pen to make free and fluent marks, in the manner of Oriental brush or Arabic pen calligraphy – but without any reference to specific letter forms. Instead, the aim is to shape the marks into sets of signs that are formally coherent, yet have no obvious or consistent reference to any common thing. A few artists – notably the Frenchmen Henri Muchaux and Christian Dotrement – have even invented whole pages of mysterious calligraphy arranged in lines, sometimes resembling Arabic script, but with none of the characters identifiable as any actual letter. The viewer projects meaning into the marks by discovering what their forms suggest to him or her. This procedure, though it may derive visually from Oriental calligraphy, stems from

6.33 JULES BISSIER
7.6.1956. Ink on paper, 9¾ × 12¼ins (24.8 × 31.2cm). Kunstsammlung Nordrhein-Westfalen, Düsseldorf.

Under the influence of Far Eastern calligraphy, this German artist sought to express subtle intuitions by means of minimal gestures of the brush.

ETOSTENDIT MIHI FLVVIVM
AQVAE VITAE, SPLENDIDVM
TAMQVAM CRYSTALLVM,
PROCEDENTEM DE SEDE
DEI ETAGNI.

6.34

6.35

6.34 Augustan inscription in the Forum, Rome, late 1st century BC.

Each individual letter follows a carefully laid out rectangular proportional design; and the rectangles occupied by each letter are linked by proportional overlaps.

6.35 EDWARD JOHNSTONE
Roman Capital MS, from *The House of David, his Inheritance: a Book of Sample Scripts*, 1914. Manuscript. Victoria and Albert Museum, London.

Johnstone, one of the leaders of the 20th-century revival of calligraphy and typographic design, based this elegant script on Roman square capitals of the 3rd to 5th centuries AD.

the custom of automatic writing by which the earlier Surrealists, such as André Masson, attempted to record messages from the unconscious mind.

Standard forms

Western letter forms have evolved from ancient Semitic scripts, by way of Roman writing. They, too, were originally pictorial; it can be interesting to explore the hidden or oblique meanings they can contain.

Our letters are arrangements of straight lines and curves. Artistic lettering and handwriting can take considerable liberties with the shapes and proportions of components, while still retaining legibility. There is a highly developed aesthetic of formal lettering, whose history goes back to Roman inscriptions and to medieval manuscript hands. In the mid-fifteenth century a new hand was invented in Italy for communication between the scribes of government and commercial offices. Called italic, it became the standard pattern for most later scripts. Great modern calligraphers, such as Eric Gill and Edward Johnstone, combined it with pure Roman capitals and devoted care and skill to the planning of the shapes of individual letters, using arrangements of the basic forms discussed in Chapter 3.

DRAWING AND DESIGN

Someone planning a design to be realized in 3D medium may use certain special drawing techniques carried out in 2D on rectangular sheets of paper. The designer normally accepts the coordinates of the sheet itself as a basic control for the design, though not all design need be done in immediate proximity to the edges.

Plans

Presentation drawings for prospective clients may include shadow effects, decorative twirls, non-essential lines, and so on, to make the plan appealing. But planning drawing normally confines itself to finely executed, clear edge lines, because accurate measurements may need to be taken from the drawings.

This is why product draftspeople and architects use fine pens, very accurate rulers, and elaborate desk apparatus. In the past it was possible for architects, say, to leave many more details to the inventive skill of craftspeople than they would nowadays; even today, in the Islamic world, for instance, there are still vault-builders and tilers who can execute designs curved in space which western designers would find virtually impossible to define in advance using their standard graphic formulae. A few highly creative modern architects, such as Le Corbusier in the roof of his chapel at Ronchamp, have invented 3D forms that cannot easily be reduced to normal drafting terms. But the conventions of measured 2D drawing have, since about 1800, conditioned the way designers of 3D objects think.

These conventions are based on sets of **right-angled coordinates**. In practice the drawn object is reduced conceptually to flat silhouettes, each of which can be drawn as a 2D plane: ground plan, front elevation, side elevation, and perhaps lid or roof plan, which are thus fully compatible with right-angled frame-construction methods. The designer can easily measure off the correspondences of structural components or interior subdivisions with the external faces of the work. The designer thus conceives objects from the outset in terms of plane faces which amount to full-sized versions of 2D measured silhouettes set up at right angles to each other, rather than as fully 3D objects that might translate only with difficulty into 2D terms. Sloping edges can be planned to join two points specified along the coordinates; and geometric curves are usually confined to one of the faces only. Such ease of conception implies low cost. It also means that the designer can draw objects he or she has never had to visualize in the round, and that computers can easily carry through design projects based purely upon schemes of lines measured along the three spatial coordinates.

The basic requirement of technical drawing – the **fine straight line** – has also had a profound effect on current design. This is naturally transferred from the drawing board to the 3D object by industrial rather than craft processes. Thin line becomes sharp edge. Three-dimensional forms conceived originally in terms of geometrically outlined flat surfaces may thus have little intrinsic 3D character. Thin, precise edges have come to be valued aesthetically as "clean line", often at the expense of the qualities of depth, bulk, or presence which less limited drawing can convey.

3D projection

There are several methods of drawing 3D **stereometric projections** of solid objects in 2D. They all operate by reducing objects to a set of silhouettes seen from three aspects, which are then laid out as planes with clear-cut edges that meet at right angles. Nowadays even complicated shapes, such as shell forms, can be relatively easily projected with the aid of machines. Our understanding of the 3D significance of projections, however, still depends on our learning to read sets of lines recording edges that are supposed to define plane-faced solids.

The first method, **orthographic projection** – also called orthogonal projection – consists of representing the front face of the object as if the line of sight meets the plane of the drawing surface at right angles everywhere, and gives the effect

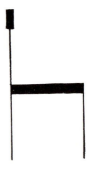

6.36   Orthographic projection.

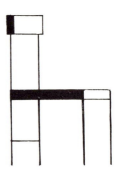

6.37   Orthographic projection with foreshortening.

6.40   Horizontal oblique projection.

6.41   Vertical oblique projection.

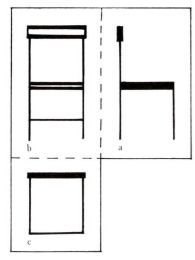

6.38 First-angle projection: (a) side (b) rear (c) top.

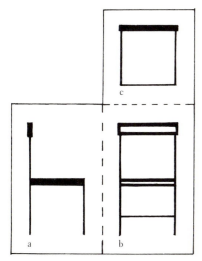

6.39 Third-angle projection: (a) side (b) rear (c) top.

of a vertical section through the object. An object that contains no overlaps (for example, the frontage of a house) will seem totally flat and belong firmly to the surface, with no sense of a third dimension. If the object is a figure, say, that has arms and clothes that overlap each other, these will be the only elements of the image suggesting spatial depth. Even the standing ground will become a single base line, as in Egyptian relief. Front and side elevations and plan views are, in principle, orthographic projections of an object from different 90° angles of view.

The earliest development of orthographic projection, called **first-angle projection**, was invented early in the eighteenth century in Europe as a way of describing engineering structures. A slightly different version, called **third-angle projection**, was later adopted in the United States. Both consist of laying out on the same sheet a set – linked by a uniformly measured grid – of three orthographic images of an object projected onto the sides of an imaginary cuboid box from three views: front, side, top, or bottom. In first-angle projection, front and side stand level, with the bottom plan-view placed below the front view, and the front edge of the side view facing out. In third-angle projection it faces in, and the top plan-view stands above the front view. Using the axes of the 2D grids as bases for measurement, it is possible to define the position in space of any point within the object. To conceive and analyze objects in terms of orthographic rectangular faces is an excellent way of transmitting information; it is much less useful for original artistic 3D invention.

You can also make an orthographic projection of an object placed obliquely to the viewer by defining the center line where the two faces that slope away meet, then keeping all heights constant and level; for if the sides were allowed to narrow by foreshortening, they could not be used for measurement.

Another kind of projection is called **oblique projection**. It has two forms: horizontal oblique and vertical oblique. Both have always had important artistic uses. They work mainly for shapes of basically rectangular cuboid form. In horizontal oblique projection, the front orthometric and side orthometric views of the same stereometric shape are joined side by side, one vertical edge of each acting as the join. Each of the two faces keeps its correct shape and its right angles. Only the front orthometric projection keeps its true measurements and correct orthometric shape, though on occasion the side face also may. Both faces stand level on the same straight base line. One special and famous form of horizontal oblique projection was adopted by Picasso in the 1930s, and borrowed by many other artists. Used for faces as well as figures, it combines orthometric images of profile and frontal silhouettes. In a face, for example, one eye may be given an indefinite generalized shape which allows it to play a part in both projected faces.

In vertical oblique projection, only the front view keeps its correct orthometric shape. A side view and a top or bottom view are extended from the appropriate edge of the front face. They may keep correct long-line measurements, but their angles have to be distorted to force them together along the edge they share. The degree of distortion depends upon which of the two attached faces has to appear wider. Each stereomorph implies its own individual volume and space. And it is impossible to draw vertical oblique projections of the exterior volume or the interior space of any rectangular box, such as an architectural construct. Lettering can be given vertical oblique projection to make it appear 3D and heavy.

Two further important types of projection are the **orthometric** and the

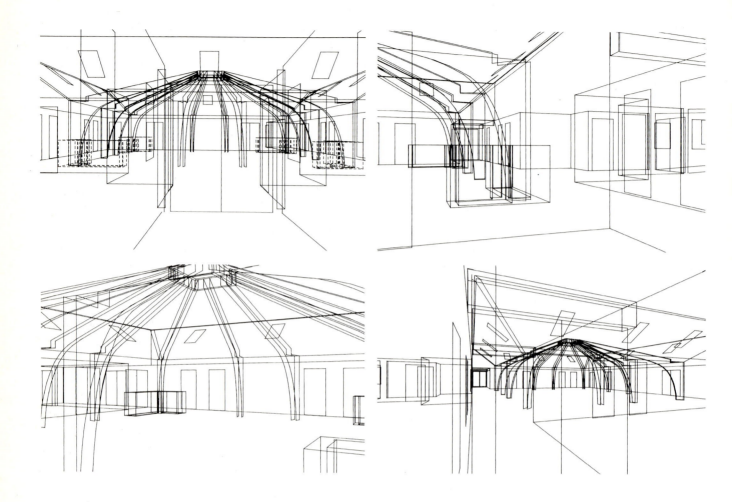

axonometric. In both of these the vertical lines remain vertical, and the actual lengths of all the axial lines remain accurate. In both the object is viewed from above, so that it is possible by "removing" the lid or roof to display something of the interior of the volume. In orthometric projection front external and rear external faces of the volume lie in a plane with the drawing surface, and their vertical right angles are constant, but the rear plane is displaced upward to one side, so that the rectangles of ground, top, and side faces are distorted into parallelograms. In axonometric projection the object is viewed from above and cornerwise so that the rectangularity of the ground plan and lid/roof is preserved, the vertical faces all being distorted into parallelograms. Axonometric projection is used especially for architecture, since it preserves the actual shape of the ground plan, which is so important in architectural planning.

Artistic uses of projections

Stereometric projections of objects have often been combined in the same artistic composition with, say, figures or trees rendered in orthometric projection – for example, in Byzantine and Indian Rajput art and in Cubist paintings of the 1910s to 1930s. One of the reasons for the strange cubified look of scenic elements such as the mountains in twelfth- and thirteenth-century Italian painting is that the artists were trying to give them the hard edges necessary for them to be read

6.42　Four views of a Cheshire Home, Marske, Cleveland, 1984. Computer drawing using the software package Capitol by Graphicsaid.

The layout of a complex architectural form can be designed in terms of points measured along 3D axes on a computer, then called up on the screen at any angle, with appropriate perspective foreshortening. It is now possible to "walk through" an entirely hypothetical building.

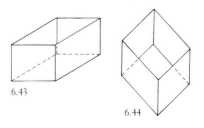

6.43

6.44

6.43　Orthometric projection.

6.44　Axonometric projection.

6.45 Vanishing point perspective.

6.46 Reverse protruding perspective.

in terms of linear projection. They also developed an oblique/vertical/oblique projection, divided along a notional center line, which can still give interesting results. The use of orthographic and oblique projections for different objects in the same picture always gives rise to strange ambiguous readings of space.

Many great figurative draftspeople have built oblique projection planes into the volumes of their bodies in order to make them seem solid. They divide up the fruit-like bulks of their bodies into faces or crystal-like facets – not always rigidly accurate ones, but nonetheless readable (see p.100). A body-bulk, say a chest, may have its front face defined with a receding face on each side clearly visible to make evident its stereomorphic volume. The outline will mark the farthest point of the recession. Receding faces may be clearly defined by, say, a shadow. To keep the overall silhouette within a "realistic" figure outline, the watersheds have to be carefully placed, and the frontal face slightly narrowed. Carvers are especially interested in this technique because it matches the way they cut their first principal slanting facets that break into the faces of a block and gives their finished work genuine 3D stereomorphic presence.

These kinds of projection offer us today a wealth of artistic possibilities which designers can explore in the context of our twentieth-century expressive freedom.

Optical perspective

The **box perspective** which we in the West now accept as normal is a projection based upon laws of optics first elaborated scientifically in Europe toward the end of the fifteenth century. It amounts to a kind of vertical oblique projection that also recognizes the correct degree of decrease in length which verticals and horizontals of equal size appear to undergo as they recede from the observer. It works best for purely rectangular blocks. Scientific perspective also adopted a device for coordinating into one space box all the diagonal receding lines of rectangles or cuboid blocks, as well as the floor. This is the single vanishing point

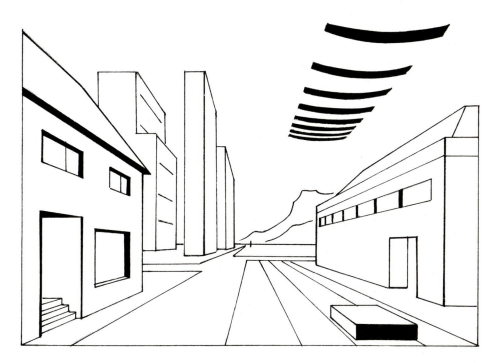

6.47 Box perspective.

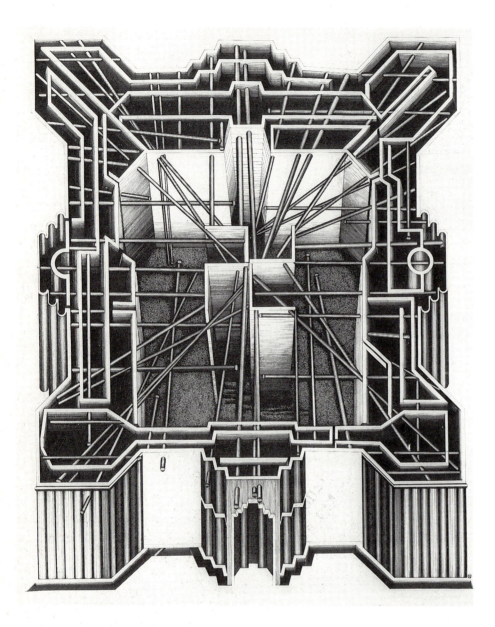

6.48 DEANNA PETHERBRIDGE
Square Inch Field of the Square Foot House, from the *Seven Citadels* series, 1974. Pen and ink on paper, 27½ × 19¾ins (70 × 50cm). Private collection, London.

A deliberately puzzling assembly of apparently consistent drawn shapes, including symbols such as the swastika. The careful two-dimensional logic produces an impossible three-dimensional object.

on the horizon or eye-line toward which all the diagonals of all the vertical oblique projections on either side of the observer converge. The space box thus seems to contain the observer, implying that he or she is looking into the box through the frame of the picture – but only through one fixed and stationary eye.

Normally the vanishing point lies at the center of the horizon, directly opposite the viewing eye. If the viewpoint is high, the horizon and vanishing point will be high, and the floor area deep in the format; if low, the vanishing point will be low, and the floor area shallow. So a perspective drawing "places" the eye of the viewer in a specific relationship to the scene. The perspective effect is enhanced if you use a complex of geometrical forms strictly aligned at right angles to the orthometric projection of their front faces, as in a street. Depending on how much your vision of the front face of the rectangle diverges from the head-on, the vanishing point will diverge to one side or the other of the center of your horizon. A perspective view of a rectangular building seen from one corner requires two vanishing points on the horizon, one for each visible face.

The evolution of perspective projection as an intellectual discipline went hand in hand with the development of **drawing machines** by artists who were trying to produce accurate likenesses of the purely optical appearance of the "real world" from the point of view of an individual, complete with foreshortening. Space conceived as a diminishing box extending behind the "window" of the drawing format also makes it possible for art to produce an impression of vast or even "infinite" distance.

We know what early drawing machines of about 1500 looked like because both Leonardo da Vinci and Dürer left illustrations of them. Some involved taking quite complex measurements with the help of an assistant. But the simplest and most effective could be used by the artist alone. They are still useful today.

The basic machine consists of a fixed frame containing a sheet of transparent material on which to draw. Between this and the artist is a peephole, through which you look with one eye. The machine is placed with the sitter or scene on the far side of the transparent sheet. Peeping through the hole, you can then trace outlines around the edges of the image you see on the sheet. The practice of drawing itself is in effect reduced to tracing outlines given by the machine.

The desire of artists for ultimate realism in their work inspired the evolution of this drawing machine through a series of stages, including the *camera obscura*. The final stage was achieved in the 1820s by William Fox Talbot, Claude Niépce, and Louis Daguerre – all artists looking for a definitive way to fix the static appearance of the real world. The first "photographs" – the word means "drawn by light" – were the result.

6.49 ALBRECHT DÜRER
Illustration from *The Art of Drawing*, Nuremberg, 1525. Woodcut.

This illustrates a drawing machine in use. The device fixes the relationship between the subject and the artist's hand and eye, and it makes easy the capturing of optically accurate proportions and likenesses.

CHAPTER SEVEN
PRINT

PRINTING BASICS

Printing can be regarded as a way of producing an image indirectly. The image may be a drawing, or some other hand-made design; or it may be the result of light acting on chemicals, as in photography. Prints are normally made by carrying out an original design on a separate form, or "matrix." From this matrix you take impressions which reverse the design – a fact you must take account of. Except for silk-screen and photography you do this by applying pigment or ink to the matrix and pressing the matrix onto paper. There are several ways of applying pressure, either by hand or by mechanical press. The paper needs to be relatively absorbent, so as to take off a clean impression which does not smear or spread. Different grades of paper are particularly suitable for different techniques. You mix the pigment to a precise consistency either with water-based glue or drying oils, and perhaps dampen the paper slightly to enable it to take up the pigment correctly.

You can execute a print design only in terms of lines and flat tone. With a few exceptions, it is only possible to vary the tonal qualities of lines or areas by retouching the matrix by hand as you print, on small print runs. Most long-run prints have their darks built up by multiplying lines as hatching and texture, plus controlled inking. It is possible to color any monochrome print by hand, either in specific areas or all over. You can also print your lines with colored pigment, on colored paper. This can produce splendid results. Hercules Seghers, an older contemporary of Rembrandt, printed versions of his designs in a variety of color combinations.

Traditionally, the printing techniques are divided into two classes: **relief printing**, in which the marks are applied to the paper from the crests of raised ridges and surfaces; and **intaglio printing**, in which the pigment is absorbed into the paper under pressure out of channels in the printing surface, the rest of which has been wiped clean. Certain modern techniques form another class by themselves; and photography, of course, has its own specific methods. For convenience we shall use the term "ink" for printing-pigment in general, and assume that it is black.

7.1   ANDY WARHOL
Mao, 1973. Acrylic and silkscreen on canvas, 192 × 96ins (487.7 × 243.8cm). The Metropolitan Museum of Art, New York, Gift of Sandra Brandt, 1977.

A gigantic silk-screen print based on a widely distributed photograph of the Chinese communist leader. It is freely brushed with acrylic pigment, turning it into a unique "original."

7.2   EDWARD HOPPER
Man's Head, 1902. Monotype, 4½ × 3¼ins (11.4 × 8.25cm). Whitney Museum of American Art, New York, Josephine N. Hopper Bequest. Acq. #70.1560.100.

This print was taken, while the pigment was still wet, from an image loosely brushed onto a non-absorbent surface – probably glass.

Tracing and pressure tracing

These are useful devices for clarifying final versions of an image to be printed. To trace, you lay a sheet of almost transparent paper over a preliminary rough and draw over it a final outline copied from part of the visible drawing. Pressure tracing consists of laying a sheet of specially coated paper face down over a fresh sheet under the preliminary drawing or a tracing from it, and then applying pressure to parts of it. This attaches some of the coating to the fresh sheet or to the printing matrix. The results of both processes are clear lines abstracted from the relative confusion of an earlier development drawing. Nowadays you can use the photocopying machine to make multiple versions of a drawing on which you can then experiment with variations.

Monotype

The simplest and most immediate technique of printing is the monotype (i.e., one-off), which is used by many artists. You draw or paint an image with printing ink on a sheet of, say, glass or paper, and then lay another sheet on top of it, to absorb the drawing medium before it has dried – a process that adds interesting qualities to the image. A monotype print is, of course, reversed from the original drawing. You can re-draw the image, either on the matrix surface or on the monotype pull itself, and reprint. This then produces a second impression, which you can develop from the first image, even changing it quite radically. By repeating the process you can work up a long series of monotypes. Edgar Degas and Richard Diebenkorn are two artists who have obtained particularly beautiful results this way.

RELIEF

Relief is the oldest form of printing. Its most primitive form is probably *frottage* (see p. 159). By about AD 900 the Chinese were relief-printing, first textiles and paper money, then books on paper from flat blocks of wood, usually one block for each pair of pages. They cut away the background to leave the writing standing as ridges. This was the method adopted soon after 1400 in Germany for Europe's first woodblock-printed books. In Europe, book-printers then began using sets of wooden type consisting of dozens of identical blocks for each letter, which they assembled into lines within special frames to print each sheet. These were the prototypes of modern letterpress.

7.3 *The Coronation of Mary*, c.1410. German woodcut. Formerly Graphische Sammlung, Munich.

In this devotional print the beautiful network of lines left standing in relief is complemented by carefully shaped empty spaces cut out of the block.

The printing block

You can make relief printing blocks out of almost any material that has a flat surface that can be cut away with knives, chisels, gouges, and V-tools. Wood is the commonest, and perhaps the best material, because the impress of its grain and even the saw-marks can give life to the final print. Many of the finest woodblocks are cut along the grain – which you need to respect. But ordinary long-grain woodblocks will only give a certain number of impressions (varying with the quality of the wood) before they get rough and fluffy and bits of the crests start to break off. By far the best wood is box, which is worked across the end grain. It is dense and strong, and you can cut it without the grain lifting. But nowadays there are few box trees old enough to give a block of any width; even in the nineteenth century, blocks had to be made up of pieces bolted together. So instead we use flooring linoleum or vinyl as substitute. Both lack the "life" of wood, but they will take fine and close cutting.

During the 1860s the commercial printers of fine woodblock illustrations for books began to use **clichés**. These are metal castings of original woodblocks. Individually they can produce long runs without breaking down, and they reproduce the qualities of the original block fairly well. Until recently, newspapers used to be printed from curved cast metal clichés mounted on rotary presses.

There are unconventional ways of producing relief-print images. One is to cut out a raised pattern of lines and areas from cardboard, and glue it down onto another piece of cardboard. You can then print a (very small) number of impressions from the raised shapes. Another method uses the acid-etching technique to bite away the ground and so produce a relief rather than an intaglio image on the metal plate (see p. 198).

Methods of inking

Any part of the surface left standing will print either as line or as area if it is inked. But to save time, it is perfectly possible to leave large areas standing and simply avoid inking them before printing. You can ink wood, linoleum, or vinyl blocks in two principal ways. The first and subtler is to paint the ink on by hand, using a brush. This is the artist's method, because it allows you to produce all sorts of ink qualities on the final print. The second is the normal commercial procedure of using a roller, first to spread the ink on a sheet of stone or glass to the right thickness and consistency, and then to roll it over the faces of the standing areas and ridges on the block. This gives a smooth, equal tone all over.

Methods of printing

The two methods of inking are matched by two methods of printing. The commercial method is, after placing the paper on the block, to pad the backs of both with felt mats, and pass them all through the press. The artist's method is to lay the paper onto the block, which lies face up, perhaps fixing it along one edge to keep it in constant relation to the block. You can then lift the paper repeatedly to look at it and brush more ink onto the ridges of the block, applying ink more densely to parts according to your aesthetic judgment. You can even

7.4   FREDERICK SANDYS
Illustration to the poem "Manoli" in *The Cornhill Magazine*, 1862. Wood engraving.

The cruel husband is walling up his wife. The design, strongly influenced by Dürer, is far sterner and stronger than most Victorian figuration.

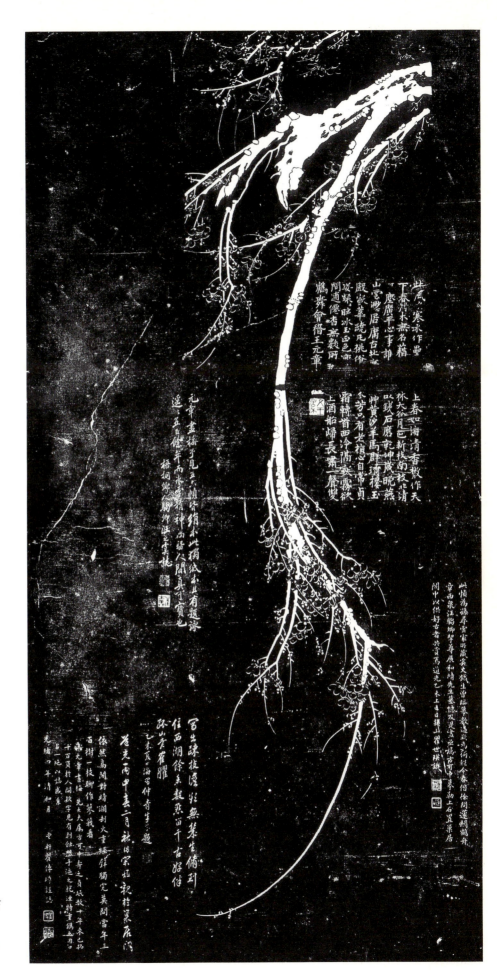

7.5 WANG MIEN
Plum Blossom, Chinese white print.
Durham University Oriental Museum.

The original design was drawn on a
board, and the drawing itself was
carefully cut out as channels. A sheet of
paper was then laid on the board and a
block of wet ink rubbed all over the
surface. The process leaves the original
drawing as white.

apply different colors to different parts of the design during the same printing. You press the paper down by hand, or rub its back gently with a pad of leather or cloth.

An easy technique which can give interesting results is **gauffrage**. You lay dampened paper on a relief block without any ink and press it down with a soft pad. This gives a "blind" printing only of the shape in relief.

Coloring by hand

Once you have printed a design you can color areas of it directly by hand, not only on the front of the sheet, but on the back of a thin absorbent sheet, such as Japanese mulberry paper. Munakata did this most effectively. You can also use different blocks to print several colors over different parts of the design. The Japanese *Ukiyo-e* printers of the seventeenth to nineteenth centuries developed and refined this technique.

It is best to use one principal block to serve as the key block which gives you the register for printing each of the other blocks. The *Ukiyo-e* usually employed the black linear design for this. They would print a set of sheets of the key block on thin paper, and stick them face down on to fresh blocks, then use that design as a guide for cutting out on each new block the areas of each colour needed. They did not often print one color over another, for fear of losing delicacy. With modern pigments, however, we can do so.

One technique employed between the sixteenth and nineteenth centuries in Europe was to use one or more extra blocks, resembling those used for color, to print areas of one or more grades of pure tone paler than a principal line block, which was itself either wood-relief or intaglio-engraved. This gives an effect of pen and wash, and is becoming popular again partly because it can resemble an effect of photographic imagery.

Drawing for relief print

Most relief printing starts with a drawing. You can draw on the block itself, or glue a drawing on paper onto the block. By using a drawing on very thin paper and placing it face down on the block, you can produce an image that is the right way around. You then cut away all the surfaces you wish to remain white. You can, in fact, draw as you cut, with few or no guidelines, if you feel confident enough. You will then actually be drawing white shapes with your cutting-tools.

The results of relief printing are marks which can have three kinds of value. First there is pure line, either black or white. You can give it all sorts of qualities of rhythm, varied width, roughness, or smoothness, by the way you cut. Black line printing can be virtually a reproduction of an original pen or brush drawing. European woodprints of the fifteenth and sixteenth centuries and the Japanese *Ukiyo-e* prints are worked as pure lines, which involves much skilled labor in cutting away all the wood not meant to print, leaving carefully shaped ridges standing. You can also draw with white cut-away lines, which appear against a black background.

Lines have their own qualities of movement which are more or less independent of tonality. But you can think of your printed black in terms of shaped areas

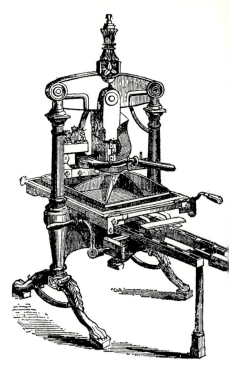

7.6 Mid 19th-century handpress. These were often beautiful objects in their own right. Many are still in use today.

7.7 LUCAS CRANACH THE ELDER
St Christopher, 1509. Woodcut, 9⅝ × 6⅞ ins (24.6 × 17.5 cm). Graphische Sammlung Albertina, Vienna.

This *chiaroscuro* print was made from two blocks. On one, the artist made a pen drawing, then cut away the rest of the block to leave only the drawn lines standing. A second block was cut, leaving raised areas for shading. Impressions were then taken, in a lighter color from the second block, then in a darker color from the first.

7.8 ALBRECHT DÜRER
The Knight, Death, and the Devil, 1513. Engraving, 9⅝ × 7⅜ ins (24.5 × 18.7 cm). The Metropolitan Museum of Art, New York, Harris Brisbane Dick Fund, 1943.

This is one of the most famous engravings ever made, a powerful allegory of the sufferings common in the late Middle Ages. Its plastic forms are worked out with almost obsessive energy. It is full of fascinating details: landscape, skull, dog, devil's horn, lizard, harness.

of dark resembling *chiaroscuro* in drawing. The white areas you cut away will then stand for light. The eighteenth-century English engraver Thomas Bewick invented a technique of cutting boxwood blocks into a black-and-white tonal image that played down the linear aspect (often called wood-engraving even though the technique is that of relief printing). Nowadays most woodcut artists use a very free combination of black (printed) and white (cut-away) drawing and rely on the physical qualities of the block and free cutting to give life and variety to their printed marks.

INTAGLIO

The essence of intaglio is that the top face of the matrix is wiped clean with a soft cloth before printing, so that ink is held only in channels, and the channel-shapes produce the black print. The wiping can be done very skillfully to control the quantity of ink held by an area of channels. Intaglio needs to be printed on a mechanical press. The two oldest versions of intaglio printing are engraving and etching. Engraving is done on either metal plates (usually copper or steel) or smooth-faced woodblocks; etching, on copper plates.

7.7

7.8

Engraving

To create an image for engraving, you push a sharp-edged tool of slanting triangular shape – a graver – over the face of the plate, cutting channels of varying depth and width. The lines thus tend to be clear-cut and decisively conceived. Copper is soft; and if you cut deeply and roughly into it you can raise a burr – a little fringe of metal shreds along the edge of the cut which holds extra ink to give an interesting blotted black. But copper has little resistance to pressure and lasts for only a few dozen impressions. Copper engraving can only give lines and so must compose areas of tonal hatching from groups of lines or chip-like dots. So it can resemble pen-drawing quite closely. Commercial engraving on steel plate, which is much harder than copper, was developed in the early nineteenth century to give longer print runs than the softer copper plates could. Because of the physical difficulty of cutting steel deep and variously, it tended to be used to produce areas of uniform tonal hatching. Machines were developed to take over some of the labor of scratching hundreds of fine parallel lines. Chemical methods of coating copper plates with a fine deposit of steel helped to improve their printing life.

Etching

In etching, chemicals rather than a tool are used to cut away the metal of the plate. This technique was developed from engraving, and it is quite common for etchers to finish a plate by means of engraving. Copper is the metal normally used for etching. You prepare the copper plate by scattering over the design surface a darkish soft ground, compounded of resins and waxes. You then hold the plate up and heat it gently from the back, so as to melt the ground into a thin, even layer. It also helps if you "smoke" the front with wax tapers or resinous pine-spills to darken it. You then paint the back and edges with an acid-resistant "stopping-out" varnish. Using a special needle-like point, you then draw the first stage of your design by scratching resin off the front. The exposed metal shows light against its ground. You then immerse the plate in a bath of dilute acid, which eats away – or "bites" – the copper only where you have exposed it with the needle. The longer you leave it in the acid, the deeper and stronger the lines become. When they have reached the desired stage, you take the plate out of the acid and rinse it off. You may want to cover up some lines with varnish to keep them as they are and maybe add other lines. You then put it back in the acid bath to bite the new lines and intensify the uncovered original ones. The deeper and rougher the biting, the darker the printed lines will be. You may clean the plate off two or three times and print an impression each time to check what it looks like at each stage, in preparation for further work. These intermediate printings are called "states": first, second, third, and final. Each state naturally emerges more complete and darker than the earlier states. You can also intensify any area of dark by working it over with an engraving tool.

   You can correct a design on copper by burnishing the soft metal smooth again, even by scraping away heavily bitten areas. If you need to scrape off a lot, you may also need to hammer up the surface from the back to make the front more or less level. There are special tools for all these jobs.

7.9 and **7.10** REMBRANDT VAN RYN
Christ Crucified between the Two Thieves (The Three Crosses), c.1653. Third and Fourth States, Etchings, each 15³⁄₁₆ × 17¹⁵⁄₁₆ins (38.6 × 45.6cm). The Metropolitan Museum of Art, New York, gift of Felix M. Warburg and his family, 1941.

There were five states of this celebrated etching. A radical transformation took place between the third and fourth states. Burnishing, re-stopping, and re-etching the plate to a far greater extent than usual, Rembrandt turned the scene into an apocalyptic vision of chaos, with darkness cascading from the sky.

Drawing on the plate

Engraving and etching both produce narrow lines. Having to push the engraving tool quite hard into the metal means that your lines have to be decisively inflected. They have the great virtue of clearness and can show your control of your hand. Western painting was long dominated by *chiaroscuro*. So the professional engravers who made the widely distributed copies of masterpieces of painting developed great skill in imitating different kinds of luminosity and shade. One major drawing technique adopted by all engravers to convey the roundness of 3D shapes was bracelet shading, invented by Albrecht Dürer (see p.161). One virtuoso seventeenth-century engraver, Claude Mellan, produced an image of the face of Christ on St Veronica's handkerchief which consisted of a single, immensely long, continuous spiral cut, beginning at the center of the nose, the depths and widths of its cutting so carefully graded that it gave an overall effect of tone.

Since etching is done with a needle, using scarcely any pressure, the lines can be soft and fluid. If you bite lightly, you can make lines as fine as a hair; if deeply, they can become broad and black. Most etchers build up masses of hatched lines, differently bitten to give areas of variegated tone. The greatest was Rembrandt, who created mysterious depths of luminous shadow from thousands of hatching strokes.

NON-TRADITIONAL TECHNIQUES

There are many different graphic techniques that use basic etching equipment. The following are among the best known.

Mezzotint

Very popular in the eighteenth century, mezzotint calls for a special conception of drawing. First you go over and over the whole surface of the wax-prepared plate with a special tool: either a *rocker*, which has a curved face covered with little points, or a *roulette*, a little wheel with similar points. As you work to and fro the points pierce the wax with thousands of tiny holes. When you put the plate in the acid bath, each of the holes lets acid in to attack the copper; so, after it is rinsed and cleaned off, the plate prints as a rich velvety black. You produce your image by burnishing and scraping the copper back smooth again, so working up lights from a dark background. Alternatively, you can actually draw on a plain plate with the rocker or roulette, which gives an effect rather like dark chalk on rough paper. This is called **crayon manner**.

Aquatint

Using this acid technique, you can lay an area of tone very much like a watercolor wash. You first pepper or dust the entire face of a copper plate with little granules

7.11 JOHN MARTIN
Illustration to Milton's *Paradise Lost*,
1827. Mezzotint.

The effect of strange distance and
supernatural light is produced by the
technique of working with lights out of
the overall velvety darkness first worked
onto the plate.

of resin. You then heat the plate just enough to melt the granules so they stick
but leave a fine network of uncovered copper between them. You varnish the
back, the edges, and all the parts you do *not* want to print, then put the plate in
the acid. It comes out with the fine network of bitten channels, which gives the
effect of an area of mottled grey. This method is often combined with an etched
line, usually produced before the plate is given its aquatint preparation. Another
option is to print from two or more plates, one etched with line, others aquatinted
with different grades of tonal density. **Color aquatint**, developed in the later
eighteenth century, and used in the twentieth century especially by Georges
Rouault, employs several plates, each printing a different color on the same sheet
to give a full-color effect.

Sugar lift

For this technique (also called lift-ground etching) you just paint your design onto
a plate using a sugary solution. You then coat the plate back and front with
varnish and immerse it in water. This gets through to dissolve only the sugar; so

7.12

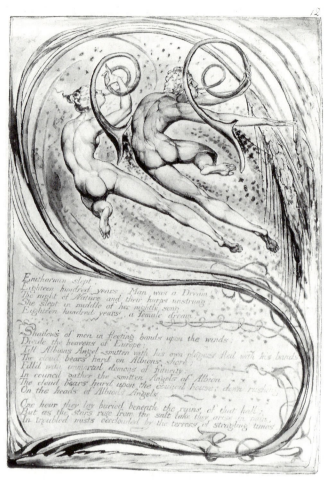

7.13

the design is left exposed on the copper. You can then retouch it if you like with varnish. Finally, you put it in the acid bath. The acid bites out the lines and areas of the original painted-on design; you then rinse and clean off the plate, then print from it.

Relief etching

Unlike other types of etching, this method produces a relief printing plate. You simply paint the lines and areas of your design on the copper plate with stopping-out varnish, and coat the back and edges with it. You then put the plate in the acid bath for so long that the acid eats away all the uncovered metal to a substantial depth. When you take it out and clean it off you have got something that resembles a relief woodblock in metal. You print it like a woodblock, spreading the ink on the crests, instead of wiping it off to leave it in the channels.

With both these techniques you can translate brushwork of any kind into printed form very faithfully. The only difference will be that the image normally comes out printed in reverse. But even this can be overcome. If you do your original drawing in varnish on thin paper, you can simply stick it face down onto the plate. The acid will dissolve the now unwanted paper along with the metal.

7.12 FRANCISCO DE GOYA Y LUCIENTES
They carried her off, trial proof before correction of title of plate 8 of the *Caprichos*, published 1799. Etching and aquatint, 8½ × 6ins (21.7 × 15.2cm). The British Museum, London.

The combination of etched line and aquatint tone produces an extraordinarily dramatic illumination for this horrifying scene.

7.13 WILLIAM BLAKE
Europe, A Prophecy: Blighted Crops, c.1821. Relief etching with watercolor, 12¼ × 9½ins (30.4 × 23.6cm). Fitzwilliam Museum, Cambridge.

Blake was equally original as both poet and artist. Using his own print technique, he illustrated his verse with figures in powerfully expressive movement and swirling decorative shapes.

Lithography

Invented in 1798, lithography was originally done on the prepared smooth face of a block of limestone (*lithos* means "stone" in Greek). Later it was done on other materials, such as a zinc sheet or even paper. You draw the image on the surface with a greasy crayon, which has the advantage of being easily removed, if necessary. Then you coat the surface with a water solution which will not "take" on the grease but dampens the bare plate. You then wipe the whole surface with greasy ink, which adheres only where it is not wet but already greasy. You then print the image onto the paper. Lithography is very popular today, partly because you can work very freely on the surface with the greasy medium, and the result can look much like an original drawing. You can counteract the reversing of the image by sticking a grease drawing face down in the same way as with sugar lift and relief etching.

A mechanical version of this artist's technique, called offset, is now widely used in the commercial printing industry.

Stencil and silk screen

One of the simplest kinds of printing is stencilling. A stencil is a design cut out of a piece of cardboard or similar material as shaped holes. These holes can be based on an original drawing. You then put your stencil over the surface to be printed and brush ink or paint freely across it; the color goes through the shaped holes to produce the image. There are obvious limitations to the kinds of holes you can cut. You cannot cut any completely closed loop, because the middle would drop out; you have to leave attaching "bridges" to hold any center piece in position. But you can later fill in the blanks left by these if you like. Despite its simplicity, stencil-cutting can be a major art form.

7.14 FRANK STELLA
Puerto Rican Blue Pigeon, from the
Exotic Bird series, 1977. Offset
lithograph, screenprint with glitter,
edition of 50, 34 × 46ins (86.3 ×
116.8cm).

These "abstract" shapes are based upon one of a set of draftsman's curves – flat shapes of wood or plastic whose contours offer a wide variety of curves to guide the drawing instrument.

Silk-screen printing is an extension of the stencil principle using extra equipment. It is extremely popular today, because almost anyone can do it and get good results, especially by enlisting the help of photography. The equipment consists of a table top with a frame hinged to it, to the underside of which you attach a sheet of strong, fairly open-weave gauze. Originally this was silk; nowadays it is likely to be synthetic, or even a fine wire screen. You make your design by blocking out areas of the gauze either with cut-out shapes stuck onto the underside or with a glutinous varnish that sets and fills its pores. You then lay the framed gauze over a paper sheet, and use a rubbery blade called a squeegee to press a full-bodied color through the gauze onto the sheet below. It passes through only where the gauze pores remain open. You can either paint the design onto the screen or apply it using a photographic technique. The latter involves painting the design on the gauze in the dark with a bichromated gelatine that hardens only when exposed to light. You then expose the coated gauze to light projected through a photographic negative or diapositive (transparency) of the design. The coat hardens only where it receives light. You then wash out the remaining soft gelatine and print as usual. Line-reduced or coarse half-tone images (see p.202) come across particularly well.

The great virtues of screen-painted images are, first, that they can be "original" works executed by the artist's own hand, at least at the stage of blocking out the image on the screen; second, that you can use very strong and thick color; third, that you can vary your color from print to print. Andy Warhol, in particular, made outstanding use of this technique.

PHOTOGRAPHY

In all the printing techniques discussed so far the original image is constructed by the printmaker out of marks laid on the surface ultimately by hand. But there is another category of printing, called **reproductive**. This depends on some kind of machine translating what is set before it into tonal or colored patches. Human judgment may control some aspects of its working; and what is set before the machine may be a humanly invented original; but the image itself is produced mechanically. The most important of these machines use the chemical processes of photography.

The camera

Basically the camera works by focusing light through a lens onto a flat film surface inside a light-proof box. This surface is coated with chemicals which change color and tone in response to light. The image is thus produced by relative degrees of chemical reaction to a pattern of light intensities over the prepared surface and subsequently fixed by the various darkroom developing and printing procedures.

The original objective of photography was to achieve impartial "accurate" images "drawn by light" directly from nature. But the camera is a device for producing images, not of things in any simple sense, but of arrangements of light. Things are recognizable in photographs only as patterns of illumination across

7.15

7.16

7.15 JACQUES-HENRI LARTIGUE
January – Paris – Avenue du Bois de Boulogne, 1911. Photograph.

A child prodigy as a photographer, Lartigue's seemingly artless snapshot becomes an instrument for acute and ironic social comment. In terms of composition of lights and darks, this is a picture of considerable sophistication.

7.16 DOROTHEA LANGE
Migrant Mother, Nipomo, California, 1936. Gelatin-silver print. Library of Congress, Washington D.C.

This is photography as social document and as a call for action. Unposed and uncropped, this haunting and compassionate image still evokes the harsh realities of the Depression.

the field. Some of the greatest twentieth-century photographers, such as Man Ray and Edward Steichen, have demonstrated how fundamentally camera art is design with shadow and light.

Black-and-white design

A black-and-white photograph consists of a mass of minute dots of black material clustered together more or less densely on the white surface of the print, to give an overall, graduated tone potentially ranging from white to black. The dots are the product of the photo-chemical action of light, first on a negative, then transferred to a positive print. Shadows, their layout and gradation, are all that you have to manipulate. **Arranging the subject** and its **lighting** – which can often mean adjusting your camera position rather than the subject – are basic factors in the design of any photo image. So too are such factors as **lens aperture**, relative **focus**, and **exposure** time. Many modern cameras control these automatically, but you may choose to control them yourself.

Shadows can be sharp-edged and strongly contrasted; or they can have a wide range of tonal gradations right across the surface. Sharply defined and contrasted shadows are particularly good with broad landscapes. In composing a monochrome image you may need to give it flat formal qualities (see p.206). You use your judgment of proportion, contrast, and structure in looking through the viewfinder to arrange the masses or networks of shadow in the subject within the picture frame before exposing the film. This is a process of selection; but the criteria the eye uses will be mainly those that it has assimilated from other forms of visual art.

Some purist camera artists hold that photographs should be conceived only within the original frame pattern – that is, without resorting to cropping when printing. With modern fast-reset cameras you can multiply the chances of getting a good frame image by shooting a long series of very similar images and selecting from contact prints – same-size prints made directly from the negative – only those that seem to have caught an interesting composition. Other photographers select and frame a small area of a negative and print it as a self-contained image.

Monochrome versus color

In full-color photography, especially diapositives, it is difficult to isolate a chosen detail of the image. It is possible in a studio to set up, arrange, and light a subject to achieve precisely the desired effect of color and shadow. But it is very expensive and time-consuming, and so usually confined to high-budget fashion and advertising photography.

This is one reason why so many art-photographers use monochrome. Another is that it is possible to control in close detail the developing and especially the printing from monochrome film. You can use different qualities of printing paper. You can vary the density of parts of the print, increasing contrast in one part, lessening it in another. You can touch out blemishes in the image on the negative so that they will not print at all – often necessary in publicity photos. You can intensify masses, softening or sharpening them up; you can pale or stiffen shadow lines, harden or soften tonal gradients across a surface, lengthening the light or dark ends according to choice. You can increase the size of the grain by adjusting your chemicals. You can enhance one or another part of a print by chemical processes. You can also employ purely chemical procedures to generate visual effects that were not given by the original subject. You can print and re-photograph several times over. If you increase the contrast on each successive print you can end up with what is called a **line-reduced image** – a pure black pattern of maximum shadow achieved by repeated re-photographing and intensifying the contrast in the image. These techniques are especially useful for silk-screen printing. Apart from chemical treatment none of these processes are available to the color photographer.

One method of treating color in photography that still offers good aesthetic possibilities is the hand-coloring of monochrome prints. This was often done in the later nineteenth century, before color photography proper was developed. Today you can use minimal touches or washes of color to great effect, without losing the elements of clear design that black and white can offer.

Photography and actuality

The camera can pick up many things the normal human eye would never be able to see – in some cases because most people could never reach the viewpoint of the camera, as with Nadar's famous early views of Paris taken from a balloon and recent pictures of the earth from satellites. In other cases the subject is one that the conditions of ordinary life would prevent most people from seeing, such as remote exotic locations, volcanic eruptions, scenes of battle, or people making love. With the aid of additional specialized equipment the camera can record images invisible to the naked eye: endoscopic pictures of diseased organs; X-rays; the surface of other planets; the structures of minute creatures photographed through microscopes. High-speed film and very short exposures can capture such phenomena as breaking waves, hummingbirds in flight, and the whorls in moving gases.

7.17 EDWARD WESTON
Pepper, 1930. Arizona Board of
Regents, Center for Creative
Photography.

Weston was a leading proponent of
"pure" as opposed to "straight," i.e.
documentary, photography. He took
infinite pains in setting up his
photographs, and works such as this
allow us to concentrate on previously
familiar objects until they reveal a
mysterious, sensuous new beauty.

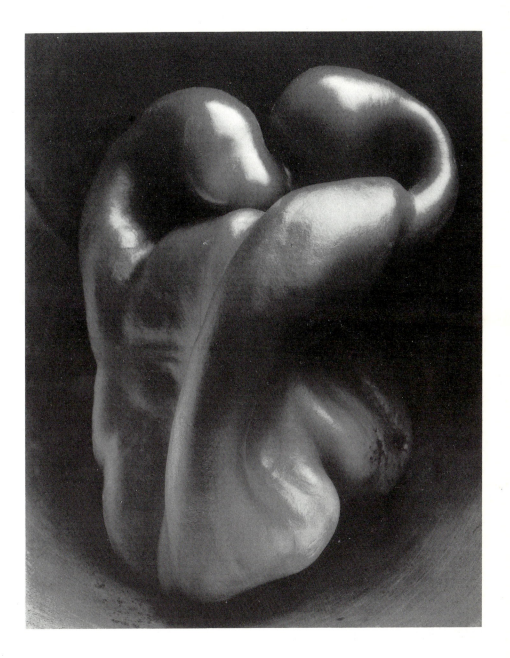

The camera can modify or exaggerate reality by means of its lens mechanism.
Edward Weston's enigmatic details of nudes and pepper fruits are famous.
Wide-angle lenses used for close-up images of the human body or face can
produce exaggerated foreshortenings, while scenes shot through a telephoto lens
can produce extraordinary compressions and distortions of relative scale between
people and environment. Social interactions and emotive situations can be
emphasized by narrowing the depth of field so that only the main participants are
in focus. Various filters can be placed over the lens to modify the quality of the
light, even in different parts of the subject, such as the sky.

Photography is normally derived from some sort of visual given, a framed
sector of reality. Our minds naturally tend to read a photographic pattern of light
and dark as parallel to distributions of light and shadow we see around us. The
act of framing the chosen sector itself constitutes a major element in the creative
process. A photograph is a thing, a sheet of paper stained with dots, not any of

7.18

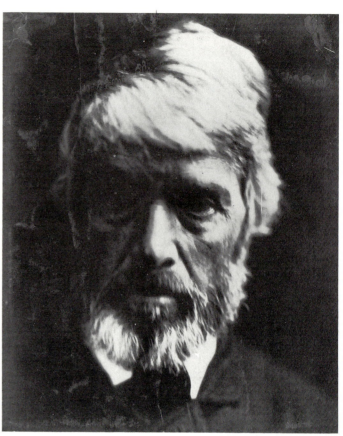

7.19

the objects it may represent. It can prompt our mind to re-create its image only by calling upon our experience of compariable actual things. Old black-and-white photographs, such as Julia Margaret Cameron's portraits, give us a relatively limited number of clues from which to reconstruct a reality-image – and may be all the stronger for that. For we have to collaborate in reading imaginatively beyond the clues, in terms of our own relevant experience.

Photographs were once able to claim an objective truth function. They could imply that such and such *was* actually before the lens at that time, and they were accepted as evidence of fact in courts of law. Today we know how it is actually possible to interfere with any image by wiping out, cropping, superimposing images, and so on.

Computers are now able to record photographic images using pixels – minute screen dots – which are smaller than the grain of the photographic image. Individual things represented in any set of photographs can be isolated and their defining pixels recombined in any way the operator desires without any break appearing in the texture of the photo field. This means that "faking" of all kinds is possible and now undetectable. The photograph has ceased to be reliable evidence of visual truth and becomes an image manufactured from elements that need originally have had no actual relation to each other.

Photography and painting

Since the earliest days of photography artists have made use of photographs in a

7.18   PAUL MARTIN
A Tramp, 1886. Victoria and Albert Museum, London.

This superb photograph calls up powerful echoes of our own physical sensations, feelings, and compassion, focussing them onto an image of an ultimate human condition.

7.19   JULIA MARGARET CAMERON
Thomas Carlyle, 1867. Albumen print, 13¼ × 11ins (33.7 × 27.9cm). National Museum of Photography, Film and Television, Bradford.

From the shadows emerges an evocation of the character of the deeply disturbed Victorian writer-sage. Cameron turned to advantage the very long exposures needed in her day, for her portraits explore the uncontrived expressions of necessarily relaxed faces; the duration of the pose seems preserved in the subject's long gaze out of the picture.

variety of ways. The camera had the obvious advantage of being able to record substitutes for actual objects difficult to study. Early nineteenth-century artists such as Delacroix and Ingres welcomed photographs of the human nude as a way of helping them to fill out accurately their sketched ideas for compositions in which nudes played a part. Images that showed people in suitable poses could serve, in the planning stage, as inexpensive alternatives to live models.

From the start, photographs were especially valued as accurate records of moments in time. In the mid-nineteenth century it came to be widely believed that the job of all art was not to create its own second nature, a world ordered according to its own system of coherence, but to record the actual environment, usually so as to reinforce a particular social point of view with some kind of sentimental emphasis. This demanded that painters be able to register a vast amount of visual detail – far more than their memories could actually retain. So they used photographs, not only to supply details, but to help them to control the balance and tonal register among those details throughout the composition. Moreover, effects produced by the camera, such as lens flares, movement-blurs, soft focus, and strongly light-soaked patches, were also taken as especially truthful to reality. The artist was often also a photographer. From the 1860s onward photography and art went forward hand in hand, influencing each other, right into this century. Today many painters, like their nineteenth-century predecessors, use photographs to expand their perceptions of the real world.

The capacity of the camera to record appearances literally had one other important function: portraiture. Portrait photography flourished in the nineteenth century. Such photographs also served as references for portrait painters, enabling them to depict well-known people – statesmen such as Lincoln, writers such as Baudelaire, successful businessmen – with detailed attention to the individual personality. Quite often artists painted portraits (and other scenes) on top of an actual photograph. They thus learned to translate effects of light on hair and subtle nuances of facial texture into paint.

Our experience of reality is not limited to moments the eye can catch. Art is therefore a matter of making, not merely of passively seeing. Nevertheless the popular idea of visual reality came, during the late 1800s, to be dominated by the camera's view. This situation still obtains today, because of the proliferation of camera images in newspapers, magazines, movies, and TV – not to mention the billions of snapshots taken each year by amateur photographers.

Movement and movies

Capturing movement and a sense of life has always been one of the main problems of the static visual arts. In Chapter 6 we looked at some of the purely graphic ways of handling this problem. But with the advent of photography other ways were evolved. Perhaps the most important were the multiple exposure shots by Marey and stop-action sequence-frames by Muybridge of people and animals in motion. These evolved into the movie image at 24 frames per second, and then into the 625-line TV image, which both seem to us (because of the physiological phenomenon of the persistence of vision) to give continuity in time. The techniques of scene-montage and sequence-cutting, as developed by Sergei Eisenstein, have helped to expand the expressive possibilities of joining dramatic action into

7.20

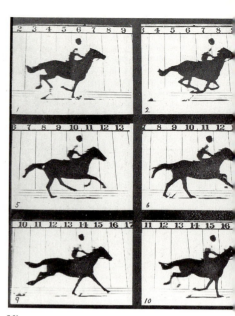

7.21

image-sequences by controlling camera angles and lighting. The special value of all such images is that they show us aspects of truth which we should never be able to witness otherwise. But we must always remember that even the movie camera can only register a narrow segment of visible reality.

Photography and design

Perhaps the most important fact about photography from the point of view of design is the way its images are already arranged as 2D plans by the machine. This eliminates a whole field of the artist's responsibility for translating 3D qualities – even 4D, if you include time – into 2D. There is thus a great loss to set off against the gains.

On the positive side, photographs can serve as formal stimuli. Painters, in particular, are enabled to move into realms of visual form that would be inaccessible without the resources of photography; for photographs that deal with commonly invisible and unintelligible aspects of reality can generate in the designer's mind fascinating new formal images. These may be interesting for reasons quite independent of the actual subject. The American painter Charles Sheeler, for instance, made many of his impressive paintings by simplifying broad forms and flattening color areas cut from photos of industrial and urban landscape. They were, to some degree, abstractions from photographic images – intended to express pride in the mechanical achievements of industry. The process of selecting and formalizing images from photographs can yield powerful works of art: a few photos of a bombed Spanish town provided Picasso with images that he transmuted into an almost audible cry of horror in his *Guernica*.

In using photographs the artist can eliminate any obvious realistic references altogether, using shapes derived from, say, aerial views of vast riverbeds or field patterns; close-ups of lichens; microscopic creatures in water. This activity is not self-justifying: you need to know why you do it and what you hope to express.

There are many methods of adapting photographic material. You can simply

7.20 *Going Along at a Slapping Pace*, early 19th century. Aquatint, English.

The traditional, and incorrect, conception of a galloping horse with all four legs extended and off the ground. Not until the advent of photography was it possible to show that this never happens.

7.21 EADWEARD MUYBRIDGE Consecutive series of photographs showing phases of movement in a horse's gallop, 1877–78. Kingston-upon-Thames Museum.

Muybridge's revolutionary stop-action photographic sequences revealed hitherto unperceived aspects of the movement of animals, and of the human body. Surprising new images of reality became available.

7.22 EDGAR DEGAS *The Jockey*, c.1884. Pastel, charcoal, and crayon on paper, 12¾ × 19⅝ins (32.4 × 49.8cm). Philadelphia Museum of Art, purchased for the W. P. Wilstach Collection.

Artists were quick to seize on the insights Muybridge's technique offered. This study by Degas of a horse and jockey is a bold experiment in the jerky dynamism that photography suggested.

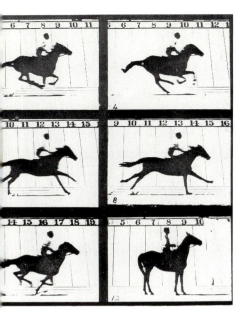

7.22

7.23   CHARLES SHEELER
Rolling Power, 1939. Oil on canvas, 15 × 30ins (38.1 × 76.2cm). Smith College Museum of Art, Northampton, MA.

A painting by the American artist which is an almost direct transcription from one of his own photographs. He made regular use of this process for his powerful pictures of industrial plant.

copy from a photo image, making a piece of pure graphic art that imitates its overall pattern of tone. You can project a transparency onto your design surface and choose which aspects to record, either tone or color, and which to leave out. You can also imitate the relative emphasis or distortion that camera lenses produce but your eye does not see naturally, and exaggerate or modify them. You can use standard techniques for enlarging images by squaring them off. You can exaggerate certain features for expressive purposes – for example, enlarge parts of bodies nearest the camera, such as feet or nose-tips, or intensify minute detail such as wrinkles in clothing or flesh, even hair follicles on a face. You can do this with pale, luminous color or with harsh tonal contrasts. Other expressive modifications

7.23

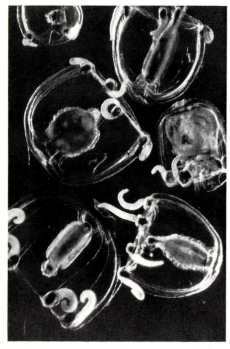

7.24

7.25

include painting out or smearing parts of the image and stressing significant details such as a grimacing mouth or unequally sized eyes.

You can also **collage** photo images, and then draw over the collage, making expressive points by means of variations in scale and emphasis. There is no limit to what you can do in this vein to make complex symbolic and iconographic points. The purely formal arrangements you employ in organizing the components of an image reinforce their meaning, both individually and collectively. The content of "reality" in any photo image used will also contribute its meaning to the design. It will make a big difference, for example, whether a V shape organizes a pair of legs or a pair of girders, and whether what it frames is, say, a monkey's face or the front end of an automobile.

7.24 Microscope view of *Hydromedusae*. Such photographs acquaint artists with forms no one can normally see, and feed their imaginations.

7.25 VASSILY KANDINSKY *Various Actions*, 1941. Oil and enamel on canvas, 35⅛ × 45¾ins (89.2 × 116.2cm). Solomon R. Guggenheim Museum, New York.

A painting by an artist obsessed with invisible forces and entities. Some of the undulating shapes in it are clearly inspired by the forms of minute water-borne organisms.

GRAPHIC DESIGN

Graphic design is the arrangement of flat layouts of text and/or images for books and magazines, newspapers, advertisements, publicity sheets, posters, and a host of other products of printing processes. It is a field that employs the skills of an enormous number of designers and it is as diverse as it is large. Two main features, however, are common to all graphic design. First is the fact that printing techniques and technologies play a crucial role in the design process. In the great majority of cases, the production route – typesetting, picture origination, printing – is determined in advance by the client, and the designer is expected to work within the constraints, and take advantage of the opportunities presented by, a particular method of production. Second is the fact that the designer is usually expected to work with elements – text or copy, drawings, photographs, or diagrams

7.26 MAX ERNST *Loplop Introduces Members of the Surrealist Group*, 1931. Cut and pasted photographs, pencil, and pencil frottage, 19¾ × 13¼ins (50.1 × 33.6cm). The Museum of Modern Art, New York.

This graphically ornamented collage of photographs suggests mysterious, dream-like connections between members of the Surrealist group, who were themselves purveyors of dream-symbolism.

7.26

– that are not negotiable. In some fields, such as advertising, the visual concept may precede and determine the actual images and words used; in others, such as book design, the graphic designer's task is to "package" existing material. These challenges and limitations have their equivalents in every field of the commercial designer's art.

Sources

In producing strong visual images for the layout of printed illustrative material, such as publicity or advertising, the graphic designer has several options. You can pose models or select and shoot scenes yourself; or you may find suitable subjects in photo agencies or archives. You can employ other sources that seem appropriate to your brief. A geographical topic may suggest the use of maps and photographs of typical landscape and cityscape, and famous historical remains. An economic or political survey may call for diagrams and graphs that turn statistics into visible form. A commercial brief may call for the presentation of products in an eye-catching fashion.

Simplification

An image can be simplified for emphasis in a number of ways. One way is to

7.27   TOM WOLSEY and HELAYNE SPIVAK
Advertisement for Karastan Rug Mills by Ally Gargano/MCA, New York, 1981.

The skillful combination of photographic images makes this award-winning ad an arresting and effective design. The Surrealists of the 20s and 30s were the first to explore the intriguing disorientation that such juxtapositions of scale can produce.

Some of us have more finely developed nesting instincts than others.

Karastan Rug Mills, a Division of Fieldcrest Mills, Inc

INVEST IN *Karastan*

7.28

7.29

7.28   JAMES NEVINS, DAVID STEVENSON and NICHOLAS SIDJAKOV
Poster by Sidjakov Berman & Gomez, San Francisco, 1984.

Bold simplification gives this elegant poster much of its impact. The undulating "ground" is both a billowing flag, and – by association with the streetcar – an immediately recognizable cityscape. A first-class example of the power of economy in design.

7.29   PAULA SCHER
Poster for the Ryder Gallery, 1983.

Lettering can be almost an afterthought when the image does all the work; or, as here, it can occupy center stage. Scher's poster for an exhibition of her own work is a contemporary interpretation of Bauhaus experiment in purely typographic design.

turn it into a pure black-and-white drawing. You can do this either by selecting and stereotyping a limited number of leading contours from the subject, usually by geometrizing them into lengths of straight line and standard curve; or by imitating the effect of solarized photographs by copying areas of shadow in a single tone. The first you can apply to virtually any image, including human figures and faces, maps, and diagrams. The second you can really only apply to the kinds of human and landscape subject that people are used to seeing in photographs and recognize easily.

Another simplification procedure applies to color. You can use individual clear, flat tints to fill in given areas of your image – perhaps only selected areas that need to be emphasized.

A fourth procedure is to imitate with clear, simple tints and/or black and white the patterns and effects of light falling on objects as it is revealed in photographs. You can grade the tints particularly well by using an airbrush. Products such as automobiles or machinery can be given a high glossy look in this way; treating especially the central feature in this way makes it stand out strongly. In fact, strong, tight treatment of any feature, contrasted with soft, blurred, or loosely brushed areas, can make it catch the eye.

There are many other means of simplification and strengthening. The aim of all of them is to make it easy for the viewer to grasp instantly what is being conveyed – which means using routines and clichés. So you may find it helpful to build up your own picture file of current illustrators' devices and learn from them. Each period has its own ways of stereotyping, for example, the made-up eyes of pretty women or the folds of fashionable garments.

Framing the image may be very effective. You produce one kind of visual impact if you leave an image **vignetted**, with its shape irregular and fading out toward the edges; quite another if you cut off the image inside a definite frame, which may emphasize it strongly. In some kinds of elaborate PR layout that combine a group of colored information diagrams, broad, heavy frames with breaks in them can be used both to stress and to interrelate the images by leading the eye from one to the next.

Typography

Typography is a vital element in all book, leaflet, and advertisement design. Typefaces consist of complete alphabets in which all the letters are designed in the same style so that they go well together in all possible combinations. Originally typefaces were derived from letter shapes standardized by the writers of medieval manuscripts. Well over 10,000 different typefaces have been designed for the

7.30 Poster for Pirelli, late 1960s.

The distortion of the lettering ingeniously reinforces the simple message. Space is at a premium here, and the designer has hit on a brilliantly inventive solution. Even the movement of the bus has been turned to advantage.

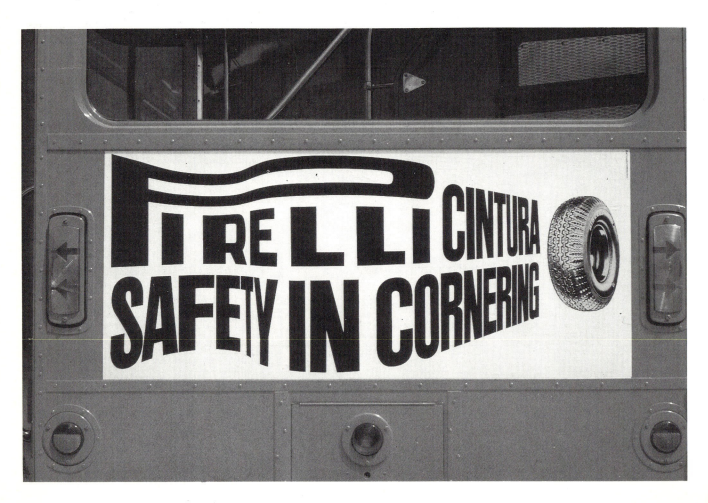

7.31 HENRI CHOPIN
J'ai le Nez Sec (My Nose is Dry), 1969.
Silkscreen.

A composition of typographic shapes
which displays the values of both visual
arrangement and textual meaning. The
lower part lists the practitioners of free
typographic art.

western alphabet. These can be broadly classified into **Roman**, based on strictly
horizontal or vertical axes with full curves, and **Italic**, slanting forward in the
direction of reading, with slightly compressed curves. Another broad division is
that between **serif** and **sans serif** typefaces – serifs being small pointed lines added
to the ends of main strokes. Many modern typefaces, including digital, are sans
("without") serif. But studies show that, in general, serif faces are more easily
read; and the whole aim of typography is to enable text to be read easily and
quickly. Studies also show that the top halves of letters rather than the lower
halves provide the main key to reading, and that the differentiation of letters in
the best faces gives a distinctive appearance to each word.

When you lay out blocks of type on the page you need to consider several
basic factors. First is the positioning of the block as a unit, its proportion relative

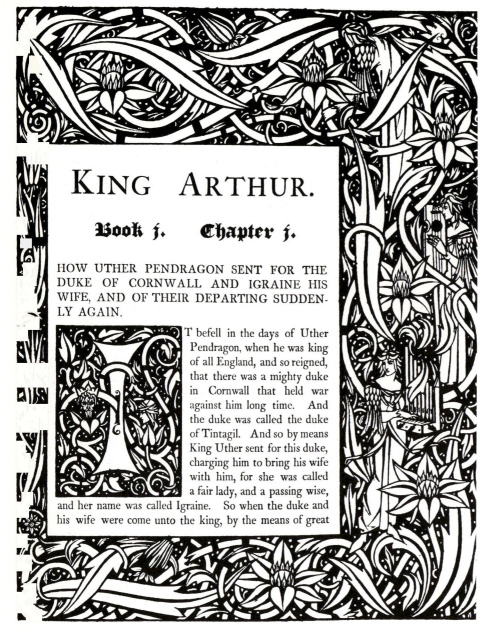

7.32 WILLIAM MORRIS and AUBREY BEARDSLEY
Page from *Morte d'Arthur*, 1893.

This fine printed edition of Sir Thomas Malory's work was decorated by Beardsley, whose technique of pure black line was perfect for combining with letterpress.

to format and margin size. This partly depends on "color" – its relative density or darkness – which arises from the thickness of the massed letter components and the spacing between individual letters and punctuation marks. Second is the width of line-spacing. Third is the relationship of any headings to the blocks of text above and below.

Typographic design has to observe strong restrictions. It has been said that, ideally, such design should be invisible, so that readers grasp the content of the text with minimum obstruction. It must use letter forms standard enough to be instantly recognizable. Mannerisms exaggerated for specific reasons, including the aesthetic appearance of the text, can make a typeface hard to read. Examples of this are the emphasis on strong, thick, concave-sided verticals in the first fifteenth-century German type (gothic or black-letter); the extravagances of some asymmetric Bauhaus poster images; and the excessive simplifications of the seven bars used for digital numbers.

Layout

Normally a layout is based on a rectangular **format**; and although its matter need not be carried up to the edges of the sheet, the format usually serves as the "given" for working out the locations of and relationships between component parts of your design.

An important technique for layout is **geometrization**. This involves compressing visual image and/or text into areas that correspond to simple geometrical shapes. The basic version is to convert their contours into straight lines, or into a series of sections which are straights, arcs, and clear angles. The most complete version is to convert the overall areas of the principal elements of your image into standard geometrical areas. You coordinate such areas by means of normal proportional and rhythmic schemes (see pp. 87–93).

A special use of geometrization, developed in the twentieth century, involves condensing areas of text into the same geometrical layout as the visual image. The basic version of this is to divide your lettering into words or phrases, each of which fits into the outline of a geometrical area. You combine such areas with the areas of the geometrized visual forms.

Computers in graphic design

It is now possible to use computer programs to generate or enhance graphic images. The various techniques computers can perform on instruction include changing the size and conformation of images; distorting, stretching, squeezing, and rotating images about their axes as if they were 3D; reversing images; multiplying copies; producing modified or sequential coloring; creating mosaic effects on any scale above that of pixel (minimum screen dot); recoloring and color-separating; embodying images in perspective grids; adding halos to shapes; creating trails or "curtains" following the image as it moves; setting up and altering images in response to drawing with a light pen on a receptor screen. Needless to say, the quality of the image-sequences that you generate depends on the capacity of your imagination to conceive a good image, or – if you discover something by pure play – to recognize its value and retain it in context.

7.33   ALAN NORTON
Computer-Generated Fractal Three-Dimensional Image, 1985. Computer graphic.

Computers can be programmed to follow given "rules" and then generate images that include a random element. The results can be startling and unearthly, as if the products of an alien imagination. Artists are just beginning to explore the seemingly limitless potential of this new design tool.

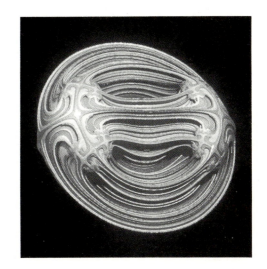

CHAPTER EIGHT
FINE ART

ART AND MEANING

Through looking at art all our lives we learn to develop and connect up our visual experience and ideas. Major works of art can be interesting every time we see them, especially when we return to them after long intervals, because we ourselves develop and become able to recognize visual ideas in them that we had not understood earlier. The language of art is of a purely visual order combining objective understanding with feeling. It may connect up with other kinds of idea, religious, social, scientific, factual, or philosophical; but it cannot be translated into such alien terms.

The term "fine arts" was invented to distinguish them from the "useful arts." People still feel an unresolved conflict between the two, and some feel that "design" has radically different meanings in each context. Industrial designers work on technological artifacts. They have to plan them to fulfill sets of prearranged intentions, which may be quite complex and limiting. An aircraft, for example, must carry a given load at a given velocity and meet other criteria such as length of take-off and landing, adaptability to climatic conditions, or suitability for weapons systems. When it is not doing any of these stipulated things, it is simply standing by, waiting to do them. It exists only for the sake of its operative functions, many of which may be quite invisible from the outside. In contrast, the fine arts convey their meaning and value entirely by their visible features. The artist's imaginative exploration of memory-reference and meaning may not be at all accessible to preliminary definition as a design-brief, and the pure art object does not have to do any physical work. The designer of environmental objects that must function actually as well as aesthetically may have to develop both regions of meaning together. Ordinary people do not need to understand how the telephone works to be able to use one themselves. But the artist's inventions can only be appreciated by people who use imagination of the same order as the artist's.

Elements

We have seen that contrast and combination are essential in good design; it articulates a challenging variety of orders and scales of form and avoids falling

8.1   WILLEM DE KOONING
The Visit, 1966–67. Oil on canvas, 60 × 48ins (152.4 × 121.9cm). The Tate Gallery, London.

Nonobjective art demands a level of involvement from the viewer that many still find daunting. But any artist's inventions can only be appreciated by people who use imagination of the same order as the artist's.

into a confusion of details. The designer of fine art therefore articulates his or her compositions from basic elements of shape, color, and rhythm, somewhat as one uses words and phrases as the basis of speaking. The individual elements of languages – visual or otherwise – cannot be totally original, for then no one else would understand them. The newness and interest is in the meaning that appears from new arrangements and articulations of familiar elements. New contexts coordinate areas of recognition and response to visual shapes that normally wait unconnected at the back of the viewer's mind.

We have examined what some of these basic units of arrangement and sense may be in Chapters 3 and 5: marks, groups, lines, shaped enclosures, positive and negative, and so on. Each of the visual fine art media also contributes its own elements. With art that is in any way figurative, one area of fundamental choice helps to determine the meaning of your image: how you divide up your image into components and what basic units of shape and color, with their particular qualities, you select to match those components in presenting your image.

This process of choosing how to divide up and shape the parts of figures defines an artistic style. One example is the classical torso, with its standard set of muscle shapes. Another is the Mayan rectangular scheme for face, features, and limbs. Some artists, such as Ingres, have chosen as their primary shapes sinuous outlines corresponding to the edges of bodies, which were then supported by modeling. The Japanese *Ukiyo-e* artists picked vital black lines corresponding with long edges, using color areas as back-up; the German Expressionists made abruptly angled strokes correspond to the gestures of limb joints and the shapes of shadows. One reason why Picasso is so interesting is that he continually found fresh shape-elements – sections of contour, areas of shape and color – to transcribe newly imagined divisions in the world, so producing new meanings. Since the shapes in even the most abstract art find references somewhere in the world of human experience, similar considerations apply even to them. The old idea that a work of art can be a "pure object" without meaning has been discredited.

Focal and subsidiary meaning

Think of a simple sentence on a page: "I have a black cat." You can look at it in all sorts of ways: as a lot of little black shapes, the letters which to a graphic designer have their special interest; as a group of compound shapes, the individual words; as a group of sounds, each with its own meaning for you; and as a whole sentence, a statement of an idea. This last meaning of the sentence – what the writer meant to say – we call its focal meaning. In order to pick it up whole we have to think beyond the other levels of meaning very fast: habitually we do it in a jump. The first levels lose their importance and become subsidiary. We cannot concentrate on the focal and subsidiary meanings at once. So when we try to concentrate on, say, the letter shapes making up the word "c a t" to study their individual formal qualities, this makes them focal for us, at least temporarily; and as designers we may try to develop them so that they contribute more powerfully to the focal meaning.

The focal meaning of a work of art is concentrated in its image. This may well be what the artist is aiming for, and for which he or she finds components with appropriate subsidiary meanings. The subsidiaries appear in the shapes and symbolisms of the unit elements, their materials and methods, each providing context for the others. The visual meaning of the image is something beyond any one of them alone, but cannot exist without them. This is why as artists we need to think about and develop the design qualities of all the subsidiary meanings, each becoming focal while we do so. We then need to adjust them so that each contributes at its own level to the focal image. In time and with practice this process becomes intuitive.

The notional image

In much of the world's greatest art the image is figurative – a **second nature** or "notional object." It is not meant to be mistaken for a piece of actual "first nature" (except perhaps in the case of *trompe l'oeil* painting), any more than the words of a poem are mistaken for the things they refer to. Second nature is a mental structure of forms whose focal meaning seems somehow to reflect our experience of first nature, but is in no sense a copy of it.

8.2 GIOTTO
Lamentation, c.1304–13. Fresco, 7ft 7ins × 6ft 7½ins (2.31 × 2.02m). Scrovegni Chapel, Padua.

Figurative art is not an attempt to deceive the viewer into believing that he or she is looking at actual people, or trees, or angels. The artist's marks create *images* of these things, evoking their counterparts in our memory, our unconscious, or our imagination.

When you work substances into shapes that indicate forms they can convey to someone else's mind a reality beyond what they actually are: that is, they become symbols (see p.134). You can arrange and work bricks, for example, to look like dancing figures. The material base, with its own logics defining its own kinds of space, sets up relations among its parts and with the viewer. These become subsidiaries to the focal meaning of the whole second-nature image and symbolize its coherence. That image does not abolish the reality of the material base – bricks as bricks – but absorbs and transforms it into the structure of the image – dancers. This is why art that strives for a perfect finish obliterating all sense of its material base is banal. It lacks evocative tension between subsidiary readings.

The symbolic object may be an external thing; but any "second nature" image can only be internal to the viewer. The artist works things into representations of scenes and people by shaping them with formal cues that evoke in the viewer patterns of response and memory. A Rembrandt drawing of a landscape with biblical figures does not look like a real landscape; it looks like other scraps of paper with scrawls on them. Its focal, second-nature image, the subject matter or message, is coded in the scrawls. You are not supposed to compare such a drawing with some original scene. That no longer exists, and may never have existed in reality. What you recognize is a construct in your mind built on the basis of the material cues. Some of the world's greatest representational works of art consist of a mere handful of strokes. Even highly elaborate paintings and sculptures actually work in the same way.

The choice of medium

In different eras and cultures, one or another of the fine art media is usually thought of as the leader; and other arts imitate its methods and effects. Most major cultures of the past have been focused around temples and cities whose imposing sculpture enjoyed special prestige. The classical Greek, Roman, medieval European, Mayan, and Indian cultures are examples of this. Often the sculpture has been colored; and accordingly paintings in these cultures may have been thought of as less evolved and less expensive sculpture. The brothers Van Eyck painted some panels of their great altarpiece in Ghent entirely in greys, to make the figures resemble stone carvings; their contemporaries, including Rogier van der Weyden, used a similar technique as underpainting and thought of painted figures as versions of the superb painted wood reliefs common in their day. On the other hand, Leonardo da Vinci and many great Chinese painters thought that the sheer physical difficulty of the sculptor's art prevented it from ever reaching as high a level as the painter's. Today, for the time being, the painters seem to be in the ascendant.

Drawing has been central to the history of western art. All western painting has been closely identified with it, and its visual patterns have assumed an important place in sculpture. Ancient Egyptian carvers worked from designs first drawn on the faces of the stone; and so, probably, did fifth-century BC Greeks. Michelangelo was one of the greatest draftsmen of all time and worked out most of his greatest sculptures first as drawings. Many other artists, including Donatello and Henry Moore, have filtered sculptural ideas through graphic thinking. But there have also been important sculptural traditions in which no sculptor ever expected to draw, as in Africa and the South Seas. In practice, a great deal of figurative painting has depended on a kind of prior 3D sculptural invention, calling on 3D mental modeling procedures to underpin pictorial method.

ART IN ITS SPACE

8.3 ROGIER VAN DER WEYDEN *Deposition*, c.1435. Tempera and oil on wood, 87 × 103ins (220 × 262cm). The Prado, Madrid.

In this wonderful painting the artist has laid out and presented his figures in the manner of the carved and painted wooden reliefs of his day. He uses modelling tone, and his colors are used to distinguish between the different things he represents.

One important attribute of any work of art is its scale in relation to the space it occupies, to the intentions of the artist, and to the people who look at it. There is a radical difference between a large work that is meant to condition the whole space in which it exists, with all its component forms visible at a distance and, on the other hand, a work whose small format, plinth, or frame creates a closed imaginative world of its own. Such differences of scale are usually lost with reproductions in books.

The artist may mean the finish and sweep of the gestures by which he or she

8.4 ANNIBALE CARRACCI
Ceiling frescoes, 1597–1600. Palazzo Farnese, Rome.

On the ceiling of this grand late-Renaissance salon the gods of Classical mythology float above our heads. Some of the supporting figures are painted purely in tone, bridging the painted world and the 3D reliefs on the walls around us.

creates the minimum shapes to be dominant and broad or, conversely, small and delicate. For the viewer, a very large sculpted or painted surface can seem rough and uncertain from close up, whereas its shapes become clear and emphatic from a distance. By contrast, the basic shapes of a tightly worked piece can be quite invisible from a distance. The different scales of working the artist adopts are major keys to the quality of feeling intended: expansive, grandiose rhetorical pronouncement in large-scale work; intimate conversation in small; with the minute touch of the miniature amounting almost to a refusal to negotiate with the immediate environment at all. In ages of faith some splendid art was placed beyond normal human vision – high on a rooftop, for example – and addressed to the eyes of spirits or the deity.

The setting in which we see works of art can be very important. In earlier ages, when paintings and sculptures were made for specific places, architects would often design appropriate settings for important works. Today, when an old building is used for an exhibition of modern art, it is often necessary to "neutralize" an assertive environment by stripping it bare and/or using temporary screening. The modern exhibition gallery needs to be an adaptable and hence neutral space, because it has to be able to accommodate temporarily a very wide variety of works without challenging or overwhelming them.

The two modes of space

In the design of all works of fine art the two modes of space (see pp. 104–7) are deeply involved. We can think of them as design from the outside in, corresponding to space as limit, or from the inside out, corresponding to space as environment. The first is quite familiar in painting, the second is more familiar today in sculpture.

Outside-in design consists of using a rectangular framework to govern the overall dimensions and interior subdivisions of a work according to sets of rectangular proportions and modules, in both elevation and plan views, with both views using related proportional and rhythmic schemes. **Inside-out design** consists of developing rhythmic measures outward from one or more centers along the components. In combining thematic contrasts into an image you may in fact find that you must either decide clearly between the two modes or devise ways to combine them, which can be far from easy.

Clearly, each mode has its own quality of expression and its own philosophical significance, which give fundamental character to an artist's work. The outside-in mode leaves nothing outside its own format, implying that the work includes and explains all its meaning within its scheme of arrangement. The format itself stands for the completeness of the scheme. The inside-out mode does not claim to understand or organize an enclosed artistic reality, but is content to live with frontiers open to the unknown. It accepts that all things may change or lead on to quite unexpected conclusions.

Art and place

Every artistic image, however represented, is attached to or springs from something else. Sculptures are attached to the earth, to buildings or public environments,

8.5 ANTONIO PISANELLO
Leonello marriage medal, 1444. Bronze, diameter 4ins (10.2cm). Victoria and Albert Museum, London.

The design, whose prototypes are Roman coins, is based on clearly phrased contours; its purpose is to glorify a young man on his marriage, claiming for him the virtue associated with ancient Rome.

8.6 GIANLORENZO BERNINI
Fountain of the Four Rivers, 1648–51.
Travertine marble. Piazza Navona,
Rome.

Water is life; and the places, at the ends
of long canals and aqueducts, where
water was dispensed to the citizens of
Rome were sacred. Here, before
Borromini's splendid frontage of
Sant'Agnese, the sanctity of place is
marked by figures of river gods,
crowned by an obelisk from ancient
Egypt.

reliefs emerge from walls, and paintings belong to the surfaces usually of interiors,
less commonly of exteriors. They therefore exhibit an inner significance of
whatever they are attached to. The great carved fountains of Rome display
triumphantly the gift of water brought in by elaborate and difficult water-works.
The high and low reliefs on Gothic cathedrals display the structure of belief that
sustained the fabric of the Church as both physical and spiritual phenomenon.
The seventeenth-century paintings in the Palace of the Doges and the Scuola di
San Rocco in Venice express the meanings of the city for its inhabitants.

Nowadays many artists have to work for indeterminate cuboid gallery spaces.
If the work is sold, it may be carried off to hang in the hall of some museum or
in a luxurious apartment thousands of miles away. In assuming a work of art to
be a portable image, we cut off any sense of a continuum of meaning between
specific environment and particular image. The image has to transform and focus
whatever place it reaches.

PAINTING

Modern fashion accepts the painter as the leading and best rewarded type of artist. The painter's materials have specific values of their own, subsidiary to the focal meaning, which painters may accept without realizing what they are. And a substantial part of the painter's skill is rooted in the sphere of drawing (see p.000).

Fresco, which is painting on still-wet plaster, has always had strong affinities with revered ancient Roman painting and major Renaissance masterpieces such as Michelangelo's Sistine Chapel. It becomes physically part of the wall surface it is painted on and so partakes of something of the sternness of architecture. There is a kind of social formality attached to **oil painting** that gives it a "definitive" character. There used to be a strong feeling that painters were not "real" painters until they could produce acceptable works in this "proper" medium.

Watercolor was once thought to be suitable only for making rough notes or sketches, even though many great artists used it skillfully – among them Durer, Constable, Turner, Sargent, and Winslow Homer.   Cezanne used to recite a little rhyme: *"La peinture à l'huile, c'est bien difficile, mais c'est beaucoup plus beau que la peinture a l'eau"* – "Oil painting's pretty difficult, but it's much more beautiful than watercolor." Nowadays we value especially the spontaneous and immediate in painting – Turner's and Cezanne's tiny watercolors, for example, as well as swift and uninhibited Japanese brush-pieces.

8.7   PAUL CEZANNE
Mont Sainte Victoire, 1906. Watercolor, 14¼ × 21⅝ins (36 × 55cm). The Tate Gallery, London.

Although he considered oil painting both a more challenging and a more rewarding medium, Cezanne continued to produce exquisite watercolors, prized for their immediacy and clarity.

Ground color

The color of the ground of a painting can itself be important. Most painters nowadays use white ground, which reflects the most light through the color layers, as well as from their own surface. Fresco and watercolor are virtually always painted on white. But some painters have returned to using colored grounds, as most artists did in earlier centuries, either covering them entirely or leaving parts of the ground color exposed to play a part in uniting the overall scheme. One common technique is to leave the ground color to serve as outlines for differently colored areas loosely brushed in over it. If you glaze transparent colors over a colored ground, you get interesting optical effects. Any color over a similar-colored ground gains strength. But a color glazed over its color-opposite gives a grey, one cancelling out the other (see p.119). Red over red thus gives a strong red. Red over green gives grey. If you lay opaque colors over a ground, its own color may matter little. Most of the pre-nineteenth-century masters of oil painting combined transparent and opaque colors in the same image, using glazes to work away from the monochrome *chiaroscuro* of the underdrawing (see p.234) over a colored and toned ground, using opaque pigments for strong colors, and loading the ground with white to give luminosity to strongly lit areas.

You can use almost any kind of support for a painting. The commonest are prepared canvases and papers (see p.158). For unconventional work, you can stitch together irregularly shaped pieces of burlap or rag or nail up pieces of rough board. Or, like Frank Stella, you can have canvases beautifully mounted on stretchers of irregular shapes – stars, figure eights, joined triangles, and the like.

Applying paint

The way paint is applied contributes to the image. You can brush it on in the traditional way with brushes of different sizes, either smoothly or with emphatic brushmarks whose kinetic qualities will be immediately read by the viewer. You can use a consistently neutral touch which unifies the surface or you can draw with strokes that suggest 3D forms. You can lay your ground flat and flood the paint on in pools. **Tachisme** consists of making a picture out of brushmarks that have specific shapes, often allowing excess paint to trickle down the surface, as in the work of Sam Francis and Pierre Soulages. **Action painting** consists of performing gestures with paint to leave traces which the viewer then interprets – as done by Jackson Pollock and Antoni Tapies, for example. Many artists have stuck other objects – sisal, feathers, gravel, glass, bits of broken crockery – into the paint, or even attacked the canvas itself with knives. One way of creating an unusual texture is to stick down folds of cloth, or pull them through slashes in the canvas, then paint them.

Color handling

There are two radically distinct ways of handling color in a painting which can be combined only to a limited extent. The first is to use a specific group of **pre-selected colors**, direct from the tube or mixed up in containers, and then lay them on in areas. With media that dry slowly, such as oil paints and thick

8.8 Jackson Pollock at work in his studio in 1950. His technique of "action painting" – using gestures not just of the arm, but of the entire body, to pour, splatter, and dribble liquid pigment onto enormous canvases laid on the floor – seemed to many people at the time to be a negation of the control and judgment an artist was supposed to exercise. But control is a matter of degree; Pollock's works are explorations of what paint can do, and of the *act* of painting itself.

gouache, it is possible to brush such colors into each other, blending their edges. With transparent paints, such as watercolors and thin acrylic, it is best to preserve each at its maximum freshness. This usually involves laying each one separately and letting it dry, starting with the palest and painting the darker over it if necessary. Water bound colors can produce interesting effects when laid side by side wet, so that they "bleed" into each other. Different thicknesses of paint, degrees of wetness, and kinds of surface can either reveal expressive brushmarks or spread the color evenly like a stain.

The second principal way of handling color is by **combining color** on the surface. You use a palette of many standard colors and mix up new tints and tones in the act of painting, either on the palette or on the surface of the picture. You can then modify what you do as you do it, adapting one color stroke and area to another. This is a traditional method of painting followed by, for example, both Chardin, the tonal modeller, and Bonnard, the pure colorist.

Variants of these techniques were developed by the so-called Pointillistes, notably Seurat and Signac. Their intention was to get over the dulling effect of subtractive color mixing by dotting in each component in a mixture on the canvas at its optimum brightness (see p. 120). They covered their carefully planned areas

8.9 PIERRE BONNARD
Evening, or *The Siesta*, or *In a Southern Garden*, 1914. Oil on canvas, 33 × 44½ins (84 × 113cm). Kunstmuseum, Bern, Switzerland.

Soft, mingled touches of oil paint produce an effect of warm luminosity. The colors register the interplay of lights from colored objects.

with small touches of bright color which blended optically only at a certain distance, to produce modulated colors and greys.

Color sequences

The scientific investigation of color constancy (see p.108) confirms one very important idea, which was developed by Paul Klee – the idea that we read color by following tracks of color areas in sequence. The research found that the brain is only able to construct each color accurately by constant reference to the sequences in which it is being read across from its neighboring colors. Klee pointed out that in some of his own works, especially the "magic square" pictures, he was trying to construct "color melodies." In these, each alignment of colors – vertical, horizontal, and diagonal – produces an effect resembling different notes of a scale arranged to produce a melody. One of the criteria for such melodies is that they should be varied and interesting and avoid repeating the same color step in a banal way. All the melodies in a work should supplement each other.

8.10 PAUL KLEE
Flora in Sand, 1927. Watercolor on Ingres paper, 9⅛ × 11¹⁵⁄₁₆ins (23.2 × 30.3cm). Private collection, Switzerland.

Klee developed the idea that areas of color should work in sequences across the surface of the painting, rather like the melodies and chords of music. He was an excellent violinist; he probably acquired the idea through his interest in Islamic art.

The color sequences, of course, are intended to set up in the viewer parallel sequences of feeling-response to the colors. Good painters have long invented their color in terms of tracks across the surface, not as static, unrelated blocks. We need to compose a picture in terms of "melodies" across its colored areas. It is the "reading phenomenon" that accounts for many of the effects that color theory has schematized. The wonderful complexities of, say, van Gogh's color come not only from his use of color opposites, but from the sequences and reading combinations in which he arranged his colors in the act of painting.

Color families

Colored areas distributed across a picture surface always appear as members of a "family group;" you give each group a characteristic arrangement of its own, by which you relate sections of a complex design that may be quite far apart. Your eye naturally picks out the shape of a scattered "family" of, say, yellow, or blue, or orange areas. You can build distributed areas of color into interlocking shapes which give them meaning within the whole. You can use this very subtly, even combining different intensities and densities of similar color. So long as you have at least four colors, you can prevent your sequences from becoming banal through constant repetition.

Uniform color areas that meet and address each other do so partly in terms of their relative dominance of size as well as shape. To read from a mass of black across a channel of white to a mass of blackish brown is quite different in effect from reading two touches of black and a passive almost-circle of brown bedded in a broad area of white. A bright yellow strip sandwiched between areas of two

8.11   SAM FRANCIS
Around the Blues, 1957–62. Acrylic on canvas, 108 × 192ins (274.3 × 487.7cm), The Tate Gallery, London.

This "tachiste" painting is executed in rough patches (*taches*) of thin, transparent oil color allowed to trickle. A fluid movement ripples through the composition.

other colors – say dull violet and blue – will have its own special value according to whether it works as a passively shaped divider or as a jagged undulation that cuts into one or both of the other areas. If you are asking your viewers to read across three colors, the effects will also be different according to the direction in which they read; so you need to take account of directions of reading in your composition.

If you build up varied color-shape transitions into quite long chains over the surface, you can give a work individual force. But at the same time you need to be careful to preserve some kind of unity in your color system – which the color-group principle helps you to do. Otherwise you may produce merely a chaotic confetti-like effect, a scatter, say, of rainbow hues with no clear threads of meaning in them.

Modulation of color

Since colors work most effectively in scanned sequences, the transitions or steps

8.12 VINCENT VAN GOGH *The Sower*, 1888. Oil on canvas, 25⅛ × 31⅝ins (64 × 80.5cm). Museum Kröller-Müller, Otterlo, The Netherlands.

The vibrancy of this painting is partly a result of van Gogh's use of color opposites in close proximity; more difficult to describe, but equally important, is the way he arranges *sequences* of color oppositions through the work.

from one area of color to another need to be carefully modulated. If you employ few colors, to choose to give every edge exactly the same transition quality over and over again – white to black, black to yellow ochre, and so on – can be boring and ineffective, even if you have chosen a brilliant and disruptive group of colors. If you are brushing your pigments freely, as in Expressionist painting, you can modulate your steps by brushing each edge differently. But you can also introduce traces of other colors into adjacent areas on one side of your transition or the other. For example, where ochre meets black (again) you can sharpen the ochre with a touch of acid yellow and the black with barely visible purple; somewhere else you can touch pink into the ochre against a faint oranging of your white.

Color dominance

One important principle in using color is that of dominance. You can use one color at its maximum intensity in combination with others that are less intense, either paler or darker, to give varied effects according to placement and quantity. This helps to show how color effects may not be *purely* coloristic. If, for example, you set a group of colors against a broad background of one color at its maximum

8.13 NICOLAS POUSSIN
The Lamentation over the Dead Christ,
c.1650–57. Oil on canvas, 38 × 52ins
(94 × 103cm). The National Gallery of
Ireland, Dublin.

A number of Renaissance artists
explored the mysterious effects of
differently colored robes arranged
sequentially across a painting. At its
most sophisticated, this technique
could produce visual "melodies,"
including the suggestion of "chords"
where the colors met, which interpreted
the subject of the painting.

intensity, you can make that color dominant where it appears with the group. But if you place only a small patch, sprinkle, or rim of that same color among the group, it can much enhance the effect not only of a less intense version of itself but also of its color opposites. It is possible to build up whole areas of resonance by subtle interweaving of colors and their mutual resonances. This is done particularly in what is called "color-field" painting. All good luminous flesh-painting, as in Titian or Rembrandt, is also based upon "fielding" colors – albeit killed (see p.126) rather than brilliant.

Hyper color

It is possible – but very difficult – to produce in free painting what we can only call "hyper color": that is, an effect of varied color brilliances that cannot be defined as specific hues. Van Gogh, Monet, Bonnard, and Klee achieved this to an outstanding degree. Different hues laid together and into each other with a mobile touch can produce vibrant sensations for which it is impossible to give any simple hue-description. Klee used to apply an area of modulated color then paint over this flocks of dots, either lighter or darker, of quite a different color range. This is related to Pointillism (see p.120), but the effects depend upon intuitive combinations of harmony and contrast (see pp. 120–2).

Color and shape

One particularly important use of color is in relation to flat shape. To apply the same color in different shapes or combinations of shape can radically alter its effects. Color and shape may build up together, and artists need to be highly sensitive to their interaction. For example, red applied as a jagged narrow blade-shape across a black background will look very different from the same pigment brushed as a loose halo around an orange disc. The reasons will not be merely optical, but connected with basically biological response. This technique of varying color can be particularly important when you are using a limited range of pigments.

Modelling with color

Late Greek and Roman painting was closely allied to sculpture (then the pre-eminent medium) and so was interested in modelling 3D shapes by means of color. The normal method – which we still use widely – was to depict modelling shadow as a darker version of the main hue of the object depicted. A pale blue robe would be given shadow of a darker blue, a pinkish face a darker red-brown. This resulted in the painted surface being broken up into distinct areas, which were integrated by the plastic unity of the figures based on underlying sculptural volumes.

In the early Christian epoch, Roman painting began to use color more freely to indicate light effects. But hardly any of this painting survives. Later Italian painting, up until the fourteenth century, followed similar methods. This approach implied a view of the world as a system of solid, different colored independent bodies in space. But it did not reveal the world as a visible unity.

Chiaroscuro

In the early fifteenth century, as we have seen (p. 226), some northern European painters executed their modelling in an underpainting, then applied transparent tints over the top. The underlying monochrome produced optical greys through the color layer that gave both modelling to the forms and an overall unity to the composition. Italian painters learned the technique; and it gradually became customary to separate the processes of modelling and coloring, usually working on a toned ground and using a single brown for all shadows and laying clear colors only where light falls.

Chiaroscuro painting is based on the overall shadow image. To our eyes, which are used to reading all tints simply as color, the brown can seem drab. But painters then felt it as warmly neutral. They painted their lights in as opaque areas of freely handled oil-pigment, brushing the edges out thinner over the colored ground and extending them into the shadow image with semi-opaque tones. The colors of flesh, garments, and trees could then be individually strong, yet remain held together by the positive color value of the brown. Painters such as Titian and Rembrandt then worked up their light areas with free color-modulation and touch.

The early *chiaroscuro* technique depended upon physically separating the two processes of transparent shadow painting, using varnishes, and painting in denser lights and colors, usually with oil, after the tonal painting was dry. About 1550 painters developed the technique of painting shadows and lights into each other in oil colors **wet-in-wet**. The gain in facility and speed was matched by a loss of distinction of quality between transparent shadow and solid light. G. B. Tiepolo, Velazquez, and Manet are among the great wet-in-wet painters who evolved individual styles.

One particular rule that *chiaroscuro* painters follow is to alternate the successive tones of their shadows, middle tones, and lights between "warm" and "cold" colors. Brown shadow is warm, grey is cold. According to the warmth or coolness of each main area tint, middle tones would be achieved by applying their color opposites. In addition, it became common for Baroque painters such as Rubens always to lay touches of brilliance into their shadows with strokes of, say, vermilion red. One observation made first by Leonardo da Vinci, and developed more fully by Delacroix, was that shadows also contain reflections of colored light from any lit object that faces them. To paint in these reflections knits together colored objects otherwise separated by areas of *chiaroscuro*.

Luminosity

Post-Renaissance European painters adopted a number of ways of controlling strong tint colors systematically. One is to establish in the picture one dominant area of hue and back it up with two lesser areas of other hues, one supporting it, the other contrasting with it. Since strong colors normally belong to specific objects such as flowers and dyed garments, such elements as flesh and landscape may be portrayed in less intense compound colors. A second way, used especially by Poussin and Persian miniaturists, is to organize figures wearing a whole series of garments of different hues into a color sequence that produces a "musical"

8.14 *Barbad Playing Music to Khusraw*, from the Khamsa of Ilyas b. Uusuf Nizami, c. 1140–41. The British Library, London, MS OR. 2265 fol. 77v.

The brilliant colors of the courtly costumes are arranged in sequences. (They should be read from right to left.) Each enhances the others. The tints were probably also burnished as they were laid down, to give them an enamel-like surface.

effect. Poussin consciously related his sequences to musical modes, each of which
has its own emotive quality.

Shadow and light

One interesting but rare way of using color in representing 3D objects is to
translate the shadow in an object into a color darker than but different from the
tint of the object, hence still offering a spatial shadow-construct to the eye. It is
also possible to translate the shadow on an object of one color into another color
that is the same brightness as or even brighter than the basic tint of the object.
And you can color the shadow on each object differently, according to the
individual tint on the lit side of the object, as Buoninsegno of Siena did in the
sixteenth century. You can also use one color for the shadows on all objects –
say, blue – and model shapes with grades of that color to arrive at a compound
final color.

Another common technique, which was developed in Venetian seventeenth-
century painting, is to use highlights of different color from the main hue of the
object highlighted: pink or pale yellow on a bluish-purple robe, for example; even
pale green on a red, invoking color harmony and discord (see pp. 120–2). White
highlights usually imply that a bleached radiance is reflected from the object.
This can be very effective if it is specifically intended, but white highlights used
indiscriminately can be damaging.

Atmosphere

Leonardo observed that the effect of distance or haze is to "blue" the colors of
objects, and by the beginning of the sixteenth century blue had become the
standard color for distant mountains. We call this technique **atmospheric perspective**. Later, Turner developed special atmospheric color methods whose implications have not really been taken up. He adapted the techniques of transparent
watercolor by adding to it occasionally some opaque body color. Turner also
achieved special effects with his use of thin oil paint, its layers and touches
appearing and reappearing through one another. The subject he wanted to paint
was the constantly moving and changing luminous atmosphere over sea and
landscape. His pictorial subjects were, so to speak, verbs not nouns, shifting
energies rather than solids.

SCULPTURE

Sculpture works with bodies of solid material in actual space, setting up relationships of scale between them. In condensing objects into intelligible units, the
artist needs to shape the faces of the material to make them join up and "move"
in 3D. Front faces, not simply edges, are the essence of sculpture. They turn the
encounter between artifact and viewer into a genuine face-to-face confrontation.
It is not enough for a piece of sculpture to be simply a common thing or collection
of things – however enigmatic. Bodies need to be articulated into continuous

volumes or arranged far apart with open, intuitively measurable distances between them. Such spacing may be very subtle and invoke all kinds of bodily memory-responses: reaching, touching, and moving through and around. The important thing is that these be consistent and reinforce each other so as to project a coherent image. The main difference between full-round sculpture and relief is that with the former it may be possible to walk around and among the components of the piece to experience their faces and intervals in sequence and add them up in one's imagination; whereas with relief distance may be coded schematically and consistently compressed – or even increased – to suggest an organized deep pictorial space from a single viewpoint.

All 3D arrangements depend upon a combination of three main factors. First is the physical character and relative size of the objective bodies that you put together. You may place a massive section of tree-trunk, for example, at the meeting of a huge spear-like iron shape and radiating ripples of fabric, all of which it is possible to see together from several viewpoints. Second is the scale and posture they adopt in relation to viewers: towering over them, say, or spread out

8.15 and **8.16**   JEAN IPOUSTÉGUY
Man Pushing Open a Door, 1966. Bronze, 78¾ × 50⅜ × 49¼ins (200 × 128 × 125cm). Galerie Claude Bernard, Paris.

A man vigorously forces his way through a door, as if passing from one region of space and reality into another. On the far side the shapes of the projecting limbs are rudimentary, and the activity seems halted.

8.15

8.16

before them, or face to face on a matching scale. Third is the way you arrange them for viewers to encounter in sequence or as a result of actual movement on their part – for example, in enclosed spaces such as illuminated tunnels, in ornamented rooms, or in the open air.

Place

A particularly important element in any sculpture's meaning is the way it relates to its place. In the past most figurative sculptures, whatever their scale, were given real or imaginary pieces of ground on which to stand. Many twentieth-century sculptors, such as Brancusi, took immense care with their bases, treating them as intermediary between the actual world and the second nature of the image. More recently sculptors have often dispensed with bases, so that scale and level have become particularly important. Artists such as Carl André and Anish Kapur spread pieces on the bare floor. Others balance forms on top of a broad surface; raise them on legs or struts; build them as walls; hang them from a ceiling, as Calder does; fill a space-cell with components; or bulldoze vast heaps and channels in a landscape. Reliefs, of course, extend from – and so belong to and modify – the wall or floor of their location; and how they are placed on it is part of their expression. They may be high up or low down; suppressed or projecting and trailing far out; made up of continuously aligned or widely separated elements. No sculpture actually treats "space" as a neutral pre-existing emptiness in which it simply stands, though the white, empty, brightly lit cuboids of modern galleries may seem to suggest it might. Every arrangement needs to create its own shape *of* space and take full possession of all three dimensions of its environment.

Materials

Sculpture is in a special sense an art of material. Whatever material you work in, either a precious one such as jade or a cheap one such as concrete, it contributes to your meaning. Jade is exceptionally hard to cut and always comes in a small size; each piece has color-inflections that your working can bring out. If you use steel girders, like Caro, or welded iron, like Chillida, these have references to our industrial world. So too does fiberglass, which is also used for surfboards, yacht hulls, and lightweight casings. Concrete has overtones of the city environment. When a sculptor these days uses stone, he or she may be establishing deliberate links with older traditions of stone building and ornament, such as the Gothic or the Renaissance Italian. To use wood implies the world of organic nature and the "primitive." One twentieth-century sculptor who sometimes combined polished metal, stone, and woods was Brancusi. The effect of his final polished metal images may be so rooted in the meaning of their medium that it can be quite surprising to see the plaster originals from which he worked. Most people nowadays are made slightly uneasy by sculpture in plaster, because they consider this material in modern contexts to be both cheap and a provisional halfway house to "final" work, despite the fact that some of the greatest Roman, Italian Baroque, German Rococo and Mayan sculpture is made of plaster.

Stones and woods have grains that give them special **surface qualities**, which can unify disparate forms. On the other hand, you can apply different kinds of

8.17

8.17   CONSTANTIN BRANCUSI
Bird in Space, 1928. Bronze (unique cast), 54ins (137.2cm) high. The Museum of Modern Art, New York.

This piece represents a supernatural being poised for flight into some transcendant region. Its superb finish and high polish make its contours absolutely continuous.

working to the same piece of any material, leaving some areas rough, others polished. Very hard stone and wood can be worked up into high gloss; but not cast stone and concrete. **Metals**, such as gold, silver, brass, carbo-bronze, and stainless steel, take the highest gloss. Brancusi polished many of his metal sculptures with immense care, so that the surfaces virtually dissolve into luminosity; for the basis of his technique in the pure linear continuity of its shell-surfaces (see p.87) ensures that every line of reflected light remains unbroken.

The special quality of **bronze** that makes it so popular a sculptural material is that where it is not polished it remains dark. This makes possible a kind of *chiaroscuro* effect, especially in relief, which is achieved by polishing only the humps into highlights, leaving the hollows dark. You can also use acid and chloride washes, lacquers, or varnishes on bronze to produce a whole range of color and tonal effects. Some twentieth-century sculptors in iron and steel, such as David Smith, have used mechanical surface treatment to give different qualities to parts of their metal surfaces: filing and scouring with rotating wire-brushes or silicon carbide disc-heads, for example.

8.18   DAVID SMITH
Becca, 1965. Stainless steel, 113¼ × 123ins (287.7 × 312.4cm). The Metropolitan Museum of Art, New York, Bequest of Adelaide Milton de Groot.

Like all of this artist's welded steel sculptures, this combination of boxes has an overall bodily expression. Its surface has been scoured gesturally with a rotary abrading tool.

8.19 GIOVANNI PISANO
St Simeon, c.1370. From the façade of
Siena Cathedral. Museo dell'Opera
Metropolitana, Siena.

This stunning piece of stone-carving
was meant to be effective at a great
distance. Its deeply channelled surfaces
"move" vigorously in three dimensions,
conveying a very specific kind of
animation.

Processes

By emphasizing the physical properties of materials through your methods of
working, you can introduce fresh levels of subsidiary meaning into any work. The
four basic categories of working – wasting, adding, molding, and constructing –
leave distinctive traces. For sculpture, wasting is essentially carving; adding is
modelling, molding is primarily casting; structural processes involve assembling
separate parts.

　　Wasting implies that your final object was somehow present in the material
block before the carving brought it out into the open. The artist "finds" the image
in the given shape of the material. The rougher the cutting, the more strongly
the viewer can grasp the original properties of the substance: granular, grainy,
fibrous, and so on. So you should not refine your cutting marks to the point
where they obliterate these properties. But when you cut roughly you need to
give the cuts expressive and informative shapes. The processes of wasting to a
surface finish consist of closer and closer chiselling, with strokes that follow each
other rhythmically, then rubbing down and polishing, bringing the surfaces ever

8.20 Unfinished *Kouros*, from Naxos,
Greece, 6th century BC. National
Museum of Archeology, Athens.

This memorial figure of a youth was
abandoned at an early stage of carving.
It shows clearly how the sculptor began
to attack the block from all four of its
faces with a point-chisel in order to
"release" the figure from the material.
Perhaps rescue proved impossible in
this case.

8.21 *Kouros*, from Tenea, c.570 BC.
Marble, c.60ins (152cm) high.
Staatliche Antikensammlungen und
Glyptothek, Munich.

This finished marble figure was
probably set up in memory of a young
man killed in war. The carving achieves
an overall linear continuity of surface,
presenting and articulating a set of
clearly identifiable volumes.

8.20

8.21

nearer to being pure functions and loci of lines (see p.87). So you need to pay ever closer attention to the precision and variety of their slopes and curves. The great ancient Greek sculptor Polykleitos of Argos is recorded as having said, "In sculpture it is the last nail's thickness that is the most difficult." Most sculptors nowadays who wish to work fast prefer to avoid such time-consuming effort, often using a general finish, such as sand-blasting, to give overall consistency to broad forms.

Perhaps the most important contribution that wasting/carving techniques make to the sculptor's forms is embodied in the "planes of reference" given by the block. Many of the world's greatest carvings have been worked from a front plane, two side planes, and a back. In stone-carving these planes may be rough-hewn on the original block. The carver may then draw on them the outlines of his or her formal propositions, so defining in terms of the plane coordinates what needs to be cut away. Cross-sections may also be planned on the base and on a top surface.

In a similar way, some African and Asian sculptors have used the cylindrical surface of a wooden log as a curved plane of reference, against which they have developed rectangular volumes. Since most "primitive" sculpture has been in wood, a dialectic between rectangular and cylindrical main planes is thus one of the main sources of its aesthetic invention, involving fascinating interplays between circular horizontal inner planes and rectangular vertical shapes.

8.22

Modelling procedures imply that the object is built up in space out of nothing, without any principal planes of reference. There are no positions and proportions already given by or implicit in a block of the original material. So the modeller's basic job is to feel for these and give them form. The positive value of this situation is that you can choose to do anything you wish, and the possibilities for variety and life in the working of the surface are enormous. Modelling produces its own special kinds of work traces, which you can vary immensely and exaggerate – as, for example, Giacometti and Matisse did, turning them into a kind of handwriting in space. Where the painter defines deep 3D notionally, through the image and the implications of its properties of tone and color, the modeller builds the 3D image according to a scale of placement that he or she personally establishes and encodes as a scale of actual depth. The relief-modeller can make particularly interesting amalgamations of both actual and notional 3D spaces.

Molding nearly always follows upon modelling, as a way of making a modelled original more permanent and valuable, perhaps also of multiplying versions of it. But you can mold from wasted work, especially that which is done in soft and cheap original material such as chalk or a lump of pre-cast plaster. You can also work up a mold directly in intaglio out of clay, plaster, or plastic. In direct intaglio work the difficulty of inventing spatial locations, humps, and hollows in reverse can lead to interesting and unexpected formal ideas.

Structural processes are dealt with fully in Chapter 2. Here we need only add that the different materials that you combine into a construction can contribute a wide range of subsidiary meanings to an image. One ancient procedure was to use gold, ivory, marble, and bronze in the same sculpture – ivory, say, for the exposed flesh of a clothed goddess, and other materials corresponding to other parts of the image. Jewellers, in particular, combine precious metals, enamels, pearls, and gemstones into comprehensive images.

8.2

8.22   Ceremonial mask with two "fish bone" wings and face screened by simulated crayfish claws. New Ireland. The British Museum, London.

This piece encloses a substantial volume of space, from within which the spirit-being it represents peers out. The different components are actual or represented natural objects which were believed to be imbued with supernatural powers.

Imaginative technique

We tend to divide up our 3D conceptualizing into three main aspects: line, surface, and volume. We have discussed them in other contexts, notably in relation to form (Chapter 3) and drawing (Chapter 6). They can, of course, be realized in any medium; and the elements discussed here can be applied in any sphere of 3D design, including architectural ornament (see pp. 310–6).

Lines always have direction and implications of movement, either in one or both directions along their length. In 3D arrangements they may be actual linear objects, such as lengths of wire, tube, cut strip, brush-drawn or incised shapes on surfaces, channels, or crests. You can give them varied rhythmic inflections, thinning and thickening them, moving them to and fro across three varying axial coordinates. You can make free linear objects twist or step across and through each other. In all linear thinking you can introduce expressively mobile undulations, zigzags, and spirals; and you can twine secondary or accompanying lines around primary lines. Secondary lines can generate a strong sense of complex energies in movement and interaction – for example, by spiralling around the volumes of bodies. Painted ornament does this on ceramics. Linear shapes at their best have several principal axes of direction, taking full possession of their space.

Where a physical linear shape comes to an end we normally feel that its movement extends beyond itself, carried out into space by its own momentum.

8.23   HENRI MATISSE
Serpentine Woman, 1909. Bronze, 21½ × 11½ × 7½ins (54.6 × 29.2 × 19.17cm). Philadelphia Museum of Art.

Modelled originally in clay, the bronze cast of this figure faithfully retains the characteristic marks and traces of the additive process, which Matisse was at pains to emphasize.

8.24   THEODORE ROSZAK
The Unknown Political Prisoner (Defiant and Triumphant), 1952. Metal, 15½ × 17 × 9½ins (39.4 × 43.2 × 24.1cm). The Tate Gallery, London.

The forms of this figure, reminiscent of thick thorns and flames, reach out into the surrounding space to express a mixture of despair, hope, and determination.

8.24

This is called its **vector**. Our eyes follow on where it seems to be heading. If we want to halt a vector-effect, we must put a stop to it: a blob or a crossbar perhaps; or we must close it around on itself so that it links either to itself, so making an enclosure, or to another line, making a junction. If we want to generate space as open environment (see p. 107), we leave the line without an end-stop.

Furthermore, you can produce lines that are invisible but felt. The most obvious form of these is in a series of objects arranged according to some linear sequence, for example, stepping stones that make a winding path. Such arrangements can be 2D or fully 3D. The relative size, projection, texture, and weight of each component can be reflected in, and balanced by, its spacing from its neighbors, so as to add all kinds of tangible qualities to the implied linear form. The arrangement can be regular, neat, tight, straight, and countable; or it can combine narrow and sprawling, rough and smooth, rounded and rectangular objects. You can arrange components so that they can be read according to several distinct and different interwoven tracks – lengthwise, crosswise, or in loops or spirals.

Linear arrangement implies both a direction of reading and a rhythm either spaced from crest to crest or from trough to trough along a continuous line, or jumping across from one prominent feature to another. Parallels among lines, protuberances, ridges, edges, and objects such as sticks, stones, or tiles can all carry rhythmic intervals. The quality you give its rhythms marks out the expressive and individual character of any work of art.

Surfaces

These can be flat, curved, or undulating along only one axis or along two; they can also twist along three. They can be handled in many ways. In theory no surface can be mathematically flat, but it may convey that meaning if it is made very smooth.

8.25 *The Wise Virgin*, c. 1280. West front of Strasbourg Cathedral.

This medieval stone carving consists, in essence, of three-dimensional developments of a network of conceptual lines resembling those of a medieval woodcut. The work conveys an extraordinary tenderness.

8.26 Male torso from Harappa, c.2400–2000 BC. Limestone, 3½ins (8.9cm) high. National Museum of India, New Delhi.

Easily held in the hand, this tiny stone carving displays a quite exceptional sensitivity, unmatched until Hellenistic times, to the qualities of flesh. Its subtle volumes can be visualised as a series of cross-sections or "slices," each of which is developed from the one above or below.

Flat surfaces, whatever their shape, imply a right-angled sightline rising from their surface. This favors the center if the surface is circular, or the intersection point of their diagonals if it is a rectangle. This is partly because such areas invite the viewer to survey and grasp them as focused planes. Looked at from the edge a surface may have the value of a straight line of given thickness. Anything that appears on a flat surface attracts special attention, whether it is drawn on it or stands up from it.

When we think of surface in terms of its mathematical definition as a locus (see p.87), a flat surface appears as the locus of a straight line moving at right angles to its own length without changing plane. Several planes arranged at angles in space make up the "geometric" solids. Planes and solids may be arranged freely at a variety of different angles. If you move a straight line around an axis to which it is parallel, it becomes a cylinder. If you twist it spirally in space, it produces one of those mobile surfaces used by Antoine Pevsner and Naum Gabo.

When you develop curved lines spatially you get shells (see p.87). Almost every dish or pot is a shell of some kind. Its surface has two curves: first the (usually) circular curve of its ground plan; second, the curve of its elevation, either exterior or interior, or both. Good pots usually have elevation-curves very different from the circle of their plan. But the most interesting surfaces are those generated by lines that change direction, often more than once, undulating perhaps along their length, while also moving as changing functions across the direction of their principal line. This is what the surfaces of Gothic and pre-Khmer sculpture do to take full possession of the three dimensions of space. Few modern artists have done it, save Arp and Brancusi. In this region the possibilities to explore are limitless.

The final mode of arranging material in unitary form we define as **volume**. Lines and surfaces are visible; volumes are invisible. They can only be implied by the artist and inferred by the viewer from what is visible, that is lines and surfaces. In implying and reading volumes, both artist and viewer have to make an imaginative jump, by which they grasp a shape of space contained within the surfaces they can see. Three-dimensional objects that do not reach toward interesting and intelligible volumes remain at a relatively low level of appeal.

The principal way to make any volume intelligible is to form it so that it gives an interesting series of changing cross-sections or plan-views, at right angles to the length of the main axis, which the eye can pick up – like the shapes of slices cut from a loaf of bread. A well-developed volume gives interesting diagonal sections too. But a regular geometric solid gives unchanging, repetitive sections. Your handling of the principal planes of the exterior of a solid form is what defines the progression of sections through its volume.

A technique invented by the Cubist sculptors was to open volumes up, defining them by sets of internal plane surfaces related axially to each other, whose ranks of outlines implied the exterior shape. In medieval and Renaissance art it was common for the cut-off ends of free-floating drapery, say, to illustrate the sections of spatial volumes. And many other techniques have been invented to illustrate volumes in terms of revealed sections, such as encircling them with obviously cylindrical bracelets, or exaggerating the enclosing curved loops of folds of flesh or cloth, or even inscribing on the face of a form "unnaturally" exaggerated 2D curves to illustrate the notional 3D section of the volume that supports them.

8.27   ALEXANDER CALDER
Black Widow, 1959. Standing stabile, painted sheet steel, 92 × 173 × 89ins (233 × 434 × 226cm). The Museum of Modern Art, New York, Mrs Simon Guggenheim Fund.

This spidery compilation of cut-steel silhouettes on a superhuman scale takes full and menacing possession of a substantial area of floor and volume of space.

Volumes may be positive, that is to say **closed**, within a body or negative, **open**, shaped by the outside surfaces of a group of other solid bodies. Negative spaces can amount to shaped recesses among solids, or holes through them, or be outlined with ranks or tiers of overlapping edges. The defining contours can belong to convex bodies or be fully concave. Good sculptors compose interesting "dialogues" of positive and negative shapes. Their negative volumes are actually what give special power to many African woodcarvings.

In generating clear volumes you need to ensure that the various sectors of your whole surface are either convex or concave in all directions, rather than flat or uncertain. You need also to fix the positions in your design of the crests or maximum lumps and of the deepest hollows. From these you are able to reason out your sets of receding planes, their lengths and angles, so as to clarify volumes lying within them, investing them with life and variety. You give character to each volume by the ways you define and combine the shapes of the differently curved surfaces enclosing each of them. You decide how much each bulge protrudes, how long each principal plane is, and its angular relations to the others. The set of angular relations are the **crystal** aspect of the form: the curving continuity of the surface its **fruit** aspect (see p. 100). According to how you stress one or the other, your volumes take on different expressive characteristics. Without any crystal aspect volumes become loose, organic, even saggy and unformed. Without any fruit aspect they can become rigid, dry, and stereotyped. Early twentieth-century imitators of "primitive" styles often allowed their emphatic shapes to remain at the level of simple surface, and not progress to implying definite volumes as they always do in, say, fine African woodcarvings.

Articulation

The culmination of all sculpture is its articulation. This means joining shaped parts together so as to connect up what they mean, at the level of formal idea. Articulation can be clear and emphatic, as in the jointed sections of Calder's stabiles; or subtle and enigmatic, as in the rocks of the Ryoanji sand garden in Kyoto, Japan, which are linked by invisible projected lines, implicit in the forms of the rocks, weaving together across the intervening spaces. Special kinds of articulation arise from the combination of different kinds of physical body in 3D, whether they are flat surfaces, ribbons, shafts, blobs, heaps, pillars, or containers of organic volume.

The first method of articulation is **simple addition**, as practiced by many modern sculptors. You simply fix two or more units together by any suitable technique such as gluing, bolting, bracketing, or welding. Your aesthetic judgment determines the precise angles, distances, and other spatial relations between the components. You can leave each component complete and unmodified, merely touching the next, so that the two can "work" upon each other. If you are dealing with volumes (see pp. 102–3), you can **intercut** or run the two together to give new and interesting shapes.

8.28 HENRY MOORE
Reclining Figure, 1951. Bronze, 90ins (229cm) long. The Arts Council of Great Britain.

Imageries of woman and of landscape are combined in this massive bronze casting. Its long, linear volumes show the slowly altering cross-sections which were a feature of the artist's technique.

In connecting any components you can **run on** at least one surface of each intelligibly into a surface of its neighbor. The run-on can be smooth or consist of sequential angular steps of plane faces – as, for example, in the underside of a stone or concrete bridge with its supporting piers, or some Cubist sculpture. Combinations of run-on surfaces can have the effect of a single compound surface that exhibits its own movement as a spatial phenomenon. Such surface run-on becomes stronger the more surfaces of bodies it connects without destroying the challenging individuality of each. Lines or channels added to such surfaces can reinforce the sense of rhythm in the run-on or emphasize the distinctness and character of components. In sculpture these can seem like additional pattern; in architecture they may appear, for example, as moldings, bands of rustication, or ornament.

As well as or instead of surface continuities you can articulate a 3D piece by relationships among the principal **axes** of its individual volumes. You first ensure that each volume has one primary axis of direction, rather like a long bone in your arm or leg; and then you arrange these so as to take possession of the three dimensions of space by the ways they either scatter or splay out into space. An extension of this principle is to combine the axes into "trees" that seem to grow through and into the space they occupy. Axes can coordinate the linear surfaces that circle around them into continuous series of varying sections, rather like highly eccentric pots running into one another. This was the basis of Henry Moore's method.

Object and image

We recognize the arrangement of shaped bulks, surfaces, and volumes composed of material as corresponding to similar arrangements of similar shapes we know from elsewhere. If the qualities of the material remain recognizable, they preserve our sense that the result is not a mere copy but a true metamorphosis of material.

Virtually all of humanity's sculptures refer, however distantly, to human or animal bodies. There are several reasons for this. Our interest naturally focuses on living things, especially our own kind. We are social beings whose lives are deeply conditioned by our reading of facial and body languages. We still feel that body images are necessary to knit together references to the deeper and remoter regions of our experience. A body image gives context and coherence to subsidiary shapes and textures that may evoke, say, cavern and cliff-face (Moore), torso and broken archaic pot (Germaine Richier), or flesh and machine (Jean Robert Ipoustéguy). A suggestion of eyes can give a sense of threat to rigidly erect "staring" forms or of life to rounded volumes. The "posture" that a sculptured figure seems to adopt in addressing the viewer also affects its meaning. It can express greeting, hostility, remoteness, or retreat. It stimulates our sympathetic human responses by implied tension and pressure, outward and upward thrust, weight and lift, internal stress and interactions of energy.

The only sculptures that actually move, of course, are mechanically or electronically operated in some way. They may be designed to signal to the viewer in enigmatic ways. But even here, the fact that such signals interest us at all depends on our interest in what they might conceivably "mean" as an unconventional and unrestricted kind of communication.

A whole sculpture or its major parts may also have some resemblance to other recognizable objects in the real world. For example, you can make a circular stone relief resemble a fossil ammonite, and so awaken feelings connected with the spiral and our imaginative grasp of geological time. The surface graining of a slab of Italian travertine stone can be polished and angled to evoke the image of a violent rainstorm and its associated feelings. A piece you cover with curling relief can evoke clouds and landscape, without being an exact "picture" of either. You can make an object resemble a group of trees, an enormous flower, a cavern, or a rock face, each of which emerges from the memory along with its associations. You can make objects that resemble things whose meanings depend purely upon cultural information. An artifact can look like a helmet, for example; a rectangular rodded grill can evoke feelings connected with imprisonment; a miniature object can resemble a large object, as a model of something resembles the full-size

8.29 DEMETRI CHIPARUS
The Hoop Girl, c.1930. Gilt bronze and ivory, brown onyx base, 10¼ins (26cm) high. Éditions Graphiques, London.

A small table-top sculpture, of a once fashionable and sexy subject, made of different materials. Each represents a substance in the subject, and lends its qualities to it: ivory, smooth whiteness of skin; gilt metal, the ridging and dotting of fabric and jewelry; onyx, the veined earth.

original (for instance, a little funeral shrine may suggest a temple); a relief carving can resemble, say, the face of a Roman sarcophagus in composition and style. These kinds of cultural reference are built into the meaning of the image.

Freestanding sculpture

The imagery of good figurative sculpture depends on techniques for formulating the relationship between work and viewer in spatial terms. A simple example will explain this. If you stand close to a cubical column, you will see either one face only or, if you stand at an angle, two faces slanting apart at 90°, separated by a shed-line where they meet. You will not be able to recognize its cubical shape immediately – what you see will be a wall or a triangular section. You will need to walk around it to compose its cubicness conceptually in your mind. The great sculptors of the past, however, to stengthen the effect of plasticity, used to widen the "back" of a cubical or "crystal" form so as to make it immediately intelligible. Michelangelo's *David* has for this reason a wider back than you would expect from the front view. The two receding side-planes remain visible along their whole length, giving to the contained volume a strong sense of perspective depth, while the frontal plane is carried forward to the viewer's attention, so establishing a strong sense of face-to-face presence.

To create a strong impression of shaped space, a sculpture needs also to lay out a set of front features locating the places of maximum projection; from these the viewer measures the deepest hollows and farthest contours of the work. Between nearest and farthest the work then offers a readable scale of depths. This is something that ordinary natural or artificial objects do not have; so they lack a vital dimension of communication. For this reason much good sculpture has the character of relief, either very deep and detached from any actual ground – what the French call *ronde-bosse*, "round-prominence" – or worked up from an actual ground surface. What gives any sculptural work its expression is the way those of its surfaces that face the viewer move in relation to each other, as sequences spaced and articulated expressively. And these can be effective only when the

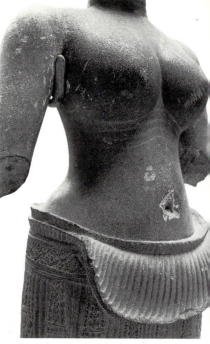

8.30 Female figure from Phnom Bakheng, early 10th century. Polished sandstone, 51¼ins (130cm) high. Musée Guimet, Paris.

The side and front surfaces of this Khmer carving of a royal goddess are worked into an almost totally convex continuity, as a metaphor for the splendor of fruit-like fullness.

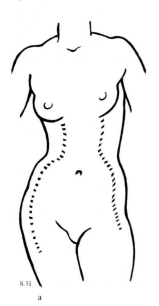
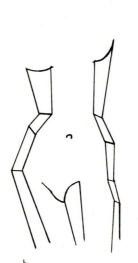
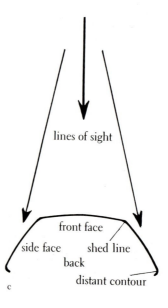

lines of sight

front face

side face   shed line

back

distant contour

8.31

a   b   c

8.31 Sculpture: (a) principal view of a sculpture in *ronde-bosse*, showing the positions of continuous "shed" lines (dotted) (b) facetting of the figure, with front and receding side faces (c) plan of the sculptural layout in relation to the eye of a viewer, allowing the full length of receding side surfaces to be seen together.

8.32 JOSEPH ANTON FEUCHTMAYER
St Christopher, 1750. Painted wood, 49¼ins (125cm) high. Reichlin-Meldegg Chapel, Überlingen, Germany.

Vivid, deep cutting, bold projections, sharp diagonal surfaces, extreme bodily posture, and drapery and hair that soar out into space characterize the technique of this masterpiece of German woodcarving.

8.32

8.33

8.33 GIOVANNI BOLOGNA
The Rape of the Sabine Women, 1582.
Marble, 13ft 6ins (410cm) high. Loggia
de' Lanzi, Florence.

Baroque sculptors explored the
possibilities of the spiral as a
compositional device. The frenetic
twisting of overlapping limbs and torsos
invites and repays viewing from many
different angles.

viewer's eyes (and hands) are able to register how far in and out and at what angles
they run.

Elaborately spiralling Baroque sculptures, such as the works of Bologna,
incorporate scales of depth from several principal viewpoints. But to build in too
many viewpoints can actually reduce the force of a work in *ronde-bosse*. To begin
with, it is only possible for powerfully receding side-surfaces to work from one
principal broad viewpoint. If you introduce an S curve or a strongly receding
pyramid of planes into one view, they are bound to be invisible from other views;
and if you develop over them shapes that are interesting for any second view, you
may be able to do so only at the cost of reducing their force from the first view.

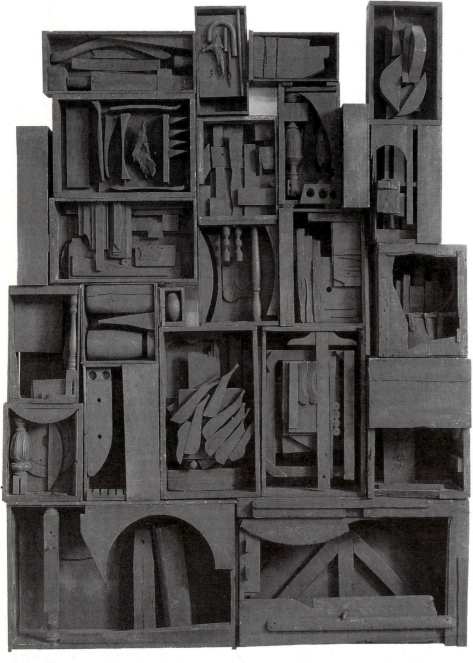

8.34   LOUISE NEVELSON
Black Wall, 1959. Wood, 112 × 85¼
× 25½ins (264.2 × 216.5 × 64.8cm).
The Tate Gallery, London.

One of this artist's boxed wooden
reliefs. Each compartment contains
enigmatic objects, sometimes odd
found scraps from workyards. The
overall color gives unity to these
fragmentary cultural totems.

8.35   Types of relief, shown in section:
(a) sunk relief (b) two-stage relief
(c) undercut (d) free modelling (e)
perspective by depth and bevel.

Relief

Whereas a *ronde-bosse* sculpture is free standing, a relief is always part of a
continuous surface and works by interacting with it. We shape and understand
its forms according to the degrees by which its surfaces stand above or below or
slant toward that ground. Reliefs have especially strong and broad front planes;
but their definition of surface and volume depends on degrees of bevel: how far
in they start, how steep or shallow their slopes are. An edge that is bevelled very
short and steeply to the ground will have the effect of a strongly separating contour;
one that is longer and shallower will stand for a recession from the face.

The ground of a relief is usually framed, either as part of an architectural
structure or as an independent panel. This makes it possible to create a convincing

notional space within the frame. Certain reliefs, such as those on Indian temples representing the realms of the gods, have elaborately molded and deeply 3D frames that bond them to the architecture. Others, such as Louise Nevelson's, may be constructed in ranks of open boxes. Yet others may emerge from a wall far into the space of a room.

There are three principal ways in which a carved relief relates to its ground. All of them rest on the assumption that the basic technique for representing notional bodies is to outline them, isolating one from another, and creating strongly formed negative spaces between them. You give the contours, of course, their own linear and rhythmic values, and can turn them into overlapping sets of lines to create depth, following drawing methods we have already discussed (see p. 161). You can even create an effect of strong relief with nothing but incised linear drawing – fine examples appear on Wei dynasty Chinese tomb lintels.

The first way, very common in ancient Egyptian art, and depending on carving techniques, is to start with a smooth face of material, outline bodies on it, cut the outlines back to a given standard depth – usually very shallow – then work only the undulating surface of the outlined bodies.

The second way is an extension of the first; you cut away the entire ground encircling the bodies to a new flat surface at a standard depth below the front face. You usually complete this before working over the surface of the bodies, so that there is an intermediate stage when they stand as raised panels, with clearly shaped negative areas around and between them. This gives a special coherence to the result. You then work the bodies with their undulating surfaces, as with the first method.

The third way involves cutting under some of the body-outlines so that they look from the front as though they were standing completely free from but against the ground.

All three methods when carved produce their images sandwiched, so to speak, between the front and ground faces of the original material. In modelling,

8.36 Sculptured sarcophagus representing Dionysos, the Seasons, and other figures, c. 220–230 AD. Marble, 35½ × 87¾ × 36¾ (90.2 × 222.9 × 93.3). The Metropolitan Museum of Art, New York, Purchase 1955 Joseph Pulitzer Bequest.

The mythical figures carved in high relief on the side of this marble coffin may refer to the mysteries of rebirth for the dead. These graceful revellers stand all but free of the ground; this remarkable technical feat required deep undercutting, probably with the aid of a drill.

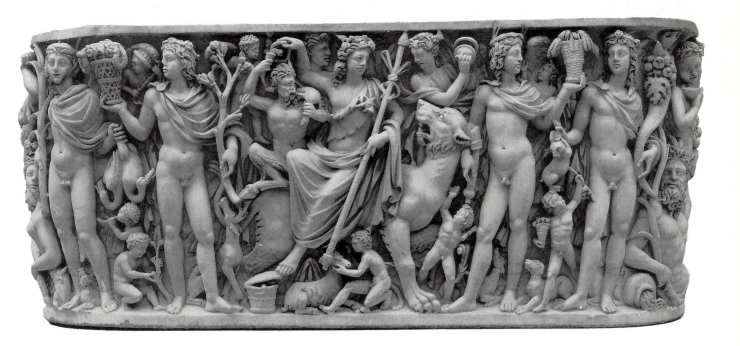

however, the relief can be as high as you wish; but without any "given" thickness of material, you will need to set up your own code of maximum prominence and hollow.

There are two chief ways in which you can think of the **supporting ground**; the first is as a neutral backing from which bodies project forward into the foreground of the viewer's own space. This is the method normally used in Byzantine and some Modernist constructed relief. The second is when the ground seems pierced like a "window," through which the viewer looks into a notional world laid out apparently according to some kind of perspective. This has been the standard European mode since about 1320, and was derived from classical Roman stucco work. With it you can convey a sense of almost infinite depth by means of the shallowest projection. One version of this kind of relief, called in Italian *relievo stiacciato*, meaning "suppressed relief," deliberately uses the minimum possible depths of cut and relies on linear channels, their overlaps, and minimally slanting bevels of surface. Donatello was the greatest master of this mode.

There are other kinds of relief often used today, which depend on constructional methods rather than carving or modelling. The first two are direct derivatives from painting and are usually colored. The third also has affinities with painting and may also be colored.

8.37   DONATELLO
The Lamentation over the Dead Christ, 1460–66. Bronze, 55ins (140cm) wide. Church of San Lorenzo, Florence.

This shallow relief, originally carried out in wax, is full of an extraordinary variety of spatial invention, including multiple overlaps, differing depths of relief, eccentric optical perspectives, and even the cutting off at the knees of one of the figures. The whole image is imbued with wild and tragic feeling.

The first kind is **silhouette relief**. You cut out flat silhouettes from sheets of material, such as board or metal. You arrange these with their flat faces at right angles to the viewer, either stacked one above the other or spaced apart by small structural components. The function of the ground may be performed by the flatness of the sheets, which implies a view of them at right angles to their surfaces. The latter method – with the sheets spaced apart – works particularly well if each silhouette is well provided with open holes through which silhouettes behind can be seen. Some surfaces may be led to and fro through these holes to link parts of front and rear silhouettes, to produce spatial enigmas. Some of Arp's and of Picasso's late works do this superbly.

The second kind of constructional relief is **collage relief**, which consists of taking a ground and jointing and sticking on to it pieces of material, the characteristics and arrangements of which convey the meaning. Charles Biedermann, for example, sticks on ranks of small slats of plastic at right angles to the ground, carefully organizing them in rectangular rhythms. Other artists may attach anything that suits their purposes in the manner of collage. Students may feel that this last is the easiest and freest mode; but it is actually far the most difficult in which to produce anything really effective.

A third kind is **cased relief**. This may be an arrangement within the space of some kind of box, either opaque and open on one side, or transparent but with one dominant face. Within the defined notional space of the box you can arrange all sorts of spatializing objects along many different axes. The objects might include lines of wire, found objects, plaques, plastic balls, loops and knots of cord, and folded fabric. This mode can develop easily into transparent showcase images, which you can walk around. A major modern master of this is the German Kurt Stenvert.

8.38   Carved door with two fish in relief, West African, 19th century. Wood, 57½ins (146cm) high. J. Müller, Solothurn.

Simple raised areas of this shallow wood relief are defined by linear loops, and areas of the fish are textured with striations and pecks. The curved rebates along the edge powerfully and economically suggest moving water.

CHAPTER NINE
INTERIOR DESIGN

BASIC CONSIDERATIONS

Good interior design reflects the lifestyle of its occupants and creates a harmonious whole, to which space, arrangement of contents, and colors all contribute. It is impossible to design interior spaces properly without having a clear idea of what kind of people you are designing for, and how they expect to live in these spaces, projecting their personalities not only to others but also back to themselves. For interiors act as a mirror reflecting who the occupants feel they are or want to be thought, confirming their sense of personal continuity and identity.

Four basic factors affect lifestyle and so interior design: climate, custom, wealth, and display.

Climate

In cold climates rooms tend to be relatively small and easy to heat, with low ceilings, small windows, and furnishings made of warm materials, such as wood and fabric. In hot climates rooms may be bigger, have high ceilings, be lined for the sake of coolness with plaster, ceramic tiles, or stone, and have furnishings made of similarly cool materials, such as slabs of marble. Windows may be shaded and stand open, so that people can walk freely onto balconies or into a garden or courtyard. In very hot climates there may be an external trellis or slatted shutters which admit air and cast a pattern of shadow on the floor.

Custom

Influenced by climate, custom is especially important in traditional societies. It governs lifestyle, including the placing and character of doors and windows, and how they are used – for instance, for watching without being seen. Some people live mainly outdoors, in courtyards, in streets and public squares, using their interiors principally as shelter and as places to cook, sleep, and dress. Tribal peoples in West Africa and Indian peasants may inhabit a scattering of modest huts in a family enclosure. Other peoples, such as the Xingu of Brazil and the Dayaks of Borneo, may house several families in one communal interior. On

9.1 STEVEN EHRLICH
Studio House, California.

Interior design is the art of creating a living space to suit the tastes and needs of the occupants, however large or small that space may be. In this case, the ground-plan of the entire house measures only 20 × 40 × 20ft (6 × 12 × 6m).

some islands of South-east Asia extended families occupy highly decorated wooden houses with socially demonstrative facades. Many tribal peoples lay out their dwellings according to a sacred arrangement. Parts of the house may be given names of parts of the body, for the house may be a metaphor for the body as sacred archetype. Some people may install the skulls and possessions of their ancestors in the house and feel that spirits inhabit parts of it, such as the roof. Property and implements may be stored in specific kinds of container and places. Certain functions, such as cooking, eating, storage, and entertainment, may even be allocated separate buildings.

A similar feeling for proprieties still affects our sense of the "natural" or "right" separation of functions into specific areas, and the keeping of certain things in particular places. Most ordinary homes today are designed around our

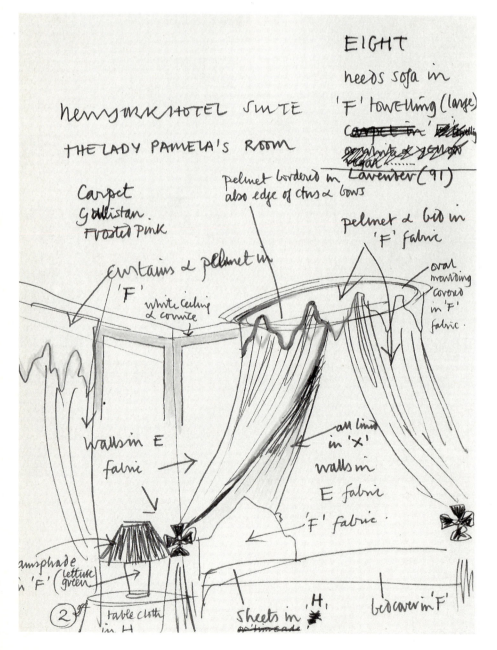

9.2　DAVID HICKS
Design for *New York Suite: The Lady Pamela's Room*. Archives of Art and Design, Victoria and Albert Museum, London.

Bedrooms present special requirements for the designer: they need at the very least to offer comfort and privacy. David Hicks, in designing a luxury suite for a New York hotel, has swathed the room in soothing fabrics to promote an atmosphere of luxury.

own standardized image of domestic activities, with appropriate spaces set aside for each: cooking, eating, watching TV, recreation, entertaining visitors, study, and so on. Conversation spaces need to be arranged so that people can communicate with each other; a TV set imposes its own restrictions on the arrangement of furniture. The dining table needs its own circulation space and serving access. Kitchen layouts, of course, must meet a great number of mainly practical criteria. Bedrooms need planning for comfort and privacy. All these factors provide a "given" for the designer, who needs to understand the order and routines of clients' individual lives and complement these in the design.

The designer also need to understand how clients expect the environment to impress both occupants and visitors. In an office, for example, the decor may be meant to give an overall impression of comfort, status, and success, yet may lack emphatic features that might distract the attention of both occupants and visitors from the business in hand.

A home may be meant to counterpoise outside public life. People who suffer from the pressures of city life and constant claims on their attention by other people and by advertising may want their home to be a restful and ordered refuge. People whose outside world is drab and grim, may want it to be a stimulating and lively place. Some people may ask that their interiors correspond as closely as possible to what the magazines tell them is conventionally accepted; others may wish to express strikingly individual attitudes. But for everyone environment needs to be friendly; and the designer's task is to make it so by the use of materials, form, and color.

Wealth

Wealth and display are not the same thing, but they cannot really be separated. Wealth affects interiors in several ways. It enables the inhabitants effectively to ignore costs of heating and lighting, and indulge in sheer size, implying grandeur in relation to the normal human scale. In courtly societies palaces were constructed with rooms numerous and large enough to accommodate vast temporary assemblies of people, as well as a permanent staff of retainers.

Wealth is usually reflected in conspicuous consumption of the labor and skill of others and in the possession of expensive and desirable objects in which cultural values are enshrined. These values may be identified in terms of sheer cost, top-of-the-market chic, or even by a manifest disdain of chic that allows individual outstanding possessions to speak for themselves. Today many wealthy people, imitated by the aspiring middle classes, are content to fill their homes with pictures, furniture, and art objects that have an accepted fashionable cachet, whether or not they have genuine aesthetic merit. Another possibility is a cultivated absence of clutter, as in traditional Japanese houses – a simplicity that can only be preserved at the expense of great discipline and effort on the part of the household.

Display

Display demonstrates not just wealth but social and cultural status. It works effectively only if those who see it recognize both its codes and the values they

represent. Wealth can be expended in sheer extravagance; whereas genuine virtue can show itself in very modest forms.

Modern interior display is the product of an historical process, reaching back into medieval European history. Aristocratic families and wealthy people had to maintain their economic position and keep the support of retainers partly by impressing society at large with their power and importance. This they did by continuous competitive display. The furnishings and decoration of interiors were carved, painted, and woven with emblems of family prestige, military strength, and recognized achievement. These included heraldic crests, images of piety and patron saints, ancestral portraits, and references to personal virtue enshrined in the current codes of cultural symbolism. These codes justified the purposeful but functionless scrolled and pierced work, crestings, and turned features added to furniture; the classical pillars and pediments on doorcases; the panelling, molding, and coffering on walls and ceilings; the rich hangings, painted walls and wallpaper, the paintings and objects that displayed the educated taste or patriotic pride of the occupants.

During the eighteenth century the Rococo palaces of southern Europe came to be filled with fantastically elaborate stucco ornament, efflorescing with emblems of abundance, of the lands, rivers, and metaphysical forces at the family's disposal. Ornamental display was meant to demonstrate a more than human glory.

By the eighteenth century not only the physical appearance of a great house but the lifestyle of the occupants was formalized into elaborate public ritual, imitated at lesser levels down through the social hierarchy. Large social gatherings included balls, where the social hierarchy was on display and reinforced. Music

9.3 LUDWIG MIES VAN DER ROHE
Farnsworth House, Fox River, Illinois, 1945–50.

The austere bareness of this interior, inspired by the traditional Japanese house, is far from being a sign of poverty: it is a statement of refined taste, which can be maintained only with very considerable self-discipline and the help of domestic staff.

was a background to the good life, and great houses maintained their own staff of musicians; some even mounted masques and plays. Meals were, as in the past, especially significant occasions; often elaborate performances preceded by processions into the dining room which the public were allowed to watch. The tables were laid out with symbolic settings of gold, silver, and porcelain, and rigid precedence in seating was followed. All the utensils and furnishings of a palace participated in the ornamental expression of social ceremony.

Most people still feel that meals have a strong ritual significance. Eating together is a most ancient way of reinforcing links, not only between individuals but between living people and their ancestors and gods. (Today's business lunch has echoes of this bonding function.) We are heirs to this whole concept of ritualized display and the decorative arts that embody it. We still expect the designs of our own tablewares to convey a ceremonial quality.

In our democratic age we have assigned most of the functions once performed in palaces to specialized public buildings; but we still feel it right that their interiors should be suitably decorated to display their importance. Concert halls, theaters, conference centers, and museums are dedicated to functions that once were rooted in the trans-personal realm of aristocratic splendor. Their designers need to aim for something beyond the utilitarian. The lobbies of big hotels such as the Hyatts

9.4   MARTIN VAN MEYTENS
Wedding of the Emperor Joseph II to Isabella of Parma, 1760, detail. Oil on canvas, 153 × 118ins (390 × 300cm). Schönbrunn Palace, Vienna.

All cultures and all ages have attached special significance to the social ritual of eating, but the palaces of 18th-century Europe took it to new heights. Vast halls had to be provided to accommodate not only the diners and all the accoutrements that went with the performance, but also the sizeable audiences of those privileged to watch.

9.5   JOHN PORTMAN
Hyatt Regency Hotel, San Francisco, completed 1967.

Public buildings now fulfill some of the roles that the great houses of the aristocracy used to do. Large and luxurious hotels offer something of the scale and splendor that were once the prerogative of the super-rich, and those who design the public and circulation areas of these buildings are often given the chance to make grand gestures.

designed by John Portman or the fancy 1930s Waldorf Astoria set out to create an effect of genuine splendor – even if it sometimes degenerates into kitsch. The sculptor Richard Lippold, whose huge yellow metal hanging "sunbursts" decorate a number of lobbies, is one of many artists who have received commissions to glorify such spaces.

FOCUS

Interior spaces are usually arranged around one or more focuses. They invite a hierarchy of levels of attention. That with the longest history is the fireplace or stove, sometimes with a picture over it and an arrangement of clock and ornaments on the mantel. In cold climates it is natural for the fireplace to be the social center. But in the era of central heating, focuses can be quite different. Nowadays a TV is often a focus; it, too, may carry ornaments.

Works of art provide a different kind of focus. Religious images or secular portraits may occupy places of honor and testify to the "sponsorship" of the house. But even secular pieces can serve as icons representing an individual's self-image: a Leger print, a Shaker cupboard, a Kachina doll, a Mexican pot, a Goya etching – or even a piece of reproduction, tourist, or jokey art. A whole interior may be designed around, and as the setting for, a few major pieces. If the occupants are collectors, the interior designer may need to grade carefully attention levels in the spaces and on the walls to allow the individual works to speak. Other people may love clutter. Family pride and affection leads many people to display extensive collections of photographs and mementos.

Wall focuses

Works of art serve as major wall focuses. The arrangement of items on a wall needs to create a rhythm and balance between flat and tactile surfaces. The distance at which a work is best viewed helps to determine the layout of the space in front of it: a large modern painting, even a print or poster, may be unintelligible at close range; whereas you may only be able to see miniatures properly from close up, or even sitting down. If the owners want a room to feature both large and small pictures together, in balance, a good solution is to use what the French call *aggroppage*. This means arranging small items in a formalized, well-proportioned group which is interesting in itself from the distance at which you see larger pieces but also allows each individual piece to be looked at from its own viewing distance. Without some kind of grouping, even interesting objects can become mere clutter.

Besides grouping pictures in pleasing ways, it is important to take their colors into consideration. These can be enhanced or killed by the colors of draperies and other furnishings in the same space, so they will inevitably influence the choice of color scheme for the room.

The same sort of considerations apply to 3D works. Small pieces may be protected in cabinets, which also need to be properly accessible. Larger pieces may need their own "habitation space." This is something you can really only

9.6 BALDASSARE PERUZZI
The Perspective Room, Villa Farnesina, Rome, 1508–11.

The owners of great houses in the Renaissance liked to display their familiarity with Classical art; visual conceits and tricks were also much in vogue. Commissioning an artist to decorate the walls of a room with *trompe l'oeil* architecture after the manner of the Romans fulfilled both requirements.

decide on for each specific object. Sculptures that are effectively reliefs may be very happy backed up against a wall. But some twentieth-century sculpture, including significant ceramics, may demand 360° of space around them and special lighting.

You can treat the actual surfaces lining an interior with different kinds of decoration. The wealthy and powerful once employed major artists to adorn their interiors with sculptured and painted schemes. Renaissance, Baroque, and Rococo ornament did amazing things with wall surfaces, opening them out into an imagery of "realms beyond." Wide perspective vistas of imaginary architecture or gardens common in classical Roman times were revived in the Renaissance. Today, people open out their walls with photographic blow-ups of forest scenes or seascapes. It can be even more adventurous to paint an entire wall – or even a floor – with *trompe l'oeil* images. This is a job many painters and installation artists welcome. Though it is most common in shops, restaurants, and boutiques today, there is no reason why it should not be done more often in private homes.

Fabrics

The importance of fabrics, especially in the home, can hardly be overstated. They can "clothe" and radically modify almost any space. Cloth is normally the material that insulates all interiors and their furniture, mediating between the human body and the architectural mass. It feels warm and its textures are grateful to the touch. It serves also to mask and adapt form. We normally hang curtains and draperies in rectangular areas. These need not match the window area precisely; and it is possible to use them to disguise badly proportioned windows.

Whereas major furniture may be fairly permanent and relatively subdued in color, soft furnishings – draperies and curtains, slipcovers, afghans, and cushions

– offer great scope for individual taste and fantasy. Even so, the colors and patterns of the fabrics must relate successfully to those of the dominant elements in the room.

STYLE

9.7   TIM BEHRENS and **JANEY LONGMAN**
Decoration in the designers' own apartment in Paddington, London, 1980.

Trompe l'oeil is back in fashion, as sophisticated and self-conscious as ever; though these days it is most often used to bring at least an illusory breath of fresh air into small urban apartments. The "views" through these "windows" are painted onto a selection of interchangeable panels.

The totality of all the choices about all the elements that make up an interior constitutes its style. It is thus usually a result, not a prescription. For with interior design many different craftspeople and producers may contribute to the final effect. Where there has been a widely shared sense of style, in societies with a strong sense of tradition and with craft-guilds, the craftspeople – potters, weavers, metalsmiths, and so on – made wares that matched the furniture and spaces naturally. They accepted current patterns as their own design resource.

It is ideal, but relatively rare nowadays, for a single designer or team to be given the responsibility for all the different artifacts that go into an interior. In the past, a few individual designers, such as Robert Adam, were able personally

9.8 ROBERT ADAM
The Music Room, Harewood House, Leeds, c.1765.

It is rare nowadays for a designer to have the opportunity that Robert Adam had, of designing every detail of an interior. Nothing here is "off the peg" or out of a manufacturer's catalog; even keyholes were specially made to Adam's design.

to design everything from the building itself down to the details of the ornament on chairs, chimneypieces and fabrics. Today major designers and design groups, such as Memphis of Milan, may occasionally do something similar. But the interior designer is usually expected to work by selecting from the very wide ranges of commercial furnishings on offer, and by relying on his or her taste to create a satisfactory ensemble.

Form

This involves a number of factors: shape, proportion, static mass, and dynamic line and surface. In interiors the **shapes** tend overwhelmingly to be rectangular – room shapes, window frames, the plans and elevations of furniture. Circular forms do occur, most commonly in table tops. Triangles may appear in the plans of corner cupboards and shelves. Oval mirrors were common in the eighteenth and nineteenth centuries, as were oval tables.

Proportion and module (see pp. 87–8) both contribute to stylistic unity. You give coherence to your space divisions and articulations, the elevations and plans of furniture by using similar proportions for the principal objects and their placing in relation to each other. An overall designer such as Adam is able to use them

9.9 CHARLES RENNIE MACKINTOSH
Hall of Hill House, Helensburgh, Scotland, 1902.

Most of Mackintosh's work was based on the use of modules, multiplied and repeated with consistent changes of scale. The harmony of this distinguished Art Nouveau interior derives from this technique.

9.10 BERNARDO FORT-BRESCIA and LAURINDA SPEAR of Arquitectonica
Spear House, Biscayne Bay, Miami, Florida, 1978.

The module established by the openings of the window are subtly echoed by the tiles of flooring.
While reminiscent of a Tudor hall in its use of space, the overall effect of this architect-designed
interior is one of coolness and light, enhanced by stone surfaces and white decor.

9.11 CHARLES MOORE and Moore Ruble Yudell
Rodes House, Los Angeles, California, completed 1979.

Color is here introduced by means of lighting rather than of painted surfaces. The effect is
deliberately "stagey" – the owner of the house called for a setting that reflected his love of the
theater. Comfortably shapeless armchairs create a feeling of homely informality, despite the volume
of the room; the overall conception seems to owe something to a studio set for a TV chat-show.

consistently down to the smallest details of ornament. You can employ an
articulating proportion, say 1:√3, for divisions of a wall space, for the height,
width, and depth of chests of drawers, for the height and breadth of mirrors; for
the height of a bed in relation to that of its headboard and its length and breadth.
You then define your module as some unit of actual measure to which all these
proportions refer. A viewer may never realize what you have done; all the objects
will just look "right" in relation to each other. *Which* proportions you use, applied
to *what* elements, will be the basis of your style. This unity of proportion can be
seen clearly, for example, in the way some Art Nouveau furniture emphasizes

the height of elements – chair backs, cupboard doors – in proportion to their width. Though it is rare for designers to conceive any totally original way of applying proportions, if they do not develop proportions at all, their forms will turn out banal and indeterminate.

Another way of connecting elements is by arranging them by means of undulating or angular **lines** (see pp. 85–7). Linear articulation of curved or undulating walls, surfaces or arrangements of furniture into a formal scheme can be very rewarding.

Color

The choice of color is a strong distinguishing feature of any style. Some designers use specific sets of colors to integrate rooms, and these may come to constitute a personal or generally fashionable style. Examples are the eighteenth-century "Pompeiian" red combined with dull green and gold; the so-called primary colors used by certain Italian designers in the 1970s; or the grey, sage and heather-dun schemes popular with designers who work with imagery closely linked to the natural world. The same designer may choose different liveries on different principles for different clients, and may also have to take into account the color schemes of paintings the occupants may wish to feature.

In deciding on a color scheme most designers will take four main factors into account. The first is the sense of space; the second is whether or not to emphasize one or more color features; the third concerns relative scale and type of pattern; the fourth, the colors themselves.

The use of **space** is based upon decisions about the proportions and relative density of the component elements. Large areas of strong color or bulky emphatic draperies can make a small space feel claustrophobic, whereas in a larger space they may work as a main articulating feature. A scheme that eliminates nearly everything 3D, closing cupboards behind solid-colored plane surfaces, may feel neat to some people, barren to others. Patterned and multicolored wallpapers produce a continuously mobile effect; uninterrupted light wall space quite another.

The **emphasis of features** can have a profound effect on the expression of any interior. In a bedroom, for example, it is possible to emphasize the bed by giving it an ornate, bright-colored headboard and a boldly patterned bedspread, subduing the surrounding colors and patterns. Similarly, in a living room a sofa or table may be featured against a subdued background if it has strongly contrasting color, tone, and/or vivid pattern. A totally different effect is produced by blending all the furniture, walls, and draperies into an equalized tonal and coloristic unity.

The use of **relative scale** and **type of pattern** can similarly stress or contrast areas. The variety of pattern types available in wallpaper, printed fabrics, and furnishings includes traditional designs that tend toward curvilinear florals or sprigging; and modern designs that feature geometrical shapes, diagonal counterchange, broad or narrow banding, or chevrons. You need to select these with regard to coherence of form as well as color and to avoid a mere scattering of types. It may be best to confine dramatic pattern or color to one object or area and offset this against plainer areas. Several fabrics with subdued grey-brown woven patterns may be combined to give a restrained, rustic effect. It is also possible to combine a multiplicity of unemphatic small sprig patterns that use the same repertoire of colors in, say, the nostalgic rural/Edwardian Laura Ashley style. But it is virtually impossible to combine many different busy and emphatic patterns in the same design scheme.

It is conventional and easy to use furniture with the same colored wood throughout any scheme; however, you can also use woods of markedly different tonalities, so long as they relate harmoniously to each other and to their surroundings.

In planning a **color scheme** you may be limited by the existing color of the walls and ceilings. White walls can accommodate virtually any color scheme carried through entirely in furnishings, whereas colored walls must be taken into account from the outset.

9.12   Art Nouveau wardrobe, c.1905.

The characteristic motifs that define a style can lend themselves to application throughout a designed interior. The sinuous curves that we recognize as distinguishing Art Nouveau, for instance, would be carried through to other pieces of furniture, wallpaper, and fabrics to give overall thematic unity.

If the walls are white, you can use one of several principles in selecting your main color group. The first option is to pick three principal, strong, and equal colors, each of which will be used in substantial separate patches of fabric or applied as paint onto furniture. Your chosen colors might be the three pigment primaries, red, blue, and yellow, or another startling combination of strong color, such as green, black, and yellow. Another approach is to select one dominant color to be used extensively, supported by a pair of second-rank contrasting but subdued or darkened colors, with touches of a strong fourth, and maybe hints of a fifth: for example, a basic deep red, with secondary ochre-yellow and pale ochre-green, plus touches of turquoise blue. You can then develop subsidiary areas in which one of the second-rank colors plays the dominant role.

If you elect to use emphatically colored walls, you start with an entirely different effect. The wall color then becomes crucial. If you choose a single color for all walls, it becomes the base color against which the furnishing colors are set

9.13 CHARLES JENCKS
The Winter Room of the architect's own house, 1978–85. Fireplace by Michael Graves.

Color is used with verve in this example of Modern Classicism, complete with architectural allusions to Greece, Rome, and ancient Egypt. Arrangements of warm, harmoniously grouped colors are offset by their opposites.

9.14 MICHAEL HOPKINS
Hopkins House, Hampstead, London, 1975–77.

Here is one contemporary solution to the question of style – and also to the problem of cost. The technology and components originally developed for large industrial buildings have been reduced to a domestic scale, resulting in an adaptable High Tech interior.

off. The easiest option then is to select a group of colors for furnishings that lie very close in terms of hue to the wall color, differing mainly by tonal density. A pinkish wall, for example, can embrace plain burnt red, brown, and purplish furnishing colors very easily. With pale blue walls, you might use deeper blue as the major furnishing color, jade green and pale turquoise as secondaries. Small punctuations of contrasting colors may set off such a harmonious group. A quite different option with colored walls is to use a single dominant furnishing color such as white, black, or violet. In this case, what matters most is how the furnishing color reacts with the wall color and the effects produced when the furnishings are positioned in different ways.

Motif

The question of the style-defining motif is closely connected with symbolism (see Chapter 5). Normally a designer employs a particularly potent image (or group of images), works variations on its characteristic shape, and adapts it to the composition and proportions of the different objects in the interior. If the motif is genuine ornament it may be fully assimilated into the structure of each piece to give an overall thematic unity. Such a process seems to be essential in all live design. An obvious example is the long elegant S-curved lily pad or pointed leaf image built into much Art Nouveau furniture, fabrics, and architectural decoration. Earlier eras employed such themes as the flat pilaster bearing a ribboned floral scroll in relief, which was featured on walls as well as furniture in the eighteenth century; the cabriole leg for different kinds of furniture; the classical pillar with Corinthian capitals supporting a pediment (much admired in the sixteenth century); the bulbous vase-like elements and grotesque masks which are a feature of seventeenth-century furniture frontages, of painted decoration, and even the horizontal stretchers of chairs; and the Chinese-Rococo motifs of late eighteenth-century design.

In the twentieth century we have passed through the era of emphatic geometrical motifs consisting of shapes clustered into ornament using parallels plus stray diagonals, brightly colored and treated with shallow textures. Now that these have lost their symbolic value the designer is faced with the problem of discovering new but valid motifs. Many original works of art have been adapted to fabric patterns; and well-known artists have provided designs for carpets (Arp, Le Corbusier, Léger) or china wares (Paolozzi for Rosenthal). Although these tend to be single focal objects rather than overall schemes, it is open to any designer to derive thematic motifs from contemporary fine art to unify the form/color structures of his or her style, clinching its total expression.

Contemporary solutions

There are three solutions often adopted for the style/matching problem today, none of which is a total design solution. The first is to create a magnificent interior by mingling **outstanding objects** in different past styles, juxtaposing or separating individual pieces so that they set each other off. In our society, which tends to be aesthetically parasitic on many others, rich people may display in the same space Central American pottery, Turkish rugs, Art Nouveau lamps, African tribal masks, twentieth-century American paintings. There does indeed seem to be something about aesthetically fine pieces that allows them to "go together," in that they inhabit a common world of exquisite form, however much their visual language and content may differ.

The second and most common solution is **modular manufacture**. It may lack any unifying symbolic motif, although the furnishings may share a common formal appearance. A commercial producer may commission complete sets of furniture in which the pieces match each other in physical structure and pro-portion. They resolve in advance the problem of stylistic matching of components – chairs, desks, shelves, cupboards – and they may be devised to fit together structurally and stylistically, so that buyers can accumulate additional pieces confident that they will go together. Modular furnishings tend to have two dominant characteristics: they are of simple and general shape, since they must appeal to a wide market; and they conform to a uniform set of measurements so as to fit together and be adaptable to all kinds of spaces. These characteristics of modular furniture, of course, greatly reduce the interior designer's scope for aesthetic development.

In practice, the designer will usually be expected simply to select **commer-cially available objects** and put them together. It is not enough simply to ensure that their form and color do not conflict. The designer has also to reconcile the symbolic echoes of all the components. Most people have quite strong – if not always conscious – associations in their minds between particular types and styles and social connotations, derived partly from TV, movies, and magazines. The plainness of modular interiors may, in a business context, imply stripped efficiency;

in a domestic context it can suggest either an uncluttered, serene lifestyle or an uncommitted impersonal bareness.

It is possible to go to the opposite extreme and select items that individually have strong but incompatible echoes of wealth and "high style." Few people may be able to afford genuine French Rococo furniture, console tables or headboards, which are so old that their gilding has mostly worn off the underlying white gesso. But much modern furniture is painted a loose overall white with touches of gilt added, vaguely suggesting the opulent original. Printed fabric designs may echo the superb patterns of early nineteenth-century Kashmiri embroidery or the prints of William Morris. Costly table lamps may be given profiled brass stems that suggest a combination of machined crankshafts and artillery shell cases. To put these three types together in the same room could scarcely be called true design; their worlds of discourse and symbolic reference (that is, content) are too incompatible. But it is often done, and it is the negation of style.

9.15 FRANK GEHRY
Spiller House, Venice, California, 1981.

Exposed rafters establish an informal, deliberately almost ramshackle atmosphere. The design is held together, however, by the discreet use of the modular rectangle established by the openings of the skylight.

ELEMENTS OF INTERIOR SPACE

The process of interior design begins with the given volumes and proportions of the existing inner spaces. These may be specifically designed in commissioned buildings; but more usually they are standard. They always provide both fundamental schemes of proportion and particular formal themes which as designer you follow through in placings and color relationships according to formal principles such as those discussed in Chapter 4. The placement and shapes of doors and windows naturally introduce proportional variations and diagonals that can pose challenges to your sense of coherence and unity. You may also have to deal with ungainly or banal shapes and spaces in apartment and office buildings and housing designed without any clear aesthetic sense.

The first stage of any design solution is to fix the location of two or more principal design elements that establish fundamental proportions and can generate at least one of the principal rectangular frames of each space. You may need, for example, to open a space by exposing rafters, lower or raise a ceiling, install a room divider, locate a focal object or main piece of furniture, define the outer rectangles of draperies to disguise ungainly windows. You may articulate the space by carefully positioning a painting on a wall or subdividing the floor with carpets and/or furniture. It is by the way you use these elements in some accord with the overall proportions of the space that you develop the unity that characterizes good design.

You can give a room character by subdividing the walls with furnishings so as to emphasize either the horizontals or the verticals or to balance the two equally. Verticals that soar way above a person's head, or even meet over it, as in a "Gothic" interior, create one kind of effect. Coordinated horizontals of shelving and worktops aligned at comfortable hand level under a low ceiling, with the main openness of the space lying just above waist height, give quite another. You can also emphasize deep window embrasures or bays to adjust the qualities of the space, breaking up what might otherwise be too simple a box.

Roofs

The way a roof is closed at the top plays an important part in creating the quality of interior spaces. Height and type of cover in relation to overall proportion is of the essence. Materials can be extremely important too, especially with regard to their acoustic and light-reflecting qualities.

There are four principal ways in which the interior of a roof can be handled: vault, open structure, girder, and ceiling.

Structural vaulting creates an organic and inviting sense of interior space. In Romanesque and Gothic Europe stone vaults were used for domestic architec-

9.16   PIETRO DA CORTONA and CIRO FERRI
Paintings on the vault of The Jupiter Room, Palazzo Pitti, Florence, 1643–46.

In Renaissance Italy ceilings were often painted with vivid pictorial imagery. While work of this quality and on this scale is hard to contemplate today, interior designers may yet turn to treating ceilings once more as an opportunity for aesthetic expression.

9.17 Vaulting in No Mosque, Shiraz, Iran, c.1600.

Brick vaulting has long been the accepted way in the Middle East of covering rooms and passageways; it lends a special sense of enclosure and a unique acoustical quality to the interiors it encloses. It is still practiced, unlike stone vaulting in the West.

ture as well as for churches. Nowadays it is hardly possible to use stone vaulting in the West save in extremely expensive, heavy structures such as banks and prisons. But in the Muslim countries of the Middle East and in Mexico, brick vaulting is still a standard technique for covering rooms and passageways; it gives the characteristic sense of enclosure and acoustic quality to the buildings of those countries.

Another way to treat the space cover is as an **open structure**. In the medieval houses and barns of England the interiors of wooden roofs were always left exposed, as were the undersides of upper floors. This may have had practical drawbacks, but the structures, with their weight-carrying brackets and complex lock joints were, and still are, interesting in themselves. In churches, Gothic roof carpentry was often carried to magnificent extremes of decoration.

Nowadays people who convert old barns or warehouses often make a feature of exposed roof support structures; and architects of modern houses in warm climates, such as Frank Lloyd Wright and Bruce Goff, have incorporated them purely for their aesthetic value. Much Californian domestic and "junk" architecture treats roof structure as a mode of aesthetic expression.

Various **girder structures**, which also give interesting interior effects, are used today for covering areas. "Space decks" made out of uniform strutting or cells are used to roof all kinds of industrial and public spaces. Their interest is limited by the fact that their shapes and rhythms are based upon identical repetition. If, however, the space to be roofed is irregular in plan, specially designed exposed girder patterns can be particularly fascinating.

By far the commonest way of covering a space is with a flat **ceiling** of panel, lath and plaster or board, concealing the roof space entirely. There have been periods when people took great interest in the aesthetic possibilities of their ceiling surfaces. In Scandinavia, for example, where the winters are long and grey, ceilings as well as furniture are often painted with flowers and birds. In Renaissance Italy ceilings were often painted with vivid pictorial imagery. Quite often the surface would be lined with panelling set in molded frames, sometimes quite elaborately carved. If such framing is deep the ceiling is then called **coffered**. Classical Roman coffering was done originally in vaults as a way of lightening the weight of the structure. But later it became a decorative feature, often painted and gilded.

From the Renaissance until the early twentieth century plaster ceilings were often decorated with quite elaborate relief designs, also in plaster. This involved techniques derived from Italy and used designs having Italian/classical overtones. Shaped coffering frames were made by running wooden profile templates along raised plaster masses whilst they were setting on the ceiling, or by precasting and then hanging them. More elaborate designs – often swags of flowers – were formed in wooden molds with details carved by hand once they were in position. There is no reason why some ceilings today should not be decorated in similar ways, perhaps with glass fiber components.

Floors

Few designers today bother much about floors. Far the simplest way of dealing with floors in public buildings is to cover them with parquet blockwork, either real or imitation, laid in schematic patterns, or with wall-to-wall carpet. Parquet tends to echo; carpet is acoustically dead – the deeper the pile, the deeper the hush. Of course there are other types of floor covering available, such as matting, or tiles made of cork, ceramic, or vinyl. In fact, the treatment of floors in a home can add greatly to the character and identity of a space – for example, by demarcating different areas with different floorings and arranging furnishings to match them.

The floor is our support and ultimate – even if indirect – contact with the earth. This is its symbolic value. Beautiful **tile** and **stone** floors have been common in many cultures, from the primitive to the most sophisticated. The examples we know best, perhaps, are Roman, Byzantine, and post-Byzantine mosaics; but similar floors inlaid with designs in cut colored stone have been made for interiors of all kinds, from modest homes to major public buildings. In Europe and the United States, in the late nineteenth century, they were often used for churches, hotels, banks, and museums. The ancient designs were based on commonly understood symbols; the later ones usually embody echoes of the earlier, for their antique connotations and prestige.

Tiles have been laid in patterns since the early Middle Ages. They can be of cut stone or ceramic – nowadays often of plastic or compressed cork. And although they are usually rectangular, they can be of other shapes that will fit closely together. You normally set them onto a solid floor in plaster or cement. Sometimes they can be carried part way up a wall or around a fireplace. Their function in temperate regions is to allow the floor to be cleaned easily, perhaps swilled down; but in hot countries they serve to keep the room cool.

Tiles are laid according to grid patterns, usually rectangular. They may all be of the same design and/or color. Or you can lay tiles of different color or design

9.18 THOMAS GORDON SMITH
Richmond Hill House, California, 1984.

Floors are often a neglected feature. Here a black concrete surface has been set with inexpensive fragments of marble to form a terrazzo in geometric patterns. The effect transforms the room.

in counterchange patterns, the commonest being the simple checkerboard black and white. Tiles may be glazed with patterns that run across from tile to tile so as to compose all-over designs. Many glazed tiles, from Byzantine and medieval times onward, carry extremely beautiful images. And in Muslim countries whole interiors have been lined with exquisitely patterned tiles glazed with beautiful colors and arranged to create a complex overall design.

The other important floor treatment is the patterned **carpet**. The history and symbolism of the carpet help to explain its appeal (see p. 71). Derived from central Asian coverings for the walls and floors of tents of nomadic peoples, it became the standard type of floor covering throughout the Middle East. Patterned knotted carpets were being exported from the Middle East to Europe in considerable numbers by the fourteenth century. The designs on most Middle Eastern carpets follow a particular type of symbolic imagery, which refers back to an ancient image of a garden paradise, anteroom to heaven, of which the peoples of central Asia dreamed. The stylized design treats the carpet as an enclosure watered by many streams, traversed by interlaced paths, bordered by trees, flowers, and birds and enclosing medallion-like beds filled with flowers.

European carpet-makers translated the flower garden on the floor into their own terms. As western garden design changed, so did western carpets. The original Muslim patterns of flower beds evolved into Baroque curlicues, reminiscent of stonework; but even when the concept of carpet as paradise finally disappeared in Europe, the floral imagery remained. Many modern carpets still depict flowers. But even if its design is completely abstract, any patterned carpet retains the potential of enhancing or enriching the space it occupies by references to the world of nature. Some famous modern artists have designed superb carpets, and abstract paintings have been used as inspiration for others. Even if a solid-color wall-to-wall carpet is chosen for a home, it can be punctuated by fine rugs which help to define the inner spaces.

In a public building, the floor covering is more problematic – quite apart from the practical considerations. Ornament becomes obtrusive the more emphatic and realistic it is. Few people share the same taste in patterns; so designers of public interiors tend to play safe and choose carpets of plain, relatively restrained colors, or those with subtle patterning. Since the carpet quite often provides the dominant color note in many offices and hotel areas, the designer has to be very careful to calculate correctly its emotive effects on the occupants.

Walls

Walls are the principal support for interior design. A number of modern architects have designed houses with walls consisting almost completely of transparent glass – in which case, of course, exterior views become the visual content of the walls. But usually this content is provided by things attached to or projecting from the walls which address the individual in terms of human scale and response.

The character of a wall emerges from the quality of its structure. You can make naked shutter-marked concrete, cut stone, handmade brick, or rough plaster features of the space they enclose, as was done in Frank Lloyd Wright's famous home and workshops called the "Taliesins" and is also done in many modern churches. Most walls today are made of flat plaster or board and are not meant

9.19

9.19   FRANK LLOYD WRIGHT
Living room at Taliesin, Spring Green, Wisconsin, 1925.

Naked shutter-marked concrete, rough or dressed stone, handmade brick, or rough plaster can be made features of the spaces they enclose. Frank Lloyd Wright exploited these effects in his Taliesin home and workshop.

9.20 and **9.21**   KISHO KURAKAWA
Nakagin Capsule Tower, Tokyo, 1972. Exterior and interior views.

There was a fashion during the early 1970s for prefabricated "living modules" of vacuum-formed fiberglass. Wall, floor, ceiling, sitting and working surfaces are continuously molded. The result is hardly inviting, but it is hard to see how such a tiny space could be made to work in any other way.

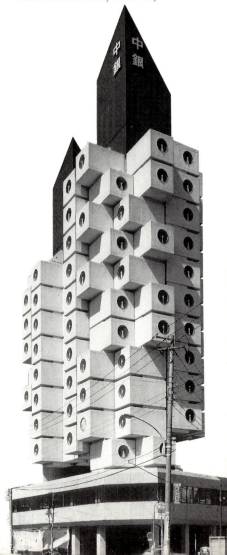

to claim much attention. But in museums, for example, walls may be deliberately neutral and plain. Some may be temporarily supported by movable structures; they may be curved or continuously undulating or have additional angles. Designers can use such devices in virtually any space. There was a fashion in the early 1970s for installing into supporting frames complete vacuum-formed fiberglass living "cells," whose continuously curved interiors, in which wall flowed into floor, ceiling, seats, recliners, and work surfaces, were designed according to a "nest" theory of living space.

In modifying any wall shape with subdivisions, the good designer takes care to relate the new work to the overall proportions of the space. The height of the space and the position and size of windows and doors can set problems for your sense of rhythm and proportion. It is all too easy for architects to dispense standard-size manufactured units of frame and board without considering their formal connection with the shape and size of the given space. The ideal solution is exemplified by the work of the Adam brothers, whose spacing of dadoes and plaster panelling and placement of harmoniously designed furniture were always integrated into the overall proportional scheme so as to generate live and varied rhythms along the entire wall area.

The treatment of wall surfaces is largely determined by the function of the interior space. There is a vast range of possibilities, each conveying its own special atmosphere and setting the tone for other furnishings. In medieval times it was customary in great houses to line large and drafty stone halls with wool tapestries woven in pictorial and heraldic designs. In more modest houses the walls themselves would be painted with patterns. The custom of lining walls with figured fabric of some kind has continued to the present day. Rich fabrics, such

as brocades, embellished elegant private and public rooms from the eighteenth century onward. Since at least the seventeenth century many people have used paper to line walls, either hand-painted or block-printed with patterns. Our modern wallpapers offer a huge variety of images. But it is possible to choose wallpapers without realizing properly the iconography and symbolism implicit in, say, their ribboned flower sprigs or hard Art Deco/Aztec shapes and colors. A good designer is always aware of the area of feeling towards which the symbolism reaches.

The plastic coverings often used to line reception areas and upper echelon offices to deaden their acoustics have their own deliberately neutral content. They convey the effect that the walls are a substantial containing environment which avoids any suggestion not only of the eccentric or cheap, but also of the individual or "unreliable."

One very important decision the designer has to make about wall coverings is how "busy" they should be in relation to the temperaments of those who will live with them. Some people like to be constantly stimulated by busy surfaces which keep active rhythms going just at, or below, the level of consciousness; others like exactly the opposite. In both homes and offices, this factor must be finely judged.

Lighting

One major problem with modern interiors is lighting. Direct overhead lighting may be harsh, but diffused lighting may destroy our sense of 3D inside the space. In most cases, both kinds of lighting must be used in some sort of combination.

One of the uses of overhead lighting is to prevent anyone from seeing what lies above it. In museum display, for example, you can use overhead lights both to accentuate specific exhibits and to cut down the apparent height of the ceiling. In the theater you can use lighting virtually to construct a stage space by defining the limits of the spectators' attention. Lighting with an upward throw that reflects from the ceiling, or that comes from many unfocused sources, may be useful in multi-purpose areas. These techniques can be adapted to domestic settings.

Light fittings themselves are quite often treated with some aesthetic care. We still live with echoes of previous centuries, when lighting was provided by candles. Their relatively feeble illumination was multiplied by means of mirrored wall sconces and chandeliers. In the eighteenth century chandeliers were festooned with strings of cut glass to multiply the light reflection. Chandeliers still have cultural prestige; and designers still make electric chandeliers for public spaces, often in a contemporary idiom.

The shapes of most modern light fittings immediately suggest the processes by which they were made, making a modernist virtue of economic fact. Fittings for tungsten bulbs are made of circular spun metal sheet and machine-molded glass and designed almost entirely in terms of pure schematic profile. Fluorescent tube, of course, can be made in straight or curved forms, and perhaps enclosed in plastic diffusers. With all these limitations virtually all one can do with lighting design is to adjust proportions, profiles, and layout, not only in terms of pure lighting quality, but also in terms of formal coherence.

9.22   WILLIAM MORRIS
Apple wallpaper, 1877. Victoria and Albert Museum, London.

Many of the beautiful wallpaper designs of William Morris are once more available, and designers can offer their clients a low-cost authentic Arts and Crafts "original."

9.23   THOMAS CHIPPENDALE
Design for a chandelier, c.1760. Victoria and Albert Museum, London.

The weak illumination provided by candles was multiplied many times over by 18th-century designs incorporating mirrors or cut glass to maximize reflected light.

9.24   DAVIDE MERCATALI and PAOLO PEDRIZZETTI
Lamp, *Basket*, 1985. Iron and aluminum, enamelled finish, double light-intensity switch. 25ins (64cm) high. Manufactured by Eleusi, Italy.

After a period of uninspired Functionalism in light fittings, designers are now producing lamps which exploit the sculptural opportunities they provide.

9.25   PAUL NASH
Bathroom for Tilly Losch, 1932. Recreation by the original constructors, for the exhibition *Thirties: British Art and Design before the War*, Hayward Gallery, London, 1980.

This elegant piece of Art Deco interior design shows what can be achieved by the thoughtful handling of light fittings, reflective and non-reflective surfaces to create a functional yet aesthetically pleasing bathroom.

9.23

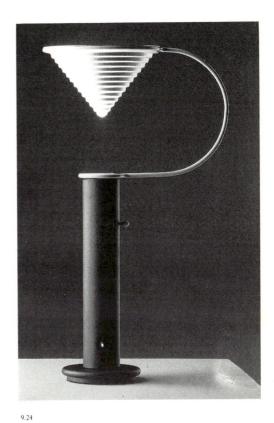

9.24

9.25

Acoustics

Acoustics is a special architectural science. Acoustic qualities are an important element in the character of any interior. Furnishings contribute by deadening echoes from walls and ceiling. Larger areas can be difficult. With modern PA systems speech is not so much of a problem, but music is much more difficult to deal with. Some halls incorporate elaborate relay-speaker systems into the ceiling structure. But most need careful arrangements of grids and slanting baffle boards suspended in the ceiling, both to absorb unwanted echoes and to distribute clear sound all over the auditorium. There is often enough leeway in the practicalities of such structures to allow for aesthetic planning that integrates them visually into the interior.

Some buildings, especially those with modern girder and concrete frames, suffer from unwanted resonance, noise, or vibration, which call for damping. Large open-plan offices are particularly vulnerable. You can vastly improve the lives of office workers by careful adjustment of acoustic levels to human tolerances, rather than to total deadness.

FURNITURE

Furniture is small-scale architecture. Its forms frequently parallel those of current architectural styles. In past epochs it could be designed to occupy specific places in a room – tall cabinets or console tables projecting from walls between windows, for example. Usually, for wealthy patrons, different pieces were at least designed *en suite* with each other, so that, for example, dining table, chairs, sideboard, and side tables followed a single style, with matching proportions and thematic decoration.

Individual pieces of furniture may possess a distinctly human expression, suggesting human attitudes and gestures. They may "threaten," "crouch," or

9.27

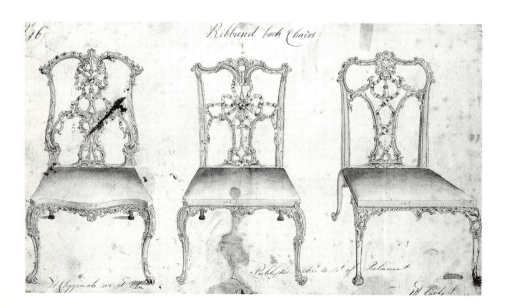

9.26 THOMAS CHIPPENDALE
Ribband Back Chairs, c.1754. Ink and gray wash, 7⅛ × 13⅜ (18.1 × 34cm). Published in the *The Gentleman and Cabinet-Maker's Director*, 1754, plate XVI. The Metropolitan Museum of Art, New York.

The famous 18th-century furniture maker Thomas Chippendale produced patterns for furniture that was at once both architectural and sculptural. Lightness and grace typify these designs.

"tower"; pieces lifted on slender legs may seem elegantly to "dance." The arrangement of furniture also articulates the space. This means that the designer must place furniture so that it not only permits ease of movement but also produces a sense of proportion and balance.

Furniture types

Although there are many types of furniture, in practice choice has always been limited. Each type combines four main elements, which are articulated and modified to complement each other in various ways, and may be elaborated decoratively. These elements are: the **platform**, a horizontal surface; the **support**, or leg; the enclosed **box**; and the vertical **frame**. Out of these the furniture designer strives to evolve beautiful structures.

Tables combine the platform with supports. The shape of the table top helps to determine the positions of the legs and whether they need to be connected by stretchers. They can be at each of four corners; or, for a circular table top, they may be a complex structural armature, a tripod, or a single stem mounted on splayed feet or running down into a pedestal.

Chairs are also platforms on supports, the simplest being stools and benches. Although usually smaller than tables, they have to carry far greater weight in relation to their size. They may have legs at their corners or pedestals of some kind, and their legs may need to be splayed and strengthened with stretcher bars. The back support fitted to the seat is a special version of the vertical frame or panel; but modern plastic chairs often combine seat and back in a single shape.

Upholstered furniture in principle descends directly from earlier all-wooden chairs and backed benches. The earliest were simply padded; later, the padding was augmented with springing, then with interlaced flexible webbing in both the horizontal and vertical planes to support cushioning. An important recent development has been the form, either hinged or molded in one piece to undulate with one or more comfortable reclining positions which is suspended in a cage-framework. Most office chairs now have adjustable seats and backs to adapt to individual body shapes and postures.

The chest is a box, often supported on feet, sometimes with a top lid. If a chest stands against a wall and has doors, it becomes a cupboard or cabinet; with sliding compartments, a chest of drawers. Usually a chest is rectangular, but it may be bow or ripple-fronted, or even circular. The front-facing elements of such pieces are an important focus for design. Handles and keyholes can be accentuated with carving or metal plaques. Vertical frames rising behind the top surface may carry, for example, mirrors or other ornament.

A desk is a combined table and chest, which is capable of considerable variation. Bookshelves are variants of table, box, and cabinet. Filing cabinets and lockers, even if they are made of metal, are still chests. Beds are a variety of platform, often with vertical frame and panel head and/or foot.

Vertical frames appear in several guises. Basically, a frame consists of extenders, constructed so as to hold a surface flat inside it. Often frames are decoratively treated, their surfaces being developed into interesting profiles. They hold window glass; they structure doors and door casings, holding panels of wood; they hold mirrors and pictures.

9.27   JONAS BOHLIN
Chair, Concrete, 1984. Steel frame, concrete panels. Edition of one hundred. 33ins (90cm) high, 22 × 19ins (57 × 50cm). Manufactured by Källemo, Sweden.

One might wonder whether concrete is really an ideal material for supporting a relaxed human body. Nevertheless, this chair has an undeniable "presence," with its suggestions of an austere and commanding throne.

A frame may also form the principal element of the screen, traditionally used for protection against drafts. Screens provide surfaces for artistic expression, in the form of painting, carving, or inlay. Some of the greatest Oriental paintings were executed on paper to be mounted on screens; and in Japan, for example, wooden screens have been, and still are, painted in colored and gold lacquer with landscape, animals, and human figures. In Europe, screens were made of painted leather and canvaswork embroidery in elaborate designs from the seventeenth century onward. Beautiful Art Deco lacquer screens were made in Paris in the 1920s. Nowadays artists of all kinds again paint screens. Less likely to be functional today – except sometimes as room dividers in open-plan interiors – screens can serve effectively as colorful and artistic focal points.

Furniture structure

The highest quality of furniture is usually a coherent casing structure, its visible parts – platform, side and front panels, and legs – being jointed together and finely finished. Cheaper furniture, however, may be constructed as a skeleton of coarse extenders carrying an industrially manufactured skin of less substantial boarding.

The style in which the components of furniture are cut and jointed plays a major part in its expression. So, too, does the surface finish. If the piece is made of thick-cut wooden members with visibly pegged joints, and the surface hand-finished fairly roughly and waxed, the effect may be strongly rustic. If all the joints are hidden by minute cutting, with fascia skirts used to conceal any under structure, the surface finished with fine French polishing, quite a different effect is created. As with architecture, the shapes and relative proportions of the component parts must be well integrated.

Slender round legs, for example, turned with necking, flanges, or spirals, need to be matched with compatible parts; broad S-curved legs with carved fronts and heavy ball-and-claw feet need other components similarly curved and carved to match them. Coherence of style is essential, and the furniture designer enters the realm of fine art by the leading of linear expression through the whole composition; by balance of parts, skillful use of proportional schemes, and surface finishes; by tactful and significant repetition of decorative motifs. Craftspeople who work from drawings prepared by others, as many eighteenth-century provincial furniture-makers did using Chippendale's published designs, achieve a quality of work proportional to their ability to articulate the stock of given elements.

A particular method of constructing furniture, very fashionable around 1900, was used for the style called **bentwood**. Long poles of wood – often ash – were steamed and bent into elaborate shapes. These were normally bolted together. The seats and backs of bentwood chairs, and even table tops, were generally made of woven cane.

Metals have been used for furniture in the past mainly for decoration such as inlay, or for hardware such as hinges, handles, and lockplates. But in the nineteenth century complete tables and chairs – sometimes highly ornate – were made of cast iron. Usually, because of the difficulty of casting iron, they were assembled from pieces each cast virtually in one plane. In the 1920s chromium-plated steel tubing began to be used to make the skeletons of Bauhaus-

9.28 ANDRÉ-CHARLES BOULLE Cabinet, late 17th century. Veneered on oak with ebony, purple wood, tortoiseshell and marquetry of various woods, pewter, brass, and copper. Supporting figures of pine, stained and partly gilt, bronze mounts, chased and gilt. 73¾ins (187cm) high, 88½ × 40ins (225 × 102cm). The Wallace Collection, London.

This masterpiece of the cabinet-maker's art shows off the skills of a wide range of craftsmen. Rare woods and expensive materials have been combined in an overall design of great distinction. Inlays include motifs of leaves, flowers, and insects, and the portrait medallion shows Louis XIV.

9.29 Burgundian armoire, in the manner of Hughes Sambin, c.1552. Walnut, carved, painted, and gilt, 97 × 61½ × 24ins (246.4 × 156.2 × 60.9cm). The Metropolitan Museum of Art, New York, Rogers Fund, 1925.

The intrinsic beauty of carved and polished walnut is here enhanced by areas of painting and gilding. Modern designers are turning once more to these examples and are rediscovering the opportunities offered by painted ornament on furniture.

inspired furniture. The tube was bent by machine into continuous shapes curved in 3D, which sustained weight by its own springy flexibility on platforms of, for instance, padded board laid across the tubing. Similar principles are still used today for furniture whose skeletons are made of bent and welded steel rod or square-section tube. The normal way of manufacturing these is to form, usually by mechanical pressure, the supporting skeleton of tube or rod designed to accept and transmit loads correctly, and then to weld, bolt, or bracket to this either sets of flat bands of synthetic board or sheets of plastic vacuum-molded to suitable shapes. Angle-iron gives the basic skeleton to millions of filing cabinets, desks and ranges of lockers made of pressed steel sheet.

Furniture decoration

All good hardwood surfaces will take polish. For a more decorative finish, much furniture is **veneered** (see p.30). The grain showing on successive slices can be laid in reverse direction to give almost symmetrical paired or quadratic figuring. Extremely elaborate designs can be composed by laying down cut sections of veneer from different woods; some of them perhaps stained. Patterns can be made in wood surfaces by laying into the veneer flat slips, either of metals, such as brass, or of distinctively colored wood, such as ebony or redwood.

Ornament on furniture can be a very important factor in any style. Purist admirers of antique furniture have held that beautiful grain, well brought out and patterned, of woods such as walnut, rosewood, and mahogany, is ornament enough; and that at most it should be pointed up by modest profiling and perhaps a few devices carved into the more solid members. But many magnificent ornamental techniques, including painted designs and motifs, have been applied to furniture down the ages, and modern designers are beginning to revive this practice.

Pieces of cast bronze ornament, often gilded and known as "ormolu," could also be inset or added to the surface of furniture. The theme of this ornament was usually flowers, fruit, and Rococo curlicues. Similar shapes can also be modelled on the surface in gesso – a mixture of glue and chalk, still used on elaborate picture frames. Furniture that was to be gilded was usually also painted first with a layer of white gesso, onto which the gold leaf was laid. These methods can be adapted to the surfaces and materials of present-day furniture.

A variety of other techniques for decorating furniture have been invented. One is **marquetry**: elaborate veneer patterns made of wood, bone, ivory, broken glazed ceramics, or colored glass. In the Far East quite large slices of beautifully veined stone resembling landscapes were often incorporated into table tops and seat backs. In the West entire table tops were made of fine marble.

Cresting is an important decorative element once used extensively in western furniture. It consists of widths of board added to and projecting beyond the tops of chairbacks, the top fronts of cabinets, the lower edges of tables, and the frames of mirrors. These are carved and pierced with elaborate profiles and surface ornament. The ornament follows the current decorative style and may be devised to continue into the surface ornament of the object. Cresting gives a piece a façade, a magnificent frontal aspect which may make it seem far larger and more important than it actually is. Great chairs in medieval halls were usually crested, and often surmounted with pinnacles as well. Much status-affirming eighteenth-century furniture was crested. Although cresting is unusual today, once one accepts the idea that it can be a worthwhile design element, there is no reason at all why modern designers should not use it in their own idiom.

Utensils

Water and food containers have always had a fundamental importance in every society. The oldest and commonest material for them has been ceramic, although metal and wood have also been used. The tall containing jar and the open bowl are the earliest and most basic forms. Although essentially utilitarian, they have given rise to beautiful elaborations of what one may call the "architecture of the vessel." People have always felt, consciously or unconsciously, a sense of the sacredness of the acts of eating and drinking and also a close personal relationship with their vessels. To express the symbolic value of these objects, potters and silversmiths have often given them magical, protective, and ceremonial shapes and decoration, some of which convey the idea of fertility.

The commonest techniques in making any utensil elegant and ceremonial are to elaborate its form by lobing, fluting, and trimming; to give it a florid, gestural shape; and to add decoration to various parts of it. One can raise jars and bowls on tall feet or narrow, bulbed stems to give them their ceremonial quality, as in the beautiful bowls and wine cups used by the ancient Greeks and the goblets used by medieval lords, from which our modern wineglasses derive. Such methods help to develop the expressive form of any vessel.

The decoration on jars tends to be vertically arranged, echoing their shape. Drinking glasses, too, may have decoration that is mainly external. But shallow bowls and plates are usually decorated from their centers across their inner surfaces and rims.

The importance of meals as ritual has always caused people to decorate their utensils with emblems and subject designs which have become symbols of status.

9.30   JOHN FLAXMAN Jr
Rum kettle with *The Dancing Hours*, figures originally modelled in 1778. Wedgwood, black basalt (high-fired stoneware). Wedgwood Museum, Barlaston, Stoke-on-Trent.

The makers of porcelain garnitures in the 18th century catered only for the rich; not until Thomas Wedgwood developed cheaper alternatives could the middle classes afford refined and elegant ware like this.

In the seventeenth and eighteenth centuries, when only the wealthy in Europe could afford genuine blue and white Chinese porcelain wares, the less prosperous used faience imitations made in Delft or Lambeth. The ideal, then as now, was to have uniform sets of tableware, with serving dishes, jugs, plates, cups, and saucers matching in proportion, shape, and design. For rich families the porcelain makers and metalsmiths also produced pieces of splendid fantasy and invention. In the houses of the nobility ceremonial meals were eaten at tables with huge symbolic centerpieces – great assemblies of precious metal or splendid porcelain figures – and the food was served from side tables decorated in similar fashion. Drawing rooms also were often embellished with urns and other containers made of precious metal or porcelain.

Today we treasure remnants from such costly garnitures from Meissen, Sèvres, or Wedgwood, setting them out in museums or on display shelves or tables at home. Our metalsmiths and ceramic artists have to take account of this weight of tradition and produce display pieces that match expectations yet count as independent works of art. Many potters, for example, have refused to make expensive single pieces, and continue to follow regional pottery traditions in making uniform types of ware for domestic use in the kitchen and at table. Others even make ironically unusable versions of traditional display pieces expressly to defeat those expectations. One famous recent venture, the huge range of feminist place settings by Judy Chicago, adapted the entire dining convention as an ironical symbol.

In cutlery, too, conventions are strong, because they are obviously useful. One needs sharp knives in the kitchen and more elegant ones at table. In medieval times people used one knife for all purposes, and spoons and forks of wood along with bowls and platters. We still sometimes use wooden utensils for bread and salads, for example; specialist craftspeople make them to feed our romantic rusticity. Knives used to be composed of parts – forged blades with added handles. Now entire sets of knives, forks, and spoons are machine-stamped from metal, sometimes with wood or plastic cheeks added to the handle.

9.31 JUDY CHICAGO
Virginia Woolf place setting from *The Dinner Party*, 1979. China paint on porcelain, ceramics, and needlework, plate diameter 14ins (35.6cm).

The conventions of dining are used for ironical effect in this famous and powerful feminist work. "Traditional" women's crafts – pottery, needlework – were carried out on a huge and collective scale to create the setting for an imaginary reunion dinner for the great women of history.

CHAPTER TEN
ENVIRONMENTAL DESIGN

THE SHAPED ENVIRONMENT

Architecture is the art of designing environmental structures and spaces, both interior and exterior. Their forms are experienced by people from a multiplicity of viewpoints – near and far, walking and sitting, observing and touching. Environmental design begins with architecture and extends into garden, landscape, and cityscape, according to the degree to which human beings can impose intelligible patterns upon them. The balance between the practical, functional aspects of a design and its aesthetic aspects is especially difficult to strike. All too often, we the public are obliged to live in surroundings whose appearance is largely accidental. Usually an architect is able to apply his or her own aesthetic criteria only to a single building – or sometimes as far as the garden of a house. Occasionally a major design commission may include a large ground-level concourse or a stretch of cityscape such as a spacious plaza. But, landscape design apart, opportunities to apply overall conceptions like these are rare. The architect usually has to conceive the unit so as to fit within a space determined by factors such as street plans and property boundaries, or make something interesting out of a more-or-less neutral patch of ground.

Like any other form of design, architecture employs the aesthetic elements of shape, proportion, rhythm, contrast, and combination; but it is also conditioned – far more than other arts – by natural forces and practical considerations. Because of its responsibility for finding comprehensive solutions to complex practical problems, architecture rarely takes giant, "revolutionary" steps into the unknown, even when it is exploring the possibilities of new materials.

Form and expression

As we scan our environment we synthesize the rhythms of projections, interpreting undulations, angles, enclosures, variations, punctuations, breaks, steps, and

10.1   Aerial view of the village of Labba Zanga, Mali.

The houses and granaries of the Dogon are laid out in complex, organic, and harmonious patterns; "modern" rectangular roofs appear among the round thatched buildings. Traditional communities all round the world arrange their living environments in seemingly haphazard yet actually pragmatic ways.

10.2   ICTINUS and CALLICRATES
The Parthenon, Athens, completed 438 BC. Detail of the west front.

A detail of the massive masonry shows how precise numerical/proportional designs come to be realized at the level of craft within the tolerances of human skill.

10.3   ANDREA PALLADIO
Palazzo Porto-Colleoni, c.1565–1569. Elevation of front (left), and courtyard (right). Dark siena and red siena drawing on paper, 11⅓ × 14⅝ins (28.8 × 37.3cm). Royal Institute of British Architects, London.

This architectural drawing shows clearly how the design is conceived in terms of rhythmically spaced solid volumes. The height of one is based on two successive Golden Sections, the other on a grid of squares.

shadows in terms of mass and hollow, weight and balance, continuity and interval. We understand space in terms of such relationships. Environmental design uses these formal concepts to order our surroundings, shaping materials – stone, brick, concrete, steel, glass, even trees and plants – and arranging them to generate spatial images.

Goethe called architecture "frozen music"; and like music and the other arts, architecture can evoke in viewers multiple responses that reflect their own bodies in action: "springing" arches, "soaring" domes, "leaping" and "spreading" vaults. Significantly, we always feel that our buildings *rise*, whereas in reality they press down. We can set up special relationships between different elements: A envelops B; B towers over C; N arches delicately several times over the space limited by X and Y; block-like B is counterbalanced by elongated C; we can go across and disappear behind Z; and so on. By this kind of reading we can grasp a whole series of different orders of form and relation implied in a piece of design.

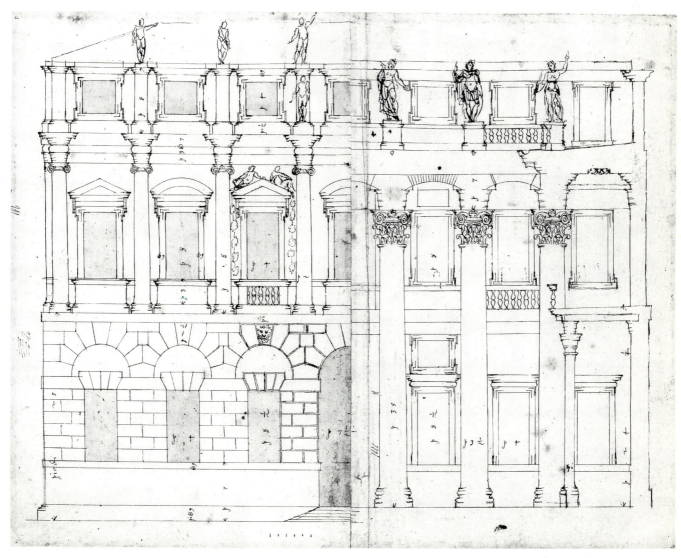

10.3

ARCHITECTURE

Dwellings

The earliest form of architecture, dwellings originated very close to nature. In southern France, Sicily, and the south-western United States, some people still live in caves – which at least offer respite from the heat. Whole communities have occupied large sites with natural caves or overhangs which they may then have quarried out and walled in. In Apulia, in southern Italy, stone houses are still roofed with great cones of flat stones piled without mortar, the houses of extended families running together like miniature mountain ranges. Elsewhere one finds clay houses, fired with brushwood like giant pots – predecessors of the molded plastic "dwelling units" evolved in the 1960s. Other houses are huge woven baskets, thatched. There are houses chiselled out of single boulders, and houses whose door frames consist of single flat boulders chiselled into openings, anticipating the gateways used in courtyards of the Chinese Ming period. Some peoples have lived beneath ground level, in rooms around big open courtyards entirely excavated into dry rock plateaus. The circular **center post** enclosure

10.4 Trulli houses at Alberobelli, Bari, Italy.

An Apulian hill village, whose linked houses are roofed with cones of dry heaped stones: a fine example of a surviving vernacular architecture.

10.5 Adobe houses, Taos Indian Pueblo, New Mexico. Late 19th-century photograph.

The outside walls are faced with mud plaster applied by hand. For safety, the different levels are reached by ladders which can easily be pulled up.

10.4

10.5

around a tree is still seen in northern and eastern Europe, once also in India and South-east Asia. Sometimes such structures house whole families. Often their floors are dug into the ground, which then provides the walls; but they may also be walled with laid stone, wickerwork, or timber.

One characteristic of "primitive" buildings is that they tend to form **clusters**. Each cluster develops naturally, as younger generations of a family grow, marry and make new homes, yet continue to work over the same land. Family life gives security, as does the village for groups of families. Villages have often evolved by a preliminary process of infilling between original clusters, which we can often trace. Both cluster and village often developed within the organic, bulging perimeter of a wall, which protected the community against the aggression of neighbors and limited its sprawl. Defensible perimeters tend naturally toward the minimum length for an enclosure, which is a circle, not a rectangle. Rectangular planning comes as a result of evolving social power structures. On hills or hogbacks, villages normally developed along the ridge-line, like many Italian hill villages. Lowland villages have been laid out along one dominant road. In these cases the houses have tended to be arranged end-to-end, perhaps sharing a common roof-line, to change eventually into what we know as the terraced house or row house with its true axis at right angles to the street frontage.

In so-called "primitive" societies powerful families inhabit large multi-family dwellings, which stand separate from each other, as among the tribal peoples of Sumatra or in northern Japan. In Europe a similar hierarchical ordering of society produced the manor house with outbuildings at the center of its lands. At the other end of the social scale, peasants lived in humble one-family dwellings, although they might in some places live in joined-up rows of cottages, such as one still sees in many British villages. In Britain, where land is relatively scarce, most people today live either in terraced houses, which range from the sordid to the splendid, or in semi-detached, or duplex, houses. In the United States, where land is plentiful, the one-family or detached house is the norm, and has been since colonial days. Many modern American houses, especially in prosperous neighborhoods, serve as vivid expressions of the individual taste of the owners.

Hall and monument

A public building has two complementary aspects: as accommodation – hall – and as demonstration of status – monument. The two may be treated separately in theory; in practice they may be combined.

The hall is one of the earliest and most important structures in many architectural traditions, including our own, serving a number of social purposes, from simply protective to political, religious, industrial, and ceremonial. An outstanding characteristic of major modern architecture is its emphasis on large, functioning, internal spaces. This has depended upon the development of new materials and methods, which allowed the size of covered areas to be greatly increased without incurring unbearable penalties of weight and cost. Pre-nineteenth century hall-architecture depended upon skilled craftspeople shaping and structuring natural materials. During the later nineteenth century, however, mass production methods were increasingly applied in building, using materials best suited to them: cast iron, forged steel, reinforced concrete, and very large sheets of glass. Architects were then able to design huge space-covering structures in terms of standard components, each one produced in calculated numbers, which could then be assembled according to a given procedure.

The earliest monument of this mass-production architecture was the Crystal Palace, built for the Great Exhibition of 1851, held in London. With its hundreds of identical iron pillars, beams straight and arc-curved, brackets, frames, and acres of glass, this was a truly revolutionary building. The great early railway stations developed the principle, requiring special sets of pillars and cantilever girders which covered huge areas by relying upon the tensile properties of metal. The Crystal Palace had no monumental frontage; the ends of its aisled hall shape were simply closed off. The railway stations very often had monumental facades added, in an accepted style, such as the neo-Gothic St Pancras Station and adjacent hotel, in London. Only gradually did it come to be accepted that the hall could be, in effect, its own monument, as today great structural halls are. Among them are Buckminster Fuller's geodesic structures, such as the Houston Astrodome and huge parabolic concrete shells, such as the TWA Terminal at Kennedy Airport, which is supported on a few girder feet. Their internal subdivisions are light, independent, and adaptable.

A monument is a public declaration in visual form. Often it is a solid memorial, reminding society of something centrally important to it. The com-

10.6 and **10.7**   JOSEPH PAXTON
Great Exhibition Building (Crystal Palace), Hyde Park, London, 1851. Perspective, and the raising of the transept roof ribs. Steel engravings from *The Illustrated London News*, 1850 and 1851.

The Crystal Palace first demonstrated how major architecture could be assembled from prefabricated standard components, in this case of cast iron and glass. The module of the entire building was derived from the proportions of the largest sheet of glass it was then practicable to produce – 49 × 30ins (124 × 76cm).

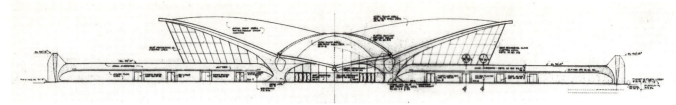

10.8

10.9

10.10

10.8, 10.9, and **10.10**   EERO
SAARINEN
Trans World Airlines International
Terminal, John F. Kennedy Airport,
New York City, 1956–62. Architect's
drawing of south elevation, exterior and
interior views.

The curvilinear exterior is carried
through into interior mezzanines and
inner structures which are, in effect,
sculptures. It is both hall – a functional
building for an airline and its customers
– and monument – a statement of a
corporation's vision of its role and its
future.

monest monuments are pillars, obelisks, plinths, long walls, and massive ornamental gateways, sometimes bearing statues, for example, of heroic victors and
other figures symbolizing triumph, peace, public sorrow, or prosperity. The
monument is meant to be looked at, not inhabited, though some monuments
contain their central image within a hall where it may be visited with reverence
– as in the Taj Mahal and the Lincoln Memorial. The point about the monument
is its emphatic rhetorical expression. Monuments can commemorate a religious
achievement – as, for instance, some Jain temples do in India, and as Christian
churches, in a sense, commemorate the Triumph of the Cross. They may also
express political or philosophical ideas. The Eiffel Tower is an intentional
monument to nineteenth-century engineering and economic power; the Statue
of Liberty, to a political idea; the Watts Towers in Los Angeles to a more personal
aim.

In later nineteenth- and early twentieth-century functional and domestic
architecture, the monument aspect is by no means abolished. The colossal
concept – drawn but never built – of Le Corbusier's *Plan Voisin*, composed of
vast vistas of concrete blocks of apartments, was intended as the rhetorical and
monumental presentation of an egalitarian democracy. Many "futuristic" concepts
have been designed supposedly to meet the demands of an exploding population,
using available engineering techniques; but the drawings show that they are also

10.11   GEORGE GILBERT SCOTT
The Albert Memorial, Kensington
Gardens, London, 1863–72.

The structure serves as a fantastic
canopy for the statue of Prince Albert;
the statue provides the justification for
the structure. It is a piece of public
mourning and political rhetoric: the
sculptured decoration refers to the
military and cultural achievements of
the British Empire.

10.12

10.13

10.12 LE CORBUSIER
Model of the *Plan Voisin* for Paris, 1925.

Le Corbusier's plan for an integrated city was never realized, save in drawings and – as here – a model. Nowadays we seriously doubt the validity of such grandiose and monumental schemes, though similar complexes have been built.

10.13 LÚCIO COSTA and OSCAR NIEMEYER
Brasilia, Brazil, begun 1956. Aerial view.

A city conceived and built from scratch deep in the Brazilian hinterland, to serve as the capital of this huge country. Administrative staff to serve the machinery of government are accommodated in these identical functional units.

10.14 LE CORBUSIER
Chapel of Notre-Dame-du-Haut, Ronchamp, France, 1950–4.

This view of one end of the great roof, supposedly derived from a crab shell, shows the monumental sculptural qualities of the building.

intended as monuments to a kind of science-fiction idealism, which may or may not correctly anticipate the future.

One artistic manifestation of the building-as-monument had a strong influence on architecture in Germany in the 1920s, and has been resurfacing recently, notably in the United States. This is the expressive fantasy piece, many unbuilt and perhaps unbuildable. Perhaps the most important fantasy artist was Hermann Finsterlein. His work consisted of drawings and 3D models which were, effectively, sculptural maquettes for colossal pieces. Pragmatic architecture can indeed benefit from such work of the free imagination, although most examples that are eventually realized tend to be the results of one patron's initiative – often his or her home.

Le Corbusier's chapel of Notre-Dame-du-Haut at Ronchamp, built in 1950–4, with its famous "crab shell" roof, is, externally, a monumental sculpture in this fantasy vein. So are some of Erich Mendelsohn's fashionably "dynamist" buildings of the 1920s, whose exterior shells resemble the streamlined fairings of aircraft – echoed in some recent Californian buildings.

Articulation of inner and outer

Architectural volumes, of course, have both inner and outer aspects. Which of these is to be emphasized is usually apparent in the architect's first sketches. The choice between them is commonly determined by the special requirements for the building. A structure that, for example, is designed to cover a very large area for colossal audiences, such as Pier Luigi Nervi's exhibition hall in Turin or Kenzo Tange's Olympic indoor swimming pool in Tokyo, will solve its primary problem of sheltering, and then rely for its external effect upon its scale and our understanding of its visible structure. Inner and outer are simply two views of the same engineering fabric. In contrast, the massively monumental stone-built banks, hotels, and offices of the early 1900s in Europe and the United States provided equally magnificent but distinctive internal spaces. Their designers thought of both primarily in terms of the balance of solid masses.

The greatest architectural works articulate formally both inner and outer aspects by means, above all, of consistent proportion and thematic development. One instance of combined space design paradigmatic in western architecture is Alberti's Church of Sant' Andrea in Mantua. Its façade is incomplete yet amounts to a set of variations, not simply upon the theme of the interior arcading but also upon the ground plan. The whole building is full of rhythmic subtleties of form carried by careful scaling even down to the coffering of the vaults. Most important of all, it combines in one composition a variety of forms, distinguished by contrasts between – among other themes – the rectangular and circular, the stepped angular projection and the smooth continuity, each of which is stated overtly in the decoration of the façade. Resolutions of the contrasts are carried through in the host of subsidiary forms, including relief patterns. And, of course, the interior can be read as a continuous dialectic between mass and void, each helping to define the character of the other.

Successful buildings resolve such thematic contrasts into unities and, by using techniques of variation, reconcile outer and inner volumes without eliminating their identity. In Gaudí's church of the Sagrada Familia in Barcelona the dynamic linearism of the Art Nouveau style weaves inner and outer surfaces into a continuous fabric. In many western buildings the internal subdivisions are carefully demarcated externally and on the frontage by geometrical formal and proportional schemes. Windows may be decorated with motifs based upon the mode of structural support, the pillar and arch, which appear inside as well as outside.

10.15   ERICH MENDELSOHN
The Einstein Tower, Berlin-Neubabelsberg, East Germany, 1919–24.

Built by the German government as an observatory and laboratory for Albert Einstein, this rare example of Expressionist architecture seeks to symbolize the poetry and mystery of the unexplored universe.

10.16   KENZO TANGE
National Stadium for the 1964 Olympic Games, Tokyo.

The roofs are suspended from huge single cables, guyed and braced out into spirals. Their function is purely that of a sheltering hall.

10.17 and **10.18**   LEONE BATTISTA ALBERTI
Church of Sant'Andrea, Mantua, begun 1470. West front and interior.

The interior is developed formally from themes and proportions established by the façade. The building exemplifies the integration of the aspects of monument and hall.

10.17

10.18

Façade and ornament

Many more commonplace buildings also strive toward monumentality, and the external imagery of the façade may be the principal focus of the architect's art. Façade simply means "face."

Just as people prepare their own façades, by means of hairstyles, make-up, clothing, and jewellery, to make a favorable impression, so buildings present façades to the public on behalf of their occupants. The tribal houses of South-east Asia, with their towering ranks of horned skulls, demonstrate that the family has been wealthy enough to sacrifice all those buffalo. The palaces and houses of the West may be fronted with towers, splendid gates, and porticos symbolizing strength, and may bear the heraldic arms and crests of nobility from whom the family claims descent; the use of classical arcades and pediments may be intended to suggest their classic moral virtues. In some places, however, façades may be

10.19 ANTONI GAUDÍ
Cathedral of the Sagrada Familia, Barcelona, begun 1883.

Gaudí began this strange complex in 1883 in recognizably Gothic style. As work slowly progressed, increasingly biomorphic forms appeared; spires rose like living coral. The building was far from completion when Gaudí died in 1926, and work continues to this day.

10.20 West front of Amiens Cathedral, France, 1220–1250.

The three west doors follow the pattern of the ancient Roman triumphal arch. From the terraces above the figures of saints look down, while the upper stories and spires reach up toward heaven.

developed only slightly or not at all, perhaps in accord with conventions of social modesty and constraint. Some Middle Eastern peoples design their homes around inward-facing courtyards. Terraced houses in cities may each offer only a modest frontal area, the terrace itself offering a unified façade on behalf of all the units.

The question of "truth" in relation to the façade has been one of the central issues in the history of modern architecture, largely because the ornament on nineteenth-century architecture, against which Modernist architects reacted, was often elaborated to an extreme degree. Forms were multiplied not for structural, thematic, expressive, or proportional reasons, or to define external space, but simply for conspicuous display, which came to seem immoral and, in a profound sense, false.

Two familiar types of European building are universally acknowledged as having the quality of "truthfulness": the medieval cathedral and the sixteenth-century Italian palace. In their different ways, these two styles of façade fulfill two important criteria: they develop themes derived from the structure of the building, and they state the meaning of the building in symbolic terms, so as to connect it with the life of the public and enhance the space it confronts.

Medieval cathedrals, both Romanesque and Gothic, were given façades based on the ancient Roman triumphal arches that still stood in the old Imperial Roman provinces in France and Germany. They thus symbolized both the classical heritage of the Roman Church and its triumphant presence in the world. These façades were not simply tacked onto the fronts of the churches but integrated with their structure; they evolved complexes of form derived thematically from elements of the basic shape. Like the triumphal gateway, the façade has three entrance doors – a large central door flanked by two smaller ones. The arches of the doors reflect the inner vault-structures and proportions of nave and aisles. They also link the circular window, placed above the central door, to the rectangular layout. In many Gothic cathedrals these arches enclose sculptured panels called tympanums and are crowned by lofty triangular frames reflecting the triangular sections of the roof. The proportions of the curved arches reconcile the main circles, triangles, and rectangles, as well as rehearsing the manner in which the weight of the roofs and towers is carried. The ornament derives from and elaborates the basic formal themes. Symbolically the door serves as a transition between the common world and the "Kingdom of God," and the statues of prophets and saints lining the passage symbolize the doctrine that leads through judgment to salvation.

The sixteenth-century Italian palace may have only a relatively modest rectangular entrance, partly in deference to its traditional function as fortress. But the proportions of the door-frame may give the key to those of its rectangular internal structure of courtyards, halls, and passageways. The positioning and scale of arched and pedimented windows reveal the height of the interior stories –

10.21 MICHELOZZO DI BARTOLOMMEO
Palazzo Medici-Riccardi, Florence, 1444–59.

The lowest story has rusticated masonry, suggesting strength. The upper stories, eaves, and all the windows follow careful geometrical and proportional layout that is evident even in this foreshortened view.

10.22   KISHO KURAKAWA
Takara Beautilion, Expo 70, Osaka, Japan.

The external skeleton of steel tube carries living-capsules. It is capable of being indefinitely extended, new components being simply bolted on, with many possible arrangements of the capsules and the empty spaces between them.

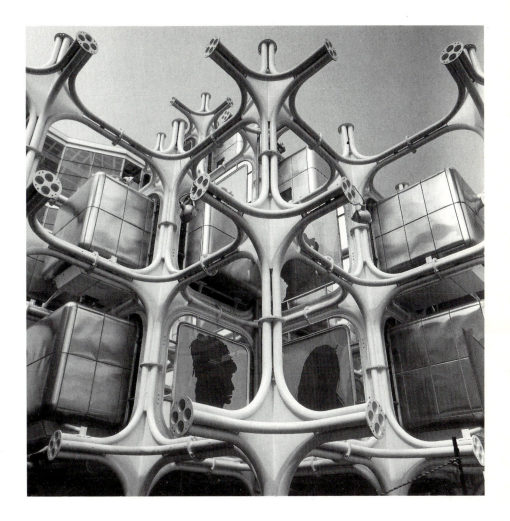

which may be immense. Rustication of the ground story suggests the strength of the rock from which the masonry comes. Everywhere the referential symbolism of Classicism prevails, down even to the proportions of details, which the learned architects probably derived from the writings of the ancient Roman architect Vitruvius, and which made these buildings powerful statements of the ethos of their time.

The role of ornament on a façade became controversial in the nineteenth century. An influential critic of that time, John Ruskin, rejected ornament for functional buildings, but accepted that it could be used on certain structures, where its beauty and expense could convey the owners' pride in their property. The Viennese architect Adolf Loos, writing in the 1920s, condemned ornament outright as a "crime". He was thinking of the pretentious ornament which covered the façades of modest apartment houses on the Vienna Ringstrasse. Loos saw its purpose as false to the building and laying spurious claims to social status. In his own buildings Loos developed special kinds of what he considered proper decoration, which was strictly limited to revealing the proportional systems of the building and the qualities of its materials. The façade, in his view, should function in exactly the same way. This became an ideal of the Modernist movement.

What, then, can the façade be for us in the late twentieth century? Inevitably, the way an architect places a doorway is a natural focus of attention, and what we see and experience as we enter a building still constitutes a major part of the

10.23 HANS HOLLEIN
Façade of the Schullin Jewelry Shop,
Vienna, 1975.

This marble frontage could have been
added to virtually any structure. Its
design is based on segments of circles
centered at points within a system of
subdivided squares.

statement made by any building. We need still to question the truthfulness and
purpose of a façade. Recently architects have begun to develop quite elaborate
façades, even lightheartedly adding non-structural features, simply to give a
building individuality or public appeal. A new museum located in open space
may have an immensely wide, strongly textured frontal wall, unbroken save for
a small semicircular entry off-center. A house in a hot climate may feature deeply
recessed and shaded entries, and windows shadowed by long eaves or by deep
coffered trellises that offer coolness. Another building may present an external
cage structure, with enclosed volumes hung inside; yet another may feature the
blunt ends of its construction girders projecting through a frontage entirely of
glass to give an effect reminiscent of modern sculpture. Even if the façade seems
to be refusing to make a strong statement, that in itself may be a statement of the
value of outward reticence, combined perhaps with an intent to surprise by the
interior. The street entrance to a hotel, say, may reveal very little externally –
possibly because of the limitations of its siting – and reserve all its impact for the

lobby. Conversely, it is now commonly accepted that a purely practical kind of shop may operate behind an elaborately designed façade whose function is to attract the right kind of customers. Such a façade may even rate as a virtually independent work of art.

Post-Modernist ornament

Post-Modernism has deliberately returned to the principle of adding ornament onto façades and elsewhere, including interiors. Much of this ornament is distinctly playful, and drawn from the repertoire of mass culture. Bright colored projecting windows and railings, decoratively designed gateways and gables, undulating glazed screens along frontages have all become familiar features. Borrowings and quotations from older styles and from Pop Art proliferate – geometrized, simplified, often vastly enlarged and added arbitrarily. These include mock pillars, dolmen-like porticos, rows of huge golden balls. Unconventional and varied claddings and finials may be added to otherwise conventional Modernist structures; a conspicuous example is Philip Johnson's AT&T Building in New York, an otherwise simple block with fine-cut stone cladding which is surmounted by a colossal, simplified cresting adapted from Chippendale furniture. This kind of decoration adds considerably to cost, so is usually commissioned only by wealthy people and organizations who can afford to make an architectural impact. The Public Services Building in Portland, Oregon, was originally designed to have a massive canopy-like projection for its façade: but this proved too expensive, so cheaper 2D decoration was substituted, consisting of a vast colored facing like

10.24 and **10.25** MICHAEL GRAVES
Public Services Building, Portland, Oregon, 1979–82. Perspective drawing, 1980, and view.

The architect's perspective shows the original intention of adding elaborate and jokey Post-Modernist decorations of gigantic swags and bows. Cost, and popular resistance, resulted in these being toned down on the finished building to virtually two-dimensional stylized motifs.

10.24

10.25

a broadly stylized eighteenth-century ribbon with bows. The structure now stands revealed as a normal girder-box office block, surmounted by the usual service gear concealed in a mock pillared shrine on the roof.

Many Post-Modern buildings – for example, in Japan – add together cuboid blocks of emphatically different sizes. Apartment buildings are built with ripple-fronts and undulating eaves-lines. A complex such as James Stirling's Neue Staatsgalerie in Stuttgart uses spectacular sloping walls of varied stone, vast ramps, and circular courtyards, whose walls are pierced irregularly with openings upon external or internal vistas, the circulation pattern being marked by bright red and blue painted handrails.

High Tech reaction

The whimsicality of much Post-Modernist ornament has produced a strong reaction in favor of a quite different ornamental style, often called High Tech, a descendant of Functionalism. This style deliberately exposes its purely engineering solutions to the problems of enclosing spaces. Many buildings, such as Richard Rogers' Lloyds Building in London, now exhibit externally not only their steel girder and truss structures but also their intestine-like service ducting. Inside, the flooring girders may be painted in bright colors. Such exposed components have

10.26   RICHARD ROGERS and Partners
Headquarters for Lloyd's, London, 1978–86.

All the essential ducting for this big office block is carried on the exterior and treated as a decorative feature, lending interest to what might otherwise have been just another big business tower.

10.27   JAMES STIRLING and MICHAEL WILFORD
New building and chamber theater for the Staatsgalerie, Stuttgart, 1977–84.

Decorative features are restrained to avoid conflict with the works of art in this open space. The banding and detailing of the massive masonry suggests Renaissance and ancient architecture. The pillar and mock gateway are entirely functionless.

10.26

the practical advantage of being easily accessible and replaceable. Interior elevator structures and machinery may also be on display and brightly painted as part of a color-scatter scheme. Vast storage areas, like that by Norman Foster in Swindon, Wiltshire, may be roofed with girdered transparent sheets suspended by cable and rod, in the manner of suspension bridges, from tall, brightly painted masts, stabilized by further cables, that suggest the rigging of sailing ships. Such structures are, in effect, huge adaptable halls that can accommodate any activity or static installation inside their airy, light-filled spaces. They have no real façades.

That this kind of treatment is meant to be, in a sense, ornamental is made clear by the many vigorous statements of their architects. They deliberately display an imagery of functional science, calling the attention of a scientifically educated and aware public to the elegance of their ideas. However, it is questionable whether these buildings offer a genuine solution to the aesthetic problem of valid ornament, since they do not allow more than one reading of their engineering image, and so do not develop true visual metaphor.

10.28 NORMAN FOSTER and Associates
Distribution centre for Renault UK Ltd, Swindon, Wiltshire, 1983.

The masts and guys of the space-roofing structure cover an adaptable interior space. Internal subdivisions play no part in the engineering. The structure can be extended indefinitely, its interior being closed off by lightweight glass panels.

ARCHITECTURAL PLANNING

In most countries there are more or less strict building and industrial environmental regulations that govern design relationships between window area, light levels, volume, height, and density of occupation, as well as service criteria such as access, escape, water, waste disposal, and temperature control. To relate all these to site-plan and cost, especially in cities, is a matter of complex calculation. These factors help to ensure the standardization of certain specific procedures for handling forms in space. These procedures are then used in routine ways which make experimental architecture relatively easy to conceive and execute. One method is structural, one conceptual. **Structural methods** now rely upon almost infinitely adaptable steel rod, girder, tube, and bar, sheet metal, and poured concrete in the form of post, beam, and arch, plus thin but rigid walling materials. The computer readily calculates optimum engineering/economic shapes. **Conceptual methods** are expressed in the graphic techniques used for 2D planning.

Conceptual methods

The routines for producing architecture in the office and of teaching it in the studio depend heavily on 2D thought. They arise naturally from geometrical outlining of plans and elevations according to right-angled coordinates laid out on rectangular sheets, using projections, including isometric and axonometric (see pp. 179–82). Three-dimensional computer images, now much used, follow essentially similar procedures. The "content" of such minimal graphic imagery consists principally of notation of measurements along axes to define areas as the edges of imaginary planes. The measured plane has thus become the prime characteristic of design.

10.29 THEO VAN DOESBURG and CORNELIS VAN EESTEREN *Color Construction (Project for a Private House)*, 1923. Gouache, 22½ × 22½ins (57.2 × 57.2cm). The Museum of Modern Art, New York, Edgar Kaufmann Jr. Fund.

This shows very clearly the outstanding character of much Modernist architecture as an assemblage of planes at right angles to each other, proportionally varied.

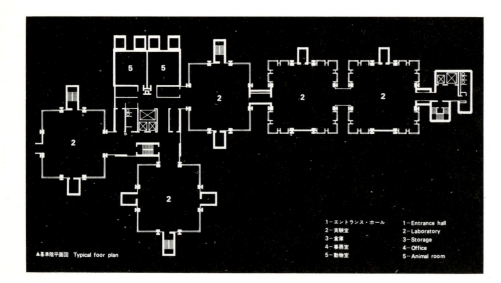

10.30 and **10.31**   LOUIS KAHN
Medical Research Building, University
of Pennsylvania, 1958–60. East
elevation and plan.

The building is developed upwards
from its ground plan; in fact, it could
equally have developed into other forms
under the control of its simple module
system.

10.31

Ground plans, elevations, story and roof levels are conceived separately from
the beginning according to one pair of the three right-angled coordinates. Such
drawing is then "three-dimensionalized," first in axonometric projection (see
p. 182) then into models assembled from uniform cardboard or other sheet. All
the boundaries of the architectural space are thus defined as flat, clean surfaces
defining large box-like volumes, whose defining features are the troughs and crests
where plane surfaces meet. There has grown up a belief that architecture is
primarily a matter of jigging together very few broad single volumes defined by
plane surfaces, and that architectural space is best conceived in terms of the cube,
cuboid, cylinder, and possibly sphere, with occasional excursions being made
into other theoretical solid forms with more faces.

Such design can be learned schematically. Its surfaces adhere closely to
measured axial diagrams, eliminating strong contrasts between orders of form and
qualities of varying bulk, mass, texture, and thickness. Such architecture often

photographs effectively, although it can sometimes be difficult for the viewer to make out whether a photo represents the finished building or its model. Interior subdivisions can easily be invented on paper by subdividing rectangular plans and elevations and deriving floor and roof plans by simple projection (see pp. 179–80). With the aid of a computer the architect can now lay out a 3D complex point by point, and then call it up sector by sector to introduce modifications with a minimum of conceptual effort. Such methods undoubtedly work; but it is part of the thesis of this book that they lead to an impoverishment of the designer's – and the viewer's – imagination.

Modular construction

This dependence on calculation and automation has also affected the substance of current architecture. Components for buildings are manufactured en masse

10.32 MOSHE SAFDIE
Habitat, Expo 67, Montreal.

The thoughtfully varied layout of essentially similar dwelling units can produce a sense of animation in what might otherwise constitute a monotonous set of apartments.

and cheaply in a factory – floors, wall slabs, even complete bathroom and kitchen modules. They are then assembled on site. The design of such work is naturally devoted mainly to ensuring that the components will fit together properly; and the assembly technique is a critical factor. The once-common practice of setting flat structural components – floors and walls – into a steel frame, or even simply bolting them together to create a stack of boxes, has proved to have dangerous weaknesses; leakage and even collapses have occurred. Improved methods are being attempted. It used to be believed that modular construction had to be more or less confined to box shapes; but more sophisticated and expensive molded modules in, for example, fiberglass can give a variety of curvilinear and angled volumes. In Japan, hostels composed of stacks of hundreds of miniature habitation modules, often of plastic, are common. At Habitat '67 in Montreal, larger but still modular multiple box-dwellings were stacked and laid out in a casual, irregular fashion, so as to give the inhabitants a feeling of variety.

Ground plan

The ground plan is usually the first given in any design. It connects and interrelates the footings of the entire structure, also establishing floor patterns. Its shape may be governed by the site or it may be a matter of purely symbolic choice.

The ground plan may be repeated, either similarly or with modified subdivisions, in higher stories of the structure, which are, in effect, bridges matching the plan – unless, of course, the whole fabric is itself subdivided at upper levels into domes or towers of various shapes. A standard rectangular post-and-beam cage can vary the spaces at its different levels by means of walling. The lower levels may be opened upward to take in extra stories; and the upper levels may also be diminished. The variation and proportional adjustment of the divisions are the chief spatial resource of the architect with all such designs.

The ground plan normally corresponds in principle to the clients' style and practical requirements. Whatever the overall conception of the building, the ground plan establishes the basic elements of the ultimate form. Frame or cantilever structures rest normally on piers or piles driven into the ground to carry the weight of the structure, and the simple geometry of their placement corresponds directly to the main supporting members.

Nearly all ground plans are oriented in relation to the frontage of the building, even when access is provided from more than one side. Apart from this, they may be relatively neutral in character. In some buildings, though, the ground plans may have one or more distinct directional focuses. This is true, for example, of some religious buildings, notably mosques and churches, which are oriented toward Mecca and Jerusalem, respectively (although in the latter case often only metaphorically). Such buildings have one end to which the attention of all the occupants is directed. Churches, which are derived ultimately from the long Roman basilica, or assembly hall, normally have an axial nave, often with aisles and sometimes with projecting side chapels. Some shrines, such as those of the Hindus and Buddhists, also derived from the basilica-type, may provide in addition a passageway so that visitors can walk around the main icon placed at the end. Nowadays it is common to give interest to the main spaces of institutional buildings and private houses by setting off their ground-axes at angles to each other.

There are a few other types of building whose ground plans have special directional features. The three most important are sports stadia, theaters, and museums. The stadium, based upon the Roman circus, is arranged so that all spectators can easily look down into the arenas where the sports are played. The theater is based on the Roman amphitheater, which originally had its seating arranged around a natural hillside formation with a stage constructed across the end; later the seating, too, was constructed. The ground plan of the traditional indoor theater features a raised stage at one end, usually behind a proscenium arch, although the earlier apron stage is being revived. Some theatrical companies have found any directional arrangement inhibiting, and have experimented with ways of performing in the round, as in a circus, although few theaters are designed completely in the round. Most museums consist of a series of galleries, some of which can be arranged, by means of partitions, for example, to accommodate group shows or sequential exhibits. The "palace" tradition which lies behind the museum concept ensures that most museums, which have no real need for such a feature, nevertheless have a grand staircase leading up from the principal foyer to a grand reception area on the second floor.

Ground plans are usually made up of rectangles or squares, either single, added together, cut into each other in different ways, or subdivided. Triangles, stars, circles, and ovals can also be used. Convention has decreed, however, that the main blocks be virtually always rectangular, modified perhaps with projections stepped-out or inset. For the rectangle provides the simplest basis for all spatial and structural calculations along axes we can define in terms that the architect can most easily communicate to the builder.

Walls

Most walls are vertical. The exceptions are "battered" walls, which lean inward on one or both sides in order to resist – or imply – outward pressures; sheet structures, which can slope purely for visual effect; and walls that are integral with special roofing-systems. Sheer verticality is only necessary, in fact, where a wall structure is a weight-bearing stack of material, or a lightweight material without added supports. Most modern sheet materials can quite easily be fixed with slots or brackets at any slant required, and in much inventive modern architecture they are. But the convenience and cheapness of rectangularity ensures that vertical walls are the norm.

Walls have an overridingly important visual function. Their height, proportions, and physical character are what mainly give a building its outer presence. Walls are also the most visible realization of the ground plan at all levels, establishing the enclosures by which the inner spaces and outer volumes are shaped. An exotic ground plan – say a star shape, or a pair of intercut ellipses – can rise vertically to create highly individual spaces.

All structural materials have their own distinctive properties, and the materials used in the construction of a wall may add symbolic references to the entire building. For example, flat frontage of brickwork will give a specific sense of scale based on our understanding of the normal size of bricks, as well as warmth of texture and color. A concrete wall cast in rough timber shuttering would create quite a different, possibly forceful presence; one of polarized glass in minimal metal frame, quite another. Each could be applied to very similar structural backing. Emphatic textures, of course, may be given to any wall to add interest and to hide an unpleasant structural material, so serving a valid ornamental purpose.

In recent times decorative 3D development of walls has been very rare. Earlier architects arranged materials into focal masses, such as piers and pilasters, and used diapers of relief or colored ornament to enliven broad expanses of wall. Nowadays many domestic architects, too, are developing ways of evoking 3D imagery by incorporating window bays, recessed entries, and offset frontages into their designs.

Roofs

In some styles of architecture the roof is the main external expressive feature. Examples of this include the steep gables and roofs of sixteenth-century Germany and the recent work of Bruce Goff in Oklahoma. In other styles the roof is not visible, a merely utilitarian covering – as in some Italian Renaissance palaces and modern flat-roof design. Conservationists rightly make much of the way in which pre-1930s city architecture considered and developed its roof-lines. Today, domestic architecture is beginning once more to challenge plan and wall surfaces with fresh formal propositions, such as pyramid shapes, vaults, and domes.

10.33   Seven-Roofed House, Memmingen, Germany, c.1560.

Heavy falls of snow in northern Europe necessitated steep roofs; as a result, traditional architecture often emphasized the roof structure, if not always as spectacularly and imaginatively as this.

10.34 GIACOMO BAROZZI DA VIGNOLA

Palazzo Farnese, Caprarola, Orvieto, Italy, 1552–1573. Lantern seen from below.

The great ascending spiral of the staircase articulates the interior levels of the building. It also defines its space by means of powerful solid bulks, rather than plane geometric surfaces.

Unifying factors

We have discussed buildings so far in terms of the bottom, sides, and lid of the notional box that frames the inhabitants. But what ultimately matters artistically is the union of all three – not just in a structural sense but in the way they constitute a whole. Obviously, there are some building shapes that eliminate entirely the distinction between wall and roof, such as the once fashionable geodesic domes. But for most practical purposes the box remains the valid and comfortable architectural conception.

Boxes of varied size can be intercut at all sorts of angles to create varied and intelligible spaces; they can be inserted into one another partly or completely; they can be added to one another so as to project internally and externally. One wall can be extended beyond its meeting with other planes – perhaps to provide a larger façade. Two or more boxes may share the same wall, adjoining different parts of it. But the imaginative articulation of genuinely continuous void volumes is always more than the addition of geometrical components.

One of the most important unifying factors can be the staircase. In primitive houses this may be no more than a ladder, giving access to upper stories either externally or internally. A more solid development of the ladder is the spiral stairway found in castles and medieval churches, often enclosed in turrets. Later, stairways were straightened out (at least slightly) and given broader treads and banisters.

The staircase normally needs a well-space of its own. This can become a major architectural feature; and the staircase itself – especially its balustrades – lends itself to rich ornamentation. Architects of earlier centuries applied great ingenuity and sense of theater to the design of staircases, especially those for grand palaces, which often led up to important reception rooms on the second floor, or *piano nobile* (noble level). These magnificent stairways could take a variety of forms: a first broad flight to a landing could diverge into a pair of further flights spiralling in both directions; or a divergent pair of lower flights could meet and cross at landing level; in some cases a pair of engaged helical spirals might cross and recross. A staircase needs to be lit, and by the eighteenth century it had become common for the stairwell to be surmounted by a dome with windows or overall glazing.

Modern stairways may lack the ceremonial dimension of such earlier examples, but they, too, can take different forms. Open-tread stairs with open banisters or metal and sheet glass balustrades are often suitable for open-plan and/ or split-level houses. Elsewhere purely functional access stairs may be preferred. Where a stairway runs along a wall, that wall is very often treated as a major display area, perhaps for works of art. Stairs provide a sloping feature, with rhythmic punctuations – maybe even a round or rectangular spiral – that needs to be resolved inventively into the rest of the design of the house.

It is significant that many large modern buildings lack staircases (save for fire-stairs), and link a series of identical floors by elevators. This eliminates the user's sense of physical contact with the ground, so reinforcing the neutrality of internal spaces.

EXTERIOR SPACES

Exterior spaces can be important elements in an architectural whole. Broadly speaking, they are those parts of a complex that are unroofed, and they include not only gardens but other open spaces.

Courtyards and terraces

The open spaces most closely integrated with the main structure are the courtyard, terrace, and open walkway. What combines them with the formal layout of the whole is their ground plan and flooring. But what gives them their primary quality is their scale in relation to the walls and roofs that frame them. Many different features can add to their aesthetic effect, depending on the climate. These include shadow; echo; axis of movement in relation to walls, windows, and moldings; steps; side passages or openings into adjacent rooms; and whether and where an exit opens on to a vista, another building, or another space. Some closed courtyards can give a sense of comfort and peace; garden courts can open onto distant landscape; wall-side terraces can enable a visitor to gain a lively sense of the fabric of the building. Interesting roof-lines against the sky can intensify the experience of contrasts.

10.35 Garden of the Villa Lante at Bagnaia, near Rome, c.1610.

In this garden the layout of closely clipped shrubs follows a symmetrically planned scheme, embodying similar curves and spirals to those used in Italian architectural and textile ornament.

Gardens

The old Greek word for garden is *paradeisos* (paradise). Gardens are still, for many people, images of paradise – as in the biblical Garden of Eden. Every paradise is an area of peace and psychological integration where the springs of life nourish flowers and fruiting trees. Middle Eastern carpets are images of the ordered gardens of the spirit. In the Far East, notably in Japan, gardens are also a major art form, symbolizing the interweaving threads and patterns of ever-changing Nature. The western view of gardens is less mystical; but there is no doubt that many people find a kind of psychological fulfillment in growing vegetables and flowers, and that the way one designs a garden can incorporate reflections of broader symbolism.

There are two principal kinds of garden. One kind – the formal garden – is conceived as a symbol of strict formal order and coherence; the other – the informal garden – as a symbol of the variety and unformulated wildness of Nature. The first embodies space as limited; the second, space as environment (see p. 107). The usual way of laying out a formal garden is to subdivide each area with paths that follow geometrical figures symmetrically laid out on grids; the spaces between the paths are filled with plants and flowering trees laid out in rows and patterns. The beds may be edged with, say, boxwood or stone; and a large garden may be subdivided with hedges of yew or box and contain flights of steps and pergolas.

10.36 Suizenji Garden in Kumamoto, Kyushu, Japan, 17th century.

The apparent naturalness of this garden is a sophisticated deception. Specific elements were required by convention, and it was in the artful artlessness of their disposition that the skill of the creator and the pleasure of the viewer lay.

The planned areas may center on special features, such as a geometrical pond, a fountain, and/or sculpture at a crossing or apex of walkways. There is a long classical tradition of placing pairs of stone urns to flank the entrances to arterial pathways or at the top of flights of steps. The greatest examples of formal gardens were those of seventeenth- and eighteenth-century Persia and India, Renaissance Italy, and France, where they complement the great châteaux from the time of Fontainebleau to Versailles. Another notable example was the English Elizabethan knot garden, whose layout was based on interlace figures.

The informal garden was developed in the Far East and was imitated, with differences, in eighteenth-century England. It is meant as an intelligible image of untamed Nature, although in fact growth in such gardens needs to be kept under very tight control. The essence of the Far Eastern garden is that nothing in its arrangement ever occurs twice. Channels of water, sequences of rocks arranged at different angles, trees in irregular groups and carefully pruned to irregular shapes, and areas of the same plant or bush trimmed to an organic contour are the elements. "Borrowed landscape" can be very important – distant views included in the image of the whole.

The English adaptation of the Oriental garden incorporated lakes of irregular shape – in practice flooded stream beds – alongside large, seemingly haphazard clumps of trees on hillsides and immense vistas onto measureless boundaries. Later in the eighteenth century neoclassic taste introduced formal features such

10.37   HENRY FLITCROFT and HENRY HOARE
The Park at Stourhead, Wiltshire, England, 1744–65.

This great garden, with architectural features placed subtly among mixed plantations, embodies an aesthetic of the natural, the irregular, and the picturesque, derived partly from 17th-century Italian and French paintings and partly from the Far East.

as symmetrical ponds, steps, sculptures, and more obviously planned garden areas. Many new plants, gathered from distant parts of the world, provided an exotic flavor of the tropics and the Far East.

Most modern gardeners, including those who work on a small scale, leave their planning to an intuition that combines both formal and informal aspects. Both approaches to garden design are worth exploring; and everyone can think up new combinations following either of the main principles.

THE URBAN ENVIRONMENT

One recently revived mode of architecture is that of combining in a single overall design groups of individual buildings. All too often, real-estate developments have consisted of lots laid out side by side along streets whose only variety is produced by gradients and awkward existing property boundaries. But it is possible to plan interesting multi-structure developments in cities under the control of local governments prepared to demolish large areas of bad building. Similarly universities and some large businesses with broad open sites at their disposal, can plan and build unified complexes. All such projects, of course, demand considerable capital expenditure and imagination. Great examples from the past have usually been under the control of a single person: Bernini's St Peter's Square in Rome; John Wood's Royal Crescent in Bath; Rockefeller Plaza in New York. Other

10.38   JOHN PALMER
Lansdowne Crescent, Bath, 1789–93.

The grand sweep of John Palmer's terrace, like those of John Wood elsewhere in this town, demanded imagination from client as well as architect. It is based on a simple formal concept, which is brought to life by the inventiveness of the detailing.

10.39 Timgad, Algeria, founded 100 AD, with the Arch of Trajan.

The Roman colonial city revealed by excavation displays the Roman passion – which we have inherited – for rectangular arrangement. The basic pattern of the axially streeted military camp was repeated on whatever scale was required.

outstanding ventures include the nineteenth-century Princes Street in Edinburgh; the Étoile, in Paris; and the "Moorish" city center, in Kansas City. There are also innumerable cities in Europe in which one major building – perhaps a cathedral or city or market hall – dominates a square, serving as the centerpiece for surrounding good buildings.

In any planned precinct, a single formal conception should shape the components. This conception needs to be genuinely visual, not purely technical, and developed with some richness of implication. If its forms are over-simple and its details monotonously standardized, it can become tyrannical. If a development is conceived as a genuine overall unity, its components can naturally vary, and it can contain some degree of diversity.

Rectangular plans

The oldest city plans we know about follow that supreme symbol of order, the rectangular grid. The excavated third-millennium BC cities of the Indus Valley had rigidly right-angled street plans; and even the main houses were focused around rectangular courtyards. Most Greek cities were rectilinear. Century after century, ordered city planning has – with a few significant exceptions – meant rectangular ground layout. Everywhere the Romans colonized and settled, the pattern of the square, axially streeted camp was established. Wherever the example of classical Roman design was adopted, including the United States, the same procedure has been followed – or at least attempted.

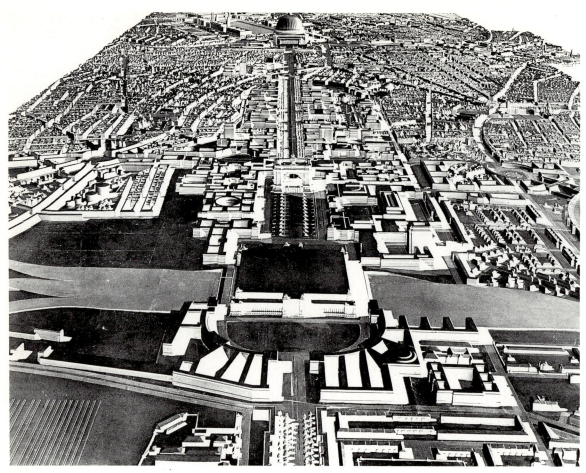

10.40

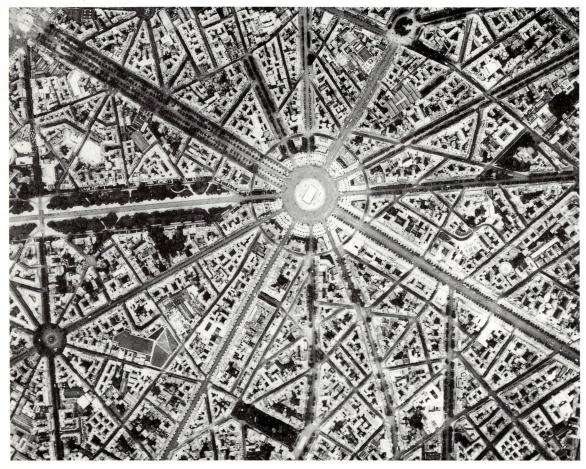

10.41

10.40   ALBERT SPEER
Model of a plan for the rebuilding of Berlin, 1937.

Hitler's capital was to have had at its heart vast spaces for ceremonial parades and mass gatherings, and what would have been the largest dome ever built.

10.41   GEORGES-EUGÈNE HAUSSMANN
Place de L'Étoile (now Place Général de Gaulle), Paris, 1853–70.

Thoroughfares of such width could never be effectively barricaded, and troops and artillery would have clear lines of fire, should the Mob ever take to the streets again.

10.42   New York, the Commissioners' Plan, 1811, detail. The New York Historical Society.

A somewhat uneasy compromise was reached between the irregular existing street plan of the old colonial settlement at the southern tip of Manhattan, and the rational grid plan considered appropriate for the Republic of the New World.

Of course, only when it is possible to build a city from scratch can a total plan be carried through. This was the case on the virgin open landscapes of the United States, when cities spread out over open land; or when disaster struck, as when German cities were razed by bombing in 1944. Radical transformations of existing city plans could be carried out when a tyranny had the power to destroy the old and impose a new order, as when Napoleon III had Baron Haussmann drive his boulevards through the medieval street-plan of Paris, maybe to expose putative rebellious mobs to lines of cannon fire; or when Albert Speer redesigned an intended 1,000-year Berlin for Adolf Hitler.

Water

Without some natural organic factor, pure rectilinear grids above a certain scale can be barren. That organic factor we can call the **water principle**. Many ancient cities in fact depended directly upon water, usually a river and its access channels.

Rivers were humanity's earliest means of transport for heavy loads. Large concentrations of people need ready access to water to drink, cook with and wash in. Cities have grown naturally along the banks of rivers or at their lowest bridging points with direct access routes running down to them from the hinterland. Some defensive cities have been, in effect, fortresses with deep-well or rain-cistern water supplies. Rome, on its seven hills, depended from early times upon an elaborate

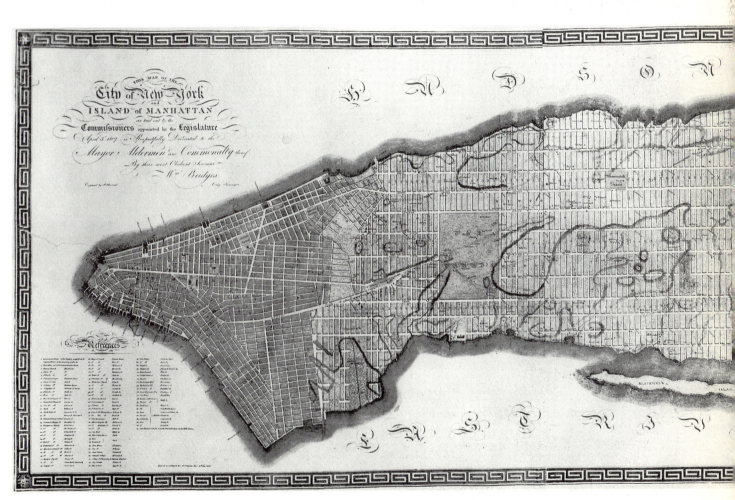

10.43 Plan of the City of P'ing-chiang (Suzhou) incised on stone, Sung Dynasty, 1129 AD. 109½ × 57ins (277 × 145cm). Rubbing. The British Library, London.

City planning in the East has long followed rectangular patterns in the name of both practical operation and cosmic order. The grid is often oriented to the cardinal points of the compass.

series of channels and aqueducts drawing water from the surrounding country as well as from the Tiber. In the desiccated landscapes of the Middle East, cities have often been sited upon buried watercourses, led perhaps for many miles from springs and wells on remote hillsides.

The cosmological diagram

In western traditions the symbolic references of the city plan are lost in the mists of time. But in other cultures we still find conscious understanding of a symbolic pattern for the city, which may vary only in detail. We can call it the cosmological diagram. This is an image of how the ordered world of humanity is supposed to be connected with the Great Principle of Reality and to control the less ordered areas lying beyond its limits. The Chinese, Mexicans, the medieval Khmers and Indians, all built an image of the axis at the center of their cities, usually a temple and/or royal palace. Through that center the rulers and their priests kept in touch with the Great Principle – often thought of as celestial. Around the center, the different areas of the city were oriented toward the four directions of the world.

Ancient Baghdad was deliberately planned from the outset as a cosmic diagram. Angkor consisted of royal temples that controlled the whole water system of the fertile plain of Cambodia. At successive Chinese capitals the emperors conducted daily rituals in their central palace-temples expressly to regulate the interaction of heaven and earth on behalf of humanity. So far as we can tell, both Mexican and Inca imperial cities worked on a similar principle. In some cultures different social groups were expected to live in specified quarters of the city – those allocated to carpenters, potters, merchants, administrators, and so on.

Economic factors

The interaction of human settlement and surrounding terrain also follows patterns resulting from the growth of the economy. On the peasant village level, individuals who are agricultural and husbandry producers are also capable of building their own houses with the help of family and neighbors. The major crafts such as potting, metalworking, and wheel-making may then come to be carried out by specialists. Before the appearance of a money economy such craftspeople might be paid for their work in kind with produce and other goods. A more developed economy entails trade between towns and between countries. But even in the early twentieth century there were still areas in Europe, as well as in North America, that were self-sufficient. A most important part of any such area was, and is, the marketplace.

The **marketplace** has always been a focus for commercial exchange and social life. In old towns it was accommodated on a main avenue, to allow access for wagons, flocks of sheep, buyers, sellers, and tax collectors. In Europe it was situated close to church, castle, and administrative center; and officials, in the past, closely supervised the communal grainstores. Once money economies had evolved, shops and bazaars sprang up, close by the areas where primary producers sold their own goods. The "business center," with its markets and malls, its inns and hotels where outsiders stayed and where bargains were struck, became the focus of town life; and remained the conceptual nucleus of city planning until

recent times. Now, however, with widespread ownership of automobiles, and with the vast increase in differential land values, rents, and taxes between center and fringe, the physical shape of the town is being radically altered. In particular, the evolution of the out-of-town superstore or shopping mall now makes it unnecessary for anyone to go into the center for ordinary shopping.

Zoning

Until after the Second World War, even in major cities, people frequently lived in or beside commercial buildings, their shops, services, and theaters being a few minutes' walk away. Animals were reared in city courtyards. Factories lay at the ends of networks of residential streets that also contained shops. Hotels were close by the railway station or business center. But now, in general, we have moved away from the mix of functions toward the zoning of specific functions into different localities. Planning authorities have conceived this as essential to deal with the twentieth-century population explosion and patterns of migration. Many towns and cities contain visible evidence of this process taking place, and the different phases of applied design embody its progress.

In old city centers the "sorting out" has been incomplete, complicated, and

10.44 Banbury, c. 1800, with major features in late medieval times. From *Historic Towns: Maps and Plans of Towns and Cities in the British Isles, with Historical Commentaries, from Earliest Times to 1800,* (General Editor M. D. Lobel), Lovell Johns, Cook – Hammond & Kell Organisation, 1969, Oxford.

Settlements on which a master plan was never imposed have grown up in ways determined by local geography, custom, and economic life. Castle, marketplace, and church still form the nucleus of many English towns.

often traumatic. In brand-new sections a high degree of uniformity and lack of variety in planning can cause their own problems for the people who work or live there. We now take it for granted that separate activities – dwelling, business, entertainment, shopping, education – are carried on in fairly distinct geographical areas. In many countries zoning laws enforce the separation quite strictly, invoking health and safety criteria. This tendency reached its peak in the planning of Brasilia, the capital city of Brazil, which was built from scratch in the interior of the country during the 1960s. All hotels, business offices, government bureaus, and so on were laid out, like with like, in groups, all cells in each group being virtually identical, the variety of organic life being banished.

People have come to accept that they need to shuttle much longer distances between the locations of each of their daily activities. Transport technology has evolved to handle this situation, in the form of train, bus, and car, and more recently aircraft. Trucking, including refrigerated vehicles, has serviced far-flung distribution centers. What were once homes in many city centers have often either been converted into offices or pulled down for rebuilding. Old factories and their associated housing have gone. After the owners and managers had first escaped to suburbia, lower-echelon workers followed them, and the commuter system grew up. Commercial city centers are now often deserted at night. In some very large cities, like New York and London, with the removal of industry and warehousing from the centers, private inhabitants are beginning to recolonize areas once given over to these other purposes.

The geographical separation of functions has gone hand in hand with the evolution of architectural Functionalism. Buildings tend now to be thought of as serving only one primary purpose. Whereas in the past a bank or store would have had accommodation for its staff, merchants and craftsmen would live over

10.45 PAOLO SOLERI
Hexahedron, No. 28 of *Arcology: The City in the Image of Man*, MIT Press, 1969.

This project-plan for a vast enclosed megalopolis is closely related to Science Fiction ideas of the cities of the future. The demands of its construction might well exceed the material, if not human, resources of any society on earth.

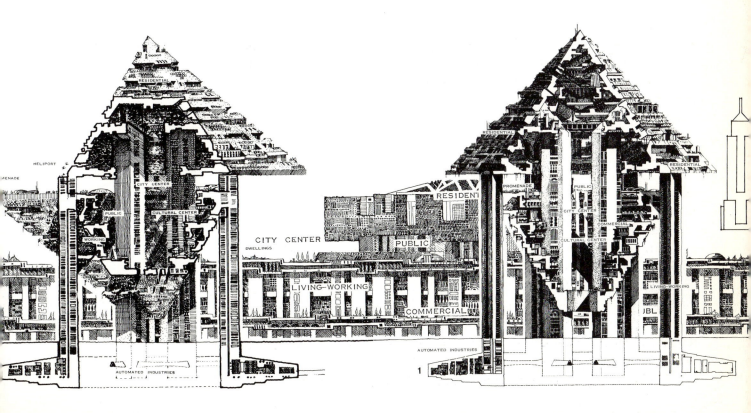

10.46 SWANKE, HAYDEN, CONNELL
Trump Tower, New York, 1979–1983. Interior.

An environment that takes account of human needs can also be an environment that makes good commercial sense. Fine materials, thoughtful detailing, and an exciting but not overpowering sense of scale invite shoppers and strollers in this showpiece mall.

and work in their shops, and supervisors and storekeepers would live in warehouses, this may no longer even be permitted. Most people now regard "living" as something they do far away from their workplace.

One of the dreams of more romantically minded planners has long been to re-integrate all aspects of life and work. Artists and craftspeople have frequently attempted such nostalgic recreations. In some of the more complex evolving cities, such as New York, they have occasionally succeeded in a kind of self-zoning. But at the level of mass-planning, relying on science-fiction projections of the likely future, architects have conceived entire cities contained within a single colossal building. Even in these, however, the functions are zoned apart, and linked by internal transport such as elevator and moving walkway.

Toward humane planning

In many countries there has been a retreat from the idea that architecture should constitute a sort of social engineering, and we are increasingly skeptical of environmental construction on a vast and inhuman scale. Certainly the financial accounting of investment and return, the costing of facilities such as roads and drainage, may seem to favor such large schemes. But analyses have shown that where space is not drastically restricted (as it is, say, in Hong Kong), it is possible economically to house as many people in individually scaled units well laid out on ground level, as in high-rise blocks and surrounding open space occupying the same area of ground. Many city authorities have gone over to the concept of the precinct for domestic developments, sometimes on neo-Georgian or Art Nouveau lines. In city centers, where high land values may decree high-rise developments, many commissioning organizations have begun to recognize the value of the goodwill generated by providing a public amenity mall or atrium offering various shops and services and a pleasant place to relax. These are now being designed into schemes from the beginning, instead of being added as an afterthought. The owners of large shopping malls are also beginning to realize the purely commercial returns on money spent on commissioning designers and artists to create friendly and aesthetically stimulating environments.

The most important thing that environmental designers and the public can do today is continue to try to restore the human element to design. Everyone needs to insist that what is built for us all to live in must relate to our human scale and give us comfort, reassurance, and even delight. Designers need to conceive their projects from the outset on that human level.

GLOSSARY

ACRYLICS A range of modern emulsions incorporating synthetic resins used as vehicles for painting pigments; mixed with water, they harden by drying out.

ADDITIVE A substance introduced into a mixture or compound to make it more effective.

ADDITIVE MIXING The mixing of colors as light, resulting in ever lighter colors (see p. 114).

ADDITIVE PROCESSES see *modelling*.

ACID-BITING Causing acid to eat away parts of a metal surface.

AGGROPPAGE A way of arranging works of art on a wall or surface in an aesthetically satisfying composition.

ALIENATION The effect of distancing people from objects so that they feel no attachment to or personal involvement with them.

ALLOY A mix of substances that improve each other's performance above that of one alone; a substance you can mix with others to improve their performance; usually metals.

ANVIL A strong, solid platform, specially shaped, on which an artifact in a malleable or ductile state is shaped by hammering.

APPLIQUÉ A method of producing 2D designs by stitching down shaped areas of one fabric onto a ground of another.

ARCADE A set of arches, usually in architecture.

ARCHETYPE A generally recognised pattern which gives shape to a variety of different phenomena.

ARCHITRAVE The band or broad beam, usually of masonry, which runs along the top of one or more openings in a wall to bond them together; it is often treated decoratively.

ARTICULATE To connect forms together logically.

AXIS (AXES, AXIAL) A principal straight line in any system of directions, e.g. the axis on which a wheel rotates; also a component in a set of directions at right angles to each other used for planning and measuring either in 2D or 3D.

AXONOMETRIC A form of drawing – projection used for delineating cuboid volumes, in which the measured lines retain their proper lengths; all right angles in the horizontal plane remain right angles, whilst right angles in vertical planes are uniformly distorted (see p. 182).

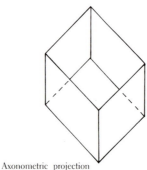

Axonometric projection

BAROQUE A period of European art history broadly between the later 16th century and the early 18th centuries; the characteristics of the kind of art produced during that period; a term loosely describing very elaborate or extravagantly convoluted art.

BENTWOOD A type of wooden structure, usually furniture, made out of wooden members bent permanently into shape, normally under heating with steam.

BINDER The ingredient in paint that holds the particles of *pigment* together and causes them to adhere to the *ground*.

BITING (WITH ACID) The process by which acids eat away metals chemically.

BLOWING (GLASS) A process whereby a craftsperson, by blowing through a hollow metal tube, inflates a bubble of molten glass which is then shaped with additional tools.

BODY (CLAY) The bulk or substance out of which ceramic wares are shaped.

BOND The attachment between two components; in bricklaying or masonry, the method of overlapping the components so that they lock together.

BOTTLE-GLASS An outdated way of making flat glass sheets by blowing glass bubbles, cutting them open and flattening them onto a stone slab.

BRACE A component used for holding rigid the other components of a structure.

BRACELET-SHADING A way of shading drawn solid shapes with arc-like loops, which emphasize the roundness of those shapes.

Detail of a woodcut showing bracelet-shading

BRACKET A component in a structure that bridges an angular joint to strengthen it.

BRASS A compound of metals, mainly copper and zinc, which has a clear golden lustre.

BRONZE A compound of metals, chiefly copper and tin, which, because it is an *alloy*, melts and pours at a lower temperature than its component metals.

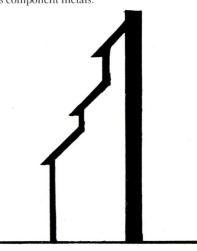

Buttress

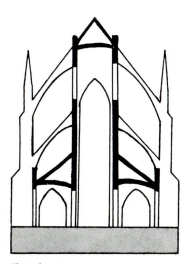

Flying buttresses

BURNISHING A process of rubbing smooth a surface, commonly metal, that is possible due to the ductile properties of its material.

BUTTRESS A shaped stack of heavy masonry constructed to resist sideways pressure in a wall.

CALLIGRAPHY The art of writing fine script; also used of linear script-like drawing.

CAMEO Originally a small carving in two-colored shell, which left figures in one color in relief against a ground of the other color.

CANTILEVER The engineering principle of using a beam to carry a weight at one end balanced by another weight resting on the other end (see p. 53).

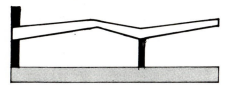

Cantilever

CAPITAL The "cushion" between the top of a pillar and the lintel it carries; often decorated.

CARTOUCHE An area of ornament isolated within a frame, which may itself be ornamental.

CARVING The process of shaping a material by cutting away with (usually) hand-held tools.

CASING (OF A DOOR) The frame constructed in a wall-opening to contain and frame a door; often ornamental.

CASTING The process of pouring a substance into a hollow mold in a fluid state, either hot (metal) or cold (plaster), and allowing it to harden before being removed from the mold (see pp. 42–5).

CATENARY CURVE The shape of curve adopted by a slack chain (Latin *catena*) or rope which is attached to supports at both ends. This shape, inverted, is the structural ideal for an arch.

Catenary curve

CENTERING A wooden structure used to support an arch while it is being built, afterwards removed.

CERAMICS Artifacts of fired clay; or the craft of making them.

CHAMPLEVÉ A technique of *enamelling*, in which glass powder is placed in troughs cut in the surface of the metal, and into which it is then melted.

CHARCOAL A drawing material consisting of wooden twigs burnt in the absence of oxygen, so as to become carbon.

CHASING Cutting shapes into the surface of metal wares.

CHIAROSCURO Meaning "light and dark", a technique of drawing or painting to render the solidity of bodies by means of representing light and shadow.

CLADDING Materials used for the outer surfaces of artifacts, especially buildings.

CLERESTORY OR CLEARSTORY A part of a building which rises higher than other roof levels, and has windows to admit daylight.

CLICHÉ In printing, a replica cast in metal of a *woodcut* block, which lasts longer than the original.

CLOISONNÉ A technique of *enamelling* in which glass powder is placed inside enclosures made of wire *soldered* to the metal surface, and into which it is then melted.

COLD COLOR Color in the range yellow-green-blue.

COFFERING Regular recessed panelling, usually in a ceiling.

COLLAGE Making a graphic image by sticking components onto a surface.

COLONNADE A rank of columns, usually supporting arches or an *architrave*.

COLOR CIRCLE A circular arrangement of areas of color following the *prismatic* order (see pp. 112–4); also called the color wheel.

COLOUR CONSTANCY A theory explaining the physical process whereby the human eye and brain perceive colors (see p. 108).

COLOR FAMILY An arrangement of areas of the same color dispersed across the surface of a painting (see pp. 230–1).

COLUMN A separate vertical support, usually in architecture.

CONCAVE A surface hollow in relation to the observer, the rim being nearer than the centers.

CONCEPT A mental unit of form or meaning, referring to a set or category of actualities.

CONCEPTUAL SPACE A picture space which is not represented but has to be imagined.

CONCRETE A substance consisting of pulverised limestone and clay, which is heated, and which sets hard when mixed with water combined with sand; also, physical as opposed to conceptual (e.g. "a concrete instance").

CONTENT (OF A FORM) The field of instances to which a form refers by being the factor of similarity between them.

CONTOUR A line defining the edge of a solid body.

CONVEX A surface whose center is closer than its rim to the observer.

COUCHING A technique in needlework for laying a flat area of stitches.

COUNTERCHANGE A regular alternation of features across a *grid*, as black and white on a chessboard.

COURSES Of masonry or brickwork, the horizontal layers in which it is laid.

CRAFT A skill of making by hand, usually in a particular material.

CRYSTAL (AND FRUIT) A clearly facetted form with sharp edges; may be given as controlling factor to the interior of a rounded organic volume (fruit) (see p. 100).

CUBISM A style of painting, collage, relief, and sculpture initiated in 1907 by Picasso and Braque which combined multiple viewpoints into a multifaceted surface of geometrical planes.

DECORATION Additional shapes developed out of basic shapes which elaborate them and enhance their expression.

DEVELOPMENT (OF LINE OR SURFACE) A geometrical procedure by which a point is conceived as moving through space to generate a line, a line to generate a surface, a surface to generate a volume (see pp. 83–7).

DIAPER An overall pattern in which a single motif is dispersed at regular intervals across a surface, usually fabric.

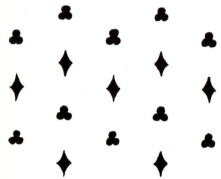

Diaper pattern

DIE An *intaglio* cut block of metal used to impress a design onto a softer metal.

DISCORD (COLOR) Two colors placed next to each other out of their "natural" or "harmonic" order of tonality (see p. 122).

DIVISIONISM A technique of painting in which pigments are not physically mixed to produce imtermediate colors, but laid on the canvas side by side as small touches, leaving the combination to be done by the beholder's eye. See also *Pointillisme*.

ELEVATION In technical drawing, a view of one vertical face of a solid artifact, usually the front, side or rear.

EMBOSS To decorate with raised ornament, usually metal.

EMBROIDER To decorate a fabric with a design composed of groups of stitches.

ENAMEL Colored glass powder melted onto the surface of metal.

ENCLOSURE (POSITIVE, NEGATIVE) A shape enclosed within continuous or interrupted outlines; positive enclosures are closed, corresponding with solid objects, negative are open, corresponding with spaces.

ENGRAVING The process of cutting channels out of metal surfaces with special tools; commonly used as a way of preparing designs for printing (see p. 194).

ETCHING A technique of *acid-biting* away lines or areas of metal surfaces; often used as a way of preparing designs for printing (see p. 194).

EXPONENTIAL CURVE A curve whose inflection regularly increases (or diminishes) along its length according to a formula such as x^2.

EXPRESSIONISM An artistic mode which attempts to translate emotion into signs, eliminating conscious deliberation.

EXTENDER A rigid long component of a structure whose function is to maintain its 3D extension.

FAÇADE The frontage or front *elevation* of a building.

FELT A fabric made by compressing fibers into a sheet.

FIBERGLASS A material made by bonding glass fibers together in a plastic compound.

FIGURE see *ground*.

FILIGREE A kind of ornamental flat metal-work full of spaces, in which the metal appears like wires or threads.

FIRING The process of heating *ceramics* in a kiln until the substance melts together and hardens when cool.

FLASHED GLASS An area of colored glass laid over glass of another color.

FLOOR In drawing, an illusory ground-level rising into the format from the lower edge, upon which the objects represented appear to stand.

FLUX A substance added to a melt which lowers the temperature at which the other ingredients melt and flow.

FOLIATE Treated ornamentally like unfolding leaves.

FORGING Hammering out metal, usually hot iron, on an *anvil* to shape it; some metals may be cold forged.

FORM A mental unit defining a shape or set of shapes (see p. 72).

FORMAT The shape and proportion of a paper sheet or artist's canvas.

FORMING PROCESSES Altering the shape of the material by pressure without altering its inner structure or removing any of its substance (see pp. 33–40).

FRESCO A painting technique involving the application of pigment to still-wet plaster.

FUNCTION The precise role an object is meant to fulfill in a mechanical system, or, by extension, a social system.

FUNCTIONALISM A theory or art, but especially architecture, which held that the entire object should be designed as if its shape was meant to fulfill a precisely defined function.

FUTURISM An artistic movement in Europe, especially Italy, before World War 1 which sought to express mechanical power and speed by means of surfaces actually, or pictured as extending violently into space.

GARNITURE A set of decorative artifacts (e.g. a clock with a pair of candlesticks or ceramic ornaments) designed to be laid out on a mantel or table top.

GAUFFRAGE Printing with a block onto wet paper without ink, the result being a scarcely visible raised or indented impression.

GIRDER A structural *extender* which is shaped so as to preserve its rigidity under stress, either solid or as an open network of interacting *braces*.

GLAZE (CERAMIC) A layer of pigment, silicates, and flux, applied to ceramic wares, which fuses when fired into a colored glassy coat.

GOTHIC A style of European medieval art between roughly 1190 and 1500.

GOUACHE Opaque *watercolor* paint in which the *pigments* are bound in gum arabic and the lighter tones contain a white pigment.

GRAIN (PHOTOGRAPHIC) The minute specks of dark color of different sizes and densities which, in aggregate, give the effects of tone in a photographic print.

GRANULATION A photographic process which enlarges the grain in a photo to make it clearly visible. Also, in metalwork, a technique of making small granules of gold partially melt onto a surface.

GRAPHIC DESIGN The design of 2D layouts, often combining text with visual imagery.

GRID A regular network of straight lines arranged at identical intervals, usually, but not always, at right angles.

GROUND The physical substance of the surface onto which artistic media are laid. Also the neutral background from which a figure is distinguished and which is perceived as lying "behind" the figure.

GROUND-PLAN The plan of the layout of its ground area which governs the vertical development of a work, usually a building.

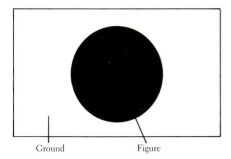

Ground   Figure

HAMMER-BEAM A roofing structure of wooden components used to cover a wide space, and capable of decorative elaboration.

HARMONY (COLOR) Colors laid next to each other in their "natural" order of *tonality* (see pp. 120–2).

HATCHING Groups of small parallel strokes in drawing which in aggregate produce the effect of a shadow-tone.

HELIX A spiral extended along its axis into the third dimension.

HORIZON In a landscape picture the level of the horizon determines the perspective, and implies the height of the viewpoint of the spectator (see pp. 183–5).

HOLOGRAM (HOLOGRAPHY) An image produced by laser technology which enables a viewer to see the object represented from several sides, visible when the viewer moves, as if the object were 3D.

HOT COLOR Color in the range yellow-orange-red-purple.

HUE The place of a color in the optical *spectrum*; its apparent identity.

HYPER-COLOR A color effect of complex radiance, compounded from several tints, which is not the same as any named tint.

IMAGE The unifying entity which focuses and co-ordinates all the components of a visual composition.

IMPRESSIONISM A style of painting developed in France during the 1860s to render the contemporary world in terms of colored light, normally using no black.

INK A fluid drawing medium made of dark substances suspended in water or oil.

INLAY The process of making designs by setting shaped pieces of distinctive material into slots cut to receive them in another material (e.g. brass into wood, cut glass into stone).

INORGANIC Materials from non-living natural sources, especially rocks and clays.

INTAGLIO CARVING Cutting shaped hollows into a surface, which may serve as stamps or molds to produce raised images when impressed onto a soft material.

INTAGLIO PRINTING The class of printing techniques that work by producing hollows in the printing surface which retain the ink when the surface is wiped clean, the ink being absorbed from the hollows when paper is applied to the surface (see pp. 193–6).

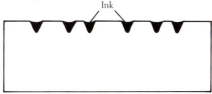

Ink

Magnified cross-section of intaglio printing plate

INTENSITY (COLOR) See *saturation*.

IRIDESCENT Reflecting a shifting array of prismatic or rainbow colors.

ISOMETRIC Methods of drawing perspective-like views of structures in which the main lines keep their correct relationships of measurement (see pp. 180–3).

JALI A trellis-like structure erected outside windows in tropical countries to admit light but exclude direct rays of the sun, developed in India.

JAMB The strong vertical side of a door-opening in a wall.

JIG An implement used to control a fabrication process (see p. 30).

JIGGERING A process in ceramics by which a fixed profile is used to shape the contour of a rotating clay body.

JOIST A secondary beam which is slotted into walls and main beams to support the boarding of floors.

KEYSTONE The central shaped stone, positioned last, which locks together the masonry of an arch.

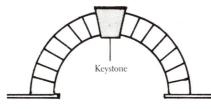

Keystone

KINETIC Having to do with movement, either actual or represented by drawn traces.

KNOT-GARDEN A layout of low box hedging and plants according to elaborate interlace patterns, especially popular in England in the 16th century.

LABYRINTH A pattern containing an elaborately convoluted pathway from the exterior to the center.

LAMINATED Composed of a series of layers bonded together.

LATHE A machine for rotating an object at speed so that its material may be shaved away by a blade held against it.

LINEAR Consisting of or based upon lines.

LINE-REDUCTION A photographic process which converts all tones into pure black and white. Also called bleach-out.

LINTEL The strong horizontal member which bridges the top of a space between pillars or the sides of an opening in a wall.

LITHOGRAPHY A process of printing, originally from the face of a flat stone (see p. 199).

LOCUS The set of successive positions in space occupied actually or notionally by a moving point to generate a line, a line a surface, a surface a volume.

LOCK-JOINT A joint for components where each is cut to a shape which fits the other, closed by a small component which sustains no major stress.

LOUVRE A framed opening in a solid wall or roof which admits light and/or air.

MALL A broad public area, often roofed, providing a range of facilities and services such as shops and cafés.

MALLEABLE Of substances, usually metals, which are soft enough to be hammered into fresh shapes without losing their internal cohesion.

MARBLING A process whereby paper can be given variegated coloring full of irregular swirls and patches.

MARQUETRY A process of decorating a surface, often in wood, by inlaying small flat sections of varied color in patterns.

MASONRY The jointing together of trimmed stones, in building.

MASS The accumulation of material in a body, which can impress a viewer by its suggestion of size and weight (see pp. 102–3).

MEANING The focal meaning of a design is what it combines and refers to as a whole; subsidiary meanings are what the parts that it combines refer to; for example, the focal meaning of a group of figures in a landscape may be a particular story; its subsidiary meaning may be conveyed by the different expressions on their faces, the kinds of clothes they wear, the attitudes of their bodies, the sky and time of day suggested, and so on.

MEDIUM The material into which a design is projected. (paint) The solvent with which *pigments* are mixed and thinned, and which is lost (usually) through evaporation.

METAPHOR In art, when a component of a design which is clearly one specific thing is shaped so as to resemble some other thing with which it has no "normal" connection.

METER An extended rhythmic pattern.

MEZZANINE A floor level which projects from the wall of a high interior space.

MEZZOTINT An *intaglio* technique of engraving which entails treating the whole copper plate with a multitude of tiny pecks, using a rocker or *roulette*, so that it prints black, and then scraping or burnishing smooth those parts which are to print light (see p. 199).

MITER A corner-joint, in which the components to make a right angle are cut each at a 45° slant, usually with an interlocking tongue and matching groove on each.

MODELLING (mental) Conceiving in the mind a logically consistent arrangement suitable to be realized in material reality. (physical) Building a reduced version to scale of an intended final artifact; or building an artifact of malleable substances.

MODERNISM An artistic movement of the first half of the 20th century committed to the belief that valid aesthetic expression was to be achieved by the use of pure geometric and mechanical shapes.

MODULE A basic unit of measure in terms of which proportional relationships are developed (see p. 88).

MOLDING (process) A technique of producing a positive shape by pressing or pouring a soft or fluid substance into a hollow negative (see pp. 41–5). (architectural component) A projecting feature on an elevation with an interesting profile, usually following a vertical or horizontal axis.

MONOCHROME Of one single color.

MONOCOQUE A technique for making a rigid 3D shape as a continuous shell, rather than as a structure of extenders and brackets, commonly used in the mass-production automobile industry.

MONOLITH Consisting of a single, unbroken stone.

MONOTYPE A technique of printing a one-off image by pressing a sheet onto a design, still wet, drawn on another surface, e.g. glass (see p. 189).

MONUMENT A structure, usually large, meant to assert the importance of a person or idea (see pp. 299–305).

MOSAIC A design of small colored glass or stone pieces, called tesserae, fixed to a surface.

MOTIF A recurring form or shape in a design.

MULTIPLE EXPOSURE In photography, taking a series of exposures of a moving object onto the same negative, so that its pattern of movement can be read.

NEO- A prefix used to signify a revival of a style (e.g. "neo-Gothic").

NEWTONIAN SPACE Space as conceived in Newton's mathematics, a constant, theoretically neutral emptiness in which all positions could be determined according to rectangular *axes*.

NIELLO A technique of inlaying a black substance into a silver surface.

NOTIONAL IMAGE see *second nature*.

OIL-COLOR Paints mixed with oils, some of which dry by evaporation (e.g. turpentine), others harden by absorbing gases from the atmosphere (e.g. linseed, poppy).

OPTICS The science of visual phenomena and perception.

ORMOLU Gilded cast bronze ornament, used lavishly in the 18th century to decorate fine furniture.

ORGANIC Of materials taken from living creatures; of shapes which are asymmetrical, irregular and/or undulating, and so reminiscent of living creatures.

OVERGLAZE In ceramics, decorative designs applied in enamel on top of the main glaze.

OXIDIZATION Chemical combination with oxygen, resulting in e.g. the blackening of silver; the firing of ceramic wares in an atmosphere rich in oxygen, which allows both body and glazes to be colored by chemical oxides.

PAPIER-COLLÉ French for "glued paper"; a technique of glueing shapes cut from paper onto another sheet.

PAPIER-MÂCHÉ French for "chewed paper," a substance consisting of pulped paper, perhaps mixed with glue, used to model lightweight artifacts.

PARAMETER In art, a numerical scheme used to generate shapes.

PATINA A surface finish produced by *oxidization*, usually on metal, which combines color with gloss.

PEDIMENT A triangular feature, resembling a gable-end, which may be mounted over e.g. porticos, windows, or niches.

PERSPECTIVE Technique for producing the illusion of spatial depth.

Pediment

PHOTO-MONTAGE A combination of photographic images, originally separate, into a single image, often by means of cutting and sticking them down, but also by treating photographic negatives.

PIANO NOBILE An Italian phrase meaning "noble level," used in palace architecture for the magnificent second story, approached by a grand staircase, on which ceremonial functions were held.

PIER A support for architectural weight.

PIERCED WORK Usually in metal, a design produced as shaped holes through the surface of a plate.

PIGMENT A chemical substance used for the sake of its color.

PILASTER A flat pillar-like support attached to the wall of a building.

PILLAR A tall architectural support which stands free in space.

PIXCEL In digitized, e.g. computer graphics, one of the minute squares from which the image field is composed.

PLANE A single surface, usually flat, which defines a 3D body.

PLASTIC (OF FORM) Formed by molding or having the appearance of something formed by molding; three-dimensional in a way that strongly reflects the act or process of shaping. (materials) Capable of being freely modelled; synthetic polymer substances.

PLASTICINE Proprietary term for a mixture of clay, non-drying oil such as glycerine, and other components, used as a modelling material which keeps its shape like water-softened clay, but does not dry out.

PLINTH A raised platform upon which an artifact may be displayed or a building elevated.

POINTILLISME A technique and movement in French painting just before and after 1900, which used crowds of small dots of brilliant colors to represent everyday scenes.

POST- Prefixed to a historical term to designate the distinctive period immediately following that period (e.g. "post-Impressionist").

PRESSURE-WELDING see *welding*.

PRIMARY One of a set of basic colors, traditionally red, blue, and yellow, from which other colors, particularly the *secondaries*, can be mixed (see p. 114).

PRISM A solid piece of glass, usually of triangular section, which will split up a beam of light directed through it into the full frequency-range of colors; prismatic colors are those that show a multiplicity of hues.

PROFILE A clearly marked line along the edge of an object.

PROJECTION The degree to which something extends towards the viewer. (drawing) The technique of representing 3D objects by drawing in 2D (see pp. 180–3).

PROPORTION A relationship of size, independent of any specific measurement.

PUNCTUATION Features that mark off intervals across design.

PURPOSE What an artifact is made for (see pp. 14–16).

RAFTER The sloping supports for the main cladding of a roof.

REALISM The artistic mode which attempts to convey a strong sense of the actuality of its subject matter.

RECEDING FACES The faces of a 3D body which slant away from the front face (see pp. 250–1).

RECESSION The apparent movement of surfaces into spatial depth.

RECTILINEAR Composed of straight lines.

REDUCTION The firing of ceramic wares in the absence of oxygen so that coloring oxides are deprived of their oxygen and reduced to plain metals.

REFERENTS Those phenomena to which artistic shapes refer, usually by resembling them, which together constitute their *content*.

REINFORCED CONCRETE Concrete in which steel rods are embedded to compensate for the concrete's relative tensile weakness.

RELIEF Sculpture, meant to be viewed from a principal aspect, the projection of which may be shallow or deep (see pp. 252–5).

RELIEF PRINTING Printing from blocks on which raised lines and shapes convey the ink to the paper from their crests (see pp. 189–93).

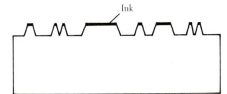

Cross-section of relief printing block

RENAISSANCE Meaning "rebirth," this term refers to the revival of Classical learning during the late 14th century in Italy, and has come to refer to the whole epoch of European culture from the waning of the Middle Ages to the rise of the modern world.

REPLICA An exact and mechanically produced version of an original work.

REPOUSSÉ Design in sheet metal beaten up from the back, perhaps finished by chiselling from the front.

RESERVED An area of a surface which does not bear design imagery.

RESIST A process of applying wax or other materials to a surface so that the covered areas do not receive a pigment or dye applied overall.

RHYTHM An arrangement of features in a sequence that is controlled by an underlying regular beat.

RIBS Long, narrow components used to support an extended surface.

RIGHT ANGLE An angle of 90°, e.g. between a vertical and a horizontal.

RIVET A small plug passed through two members, its ends being then spread, so holding the members together.

ROCOCO A style of European art in the 18th century, marked by vividly active decoration and moving figures.

ROMANESQUE A style of European art, between roughly 1050 and 1190, marked in architecture by solidity and solemnity, and supposed at the time to have close affinities to the arts of Rome.

RONDE-BOSSÉ The French term for 3D sculpture, meaning "round-prominence" (see p. 250).

ROULETTE A small toothed wheel or roller on a handle, used in *etching*.

RUSTICATION Heavy artificial roughness applied to architecture.

SATURATION The relative purity or intensity of a color; the grayer the color, the lower the saturation.

SCALE A basic grading of components of designs in a given order which gives unity to the different parts of the whole (see pp. 103–4).

SCREENING The conversion of a continuously toned original to half-tone by photographing it through a fine grid of lines, thus producing a pattern of dots from which a printing plate can be made.

SCREEN PROCESS See *silk screen*.

SECOND NATURE The imagined reality which the imagery of art may project; also

called notional image (see pp. 219–220).

SECONDARY COLORS The colors obtained by mixing any two of the *primary colors*.

SERIGRAPHY see *silk screen*.

SGRAFFITO A design produced by scratching a surface.

SHELL A continuous surface generated as the *locus* of a moving line, which may or may not change shape as it moves (see pp. 62, 87).

SHUTTERING The structure of wooden boards and beams into which concrete is poured, used as a mold for casting architectural members.

SILHOUETTE The overall shape of an object seen as flat, without any suggestion of the third dimension.

SILK SCREEN A technique of printing which uses a woven screen of fabric or metal on which a design is "stopped out" with a material that blocks the holes, and prints the design by pressing colour through the open holes onto a surface laid beneath (see p. 200). Also called serigraphy.

SLIP Clay in a fluid state (see p. 34).

SOLDERING A process of joining metal to metal by using another metal that melts at a lower temperature as adhesive.

SPECTRUM The range of frequencies or colors into which light can be broken up by a variety of optical devices, including glass prisms, so as to appear as a succession of color-bands.

SPINNING The process of making thread by twisting fibers together; or forming ductile metal by pressing into shape a piece spinning on a lathe.

SQUARE-ROOT RECTANGLES Rectangles used to generate proportions, their pairs of sides bearing the relation of length to each other of $1:\sqrt{2}$, $1:\sqrt{3}$ etc. (see pp. 88–9).

STAINED GLASS Designs composed of pieces of colored glass; in the Middle Ages the pieces were flat, and mounted in lead; more recently, glass designs may be stuck with modern adhesives.

STAKE A special T-shaped *anvil* used for hammering up hollow wares, especially in gold and silver.

STAMPING The process of using a *die* to press out a convex image, by hand-striking (as in ancient coinage) or by machine.

STENCIL A sheet with a design cut out from it, over which pigment is brushed, thus allowing the color to reach a second sheet of material laid beneath (see p. 199).

STEREOMETRIC A shape constituted by straight lines or flat surfaces meeting at clear angles.

STOP-ACTION PHOTOGRAPH A high-speed exposure, which captures an instant from a process of continuous movement.

STOPPING-OUT Painting a surface with a resistant, impermeable substance, as in *etching* or *silk screen printing*.

STYLE A distinctive way of conceiving and executing designs characteristic of a person or a period.

STYLING Covering an artifact with an exterior casing intended to look fashionable without regard to the character of its inner workings.

SUBTRACTIVE MIXING The mixing of colors as pigment, resulting in ever darker colors (see pp. 114–5).

SUBTRACTIVE PROCESSES see *wasting*.

SYMBOL Something which means more than it is, the focus of a meaning otherwise inaccessible, often abstract or belonging to the realm of feeling (see pp. 134–53).

TACTILE Working through or appealing to the sense of touch.

TANGRAM A Chinese game in which a standard group of paper cut-out shapes is used to compose images.

TAPESTRY A fabric design woven in varied color; or, more loosely, embroidered upon a plain cloth base with colored stitches.

TEMPERA A *binding medium* for painting pigments which combines an oil with a water-based adhesive (e.g. egg-tempera, a natural emulsion of oils and water) (see p. 35).

TEMPLATE A physical shape produced as a pattern to guide the making of other similar shapes.

TIE-AND-DYE A technique of tying up sections of a fabric tightly with waxed thread before dyeing, which then refuse to take up the dye and so produce a pattern of the color of the undyed fabric.

TONE/TONALITY Degrees of dark and light in the pigments or inks used to execute a 2D design.

TOPOGRAPHY The production of images of places to describe their literal appearance and record facts about them.

TRACERY Linear designs and geometric shapes executed in pierced work, especially the stonework in Gothic windows.

TRANSFER PRINTING The taking of a printed impression from a previous impression, itself printed; used especially in decorating ceramic wares.

Tracery

TRIUMPHAL ARCH A type of built structure, originally Roman, consisting of a set of three vaulted arches side by side, crowned by a deep *architrave*, through which victors in battle or public heroes were supposed to ride in triumph to approach the public square; later adopted as a pure architectural pattern.

TROMPE L'OEIL French for "deceives the eye," used of painting which sets out to imitate the appearance of things so exactly that they seem real rather than painted.

TRUSS A structural extender which connects main beams so as to support weight.

TURNING Shaving off part of the material of an object as it rotates, as in *lathe*-turning.

TYPOGRAPHY The design of printed text.

UNDERGLAZE DECORATION On ceramics, a design drawn onto the body and then covered with a layer of transparent glaze, through which it is visible after firing.

VANISHING POINT The point on the horizon in a perspective image towards which lines parallel to the line of sight converge (see pp. 183–5).

VAULT A concave curved ceiling, normally of masonry.

VENEER Thin slices of finely patterned wood, cut by a special machine, which are

glued to the surface of plainer wood, in furniture making.

VERANDAH A covered open terrace projecting from the side of a house.

VIRTUAL MOVEMENT Suggested by shapes which do not actually move.

VOLUMETRIC The property of revealing volume.

WARM COLOR Color with a reddish tinge.

WARP The longitudinal threads in a woven fabric, set up first on the loom, through which the transverse *weft* threads are woven.

WASTING The subtractive processes of shaping by cutting material away.

WATERCOLOR Pigments mixed with water-soluble gum, applied as a transparent wash.

WATTLE-AND-DAUB An old way of filling the spaces between the wall-frames of wooden buildings with interwoven twigs and branches daubed with clay and lime.

WEAVING The principal way of turning thread into fabric by criss-crossing longways and crossways threads (*warp* and *weft*) (see pp. 66–8).

WEFT The transverse threads in weaving which are passed between sets of *warp* threads.

WELDING A process for joining metal components by combining their substances into one where they meet; soft metals can be made to flow together by sheer pressure (pressure welding); others can be made to flow together by intense heat.

WOODCUT A type of print taken from a smooth block of wood, cut with a design in relief (see pp. 190–3).

WOOD ENGRAVING A form of *woodcut* in which the design is cut into the end-grain of a polished block of very hard wood.

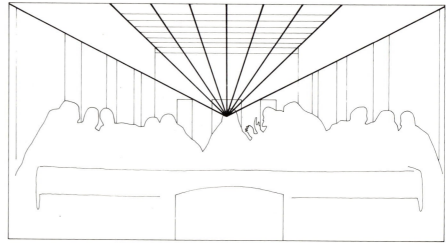
Vanishing point

CREDITS

INDEX

A

Aboriginal branch shelter **1.3** (13)
acoustics 286
action painting 226, **8.8** (227)
ADAM, ROBERT 26, 265, 282; Music Room, Harewood House **9.8** (266); Stowe House **1.23** (27)
adobe structures 48, **10.5** (298)
advertisements, designing *see* graphic design
African woodcarvings 102, 242, 246, 247
Agam, Yaacov 175
ALBERS, JOSEPH 175; *Planar Sections* **6.27** (175)
Albert Memorial, London **10.11** (303)
ALBERTI, LEONE BATTISTA: Sant' Andrea (Mantua) 306, **10.17**, **10.18** (307)
Alfriston Clergy House, Polegate **1.8** (17)
Alhambra, The (Granada): tile decoration **3.31** (90)
Amiens Cathedral **10.20** (309)
amphora, Athenian **3.23** (87)
André, Carl 238
Angkor Wat 102–3, 333
appliqué work 70–1
Apulian villages 298, **10.4** (298)
aquatints 196–7
arches 52, 56, 60, **2.30** (52)
archetypes and symbolism 143–4
architecture 294, 297; articulation of inner and outer aspects 306; of courtyards and terraces 324; of dwellings 298–9; façade and ornament 308–16; "futuristic" concepts 303; ground plans 320–1; halls 299–300; modular construction 319–20; monuments 300, 303, 305; planning methods 316–19; roofs 322; and structural engineering 52–61; unifying factors of buildings 323–4; walls 321–2. *See also* gardens; urban planning
armature structures 54, **2.33**

(54); casing for 60–1
Arp, Hans 245, 255, 274
art, fine: definition 216; choice of medium 220–1; elements 216, 218; focal meaning 218–19; notional image 219–20; and relation to its space 221, 223–4
Art Nouveau 273; wardrobe **9.12** (271)
asymmetry *see* balance
atmospheric perspective 236
automobile construction 62, **1.6** (16), **2.43** (62)
axonometric projection 182, **6.44** (182)

B

balance in design 103–4
ball and socket joints 55
BALLA, GIACOMO 171; study for *Passing Car: Abstract Speed* **6.22** (171)
Banbury, England (c. 1800) **10.44** (334)
Baroque sculpture 151, 251
Barry, Sir James 148
basket making 64, 66
Bath, England 328, **10.38** (328)
Bauhaus School 19, 214
BEARDSLEY, AUBREY: page from *Morte d'Arthur* **7.32** (214)
BEGGARSTAFF BROTHERS, THE (William Nicholson and James Pryde): poster **4.24** (127)
BEHRENS, TIM: own apartment **9.7** (265)
BELLOSILLO, JAVIER: *Figure* **4.13** (117)
bentwood furniture 288
BERNINI, GIANLORENZO: *Fountain of the Four Rivers* **8.6** (224)
Bewick, Thomas 193
Biedermann, Charles 255
BISSIER, JULES: *7.6.1956* **6.33** (178)
black, associations of 125–6
BLAKE, WILLIAM: *Europe, A Prophecy: Blighted Crops* **7.13** (198)

BOCCIONI, UMBERTO: *Unique Forms of Continuity in Space* **1.13** (19)
body images 151. *See* human body
BOHLIN, JONAS: *Chair, Concrete* **9.27** (287)
BOLOGNA, GIOVANNI 251; *The Rape of the Sabine Women* **8.33** (251)
bolts 54–5
bonds, bricklaying 50; Flemish **2.27** (50)
BONNARD, PIERRE 233; *Evening* **8.9** (228); *Still Life with Fruit* **6.16** (165)
BOSCH, HIERONYMUS: *Adoration of the Kings* **2.23** (47)
BOTTICELLI, SANDRO 132, 148; *The Birth of Venus* **5.14** (148)
BOULLE, ANDRÉ-CHARLES: cabinet **9.28** (288)
box perspective 183–4, **6.47** (183)
bracelet shading 161, 196, **6.11** (161)
bracers 56, 59–60
brackets 56, 59
brain, human 23–4, **1.18** (23); and perception of color 108, 110
BRANCUSI, CONSTANTIN 238, 245; *Bird in Space* **8.17** (238)
Braque, Georges 168
Brasilia, Brazil 335, **10.13** (304)
brass 44
bricklaying 50, **2.27** (50)
brickmaking 49–50
bridge construction 18, 56, 59, **2.20** (46), **2.37** (58)
Briosco, Andrea *see* Riccio, Il
Bristol, England: Clifton Suspension Bridge **2.20** (46); Temple Meads Railway Station **1.2** (12)
BRODERICK, PAT: *Lords of the Ultra-Realm* **5.9** (142)
broderie anglaise 71
bronze 44, 239
Brown, Lancelot ("Capability") 107

BRUNEL, ISAMBARD KINGDOM: Clifton Suspension Bridge **2.20** (46); Temple Meads Railway Station **1.2** (12)
BRUNELLESCHI, FILIPPO: Pazzi Chapel, S. Croce **3.3** (75)
Buckminster Fuller *see* Fuller
bulk (in design) 102, 103
Bulfinch *see* Thornton
Buoninsegno of Siena 236
Burgos Cathedral, Spain **3.13** (81)
Byzantine art 130

C

cage structures 54, **2.33** (54)
calamanco, pieced **2.51** (70)
CALDER, ALEXANDER 247; *Black Widow* **8.27** (246)
CALLICRATES: The Parthenon, Athens **10.2** (296)
calligraphy 177–9
camera art *see* photography
CAMERON, JULIA MARGARET: *Thomas Carlyle* **7.19** (204)
CANALETTO (Giovanni Antonio Canale, *called*) 167; *Venice: A Regatta on the Grand Canal* **5.4** (138)
cantilevers, principle of 54, **2.32** (53)
Capitol, The (Washington) 26, **1.24** (27)
Caro, Anthony 238
Carpenter, Barrett 120
carpet-making 71
carpets, patterned 281; *Simonetti Carpet* **2.49** (69)
CARRACCI, ANNIBALE: ceiling frescoes **8.4** (222)
carving 241–2
cased reliefs 255
casing (for structures) 60–1
CASSON, MICHAEL **2.1** (29)
casting *see* molding
catenary curves 59–60, 84
cathedrals, medieval 309–10
ceiling decoration 278–9

cement: casting 44–5; modelling with 33, 34
ceramic casting 45
CÉZANNE, PAUL 126, 225; *Mont Sainte Victoire* **8.7** (225)
chairs 287, 288, **9.26** (286), **9.27** (287)
champlevé enamels 40
charcoal drawing 154, 156
Chardin, Jean-Baptiste 228
Chartres Cathedral: flying buttresses **1.1** (11); rose window **5.11** (145); stained-glass window **4.28** (132)
chests 287
Chevreul, Michel-Eugène 116–17, 118
chiaroscuro: painting 234; printing 193, **7.7** (193)
CHICAGO, JUDY: place setting **9.31** (293)
Chillida, Eduardo 238
Chinese calligraphy 177–8
Chinese ink 154
Chinese painting, traditional 107, 174
CHIPARUS, DEMETRI: *The Hoop Girl* **8.29** (249)
CHIPPENDALE, THOMAS 288; chandelier **9.23** (285); *Ribband Back Chairs* **9.26** (286)
CHO CHUNG-YUNG: crystal stele **2.13** (39)
CHOPIN, HENRI: *J'ai le Nez sec* **7.31** (213)
circles 76, 79–80, 90
cire-perdue casting 42
cityscapes 167
CLAUDE LORRAINE (Claude Gellée, *called*) 167; *Landscape with Narcissus and Echo* **6.12** (162)
clay modelling 33, 34–5
clichés, printing 190
CLODION (Claude Michel, *called*): *Cupid and Psyche* **2.8** (35)
cloisonné enamels 40
cloth *see* fabric in the home; textiles
coins 45, **2.19** (45)
collage 33, 159, **2.6** (32); of photo images 208
collage relief 255
color: additive mixing of 114; constancy 108, 229; to disrupt convention 129–30; emotional response to 123–6, 129; enhancement of 118–19, **4.15** (119); Goethe's color circle 123–4; and the light spectrum 112–14; Newton's optical color circle 113–14, **4.7** (114); opposites 116–18; perception of 108,

110; primary 119; Rood's color circle 120, 122; secondary 119–20; as splendor 130, 132–3; and substance 110–12; subtractive mixing of 114, 116; tertiary 120; warm/cold 119, 126. *See also under* interior design; painting
color aquatint 197
colored line 130
comic strips 168
computers: and architecture 317; and graphic design 215; and photography 204
concrete 238; making mold for 42; reinforced 53
cones 83
Connell *see* Swanke
Constable, John 225
Constructivism 19, 140, 174
content and form 75
contrasting forms 93–4, 96–7; combinations of 97–100
copper 36; engraving 194; etching 194
cord making 64
Cordoba, Spain: Great Mosque **3.14** (82)
Coronation of Mary, The (woodcut) **7.3** (189)
COSTA, LÚCIO: Brasilia **10.13** (304)
courtyards 324
Cozens, J. R. 167
CRANACH, LUCAS (The Elder): *St Christopher* **7.7** (193)
crayon manner (painting) 196
cresting (on furniture) 291–2
Critchlow, Keith 25
Crown of Charlemagne **5.1** (135)
Cruz-Diez, Carlos 175
crystal aspect of form 100, 246
Ctesiphon, Iraq: Palace of Chosroes **2.40** (59), 60
cubic shapes 79
Cubism: painting 168, 171, 182; sculpture 245, 248
curves 84–5
cutlery 293
Cyclopean masonry 49
cylinders 83

D

Daguerre, Louis 185
Dartington Glass, England **2.12** (38)
dazzle effects, optical 93, 175
DEGAS, EDGAR 167, 189; *Dancer Adjusting her Stocking* **6.17** (166); *The Jockey* **7.22** (207)
Delacroix, Eugène 126, 205, 234

Delaunay, Robert 174
DELAUNAY-TERK, SONIA 174; *Study in Light: Electric Prism* **4.10** (115)
Delphi: Polygonal masonry **2.25** (49)
diagonals 89–90, 100, 102
diamonds: cutting 31–2; The Regent Diamond **2.5** (32)
Diebenkorn, Richard 189
die-stamping 45
DOESBURG, THEO VAN: *Color Construction* **10.29** (317)
Dogon dancers **5.5** (139)
DONATELLO 220, 254; *The Lamentation over the Dead Christ* **8.37** (254)
Dotrement, Christian 178
drawing: dramatic composition 166, 167; free form 172–4; landscape 167; lines 159–60, 161, 163; media 154, 156–8; and photography 171–3; shading 161; story-telling 167–8; surfaces and supports 158; technical 179–83; techniques 164; tone and texture 157–8, 160–1; viewer's interpretation 163–4; and virtual movement 174–5, 177
drawing machines 185, **6.49** (185)
drawn-thread work 71
dressmaking 71
DREW, DAVID **2.45** (65)
dry-stone walling 49, 50, **2.26** (49)
DUCHAMP, MARCEL 146, 171–2; *Bottle Rack* 140; *Fountain* 140, **5.6** (140); *Nude Descending a Staircase* 171
DUFFEY, JUDITH: *Masquerade: Sheep in Wolf's Clothing* **2.47** (67)
DÜRER, ALBRECHT 161, 225; drawing machine **6.49** (185); *Head of Apostle Wearing a Hood* **6.1** (155); *The Knight, Death and the Devil* **7.8** (193); woodcut from *Six Knots* series **2.46** (66)
Durham University: Oriental Museum **2.41** (60)

E

Eakins, Thomas 171
EAMES, CHARLES: *Competition Drawings* **1.5** (15)
ears, human 22

EESTEREN, CORNELIS VAN: *Color Construction* **10.29** (317)
Egyptian boxwood figure **2.2** (30)
EHRLICH, STEVEN: Studio House **9.1** (257)
Einstein Tower, Berlin-Neubabelsberg **10.15** (306)
Eisenstein, Sergei 205
electrolysis 45
Eliade, Mircea 143–4
Emakimono 168
embroidery 69–70; on canvas 70
enamels 40
ENDER, BORIS: *Untitled: 19 July 1924* **6.24** (172)
engraving 193, 194, 196
ERNST, MAX: frottages **6.5** (158); *Loplop Introduces Members of the Surrealist Group* **7.26** (209)
ERTÉ: letters from *The Alphabet* **5.12**, **5.13** (147)
etching 193, 194, 196; relief 198
Expressionism 129, 130, 218, **4.25** (128)
extenders 53–4
Eyck, Hubert and Jan van 220
eyes, human 21–2; and color perception 108, 110, 117

F

fabrics: in the home 264–5. *See also* Textiles
façades, architectural 308–13; High Tech 314, 316; post-Modernist 313–14
facial expression, symbolism of 149–50
Falling Water, *see* Kaufmann House
Farnese, Palazzo (Orvieto) **10.34** (323)
Farnsworth House, Fox River **9.3** (260)
Fauvists 129
felting 63
FERRI, CIRO: ceiling paintings **9.16** (277)
FEUCHTMAYER, JOSEPH ANTON: *St Christopher* **8.32** (251)
Finsterlein, Hermann 305
FLAGG, JAMES MONTGOMERY: recruiting poster **5.10** (143)
FLAXMAN, JOHN, Jr: rum kettle **9.30** (292)
FLITCROFT, HENRY: The Park, Stourhead **10.37** (327)
floors: coverings 279, 281; structure 60
Florence: The Baptistery **1.21** (26); Palazzo Medici-Riccardi

Florence: – cont.
10.21 (310); Palazzo Pitti
9.16 (277); Pazzi Chapel, S.
Croce 3.3 (75); S. Miniato al
Monte 3.1 (73)
Ford Fiesta assembly line
2.43 (62)
form (of design) 13–14, 72, 74;
and content 75; contrasting
93–4, 96–100; geometric
76–83; linear 83–7; and
meta-form 72; and pattern
91, 93; and proportion 87–91
forming processes 33–40
FORT-BRESCIA,
BERNARDO: Spear House,
Miami 9.10 (268)
FOSTER, NORMAN: Renault
Distribution Centre 316,
10.28 (316)
FOUQUET, JEAN: Portrait of a
Papal Legate 6.4 (157)
framing 167, 212
FRANCESCO DI GIORGIO:
church ground plan 3.25 (88)
FRANCIS, SAM 226: Around
the Blues 8.11 (230)
frescoes 225, 226
frottage 96, 159
fruit aspect of form 100, 246
FULLER, RICHARD
BUCKMINSTER 300;
United States Pavilion,
Expo 67 2.42 (61)
function (of design) 14–16
Functionalism 18, 335
furniture 286–91; decoration on
291–2
Futurism 19, 171

G

GABO, NAUM 87, 245; Linear
Construction No. 2 3.20 (86)
Ganllwyd, Wales: black tin
chapel 1.9 (17)
gardens 326–8, 10.35 (325),
10.36 (326)
GAUDÍ, ANTONI 107; church
of Sagrada Familia 306,
10.19 (308)
gauffrage 192
GEHRY, FRANK: Spiller
House, Venice (Calif.) 9.15
(275)
Gellée, Claude see Claude
Lorraine
gemstones: setting 36; shaping
31–2
geodesic constructions 61, 2.42
(61)
geometric forms 76–83; and
proportion 87–91
GIACOMETTI, ALBERTO
15–16, 242; Walking Man
1.7 (16)

Gill, Eric 179
GIOTTO: Lamentation 8.2
(219)
girder structures 278
Girtin, Thomas 167
glass 37; blowing 37; coloring 38;
cutting 39; flat 38; stained
39–40, 132, 4.28 (132)
Goethe, Johann Wolfgang von
297; color theories 120,
123–4, 126
Goff, Bruce 278, 322
GOGH, VINCENT VAN 119,
126, 164, 230, 233; The
Night Café 4.14 (118); The
Rock: Montmajour 6.15
(165); The Sower 8.12 (231)
gold 36, 2.10 (36)
Golden Section, the 89, 3.28,
3.29 (89)
GOTTLIEB, ADOLPH 98;
Thrust 3.36 (97)
gouache 35; color handling 228.
See also painting
GOYA Y LUCIENTES,
FRANCISCO DE:
Self-Portrait with Dr Arrieta
5.2 (136); They carried her off
7.12 (198)
graphic design 208–9; and
computers 215; layout
213–14, 215; simplification
of image 210–12; sources of
subject 210; typography
212–14
GRAVES, MICHAEL: fireplace
9.13 (272); Public Services
Building, Portland 313–14,
10.24, 10.25 (313)
grids: role in design 91, 93
GROMAIRE, MARCEL: Nude
Study 6.13 (162)
ground plans 53, 320–1
Guardi, Francesco 167
Gudea, portrait sculpture of 1.17
(22)
Guggenheim Museum, New
York 3.19 (85)

H

Habitat 67, Montreal 320, 10.32
(319)
Hadfield see Thornton
Hallet see Thornton
halls, public 299–300
hand-modelling 47–8
hands: as source of design 22–3
HANSEN, THEOPHIL VON:
Heinrichhof, Vienna 1.11
(18)
Harappan male torso 8.26 (245)
Harewood House, Leeds 9.8
(266)
Harlequin and Columbine
(Meissen) 2.18 (44)

hatching 158, 161
HAUSSMANN,
GEORGES-EUGÈNE 331;
Place de l'Étoile, Paris 10.41
(330)
Hayden see Swanke
heap structures 47–9
helix 85, 3.17 (84)
hemispheres 80
hexagons 83
HICKS, DAVID: design for New
York Suite 9.2 (258)
High Tech style 314, 316
Hill House, Helensburgh 9.9
(267)
hinges 55
history and design 24–7
HOARE, HENRY: The Park,
Stourhead 10.37 (327)
HOLLEIN, HANS: Schullin
Jewelry Shop 10.23 (312)
Homer, Winslow 225
HOPKINS, MICHAEL:
Hopkins House, Hampstead
9.14 (273)
HOPPER, EDWARD: Man's
Head 7.2 (188)
hu (wine vessel) 2.16 (42)
human body: as source of design
20–4; and symbolism 149–53
Hyatt Regency Hotel, San
Francisco 9.5 (262)

I

IBN AL-BAWWAB: page from a
Koran 6.32 (177)
iconography 148
ICTINUS: The Parthenon,
Athens 10.2 (296)
Impressionists 167
Indian art 111, 4.4 (112)
Ingres, Jean Auguste Dominique
205, 218
ink, drawing with 154, 156–7
inside-out design 223
intaglio molds 41–2
intaglio printing 186, 193–4,
196
interior design: and acoustics
286; and climate 256; color
schemes 270–3; contemporary 274–5; and
custom 256, 258–9; and
desire for display 259–61,
263; effect of wealth on 259;
fabrics 264–5; furniture
286–92; lighting 284, 9.23,
9.24, 9.25 (285); motifs
273–4; proportion 266, 268,
270; style 265–6; walls
263–4, 281–2, 284
I-pin drawings 164
IPOUSTÉGUY, JEAN
ROBERT 248; Man Pushing
Open a Door 8.15, 8.16 (237)

iron, forging 36–7
Ironbridge, Shropshire: Bridge
2.37 (58)
irrational proportions 88
italic lettering 179
ITTEN, JOHANNES:
Representation of Contrasts
3.34 (95)

J

Jacquard loom 68
jade sculpting 238
Jaguar SS100 1.6 (16)
Japanese painting, traditional
107, 174
Japanese printers 192, 218
JENCKS, CHARLES: Winter
Room 9.13 (272)
jewelry 242; molding metal 42;
shaping stones 31–2
JOHNS, JASPER 124, 146;
Figure 3 4.22 (124); Figure 7
4.23 (124)
JOHNSON, PHILIP: AT&T
Building, New York 313;
Seagram Building, New York
3.6 (76)
JOHNSTONE, EDWARD 179;
Roman Capital MS 6.35
(179)
jointing techniques 54–6
JONES, INIGO: Tulip
Staircase, Queen's House,
Greenwich 3.18 (84)
JUAN DE COLONIA: Burgos
Cathedral 3.13 (81)
Jung, Carl Gustav 143–4

K

KAHN, LOUIS: Medical
Research Building, Univ. of
Pennsylvania 10.30, 10.31
(318)
KANDINSKY, VASSILY 126,
173–4; Point to Line and
Plane 6.23 (172); Various
Actions 7.25 (208)
Kapur, Anish 238
Karaori kimono 4.27 (131)
Kaufmann House, Bear Run
3.49 (106)
KIRCHNER, ERNST
LUDWIG: Self-Portrait with
Model 4.25 (128)
KLEE, PAUL 154, 229, 233;
Flora in Sand 8.10 (229);
The Thinking Eye 6.2 (154)
KLINE, FRANZ: Vawdavitch
3.35 (96)
knitting 66
knots 66
Konarak, Temple of 2.4 (31), 3.8
(78)

KOONING, WILLEM DE: *The Visit* **8.1** (217)
KORYUSAI: *Girl Teasing her Dog* **6.18** (167)
kouros **8.20**, **8.21** (241)
Koya, Mount (Japan): Great Central Pagoda **2.38** (58)
KUO HSI (*after*): *Winter Landscape* **3.48** (106)
KUROKAWA, KISHO: *Agricultural City Project* **3.37** (98); Nakagin Capsule Tower, Tokyo **9.20** (282), **9.21** (283); Takara Beautilon **10.22** (311)

L

Labba Zanga, Mali **10.1** (295)
landscapes 167
LANGE, DOROTHEA: *Migrant Mother* **7.16** (201)
LARTIGUE, JACQUES-HENRI: *January – Paris – Avenue du Bois de Boulogne* **7.15** (201)
Lascaux cave site 107
Latrobe *see* Thornton
LEBRUN, CHARLES: *Expressions of the Passions of the Soul* 150, **5.15**, **5.16** (149)
LE CORBUSIER (Charles-Édouard Jeanneret) 18, 100, 274; *Modulor* **3.24** (88); Notre-Dame-du-Haut, Ronchamp 180, 305, **10.14** (305); *Plan Voisin* 303, **10.12** (304)
LÉGER, FERNAND 112, 274; *Two Women Holding Flowers* **4.5** (113)
legs: and stability 153
Leibniz, Gottfried Wilhelm 113
LEONARDO DA VINCI 185, 220, 234; plan of church **3.10** (80); studies of water **3.2** (74); *Vitruvian Proportions derived from the Human Body* **1.15** (21)
lettering 177–9. *See also* Typography
letters: as conventional symbols 146–7
lift-ground etching *see* sugar-lift etching
light spectrum 112–14
lighting, interior 284, **9.23**, **9.24**, **9.25** (285)
lines: characteristics in drawing 159–60, 162–3, **6.8** (160); dynamic expression of 85–6; as *locus* of moving point 83–5; 3D functions of 86–7, 164, **3.21** (86)
lintels 52, **2.29** (52)

LIPCHITZ, JACQUES: *Figure* **5.21** (153)
Lippold, Richard 263
lithography 199
Lloyd's Headquarters, London 314, **10.26** (314)
Logothetis, 175
London: Albert Memorial **10.11** (303); Crystal Palace 300, **10.6** (300), **10.7** (301); Hopkins House, Hampstead **9.14** (273); Lloyd's Headquarters **10.26** (314)
LONGMAN, JANEY: own apartment **9.7** (265)
LOOS, ADOLF 311; Goldmann and Salatsch Store, Vienna **1.12** (18)
Lorraine, Claude *see* Claude Lorraine
Los Angeles: Ennis House **1.20** (25); Rodes House **9.11** (269)
lost-wax casting *see* cire-perdue casting
lug and slot joints 54
Lüscher Color Test 125

M

MACKINTOSH, CHARLES RENNIE: Hill House, Helensburgh **9.9** (267)
macramé 66
MAGRITTE, RENÉ: *Mental Calculus* **1.19** (24)
MALEVICH, KASIMIR 174; *Splitting of Construction* **6.28** (175)
Manet, Édouard 234
MARC, FRANZ 130; *Blue Horses* **4.26** (129)
Marey, Étienne-Jules 171, 205
marquetry 291
MARTIN, JOHN: illustration to *Paradise Lost* **7.11** (197)
MARTIN, PAUL: *A Tramp* **7.18** (204)
MASACCIO 111; *The Rendering of the Tribute Money* **4.2** (110)
mass (of design) 102, 103
Masson, André 179
MATISSE, HENRI 129, 242; *Serpentine Woman* **8.23** (242)
matrix 186
Medici-Riccardi, Palazzo (Florence) **10.21** (310)
Meissen: *Harlequin and Columbine* **2.18** (44)
Mellan, Claude 196
Memmingen, Germany: Seven-Roofed House **10.33** (322)
Memphis of Milan 266
MENDELSOHN, ERICH 305;

Einstein Tower **10.15** (306)
MERCATALI, DAVIDE: Lamp, *Basket* **9.24** (285)
meta-form 72
metals: bending 36, 40; casting 44; chasing 33; electrolysing 45; forging 36–7; jewelry making 42; riveting 55; as sculptural material 239; shaping 36; stamping 45; welding 37, 55
metaphor 136, 139
MEYTENS, MARTIN VAN: *Wedding of the Emperor Joseph II* **9.4** (261)
mezzotints 196
Michel, Claude *see* Clodion
MICHELANGELO BUONARROTI 111, 151, 220; *David* 250; *Day* **5.19** (152); Porta Pia, Rome 19, **1.14** (20); *Slave* **2.7** (33)
MICHELOZZO DI BARTOLOMMEO: Palazzo Medici-Riccardi (Florence) **10.21** (310)
MIDDLETON, PHILIP: Oriental Museum, Durham University **2.41** (60)
MIES VAN DER ROHE, LUDWIG: Farnsworth House **9.3** (260); Seagram Building **3.6** (76)
MIRÒ, JOAN: *Foundation's Tapestry* **4.1** (109)
Modernist architecture **3.6** (76), **10.29** (317)
modular building construction 319–20
MOENCH, DOUG: *Lords of the Ultra-Realm* **5.9** (142)
MOHOLY-NAGY, LÁSZLÓ: *Light Space Modulator* **2.21** (46)
moiré effects 93, 175
molding 41; intaglio technique 41–2; materials 42; poured 44–5; press 44; shaping mold 41–2; vacuum 45
MONDRIAN, PIET 119, **3.5** (77); *Composition with Red, Yellow and Blue* **3.4** (76)
Monet, Claude 233
monotype printing 189
monuments 300, 303, 305
MOORE, CHARLES: Piazza d'Italia, New Orleans **5.7** (141); Rodes House, Los Angeles **9.11** (269)
MOORE, HENRY 220, 248; *Reclining Figure* **8.28** (247)
MORAN, ROBERT 175; *Four Visions* **6.30** (176)
MORRIS, WILLIAM: *Apple* wallpaper **9.22** (284); page from *Morte d'Arthur* **7.32** (214)

mosaics 40
movies 205–6
Muchaux, Henri 178
MU-CH'I: *View of the Hsiao Hsiang* **6.25** (173)
musical graphics 175, 177, **6.30** (176)
MUYBRIDGE, EADWEARD: stop-action sequences 171, 205, **7.21** (206)

N

nailed joints 54
Nakagin Capsule Tower, Tokyo **9.20** (282), **9.21** (283)
NASH, PAUL: bathroom **9.25** (285)
needlepoint *see* embroidery on canvas
Nervi, Pier Luigi 306
NEVELSON, LOUISE 253; *Black Wall* **8.34** (252)
NEVINS, JAMES, STEVENSON, DAVID and SIDJAKOV, NICHOLAS: poster **7.28** (211)
New Orleans: Piazza d'Italia **5.7** (141)
New York: AT&T Building 313; Commissioners' Plan **10.42** (331); Guggenheim Museum **3.19** (85); Seagram Building **3.6** (76); Trump Tower **10.46** (336); TWA Terminal, J. F. Kennedy Airport **10.8**, **10.9**, **10.10** (302)
Newton, Isaac 113; optical color circle 113–14, **4.7** (114)
Nicholson, William *see* Beggarstaff Brothers, the
NIEMEYER, OSCAR: Brasilia **10.13** (304)
Niépce, Claude 185
No Mosque, Shiraz: vaulting **9.17** (278)
NORTON, ALAN: *Computer-Generated Fractal Three-Dimensional Image* **7.33** (215)
Núpsstadur, Iceland: chapel **2.22** (47)

O

oblique projection 181, 183, **6.40**, **6.41** (180)
octagons 83
oil painting: color handling 226; ground color 226; paint 35. *See under* painting
Oldenburg, Claes 140
Op Art **6.29** (176)
Oppenheim, Meret 140
optical theory, modern 132–3

Organic Design in Home Furnishing **1.5** (15)
ornament 19–20; architectural 308–16
orthographic projection 180–1, **6.36** (180), **6.38**, **6.39** (181)
orthometric projection 182, **6.43** (182)
Ottonian illuminators 111–12, **4.3** (111)
outside-in design 223
ovals 80
ovoids 80

P

painting 225; applying paint 226; atmospheric perspective 236; *chiaroscuro* 234; color dominance 232–3; color families 230–1; color handling 226, 228–9; color modulation 231–2; color sequences 229–30; color and shape 233; ground color 226; highlights 236; hyper color 233; luminosity 234, 236; modelling with color 233; paint types and pigments 35–6; shadows 236; supports 226. *See also* color
palaces, Italian 309, 310–11
Palazzo Farnese, Orvieto **10.34** (323)
Palazzo Pitti, Florence **9.16** (277)
Palazzo Porto-Colleoni **10.3** (297)
PALLADIO, ANDREA 26; Palazzo Porto-Colleoni **10.3** (297); Villa Rotonda **1.22** (26)
PALMER, JOHN: Lansdowne Crescent, Bath **10.38** (328)
Paolozzi, Eduardo 274
paper: drawing 158; printing 186
paper-making 63–4
parameters 93
Parthenon, The (Athens) **10.2** (296)
patchwork 71
pattern development 9, 93
PAXTON, JOSEPH: Crystal Palace 300, **10.6** (300), **10.7** (301)
PEDRIZZETTI, PAOLO: Lamp, *Basket* **9.24** (285)
pegged joints 54
Perennial Philosophy, The 144
perspective, optical 183–5
PERUZZI, BALDASSARE: Perspective Room, Villa Farnesina, Rome **9.6** (264)
PETHERBRIDGE, DEANNA: *Square Inch Field of the Square Foot House* **6.48** (184)
Pevsner, Antoine 87, 245

pewter 44
Phnom Bakheng, female figure from **8.30** (250)
photography: and actuality 202–4; as art 140; black-and-white (monochrome) 201–2; the camera 200–1; color 202; and design 206–8; and drawing techniques 171–3; evolution of 185; and painting 204–5
PICASSO, PABLO 130, 146, 168, 181, 218, 255; *Guernica* 206; *Nude* **6.21** (170)
PIETRO DA CORTONA: ceiling paintings **9.16** (277)
Pirelli poster **7.30** (212)
PISANELLO, ANTONIO: Leonello marriage medal **8.5** (223)
PISANO, GIOVANNI: *St Simeon* **8.19** (240)
plaiting 66
plans, drawing 179–80; 3D projection 180–3
plaster: casting 44–5; making mold for 42; modelling with 33, 34
plastic, casting 45
Pointillistes 120, 228, **4.18** (121)
POLLOCK, JACKSON 226, **8.8** (227)
Polykleitos of Argos 242
Portland, Oregon: Public Services Building 313–14, **10.24**, **10.25** (313)
PORTMAN, JOHN 107; Hyatt Regency Hotel **9.5** (262)
Porto-Colleoni, Palazzo **10.3** (297)
posters **4.24** (127), **5.10** (143), **7.28** (211), **7.29** (211), **7.30** (212). *See also* graphic design
Post-Impressionists 167
pottery 34–5, 293
POUSSIN, NICOLAS 148, 167, 234, 236; *The Lamentation over the Dead Christ* **8.13** (232)
press molding 44
pressure tracing 188
printing 186; aquatints 196–7; intaglio (engraving, etching) 186, 193–4, 196; lithographs 199; matrix 186; mezzotints 196; monotype 189; paper 186; relief 186, 189–90, 192–3; relief-etching 198; silk-screen 200; stencilling 199; sugar-lift etching 197–8
prisms 83; and diffraction of light 113–14, **4.6** (114)
PRITCHARD, THOMAS FARNOLDS: Ironbridge **2.37** (58)
proportion 87–91; and interior decoration 266, 268, 270

Pruitt Igoe housing complex 18, **1.10** (17)
Pryde, James *see* Beggerstaff Brothers, The
pyramid 83

Q

Qalbloré, N. Syria **2.28** (51)
quilting 70, **2.50** (69)

R

Racine, Wisconsin: Johnson administration building **2.34** (54)
Raphael: *The School of Athens* 140
Ray, Man 201
rectangles 76, 77, 79, 88–90
red, significance of 126, 129
Regent Diamond, The **2.5** (32)
relief: carved 252–4; cased 255; collage 255; silhouette 255
relief-etching 198
relief-printing 189; coloring by hand 192; drawing for 192–3; inking 190; making block 190; methods 190, 192
REMBRANDT VAN RYN 164, 196, 220, 233, 234; *Christ Crucified between the Two Thieves* (*The Three Crosses*) **7.9**, **7.10** (195)
RENARD, C.: "At the Middle of Cymbiola" **6.20** (169)
rhombuses 83
RICCIO, IL (Andrea Briosco, *called*): *A Satyr and Satyress* **2.15** (41)
Richier, Germaine 248
Richmond Hill House, Calif. **9.18** (280)
RIDOLFI, BARTOLOMEO: fireplace **5.20** (153)
RILEY, BRIDGET 175; *Right-Angle Curve* **6.29** (176)
Rivers, Larry 146
riveting 55
ROGERS, RICHARD: Lloyd's Headquarters, London **10.26** (314)
ROGIER VAN DER WEYDEN 220; *Deposition* **8.3** (221)
Rome, Italy 224; Porta Pia 19, **1.14** (20); Villa Farnesina **9.6** (264)
Ronchamp, France: chapel of Notre-Dame-du-Haut 180, 305, **10.14** (305)
ronde-bosse 250, 251, **8.31** (250)
Rood, Ogden Nicholas 120, 122
roofs: structure of 52, 60;

treatment of interiors 276, 278–9
rope making 64, 66
rose windows 144, **5.11** (145)
ROSZAK, THEODORE: *The Unknown Political Prisoner* **8.24** (243)
Rothko, Mark 126
ROUAULT, GEORGES 133, 197; *Grégoire* **4.29** (133)
roundels, Chinese **2.48** (68)
RUBENS, PETER PAUL 234; *Landscape with Rainbow* **4.11** (116)
Ruskin, John 20, 311

S

SAARINEN, EERO: *Competition Drawings* **1.5** (15); TWA Terminal, J. F. Kennedy Airport **10.8**, **10.9**, **10.10** (302)
SAFDIE, MOSHE: Habitat, Expo 67, Montreal **10.32** (319)
Sagrada Familia, church of (Barcelona) 306, **10.19** (308)
St Louis, Missouri: Pruitt-Igoe public housing complex 18, **1.10** (17)
St Paul de Vence: Fondation Maeght **2.17** (43)
SAMBIN, HUGHES (*in the manner of*): armoire **9.29** (290)
SANDYS, FREDERICK: illustration to "Manoli" **7.4** (190)
Sant' Andrea, church of (Mantua) 306, **10.17**, **10.18** (307)
Santa Croce, church of (Florence) **3.3** (75)
San Marco, Cathedral of (Venice) **3.41** (101)
San Miniato al Monte, church of (Florence) **3.1** (73)
Sargent, John Singer 225
scale (of design) 103–4
SCHER, PAULA: poster **7.29** (211)
SCHUITEN, FRANCIS: "At the Middle of Cymbiola" **6.20** (169)
SCHWARZ, JULIAN: *Eight Inch Circle* **2.36** (57)
SCHWITTERS, KURT: *Red on Red* **2.6** (32)
SCOTT, GEORGE GILBERT: Albert Memorial, London **10.11** (303)
screens 288
screwed joints 54
scripts, pictorial imagery of 147

sculpture 236–8; articulation 236–7, 247–8; carving techniques 30–1, 241–2; free-standing 250–1; linear shapes 243–4; materials 30–1, 238–9; modelling 242; molding 242; recognizable qualities 248–50; and relation to place 233–4, 238; reliefs 252–5; structural processes 242; surfaces 244–5; volume 245–7
Scythian saddle cover **2.44** (63)
Seghers, Hercules 186
semicircles 80
SERT, JOSÉ LUIS: Fondation Maeght **2.17** (43)
SEURAT, GEORGES 118, 228; study for *Le Chahut* **4.18** (121)
Seven-Roofed House (Memmingen) **10.33** (322)
Severini, Gino 171
sewing 68–9
sexual organs and symbolism 153
Seyssaud, René 133
shading, tonal 161, 196, **6.11** (161)
SHEELER, CHARLES 206; *Rolling Power* **7.23** (207)
shell construction 62
SIDJAKOV, NICHOLAS *see* NEVINS, JAMES
Signac, Paul 126, 228
signs 136–7, 146
silhouette relief 255
silhouetted shapes 33
silk-screen printing 200
silver-plating 45
silverpoint 158
Simonetti Carpet **2.49** (69)
simulacra 150
Skara Brae, Orkney Islands: house **2.24** (48)
skeleton structures 52–4, **2.33** (54); bracers 56, 59–60; casing 60–1; extenders 53–4; joints 54–6
sleeve joints 55
SMITH, DAVID 239; *Becca* **8.18** (239)
SMITH, THOMAS GORDON: Richmond Hill House, Calif. **9.18** (280)
SOLERI, PAOLO: *Hexahedron* **10.45** (335)
Soulanges, Pierre 226
space 104–5; art in relation to 223–4; conceptual (in drawing) 161; limitations of 105, 107; as open arena 107, 166; visual (in drawing) 161
space deck 60–1, **2.41** (60)
SPEAR, LAURINDA: Spear House, Miami **9.10** (268)
SPEER, ALBERT: plan for rebuilding Berlin **10.40** (330)

spheres 80
spinning 64
spirals 84–5
SPIVAK, HELAYNE: advertisement for Karastan Rug Mills **7.27** (210)
stained glass 39–40, 132, **4.28** (132)
staircases: as unifying factor 323–4
Steichen, Edward 201
STELLA, FRANK 226; *Puerto Rican Blue Pigeon* **7.14** (199)
stencilling 199
Stenvert, Kurt 255
stereometric projections, 3D 180–3
Steuben Glass **2.13** (39)
STEVENSON, DAVID *see* NEVINS, JAMES
STIRLING, JAMES: Neue Staatsgalerie, Stuttgart 314, **10.27** (315)
stitches, sewing 69
stone: cutting 30–1, 50; laying 50; as sculptural material 238–9
Stonehenge **3.9** (79)
story-telling, pictorial 167–8
Stourhead, Wiltshire: The Park **10.37** (327)
Stowe House, Buckinghamshire **1.23** (27)
Strasbourg Cathedral: *The Wise Virgin* **8.25** (244)
strip cartoons 169
structural processes 46–62
stumpwork 70–1
Stuttgart, Germany: Neue Staatsgalerie 314, **10.27** (315)
Suarès, Carlo 119, **4.16** (119)
sugar-lift etching 197–8
Suizenji Garden, Kumamoto **10.36** (326)
Sunburst Carrier Shell (*Stellaria solaris*) **3.17** (84)
Sung Dynasty: plan of P'ing-chiang **10.43** (332); wine ewer **2.9** (34)
surface: of design 102; and linear expression 86–7; of sculpture 244–5
Surrealism 140
SWANKE, HAYDEN, CONNELL: Trump Tower, New York **10.46** (336)
Sydney Opera House **1.4** (13)
symbols and symbolism 16, 18; actual object as 139–40; archetypal 143–4; combining images of objects as 141–2; context and 137–8; conventional 146–7; and cultural echoes 148–9; definition 134; energetic qualities as 144, 146; and the human body 149–53;

iconographical 148; imaginary object as 142; personification and 142–3; physical qualities as 144, 146; represented object as 140–1; and signs 136–7; stereotyping of 146; structural analogies 134, 136

T

tables 287
tachisme 226, **8.11** (230)
tactile qualities (of design) 22–3
tailoring 71
Talbot, William Fox 185
Taliesins, Spring Green, Wisconsin 281, **9.19** (282)
TANGE, KENZO: National Stadium, Tokyo 306, **10.16** (307)
Tangrams, Chinese 163, **6.14** (162)
TAO CHI: *Lone Boat on a Stream* **6.3** (156)
tapestry *see* embroidery on canvas
Tapiès, Antoni 226
technical drawing 179–82
Teotihuacán pyramid, Mexico **3.47** (105)
terraces 324
tetrahedrons 83
textiles: processes 63–71
texture (in drawing) 160–1
THORNTON, HALLET, HADFIELD, LATROBE and BULLFINCH: The Capitol, Washington **1.24** (27)
3D: combinations of shapes 99–100; conveying from 2D drawings 179–82; functions of line 86–7, 164, **3.21** (86); projections of geometrical forms 79, 80, 83, 85
Tiepolo, Giovanni Battista 234
TIFFANY, LOUIS COMFORT: glass vase **2.11** (37)
TIKKANEN, MAISA: *Broken Red* and *Broken Blue* (wall hangings) **4.21** (123)
tiled floors 279, 281
Timgad, Algeria **10.39** (329)
TITIAN 233, 234; *The Rape of Europa* 141–2, **5.8** (142)
Tokyo: Nakagin Capsule Tower **9.20** (282), **9.21** (283); National Stadium 306, **10.16** (307)
tonal harmony 120, 122
tone (in drawing) 160–1
tortoiseshell, bending 40
Toulouse-Lautrec, Henri 167

town planning *see* urban planning
tracing 188
trapezoids 83
triangles 76, 80, 90–1
trompe l'oeil 264, **9.7** (265)
Trulli houses **10.4** (298)
Trump Tower, New York **10.46** (336)
Tumbaga pendant **2.10** (36)
turf houses 48, **2.22** (47)
TURNER, JOSEPH WILLIAM MALLORD 174, 225, 236; *A Swiss Valley* **6.26** (173)
TWA Terminal, J. F. Kennedy Airport **10.8**, **10.9**, **10.10** (302)
typography 212–14

U

Ukiyo-e prints 192, 218
unit-modules 88
urban planning: and cosmological diagrams 33; economic factors in 333–4, 337; "futuristic" concepts 303–5; human element in 337; rectangular grid pattern 329, **10.39** (329), **10.43** (332); unified complexes 328–9; and the water principle 331, 333; and zoning 334–5, 337
utensils 292–3
UTZON, JØRN: Sydney Opera House **1.4** (13)

V

vacuum molding 45
Valéry, Paul 47
VAN DER ROHE, LUDWIG MIES *See* MIES
VAN GOGH, VINCENT *see* GOGH
VANTONGERLOO, GEORGES: *Construction of Volume Relations* **2.3** (31)
VASARELY, VICTOR 175; *Supernovae* 93, **3.33** (92)
vaulting, structural 276, 278
Velazquez, Diego 234
veneers, wood 30, 291
Venice 224; San Marco **3.41** (101)
VESALIUS, ANDREAS: *The Thirteenth Plate of the Muscles* **1.16** (22)
Vienna: Goldmann and Salatsch Store **1.12** (18); Heinrichhof, Ringstrasse **1.11** (18); Schullin Jewelry Shop **10.23** (312)
vignetting 212

VIGNOLA, GIACOMO BAROZZI DA 103; Palazzo Farnese **10.34** (323)
Villa Farnesina, Rome: Perspective Room **9.6** (264)
Villa Lante, Bagnaia: garden **10.35** (325)
Villa Rotonda, Vicenza **1.22** (26)
volume, concept of 87; in drawing 161; and void space 102–3

W

walls, dry-stone 49, 50, **2.26** (49)
walls, exterior 321–2; structural elements 52
walls, interior 281–2; arranging items on 263–4; coverings for 282, 284; painting 264 (*see also* frescoes)
WALTER, THOMAS USTICK: The Capitol, Washington **1.24** (27)
WANG MIEN: *Plum Blossom* **7.5** (191)
WARHOL, ANDY 124, 200; *Mao* **7.1** (187)
Washington, DC: The Capitol 26, **1.24** (27)
wasting processes 28, 30–3
watercolor painting 225; color handling 228; ground color 226; paint 35. *See also* painting
wattle and daub 49, **2.23** (47)
wax: *cire-perdue* casting 42; modelling with 33, 34, 42
weaving 66–8
welding 55
WÊN CHÊNG-MING: *Old Pine Tree* **6.7** (160)

WESSELMAN, TOM: *Great American Nude #2* **6.6** (158)
WESTON, EDWARD 203; *Pepper* **7.17** (203)
white: primary color mix to make 114, **4.8** (114); symbolism of 125
WILFORD, MICHAEL: Neue Staatsgalerie, Stuttgart 314, **10.27** (315)
WOLSEY, TOM: advertisement for Karastan Rug Mills **7.27** (210)
wood 30; bending 40; grain patterns 30, 238; jointing methods 55–6; as sculptural material 238–9
words as conventional symbols 146
WRIGHT, FRANK LLOYD 107, 278; Ennis House, LA **1.20** (25); Guggenheim Museum, NY **3.19** (85); Johnson's Wax Building 54, **2.34** (54); Kaufmann House, Bear Run **3.49** (106); Taliesins 281, **9.19** (282)
writing *see* lettering

Y

YAKASAKI, MINORU: Pruitt Igoe housing development 18, **1.10** (17)
yellow, significance of 126
Yoruba altar figure **3.42** (102)
Yoshimura House, Habikino, Japan **3.5** (77)

Z

zoning 334–5, 337